Multilingual Subjects

MULTILINGUAL SUBJECTS

On Standard English, Its Speakers, and Others in the Long Eighteenth Century

Daniel DeWispelare

PENN

UNIVERSITY OF PENNSYLVANIA PRESS

PHILADELPHIA

Published by
University of Pennsylvania Press
Philadelphia, Pennsylvania 19104-4112
www.upenn.edu/pennpress

Printed in the United States of America
on acid-free paper

1 3 5 7 9 10 8 6 4 2

Library of Congress Cataloging-in-Publication Data

Names: DeWispelare, Daniel, author.
Title: Multilingual subjects : on standard English, its speakers, and others in the long eighteenth century / Daniel DeWispelare.
Description: 1st edition. | Philadelphia : University of Pennsylvania Press, [2017] | Includes bibliographical references and index.
Identifiers: LCCN 2016050486 | ISBN 978-0-8122-4909-5 (hardcover : alk. paper)
Subjects: LCSH: English language—Political aspects—English-speaking countries—History—18th century. | English language—Political aspects—Great Britain—History—18th century. | Multilingualism—English-speaking countries—History—18th century. | English language—Social aspects—English-speaking countries—History—18th century. | Sociolinguistics—English-speaking countries—History—18th century. | English language—English-speaking countries—Standardization—History—18th century. | English language—English-speaking countries—Variation—History—18th century. | Language policy—English-speaking countries—History—18th century. | Language and languages—Philosophy—History—18th century. | Translating and interpreting—English-speaking countries—History—18th century.
Classification: LCC P119.3 .D487 2017 | DDC 306.442/21—dc23
LC record available at https://lccn.loc.gov/2016050486

To my father

Daniel DeWispelare
March 29, 1949–September 25, 2010

If I know not the meaning of the voice, I shall be unto him that speaketh a barbarian; and he that speaketh *shall* be a barbarian to me.

—1 Corinthians 14:11, King James Version

Opacities must be preserved; an appetite for opportune obscurity in translation must be created; and falsely convenient vehicular sabirs must be relentlessly refuted.

—Édouard Glissant, *Poetics of Relation*

CONTENTS

INTRODUCTION

Multiplicity and Relation

Toward an Anglophone Eighteenth Century

Johnson, Scott, and the Highlanders

> By subsequent opportunities of observation, I found that my host's diction had nothing peculiar. Those Highlanders that can speak English, commonly speak it well, with few of the words, and little of the tone by which a Scotchman is distinguished. Their language seems to have been learned in the army or the navy, or by some communication with those who could give them good examples of accent and pronunciation. By their Lowland neighbours they would not willingly be taught; for they have long considered them as a mean and degenerate race. These prejudices are wearing fast away, but so much of them still remains, that when I asked a very learned minister in the islands, which they considered as their most savage clans: "*Those*, said he, *that live next the Lowlands.*"[1]

This passage from Samuel Johnson's *Journey to the Western Islands of Scotland* (1775) registers a charge surrounding the two dimensions of eighteenth-century linguistic multiplicity that this book explores at length: (1) heteroglossic diversity among disparate versions of the English language and (2) polyglossic interaction between these varied forms of English and other languages encountered on the global stage of travel, commerce, and empire.[2] In this passage, as elsewhere, Johnson tarries in the multiplicities of orality, allowing his reflections to generate descriptive detail about the relationships among various groups within Britain. Each group is marked with a particular linguistic character relative to the others. To every group its shibboleths. This is one of the main premises of eighteenth-century writing about language.

By starting with this brief example of metalinguistic writing—by which I mean descriptive writing that takes language itself as its topic—I want to suggest that Johnson's passage deconstructs the coherence of the term "English" so thoroughly that the term's analytical value is thrown into suspicion. In other words, by yoking together several forms of lively linguistic multiplicity under the limiting term "English," Johnson's deductions about these linguistic practices reveal their own contingency. In fact, the passage permits a reading that acknowledges the insufficiency of this term for naming the many interpenetrating language forms that people past and present have employed for speaking, writing, and creating literature. By capturing linguistic alterity in many forms, Johnson relativizes his own subject position. Against the precession of these other anglophone tongues, Johnson's English is just one form among many.[3]

That literature is, among other things, a name for the aesthetic experience that arises from an encounter with languages and voices as they are rendered in print is a bequest of the global long eighteenth century.[4] It was during this period that anglophone writers learned to evaluate themselves and others by parsing the linguistic multiplicities around them. It is my contention in *Multilingual Subjects* that scholars of cultural and literary history need to do more with the linguistic multiplicity of the past as it is encoded in the literary and nonliterary alike. We need to be able to see not only that the term "English" language is insufficient, as in the epigraph above, but also that the insufficiency of this term is a lived condition that generates descriptive texture and narrative momentum in Johnson's writing as well as that of his contemporaries.[5] We need to understand linguistic multiplicity better; we need to name its contours more accurately; we need to explore its fissures in detail; we need to explore its role in narrative more accurately; and, generally, we need to think more creatively about how the always-existing multiplicity of language is a dimension of identity that influences literary representation and reception. There are also obvious political opportunities in a better understanding of how linguistic multiplicity is characterized in (and characterizes) the period. Those questions I broach alongside the aesthetic in coming chapters.

Four discrete types of linguistic identities—and, for Johnson, cultural identities—are invoked in this four-sentence passage. Three different varieties of "English" are clearly identifiable. One non-English language appears implicitly—or possibly two non-English languages, depending on how one counts. First, and most obviously, there is the studied language of Johnson's own narrative voice, an example of Standard English within which the other languages in the passage are contained.[6] Irrespective of the fact that Johnson might here be accused of a grammatical gaffe—because "those Highlanders who can speak English" is arguably preferable to the deanimating "those Highlanders that can speak English"—his particular form of "English" is the default or framing language. From the reader's perspective, Johnson's language is normative, nothing less than what we should expect from English's first great lexicographer, and, perhaps, literary celebrity, of a certain sort.[7]

From the perspective of Johnson's elite language, the other forms of "English" appear on a spectrum from unremarkable to deviant or debased in some way. In order of appearance, the second form of language that occurs in this passage is the "English" of multilingual Highlanders who have "learned it in the army, or the navy." Or, presumably, they have learned it via cross border colloquy with exemplars of "accent and pronunciation," like Johnson, for these Highlanders "commonly speak it well." The third form of "English" is that of the Highlanders' "Lowland neighbours." These neighbors speak an "English" marked by those shibboleths of "words" and "tone" by which "a Scotchman is distinguished." According to Johnson's metalinguistic reportage, the Highlanders consider their lowland neighbors a "savage," "mean and degenerate race," certainly not the right people to teach the Highlanders "English," and, according to the rhetoric of "savagery" here invoked, perhaps not people at all.

Adding another dimension of multiplicity and difference to this already-composite ecology of tongues, some of the Highlanders are multilingual. Johnson is outside their multilingualism, and all he can do is refer to it without examining it. What I mean is that the passage alludes implicitly to the Scottish Gaelic spoken by those Highlanders who cannot speak English just as it alludes explicitly to those Highlanders who can speak both languages. I say this by inference, for if there are some Highlanders "that can speak English," then there are also some who cannot, and, perhaps, also some who will not. That some Highlanders can speak English while others cannot or will not sketches an important intra-Gaelic linguistic division. Johnson does not expound on this division here, but it comes to the surface in other texts of the period, in particular, Sir Walter Scott's *Waverley* (1814).

Waverley is a novel that, similar to Johnson's travel narrative, orders its characters in terms of complex and overlaid linguistic identities. In one famous scene, for example, Waverley tries to speak to the nonanglophone Highlanders: "Our hero now endeavoured to address them, but was only answered with 'Niel Sassenagh,' that is, 'no English,' being, as Waverley knew, the constant reply of a Highlander when he either does not understand, or does not choose to reply to, an Englishman or a Lowlander."[8] Waverley's investigations are stymied by his inability to interact in the language his interlocutors prefer. But he seems to know in advance that this would be the case. Instead of letting a dialogue reveal information about the story's unfolding, Scott uses an expression of linguistic refusal ("Niel Sassenagh") and an English translation of that refusal ("no English") to characterize the intercultural dynamics at work in Waverley's interactions with the Highlanders. This small metalinguistic moment says a great deal. Waverley is frozen, knowing only that his interlocutor refuses the only linguistic medium Waverley knows. His next brief appeal is also rebuffed: "Neither did this produce any mark of recognition from his escort."[9] The moment as a whole stands in as a larger metaphor for Waverley's ongoing attempts to comprehend events that he cannot grasp in an environment that is foreign for him, less welcoming than the legible library in which he has been raised.

Johnson and Scott's English. The Highlanders' English. The Lowlanders' English. Can the diverse linguistic forms that are disambiguated in this passage properly be referred to by the concept "English"? The easy answer is that, yes, of course they can. But this answer is unconcerned with the interpretive flattening that imagining such an implausibly unitary idea of "English" creates. My answer to the question is the long one: no, the term "English" here and elsewhere is insufficient. As a question of interpretation, it matters that we attend to representations of linguistic multiplicity, however subtly they appear. It matters that writers like Johnson, Scott, and others generate descriptive texture and plot developments by differentiating among groups of people in terms of language. My contention is that salient contextual details disappear when we fail to attend to the way that literature of the long eighteenth century actively charts linguistic difference as a way to communicate alterity of many dimensions. Language difference, after all, is one of the long eighteenth century's most important tropes and topoi. Writers, novelists, poets, and playwrights of the period make it matter.

Johnson and Scott's English. The Highlanders' English. The Lowlanders' English. This chain also represents a cultural hierarchy in which the first form explains and glosses all the others. This is to say nothing of the fact that non-English tongues like Scottish Gaelic are always crisscrossing the chain of English languages here enumerated. The multilingualism of the Highlanders in both Johnson and Scott is tremendously significant, as significant as the internal differences and corresponding subject positions of English forms and speakers in these texts. Moreover, the reader must remain aware that such representations disclose important aspects of a text's descriptive, narrative, and characterological architecture. It is the reader's job to interpret these representations of difference and multilingualism. That Johnson's Highlanders speak English in addition to their native Scottish Gaelic communicates their nobility as well as their tense relationship to the Union of England and Scotland after the rebellions of 1745. These multilingual language skills might attest to some experience in the imperial army or navy, Johnson surmises, for these institutions encourage linguistic compliance and pro-British sentiment. In Scott, Scottish Gaelic signifies in different ways. Fergus Mac-Ivor and Flora Mac-Ivor's choice of language in different communicative contexts is a narrative strategy for getting at Waverley's monolingual alterity to the multilingual Highlanders' culture. Like the reader, Waverley is ignorant and unaware of what is to come; his language deficiencies leave him sealed off from the plot's intrigue.

This linguistic and thus subjective isolation is literally enacted by the "Stag Hunt," a scene in which "the word was given in Gaelic to fling themselves upon their faces; but Waverley, on whose English ears the signal was lost, had almost fallen a sacrifice to his ignorance of the ancient language in which it was communicated."[10] The multilingual context of Waverley's northern *Bildung* is ever present to the reader, for the evocation of language's heteroglot and polyglot textures is a narrative technique Scott executes confidently and to multiple effects.[11] A brief additional example that is central to the plot of the novel is the fact that certain of the Lowland and Highland Scottish characters also have linguistic ties to the French. The French abilities of characters like Fergus and Flora evoke their rebellious, extra-British alliances while those of the Baron of Bradwardine and Rose Bradwardine signify a kind of modern civility. The external ties of the rebels resonate with the tensions of Franco-British relations in the early nineteenth-century moment in which *Waverley* was written just as Rose's education in French, Italian, and English delineates a set of linguistic qualifications that marked women as accomplished in the period.

I dwell on the linguistic dimensions of Johnson and Scott in order to open into a much broader discussion of metalinguistic writing in the long eighteenth century and its relationships to the present. In both time periods, metalinguistic writing is a form of xenotropism, one that writers find particularly powerful for capturing the interrelationships of groups presumed to be different.[12] At times, and depending on the writer, a curious combination of xenotropism and xenophobia resides in the will toward metalinguistic writing. Metalinguistic writing is by nature xenotropic, as it stresses differences communicated by one's linguistic habits. But it can also be xenophobic to the degree that it uses linguistic difference as a sign of unbridgeable human difference for aesthetic ends. Insofar as one sees language as a salient vector of interpersonal difference, this curious combination does a great deal of cultural work.

Multiplicity and Metalinguistic Writing

Multilingual Subjects extends ongoing conversations about the global scene of long eighteenth-century culture by documenting the importance of "dialect" writing, multilingual writing, and translation to aesthetic and political practices that emerge during the period.[13] Even though "dialect" writing is rarely discussed alongside multilingual writing and translation practice, I argue over the course of this book: (1) that these forms of writing are intimately related; (2) that they constitute a robust counterarchive of anglophone rather than "English" linguistic identities; and (3) that this counterarchive of linguistic lives and aesthetic practices allows us to reinterpret the monolingual conjunction of language and nation that is associated with the long eighteenth century's end.

Multilingualism signifies in texts by generating descriptive, characterological, and narrative possibilities, often in complex ways. Representations of multilingualism in the form of metalinguistic writing speak to cultural worlds beyond the text that are distinct from a narrower cultural world rooted only in a "normal" or "normative" form of Standard English. When they appear, multilingual subjects open Standard English writing onto worlds with which it is not coextensive, whether anglophone or not, thereby showing the imbricated nature of the eighteenth-century linguistico-cultural field. But the representation of linguistic multiplicity can also enfold inassimilable worlds into the world of the English-language text. As exemplars of the eighteenth-century archive, Johnson and Scott are part of a lineage of anglophone writers who attempt to make aesthetic meaning from the topos of linguistic multiplicity. The phenomenon of writing about the internal diversity and external relations of the English language, however, is by no means restricted to discussions of fictive descriptions, narrative momentum, or aesthetic effects. In fact, it is a feature common to all types of writing because generalized concern about the relationship of linguistic difference to cultural, racial, and economic difference is one of the generative engines of the eighteenth-century publishing industry.

James Adams, author of *The Pronunciation of the English Language Vindicated from Imputed Anomaly and Caprice* (1799), uses the word "literary" in the sense of "written in books, fictional or nonfictional" when he retrospectively declares, "No literary subject has been so much handled by British writers within the course of the present, expiring century, nor so frequently been distinguished by the exertions of learning, wit, and ingenuity, as grammatical systems of the English language."[14] Adams does not supply the quantitative data to back up this claim, but as anecdote, he is on the mark. The eighteenth-century anglophone publishing industry witnesses the publication of unprecedented numbers of English dictionaries, grammars, style guides, elocution manuals, translation treatises, and translations, metalinguistic writing all.[15] These texts sought, through different means, to make sense of the linguistic facts on the ground in anglophone and nonanglophone spaces. Additionally, the period is also marked by an efflorescence of travel writing, ethnographies, and pseudoethnographies, as well as protoscientific, analogical approaches to language and culture like Sir William Jones's famous "Third Anniversary Discourse," which contains the famous metalinguistic claim, "The Sanscrit [*sic*] language, whatever be its antiquity, is of a wonderful structure; more perfect than the Greek, more copious than the Latin, and more exquisitely refined than either. . . . No philologer could examine them all three, without believing them to have sprung from some common source, which, perhaps, no longer exists."[16] I continue with the entwined local and global aspects of the long eighteenth-century metalinguistic archive in later chapters, but for now I want to reiterate the main impetus behind the present work: linguistic multiplicity, linguistic difference, and the possible meanings of these cultural facts occupy eighteenth-century readers and thinkers in unprecedented, diverse, and aesthetically productive ways.

By thinking broadly about linguistic multiplicity and linguistic difference as centers of eighteenth-century aesthetic and political concern, this book invites scholars from diverse periods to engage creatively with the subjects that I group under the category "multilingual subjects."[17] Starting with the title, *Multilingual Subjects* links the prevailing concerns of eighteenth-century scholarship with contemporary linguistic politics and aesthetics by stressing linguistic habits as an important dimension of identity, then as now. For one, I use the title phrase to refer to code-switching "multilingual subjects," individuals like Robert Burns and Maria Edgeworth who were able to generate unique approaches to literary composition by capitalizing on (in Burns's case) or ventriloquizing (in Edgeworth's case) linguistic multiplicities with which they were familiar. Other "multilingual subjects" can be identified among the period's new and voluble breed of vernacular grammarians and prescriptive stylists. Schooled in Latin, Greek, and sometimes Hebrew linguistic traditions, among others, scholars and translators like Robert Lowth actively tried to standardize English in order to formulate an internally cohesive and externally reputable medium for a noticeably diverse anglophone sphere and an increasingly polyglot imperial context.[18] Just as this type of advanced scholarship depends on specific forms of institutional multilingualism and multiliteracy, multilingualism also correlates with the most precarious forms of vernacular cosmopolitanism in the period, as it does in our own. Other "multilingual subjects" were, like Olaudah Equiano, Phillis Wheatley, and so many other servants and slaves—"multilingual subjects" who became so by force, not unlike the multitude of contemporary people who are pushed or pulled into anglophony by the economic and political logics of the present.[19]

Beyond referring to individual human beings whose biographies lend coherence to the long history of anglophone multilingualism, the phrase "multilingual subjects" is also meant to invoke ways of writing about language like grammar, elocution, and translation theory. Monolingual in orientation and yet filled with multilingual substrates and residues, these booming eighteenth-century pedagogical discourses had the aggregate effect of restricting multilingualism and multilingual contact during the period. Studied as part of an individual's passage into "proper" literacy, the existence of these discourses alongside experimental forms of dialect writing in the period dramatizes the culture at large wrestling with newly monolingual forms of literacy and literary composition.

As discourses of Standard English normativity flourished, the period witnessed a proliferation of descriptive, characterological, and narrative strategies for rendering the linguistic habits of diverse individuals and cultures in print. Metalinguistic description—by which I mean the purposeful narration and description of language itself—is one of the long eighteenth century's most pronounced developments in writing technique, a development the book tracks closely. Indeed, more writing of the period than is commonly acknowledged straightforwardly thematizes linguistic difference. So in the same way that the "subject of a painting" is the matter of its content, eighteenth-century writing is replete with other unexamined "multilingual subjects," the most important of which are examined in this book as rhetorically generative tropes and topoi. Finally, I show that the many divergent and yet coexisting forms of the English language are themselves crucially important eighteenth-century "multilingual subjects." Put another way, metalinguistic writing that addresses the internal differences and external relations of the English language is the book's most frequently recurring and contentious "multilingual subject."

With all these meanings in tow, *Multilingual Subjects* lays out the case for paying close attention to the changing cultural meanings of linguistic multiplicity in long eighteenth-century culture, especially insofar as these meanings proleptically announce some of the aesthetic and political dimensions of language and globalization in the present. Far from being minor or peripheral, the interpolation of linguistic difference and diversity into texts of the eighteenth century represents a set of market-oriented aesthetic strategies just as it represents a set of political assumptions relative to language, culture, and identity.[20] Grasping linguistic multiplicity as it interacts with literary practice and aesthetic evaluation in the eighteenth-century world of empire and overseas adventurism can helps us critique and understand our own situation, one in which English in its many deterritorialized forms "must nestle everywhere, settle everywhere, establish connexions everywhere," to quote Marx's most famous descriptions of the European bourgeoisie.[21] Standard English in the eighteenth century and in the contemporary world: disrupting culture even as it enables it, subverting nonnormative forms of language even as it gives birth to new ones. Insofar as this work's claims are presentist, then, they are also interested in the patterns of linguistic identity that we can recuperate from the eighteenth-century past as a way to think differently about the future.[22]

In keeping with the main premises of the last few decades of eighteenth-century research, Susan Buck-Morss's *Hegel, Haiti, and Universal History* (2009) evokes "the Atlantic as an expanded social field, shared by millions of heterogeneous, previously unconnected people," a description that is true to the period in question just as it is obviously informed by the moment of her book's composition.[23] In Buck-Morss's words, "The collective experiences of concrete, particular human beings fall out of identifying categories of "nation," "race," and "civilization" that capture only a partial aspect of their existence, as they travel across cultural binaries, moving in and out of conceptual frames and in the process, creating new ones. Porosity characterizes the ordering boundaries of their world (as it does ours today)."[24] Charting their interconnections, and showing how those interconnections challenge the disciplinary boundaries by which we understand the heterogeneous subjects of the past, Buck-Morss asks scholars to focus on identity's porosity in that earlier world and in our own. By "porosity," she means the tendency of subjects to slip inside and outside the categories that we use to define them, categories like " 'nation,' 'race,' and 'civilization,' " a list to which we should but often enough do not add "language." Thinking with Buck-Morss, a category's tendency toward porosity becomes more important than the category itself. Concretely, the archive and the present both demonstrate that one can slip in and out of linguistic categories—through language learning, intercultural experience, or mere communicative adjustment, as sociolinguistics also demonstrates. Porosity is thus another way to figure the multilingual subjects of the eighteenth century, as forms of reading, writing, and speaking that allow for and productively encourage slippages of nation, race, civilization, and also language.

For scholars and students in the present, a critical examination of histories of multilingualism and linguistic porosity are timely in several senses. Such examinations speak to the institutional and pedagogical demands of the present by allowing scholars to connect for students and society at large the diversities of the globalizing present with the diversities of the past. Many different stories culminate in the history of our own present. Too many of those stories are invisible because of the specific historical trends that we choose to privilege. If as scholars we are generally comfortable with the idea of porosity, then this comes as a result of the work of others who have brought that texture out of the past and showed how it conditions the present. Insofar as one of the jobs of the humanities is to attune students to the demands of globality, then critical histories of porosity have already partially served these goals. To the degree that multilingual and porous histories are sometimes invisible in the frameworks with which we train students to think about cultures of the past, students of the present find their cultural lives unaccounted for in some ways. They ought to have some sense that the period they live in has long ties to the linguistic diversity of the past, within the anglophone world and without.

Anglophones and Anglophony

During his tenure as editor of *PMLA* from 2011 to 2016, Simon Gikandi used several of his editor's columns to reflect on the past and present of global linguistic diversity.[25] Among other things, Gikandi's columns investigated global linguistic diversity's relationship to contemporary culture and politics. The specter of "the powerful myth of English as the global language" was never far from his mind. For example, on more than one occasion he puzzled over the way "English-only movements thrive in large parts of the United States."[26] Likewise, in several instances he ruminated on precarious languages in the process of disappearing: "Letting a language die is an injustice, a denial of will to those who speak it."[27] Interrogating the power of English in a world where "the global linguistic map appears to be a simple division between those with English and those without it," Gikandi invoked Dipesh Chakrabarty in order to argue that English as a language should be "provincialized" in the interest of a new global order of relationality.[28] Gikandi's goal has been to "deprive the [English] language of the ecumenical status of the global and to represent it as one language among many . . . not as part of a global drive toward monolingualism but as part of the diversity and plurality of world languages."[29] In this respect, his essays are stimulating and provocative reading for their dogged insistence that English must be provincialized, pluralized, and sufficiently reconceptualized to account for the multilingualism of the present.

In keeping with this, I discuss the breadth of linguistic multiplicity that characterizes the eighteenth century and subtends its aesthetic production by employing the interpretive category "anglophony." Common in contemporary studies, this term crops up only occasionally in literary and cultural histories that focus on periods before the twentieth century, most often as a way to disambiguate Britain from other areas of anglophone population density like North America.[30] Calqued from the French postcolonial and neocolonial grouping *francophonie*, I use the noun "anglophony" to upend normative linguistic and cultural hierarchies—insofar as upending those hierarchies is possible—while also throwing the assumptions of those normative linguistic and cultural hierarchies into high relief. As in the context of francophonie, anglophony is a term that can be used to take together the "domestic," colonial, postcolonial, and neocolonial. As a way of provincializing English, this term acts as a supracategory of linguistic participation, a category comprising everything from laterally interacting and constantly evolving anglophone forms to the nonnormative forms of speakers from unrelated linguistic backgrounds to the class argots and anti- or cryptolanguages of subaltern populations.[31] Typically, the languages of these diverse linguistic identities are referred to by the difference-effacing term "English" or the normative and subordinating terms "dialect English," "regional English," "provincial English," "substandard English," and more, all of which evaluations presuppose Standard English is a transcendental category of reference rather than a conventional form among others.

When one thinks of anglophony, not in spatial terms, but instead as an irreducibly complex sonic ecology with a variety of speakers, forms, and abilities, Standard English appears merely as anglophony's most recognizable acrolect (my term for the prestige form of standard written English). In the present, nationally based Standard Englishes appear as the creations of two and a half centuries of metalinguistic debate and coercion rather than a realistic representation of linguistic homogeneity in the world.[32] Standard English may very well be the anglophone form that the majority of canonized texts have been composed in, but the preponderance of acrolectic Standard English in the literary canon is no reason to overlook other forms of language that generated texts, animated lives, and circulated in public at the same time and in the same spaces. In fact, when we look closely at anglophone texts, we see that most are chock-a-block with what Bakhtin identified as heteroglossia.

Writers who composed in acrolectic Standard English have regularly occupied privileged positions within anglophony as arbiters of the aesthetic, not to mention the political, social, and legal. This is why notable eighteenth-century Scots worked so hard to "perfect" or delocalize their English. Doing so meant gaining privilege, cultural capital, and occupational advancement.[33] The achievements of those peripheral to Standard English notwithstanding—and language learning truly is an achievement, mental and physical—the privileged position of acrolectic anglophones within our literary canons is something we should challenge archivally rather than reproduce pedagogically. Acrolectic privileges are something we perpetually reinscribe if Standard English is the only anglophone variety that receives regular critical study as meaningful and aesthetic writing. Of course, there are obvious exceptions to the claim that acrolectic Standard English is all that scholars teach as meaningful and aesthetic writing. I discuss Robert Burns, who is one of the best late eighteenth-century examples of such an exception, in the first chapter. More generally, though, I am interested in seeking out those forms of nonnormative linguistic identity that were not and have not been seen as meaningful or aesthetic, but instead as "vulgar" and "provincial," or worse, always in the process of becoming extinct.

Because *Multilingual Subjects* explores the politics and aesthetics of nonnormative anglophone languages as literary media, especially in the fourth chapter, my use of "anglophony" is intended both as a piece of terminology as well as an argument. As a term, and one with important limitations, "anglophony" helps scholars eschew awkward and unhelpful demonyms, ethnic monikers, and metropole-periphery binaries while revealing anglophone texts that allow us to examine overlooked relationships between linguistic subjectivity and aesthetic practice in the period.[34] As an argument, my use of the term "anglophony" is meant as an antidote and countermodel to unserviceable, misrepresentative, and sometimes messianically deployed terms like "World English" or "Global English," terms that I discuss in the conclusion as one of the logical extensions of eighteenth-century ideologies of Standard English. Anglophony, which should be understood as always multilingual, enables us to grasp the linguistic and cultural dynamics of the present in a way that these other terms cannot. As an added benefit, the many possible pronunciations of the term "anglophony"—some will voice this word as two trochees, others as two iambs, and still other enunciative possibilities exist—enact the differential character of the linguistic environment it purports to describe.

The objective sonic characteristics of eighteenth-century anglophony are beyond the scope of this book. I focus on representations of anglophony in print, especially insofar as these representations clash with and subvert acrolectic Standard English. For example, anglophony can take shape in print as in the following wry line from Hume, a Scottish anglophone and eminent master of the acrolect: "But the life of man is of no greater importance to the universe than that of an oyster."[35] Anglophony can also appear in print as in John Collier, a near contemporary of Hume who was born and bred in Lancashire and who made a career out of local linguistic forms and semiradical politics: "Odds me Meary! whooa the Dickons wou'd o thowt o' leeting o' thee here so soyne this Morning? Where has to bin? Theaw'rt aw on a Swat, I think; for theaw looks primely." ("Bless me! Mary, who the deuce would have thought of finding thee here so soon this morning? where hast thou been?—thou art all in a sweat I think, for thou looks primely.")[36] The archive of this sort of linguistic diversity is vast and full of incommensurable forms. One finds, for instance, that eighteenth-century anglophony can also appear in print as in this line from the diary of West African slave trader Antera Duke: "I go Bord Captin Loosdam for break book for 3 slave so I break for one at Captin Savage so I take goods for slav at Captin Brown and com back." ("I went on board Captain Langdon's ship to 'break book' [make an agreement] for 3 slaves. I 'broke trade' for one slave with Captain Savage. Then I took goods for slaves from Captain Burrows and came back.")[37] I investigate the political and aesthetic parameters of these and other examples as the book progresses, but the point here is to give some forward-looking textual examples of anglophone diversity in its eighteenth-century plenitude.

With this chain of divergent examples, I am suggesting that the primary way I conceive of the term "anglophony" is as a linguistic supracategory, one that links together a great many varieties and is irreducible to none. Gilles Deleuze and Félix Guattari's theory of rhizomatic systems helps us conceptualize eighteenth-century anglophony in spite of the fact that unrecorded communities of sound are impossible to map. Deleuze and Guattari discuss language as a politico-organic entanglement made up of intersecting varieties: "Il n'y a pas de langue en soi, ni d'universalité du langage, mais un concours de dialectes, de patois, d'argots, de langues spéciales. . . . N'importe quel point d'un rhizome peut être connecté avec n'importe quel autre, et doit l'être." ("There is no such thing as language in itself, nor is there universality in language, but rather a competing throng of dialects, of patois, argots, and jargons. . . . Any point of a rhizome whatsoever can be connected with any other point, and should be.")[38] Anglophony was (and is still) an interconnected network of differential comprehensibilities that is irreducible to geographic containers. Deleuze and Guattari's nonjudgmental chain of equivalent forms—"a competing throng of dialects, of patois, argots, and jargons"—offers the useful vision of a radically dehierarchized linguistic field with countless and mobile contact points. The eighteenth-century archive reveals these contacts often and unambiguously. A Connaught Irishman meets an English-educated Edinburgh Scotsman on an East Indiaman bound for Calcutta. A British-born West Indian plantocrat speaks with his

Caribbean-born, mixed-race overseer in some anglophone variety, and this overseer then communicates with the plantocrat's slaves in an anglophone or other creole. A young polymath poet in London employs as Hebrew instructor a Sephardic rabbi whose language background is a complex mixture of Yiddish, German, Dutch, and Spanish and whose native city is Amsterdam. They communicate.

A few more terminological points are in order. From this point onward, I will use different terms to refer to anglophone difference in lived reality and anglophone difference in text. With regard to spoken language, I use a term culled from sociolinguistics: "lect," that is, a form of speech with no value attached. By contrast, in order to discuss the imitation of lectic speech in writing as a literary device, I use terms like "acrolect," "dialect," "ethnolect," "chronolect," "regiolect," "sociolect," and so forth. My specific literary claim throughout this book is that dialect is not an actually existing set of interactional protocol in the social world that can be transparently represented on the page. Instead, dialect as we should understand it in literature is, to paraphrase Wordsworth, the written imitation of half created and half perceived linguistic attributes, attributes that are called on to signify linguistic and extralinguistic alterity.

Deleuze and Guattari's dynamic description of language as a rhizomatic system also provides a conceptual model for understanding power relations that work to conceal the multilingual complexities of a linguistic system like anglophony. They write, "Il n'y pas de langue-mère, mais prise de pouvoir par une langue dominante dans une multiplicité politique. La langue se stabilise autour d'une paroisse, d'un évêché, d'une capitale. Elle fait bulbe. Elle évolue par tiges et flux souterrains, le long des vallées fluviales, ou des lignes de chemins de fer, elle se déplace par taches d'huile." ("There is no mother tongue but instead a power seizure by a dominant language within a political multiplicity. Language is stabilized around a parish, a bishopric, a capital. It bulges. It progresses by way of stems and subterranean flows, along river valleys or railroad lines; it spreads like an oil stain.")[39] In this short passage, the writers overturn commonplace notions of language as a system of filiation where one self-contained tongue naturally gives birth to another and where each gains cultural and political power according to the logic of natural selection. When we think without the profitable pretense of a nationally sanctioned "mother tongue," as Deleuze and Guattari suggest we should, then it is easier to see historically contingent usurpations of linguistic and cultural authority that have always been carried out in loci of power like parishes, bishoprics, or capitals. Armed with the powers invested in these and other institutions, a dominant dialect or acrolect seizes power. Deleuze and Guattari offer nonessentializing ways to think of language as a space of lateral linguistic mixing and nonhierarchical cross-pollination. Their emphasis on contact and contingency helps reveal the complexity of eighteenth-century anglophony even if power relations try to occlude it.[40]

The passage quoted above provides two metaphors for language that help flesh out the methodological openings offered by the term anglophony as this book uses it. First, language is a series of networks that mimic commercial networks. A dominant language moves by subterranean flows, up river valleys, and along train tracks, which are also often the primary routes of trading activity. In this way, a dominant language is the copilot of commerce and communication, traveling wherever the two can be facilitated together, inundating spaces where other linguistic varieties or lects intermingled before. This is why understanding the British Empire's metastatic eighteenth-century growth and hardening—both overseas and within the British Isles—is obligatory for grasping the linguistic and aesthetic texture of a period that sees Standard English gradually becoming a disciplinary pedagogical space in Britain and abroad. A dominant language form greases the arteries of exchange. Like trade, it traces the globe's geographical contours and overcomes geographical obstacles where profitable. Any study of literature of the long eighteenth century that foregrounds anglophony as a conceptual category must take into account the interstitial spaces where Standard English is emergent and other interpenetrating linguistic forms are perceived as residual or moribund.

The second metaphor that is methodologically pertinent here concerns the idea that a dominant language can be conceived of like the random pattern of an oil stain, a splotch here, a blotch there, scattered densities cast on a surface in the shape of an archipelago. We can see this splotchy design of dominant language by considering the silos of educated, acrolectic Standard English speakers and writers in irreducibly multilingual places like London, Edinburgh, Philadelphia, Kingston, Bridgetown, Calcutta, and beyond.[41] The metaphor of a dominant language superimposed over the language system as an oil stain enables scholars to think of the coming of standardized English as a spray of intermittent, separated, and ineradicable linguistic blots superimposed over the diverse and ever-changing surface of global linguistic practice. This insight forces network thought, a kind of thought wherein individualized trajectories through disorganized linguistic space become meaningful. Geographical containers like the nation, the British Isles, and even the imperium are here assumed to be innervated with linguistic difference from every direction. As such linguistic difference must negotiate the oily congelations of linguistic propriety that increasingly disperse on its surface.

To recapitulate the justification for the term anglophony I have been advancing until now, when applied to eighteenth-century literature, the term "English" hides more than it reveals. Intended to connote an internally coherent tradition of language and nation—and hence teachable traditions of literature and history—"English" as a category has long been recognized as too limited. More idealization than historical or empirical reality, the flattened and flattening term "English" is a detail-obliterating abstraction whereas anglophony is a detail-recovering one. Other scholars have sought out replacements for "English" that offer increased granularity, terms like "British," "Archipelagic," and even "Imperial" English.[42] In this book I opt for "anglophony" because I relish the conceptual work this term does as well as the methodological practice it encourages. I am also suspicious of objectifying and geographizing language, for language is a process and not an object or space. One aspect of my argument, for example, is that by prizing Standard English over difference and multiplicity, anglophony disavows its unmappable and ongoing interlinguistic contacts—and to its own aesthetic detriment.

The fact that the term anglophony is derived from and has analogues in French postcolonial vocabularies thus intentionally enacts the multilingual intervention I hope to make here. By self-consciously using this borrowing as a borrowing, I want to disrupt any inference that the term is a product of critical parthenogenesis. If it is true, as I claim, that one of the tendencies of anglophone aesthetics and linguistic history has been to naturalize borrowings in such a way that their origins in external and subaltern linguistic systems are effaced, then the traces of the term *anglophony*'s explicit borrowedness start us down a road toward unraveling those aesthetic and historical tendencies. My point is that, in the present, it is obligatory that students of literature have a better model of what language is, how it changes, how it spreads, and how—following an insight made by sociolinguistics long ago—language rapidly communicates subject positions as well as semantic meaning in any interaction as in any moment of reading.

As an additional benefit, the term *anglophony*'s third and fourth syllables etymologically foreground voice and sound as salient components of linguistic interaction—and thus aesthetic and cultural exchange. This gesturing to voice (φωνή / phōnē) informs the close readings of dialect writing that occupy parts of subsequent chapters. Even so, the preservation of the endonym "anglo-" in the term "anglophony" might give some readers pause. This preservation might seem to circumscribe the diverse linguistic practices I discuss within narrowly construed ethnic or national frameworks. This is not at all my intention, as this book takes as axiomatic the fact that non-English users of different forms of anglophony have always been critically important to anglophone aesthetics. Yet, the "anglo-" in "anglophony" seems to me to serve practical as well as analytical functions. On the practical side, I am using this term to name a dynamic spectrum of semimutually intelligible linguistic forms. If there is a unifying core to the linguistic forms that I will discuss here, then the "anglo-" in "anglophony" captures that grammatical and dictive core, however infelicitously. It does so not by way of ethnicity or nation, however, but instead, by way of invoking the exclusive ethnic and national claims against which many anglophones must constantly fight. On the analytic side, then, the "anglo-" in "anglophony" evokes a specter of English homogeneity that the ongoing deterritorialization of the language constantly contradicts.

Faithful to the idea of the specter, I have also chosen to preserve the "anglo-" in "anglophony" because this allows the word to serve as a ludic, bifurcated pun that throws into question the ontological reality of its first part: "anglo-phony," wherein "phony" is taken not to mean voice or sound but instead "fake," "ersatz," "simulated," or "parodic." In the interest of continually emphasizing anglophony's multilingual texture, it bears noting that the word "phony" is the etymological derivative of the slang Irish word *fawney* meaning "ring finger," a metonym for the trick of selling a brass ring as a gold one—or so lexicography tells us. The word has been absorbed into English as a noun that indicates the artificial and inauthentic simulacrum of a particular thing. The "anglo-" in "anglophony" represents a simulacrum of Englishness in a world where the vast majority of anglophones are not and have not been English since the late eighteenth century.

As a piece of terminology, I see the way in which the term "anglophony" subverts and dissects itself as methodologically liberating and also new. To refer to an eighteenth-century subject as an anglophone existing within anglophony is not to say that person is English, far from it. Instead, this usage can be taken to insist constantly and unwaveringly on the fungibility and historical contingency of the term "English." Likewise, to refer to an eighteenth-century subject as an anglophone need not carry any racial, ethnic, class, or gender implications. Instead, the term opens up an analytical field for examining representations of different identities as they are reinforced by linguistic practices and aestheticized in text. Finally, to refer to an eighteenth-century subject as an anglophone makes no claim that this is an exhaustive accounting of that subject's linguistic skills or affiliations. One can be an anglophone as well as an arabophone, a francophone, a lusophone, a sinophone, et cetera. In fact, it is these sorts of linguistic multiplicities within people that have for too long been overlooked. They have also too infrequently been invoked as tools that can open up texts we know—as well as ones we have yet to study well—in exciting ways. As a broad and multivalent term, then, "anglophony" represents a range of imbricated and always-evolving communicative procedures, many of which are salient elements in the definition of what counts as eighteenth-century literary and verbal art.

The present moment is one in which some anglophones are telling themselves triumphal, depoliticized stories about their language's global importance, economic relevance, and aesthetic peerlessness. This is occurring while the globe is also witnessing the most thoroughgoing die-off of nonanglophone languages that it has ever known. Anglophone scholars (and others, one hopes) might chasten histories of anglophony and its subjects, its cultures, and its literatures by striving for what Édouard Glissant called "Relation." Rather than a monolingual and neoimperial global public, Glissant asks humans to attune themselves to the dynamics of creolization by considering the following question: "how many languages, dialects, or idioms will have vanished, eroded by the implacable consensus among powers between profits and controls, before human communities learn to preserve together their diversities?"[43]

The Poetics (and Prose) of Relation

When we think with the porous framework of anglophony, multilingual subjects constellate themselves in productive ways. These constellations show that multiplicity—perennially contentious and always subject to grave impositions—has always been a generative and indeed essential part of anglophone cultural life, an idea that stands in tension with Benedict Anderson's more general historical claim in *Imagined Communities* (1983) that "in the sixteenth century the proportion of bilinguals within the total population of Europe was quite small. . . . Then and now, the bulk of mankind is monoglot."[44] My argument is not that Anderson is wrong and that actually there were scores of bilinguals, trilinguals, and multilinguals throughout history.[45] Instead, my claim is that Anderson's term "monoglot" is overly limiting. Its fixity papers over the porous interstitial spaces between "bilingualism" and "monolingualism," an infinite series of gradations where linguistic knowledge is always in formation.

Moreover, Anderson's categories treat linguistic knowledge as something one can "acquire" in a perfect or complete form only over a long period of time. "If every language is acquirable," he writes, "its acquisition requires a real portion of a person's life: each new conquest is measured against shortening days. What limits one's access to other languages is not their imperviousness, but one's own mortality."[46] But what about people who learn a word, a phrase, a set of phrases, a passive understanding, an operational but perhaps limited ability in another language or languages? Put otherwise, a "bilingual" who has "acquired" another language by investing "a real portion of his life" over a long period of time is not the only subject who displays and draws on linguistic difference, and this is to say nothing of disability as it relates to language, a topic that is unfortunately outside the purview of this book. Taken in this more flexible way, multilingual pasts are recuperable and meaningful. Moreover, lineages can be drawn from these multilingual pasts to anglophony's lively (but often disavowed) multilingual present.

Glissant's account of the ways that monolingual thought is central to imperial practice is an important element of the theoretical apparatus that *Multilingual Subjects* puts forth going forward. This is because Glissant's conclusion that "Relation . . . is spoken multilingually" advocates for multilingual forms of knowledge, education, and interaction that are under threat in the globalizing present.[47] Departing from the notion that "the extinction of any language impoverishes everyone," Glissant holds up the creolization of language in the colonial and postcolonial Caribbean as a model for future forms of human relationality. He rightly diagnoses the sick present of global language politics, a present in which Standard English users too often assume that the rest of the multilingual world has facility in its communicative forms. "Whatever the degree of complexity, the one thing henceforth outmoded is the principle (if not the reality) of a language's intangible unicity," Glissant writes, later concluding that treating or teaching language and literature as though its "unicity" were real is an "epistemological anachronism," although one might also call this an epistemological error.[48]

The history of anglophony suggests that anglophones evade their own definition in aesthetically productive ways. Chosen for their exemplarity—in the contranymic sense of "exemplary" as totally unique but also utterly typical—the historical figures whose stories unfold in this book offer glimpses of anglophone life and aesthetics in forms that are otherwise difficult if not impossible to access. After this introduction, this book contains five chapters and a conclusion. Each of the chapters is organized around a particular form or genre of nonstandard, multilingual, or metalinguistic writing—linguistico-political writing, standardization theory, translation theory, intralingual translation, and interlingual translation. As such, the form of argumentation in each chapter conforms to the archive it studies. In addition, intercalated between each of the five chapters are short biographies of multilingual subjects of the long eighteenth century, human actors whose linguistic identities recapitulate the preceding chapter and anticipate the coming one. These biographies also attempt to refract the argument of each chapter in different and sometimes contradictory directions. In these short interludes, my own forms of metalinguistic writing come to the fore.

The short prelude to Chapter 1 examines the diverse linguistic identities of four escaped slaves who appear in a fugitive advertisement that was purchased by George Washington and published in the *Maryland Gazette* in 1761. Following on this first invocation of language, labor, and power, the first chapter begins with the uncanny similarity between a description of the coercive technologies used to teach English in Ireland during the 1790s and Ngũgĩ wa Thiong'o's famous description of colonial Kenyan children being "taught the lucrative value of being a traitor to one's immediate community" via linguistic pedagogy.[49] After tracing the representation of language and body in the eighteenth century through the emergent discourse of fugitive advertising, this chapter inverts the main terms of Derrida's *The Monolingualism of the Other* (1996)—as well as recent responses to this book by Yasemin Yildiz, Thomas Bonfiglio, and others—in order to refigure eighteenth-century approaches to the multilingualism of the other as a curious pairing of aesthetic interest and political demonization. Highlighting this ambivalence between the aesthetic and political, I then argue that eighteenth-century cultural incursions made in the name of linguistico-imperial thought were anticipated, critiqued, subverted, and challenged. I make this case through close readings of Robert Burns and Phillis Wheatley, two multilingual anglophones who are rarely discussed together because as subjects they appear dissimilar. As multilingual subjects, however, the aesthetic and political terms of their fame have surprising commonalities.

The interlude between Chapters 1 and 2 examines an Irish clergyman's fatalistic lament that Irish language and literacy were dying. This lament functions as a transition into the second's chapter's discussion of Jacques Rancière's *Aisthesis: Scenes from the Aesthetic Regime of Art* (2013), a book that enables a discussion of the forms of eighteenth-century multilingualism that were permitted to rise to the level of aesthetic and literary appreciation during the century, as one sees in the case of Burns. In order to begin this discussion, I elaborate on how eighteenth-century anglophony was all at once aesthetically interested in and yet politically resistant to the multilingualism of the other. The texts of the English standardization movement, I show, paradoxically criticized *and* valorized the English language by noting its "copiousness," a polysemic term that yokes together the language's perceived imperial belatedness and grammatical impoverishment (when compared to Greek, Latin, and French) with its abundant array of words and forms. At its heart, this chapter tracks the multilingual implications of the term "copiousness" as a metalinguistic description and idea relating to anglophone cultural identity.

Dorothy or "Dolly" Pentreath, a woman who has been mythologized as the last native speaker of the Cornish language, is the subject of my third biographical interlude. I tell Pentreath's story through the textual record of antiquarian Daines Barrington's effort to locate and converse with her in the 1770s. The third chapter addresses eighteenth-century theories and methodologies of translation in order to show that discourses of standardization and translation are mutually constituted over the course of the period. As I show, the ambivalence that characterizes standardization's negotiation of linguistic multiplicity also marks the period's translation theory. Translation theorists of the eighteenth century engage with linguistic multiplicity internal and external to anglophony by focusing on the translator's imperative to eschew "the servile path," so as not to fall under the control of the source language's characteristics. The regular injunction to pursue "free" or "liberal" translation coupled with the constant caution against "servile" or "slavish" translation amounts to a roundabout way of warning against unauthorized transportation of cultural material from other linguistic realms into anglophony. It also offers an additional, period-specific binary—free or slavish—within which to understand translation practice.

The primary conceit of popular outsider-looking-in texts like Oliver Goldsmith's *The Citizen of the World* (1760), or, a generation later, Elizabeth Hamilton's *Translation of the Letters of a Hindoo Rajah* (1796), is language's ability to situate a subject, even in writing. The interlude that links Chapters 3 and 4 considers Joseph Emin, a polyglot traveler who, despite "not being very well versed in the English language," wrote and published his own biography in 1792. Emin's fear of being judged through his language offers a way to think about anglophony and "dialect," a concept I purse in the fourth chapter. This chapters focuses on demotic "dialect dialogue" writing in Andrew Brice's *Exmoor Scolding In the Propriety and Decency of the Exmoor Language* (composed ca. 1727; first extant print edition 1746), John Collier's regularly reprinted *A View of the Lancashire Dialect by way of Dialogue* (1746), and, later, Maria and Richard Lovell Edgeworth's *Essay on Irish Bulls* (1802). By reading the aesthetics of Brice and Collier's work, as well as their Standard English translation histories, I frame these dialogues as deliberate critiques of the spread of Standard English literacy during the period.

Between Chapters 4 and 5 I discuss Ntiero Edem Efiom, a West African slave trader whose anglophone idiolect is a good model for the active rescripting of language and meaning through multilingualism that is discussed in the fifth chapter by way of interlingual translation. Whereas the fourth chapter focuses on intralingual translation, or, translation from one anglophone form to another, the fifth and final chapter positions interlingual translation in commercial terms. The works of Alexander Fraser Tytler, Sir William Jones, William Julius Mickle, and George Campbell show that interlingual translation of the period—like intralingual translation—stresses "free" and legible rather than "servile" translation. I intervene into analyses of imperial translation practice and aesthetics by suggesting that the effects of this ideology of translation are crucially related to the period's ideas of the commodity value of particular languages.

This book closes by considering the life and inventions of Sequoyah, a man well known for his invention of the Cherokee syllabary in 1821. This rumination on Sequoyah's desire to escape from and provincialize Standard English paves the way for the conclusion's discussion of contemporary conversations about the past and future of the English language. I discuss popular and potentially hyperbolic accounts of English's spread and influence in order to argue that the counterarchive of long eighteenth-century "dialect" writing, multilingual writing, and translation theory that the book has just surveyed offers a different view for the future of anglophony and the humanities more generally.

MULTILINGUAL LIVES

Peros, Jack, Neptune, and Cupid

On August 9, 1761, four male slaves escaped from Dogue Run farm in the Colony of Virginia. This event is remarkable for several reasons, the most notable of which is that Dogue Run farm made up part of the Mount Vernon plantation complex owned by George and Martha Washington, a couple who had married and combined their holdings two and a half years prior to the escape. In an effort to recapture those whom Washington viewed as his rightful property, he did like many other "victims" of this peculiar species of labor "theft." He took to the literate public sphere of newspapers and narrated the men into brief but vivid existence for the regional community of readers.[1] Specifically, Washington undertook the common act of purchasing a fugitive slave advertisement that described these four men in detail.[2] His advertisement, dated two days after the escape, appeared in an edition of the *Maryland Gazette* that was printed in Annapolis on August 20, 1761.[3]

Washington's roughly five-hundred-word advertisement, which has been usefully annotated by the editors of the *Papers of George Washington*, reads as follows:

> *Fairfax* County *(Virginia) August* 11, 1761.
>
> RAN away from a Plantation of the Subscriber's, on *Dogue-Run* in *Fairfax*, on Sunday the 9th Instant, the following Negroes, *viz.*
>
> *Peros*, 35 or 40 Years of Age, a well-set Fellow, of about 5 Feet 8 Inches high, yellowish Complexion, with a very full round Face, and full black Beard, his Speech is something slow and broken, but not in so great a Degree as to render him remarkable. He had on when he went away, a dark colour'd Cloth Coat, a white Linen Waistcoat, white Breeches, and white Stockings.

> *Jack*, 30 Years (or thereabouts) old, a slim, black, well made Fellow, of near 6 Feet high, a small Face, with Cuts down each Cheek, being his Country Marks, his Feet are large (or long) for he requires a great Shoe: The Cloathing he went off in cannot be well ascertained, but it is thought in his common working Dress, such as Cotton Waistcoat (of which he had a new One) and Breeches, and Osnabrig Shirt.
>
> *Neptune*, aged 25 or 30, well-set, and of about 5 Feet 8 or 9 Inches high, thin jaw'd, his Teeth stragling and fil'd sharp, his Back, if rightly remember'd, has many small Marks or Dots running from both Shoulders down to his Waistband, and his Head was close shaved: Had on a Cotton Waistcoat, black or dark colour'd Breeches, and an Osnabrig Shirt.
>
> *Cupid*, 23 or 25 Years old, a black well made Fellow, 5 Feet 8 or 9 Inches high, round and full faced, with broad Teeth before, the Skin of his Face is coarse, and inclined to be pimpley, he had no other distinguishable Mark that can be recollected; he carried with him his common working Cloaths, and an old Osnabrigs Coat made of Frockwise.
>
> The last two of these Negroes were bought from an *African* Ship in *August* 1759, and talk very broken and unintelligible *English*; the second one, *Jack*, is Countryman to those, and speaks pretty good *English*, having been several Years in the Country. The other, *Peros*, speaks much better than either, indeed has little of his Country Dialect left, and is esteemed a sensible and judicious Negro.
>
> As they went off without the least Suspicion, Provocation, or Difference with any Body, or the least angry Word or Abuse from their Overseers, 'tis supposed they will hardly lurk about in the Neighbourhood, but steer some direct Course (which cannot even be guessed at) in Hopes of an Escape: Or, perhaps, as the Negro *Peros* has lived many Years about *Williamsburg*, and *King William* County, and Jack in *Middlesex*, they may possibly bend their Course to one of those Places.
>
> Whoever apprehends the said Negroes, so that the Subscriber may readily get them, shall have, if taken up in this County, Forty Shillings Reward, beside what the Law allows; and if at any greater Distance, or out of the Colony, a proportionable Recompence paid them, by
>
> GEORGE WASHINGTON.
>
> *N.B.* If they should be taken separately, the Reward will be proportioned.[4]

Washington's notice typifies the variety of document a slave owner might be expected to compose upon the event of a slave escape. His prose follows the conventions of anglophone fugitive advertising from the seventeenth, eighteenth, and nineteenth centuries, conventions that I discuss at greater length in the next chapter. In brief, Washington's ad describes the age, dress, embodiment, and likely provenance of four people who will be hunted on the strength of those details. It also offers a sizable reward.

Additionally, and crucial for the argument of this book, Washington's ad follows the generic conventions of a subset of fugitive ads that attend meticulously to the language practices of the people who are described.[5] As a case in point, Washington includes pointed assessments of each one of his quarries' linguistic features. In the absence of the shorthand visual judgments that photographic technology makes possible, linguistic features are of obvious significance in the identification of an unknown person during the eighteenth century, especially insofar as linguistic features overlap with and buttress related perceptions about age, dress, embodiment, and provenance. Indeed, this unsystematic rendering of perceived linguistic features is a perfect example of what I mean by the term "metalinguistic writing," and so I am particularly interested in advertisements that include these details. This ad's premises are clear: one must listen in on elements of language that disclose other people's identities; these clues are revealed in speech's varied contours; and, furthermore, linguistic particularities combined with other signs of difference can be used to gloss a person's public character. In order to locate escaped slaves who are present in Washington's own account books only as made-up names and purchase prices, the ad above endows these four men with bodies and accompanying sounds. Even as those bodies and sounds are merely figments of text, they are meant to be recognizable to readers as sortable linguistic types.[6]

That the duly respected general and first president of the United States owned, managed, and pursued slaves in a way that is conventional and tedious (rather than atypical or benevolent) should come as no surprise. After all, the gap between enlightenment humanism's vaunted rhetoric and slavery's barbarities is one of eighteenth-century culture's most basic cultural conditions (rather than contradictions).[7] In Washington's case, the logistics of his long history as a slave owner are all at once mundane and shocking.[8] The people Washington held in bondage powered a lucrative system of farms that grew over the course of the proprietor's lifetime from two thousand to eight thousand acres. A total of 317 slaves were enumerated in a census undertaken simultaneous to the writing of Washington's last will and testament in 1799.[9] The contemporary visitor to Washington's Mount Vernon plantation museum might hear from a tour guide or read on a placard that Washington manumitted all his slaves upon his death. These historical approximations encourage the misconstruction that Washington himself purposefully manumitted 317 individuals in 1799. In fact, the details are more complex, the dates later, and the numbers less comprehensive.[10]

Returning to the escape of Peros, Jack, Neptune, and Cupid in 1761, the editors of the *Papers of George Washington* report that two of the four men who appear in the advertisement—Peros (a.k.a. Parros) and Jack—had come to Washington's plantation as dower slaves via his wealthier bride.[11] The other two—Neptune and Cupid—appear only in Washington's account books after 1760, a fact that lends credence to the ad's claim that these men "were bought from an *African* Ship in *August* 1759."[12] The editors further note that three of the four men—Peros, Jack, and Cupid—are included on a list of slaves at Mount Vernon that was composed in 1762, a year after the initial escape.[13] Regarding the slave referred to as Neptune, the situation is foggier. He does not appear on the 1762 list referenced above. However, in May 1765, Washington's account books include a debit to one of his overseers for 3l. 7s. 3p. for "pd Prison Fees in Maryld Neptune."[14] It is unlikely that the Neptune who was bailed out of a Maryland prison and returned to Washington's human holdings in 1765 is the same man as the Neptune who escaped in 1761. The details of how the other three escapees—Peros, Jack, and Cupid—were returned to bondage under Washington such that they were enumerated in the next year's census are also obscured.

There are two main reasons why I have traced the broad outlines of this escape and its aftermath here. First, I want to use a common genre of eighteenth-century writing, fugitive advertising, in order to show that linguistic difference was a salient aspect of interpersonal interaction in the eighteenth-century anglophone world. Linguistic difference was also a salient aspect of the representation of such interactions after the fact. People sorted and identified one another with attention to linguistic particularities. Then, as now, "Everything is summoned by an intonation," as Derrida writes.[15] Or, in the words of the contemporary poet Elizabeth Alexander, "We encounter each other in words, words / spiny or smooth, whispered or declaimed / words to consider, reconsider."[16] The second point I want to make by way of Washington's advertisement is that linguistic difference was and remains narratively generative. Fugitive ads show this plainly. Across many forms and genres of writing in the period, narrative strategies were developed in order to represent the complexities of interpersonal interaction in a realm of anglophone heterogeneity. Rhetorical strategies for naming social relationships made visible through linguistic difference flourished, as this book's chapters show. As writers developed descriptive techniques for encoding in text whether another person spoke well or badly, rapidly or slowly, with what quirks and disabilities, and in what kind of accent, the characterological and narrative landscape of eighteenth-century anglophone writing widened dramatically.

Consider, for example, the way that Washington's ad can be read against the grain as four miniscule and partial biographies. Their bodies, clothes, origins, and linguistic particularities appear as the fleeting details of subjectivity—paltry details, certainly, but details nonetheless. For my purposes, I want to stress here that the linguistic particularities Washington ascribes to Peros, Jack, Neptune, and Cupid reveal several dimensions of anglophony's eighteenth-century texture, especially as they relate to embodiment. As a case in point, Washington's ad claims that Neptune and Cupid, who are new to North America, "talk very broken and unintelligible *English*." Put another way, they are multilingual subjects and their English has been acquired recently, informally, and under the duress of trying to adapt to enslavement. They "talk" English, but unintelligibly, which, aside from being a contradiction, is a judgment on these men's social and even civilizational statuses relative to Washington. By contrast, Jack "speaks pretty good *English*, having been several Years in the Country." His body is "well made" and marked with the residues of severed familial and community allegiances by "Cuts down each Cheek, being his Country Marks." With "pretty good English" and a marked face that attests to other cultural loyalties, Jack appears in the *Maryland Gazette* as a quintessential multilingual anglophone subject of the eighteenth century.

A tantalizing and subtle detail of the ad links Jack, Neptune, and Cupid together as a conspiratorial group. The three are "countrymen," a nebulous indication by Washington that perhaps these men communicated in versions of the same African language or in African languages that were mutually intelligible or pidginized to the degree that each could make himself understood to the others.[17] Read in this way, it is possible to surmise that

Washington heard the African languages of these and other slaves with some regularity, or at least that his overseers did. This idea is further supported by the fact that, as Donald Sweig notes, Washington was regularly purchasing slaves "from the mid-1750s until about 1770."[18] It is also likely that Washington is openly suggesting to the reader that a shared set of African linguistic protocol helped facilitate the men's planning and eventual escape. Be on guard against slaves speaking to each other in languages you do not understand, Washington's ad warns the reader. Be on guard against the multilingualism of certain others. Through these short descriptions, it is clear that Washington's ad pitches linguistic difference as both apparent and subversive, especially insofar as it overlaps with and reinforces other vectors of stigmatized identity like race.[19]

The slave named Peros stands apart from the other three. For one, he is the oldest and the most experienced with the life of a slave in the mid-Atlantic colonies. This is attested to by Washington's laudatory but paternalistic evaluation that Peros "speaks much better than either, indeed has little of his Country Dialect left, and is esteemed a sensible judicious Negro." In the present, some will feel a specter of palpable linguistic loss in Peros's story, but Washington sees only improvement in the form of civilizing and (perhaps) humanizing achievement. In fact, his description implies that to the degree that Peros's "Country Dialect" has dissolved, his ability to speak and comport himself properly has improved. Peros's stable command of an anglophone language likely even encourages Washington and his overseers to view him as "sensible" and "judicious," though that reading is more assumption than conclusion. Whether or not Peros can also communicate with Jack, Neptune, Cupid, or others in another African language remains unclear but is suggested in this ad. It is not implausible that Peros should have "little of his Country Dialect left." Linguistic skills atrophy if they are unused. However, Washington does not speak Peros's ancestral language or languages. His claim that Peros has lost that unnamed language is difficult to verify and perhaps better reflects Washington's own affective investments than real linguistic facts on the ground.

Indeed, in the picture that Washington draws of Peros, the writer's linguistic evaluations take on a note of narrative excess. In addition to the paragraph near the end of the advertisement in which he gives a general accounting of the language skills of the group as a whole, Washington's initial description of Peros insists on including the detail that his "Speech is something slow and broken, but not in so great a Degree as to render him remarkable." Peros, in other words, speaks with quirks that, paradoxically, a reader of the *Maryland Gazette* will never notice because these features do not "render him remarkable." Washington admits that Peros's linguistic particularities are below detection, somehow only knowable or noticeable to the ad's author. And yet they are mentioned in this short text as though they signify something more. What could Peros's "unremarkable" linguistic "slowness" and "brokenness" be doing in a text that is purchased, written, and designed to efficiently highlight those features that *are* remarkable about him as the object of a manhunt? By the author's own admission, these details are superfluous to the task of finding and identifying the man in question. So why are they there?

Washington's inclusion of these details about Peros's linguistic identity signifies something about the context of eighteenth-century anglophony even if it says little of interest about Peros as a historical person and embodied linguistic subject. Emergent characterological and narrative forms (of which the fugitive ad is only a narrow example) played a role in making the linguistically unremarkable remarkable as an index of identity. These forms of writing bring nonnormative language into being in new ways. The slave hunter who catches Peros and his band of differentially skilled anglophone multilinguals is to know that the oldest, most "sensible," and most "judicious" among them is not actually "sensible" or "judicious" at all. His language is to be judged "slow" and "broken" even if it is not experienced as such by an interlocutor. These details consolidate the more general eighteenth-century phenomenon whereby the experience of linguistic difference is mediated by metalinguistic descriptions emphasizing normativity. Wherever they are found, these descriptions enumerate qualities like body shape, mental acuity, and behavioral quirks in such a way as to conceptually align them with linguistic difference. The inclusion of these "unremarkable" linguistic details as remarkable, in other words, is a scaled-down version of a more comprehensive process. Eighteenth-century anglophone writing that is about or concerning anglophony forecloses certain ways of experiencing linguistic difference during this period. By giving readers a linguistic scrim through which all experiences of otherness must pass, eighteenth-century texts precede and undermine human interactions that may or may not feature linguistic difference. Metalinguistic commentary comes to predict and predefine character types, in other words, and linguistic difference becomes a prominent clue in the larger labyrinth of public identity as it unfurls in the eighteenth century's transoceanic spaces.

Conversely, in the absence of apparent linguistic difference, other vectors of identity are called on to project any likely linguistic differences that may exist even when on the surface they are undetectable or "unremarkable."

As part of the passage to a more elaborate discussion of the multilingualism of the other as it appears in eighteenth-century texts, I begin with the ephemeral evocation of these four men's voices and linguistic identities because the truth of these voices and linguistic identities is something that can be neither confirmed nor denied. Washington's evaluation of these multilingual subjects is eternally suspended in the swollen archive of the U.S. slave economy just as it is forever inscribed in an anglophone history of representation involving what type of person is commonly believed to speak in what types of ways. We cannot *hear* Peros, Jack, Neptune, or Cupid speak on their own terms. Even if we could hear them, their speech would already be mediated, just as the works of liminal anglophone subjects like Ignatius Sancho and Phillis Wheatley were, at the moment of their publication, predigested through the assumptions of racist categorization, some of which were built around and buttressed by linguistic reception criteria, a point I address in the following chapter.[20] Washington's ad in the *Maryland Gazette* has spoken for these four men. In its even more powerful way, the mesh of embodied, ethnolinguistic identities that takes shape against the regime of eighteenth-century Standard English and its writing practices has, in its powerful way, already prefigured them too.

CHAPTER 1

The Multilingualism of the Other

Politics, Counterpolitics, Anglophony, and Beyond

Violent Bequests

> The Irish language and the Irish people were proscribed together. It was penal to teach and penal to learn the energetic dialect of our country. All of you recollect when it was a crime to speak it in the hedge schools, where we received the first rudiments of knowledge; and when the square bit of timber, called *the score*, suspended from the neck of each new scholar, gave intimation to the master, by a notch on its angles, when the stammering urchin relapsed into his mother tongue at home.[1]

> Thus one of the most humiliating experiences was to be caught speaking Gĩkũyũ in the vicinity of the school. The culprit was given corporal punishment—three to five strokes of the cane on the bare buttocks—or was made to carry a metal plate around the neck with inscriptions such as I AM STUPID or I AM A DONKEY. Sometimes the culprits were fined money they could hardly afford. And how did the teachers catch the culprits? A button was initially given to one pupil who was supposed to hand it over to whoever was caught speaking his mother tongue. Whoever had the button at the end of the day would sing who had given it to him and the ensuing process would bring out all the culprits of the day. Thus children were turned into witchhunters and in the process were being taught the lucrative value of being a traitor to one's immediate community.[2]

Although drawn from different periods and spaces, the scenes of learning above bear witness to violent and "humiliating" episodes of linguistic coercion. The first conjures up anglicization in Ireland during the 1790s while the second recalls the stiffening of British education policy in colonial Kenya after 1952.[3] Taken chronologically, these two scenes portray language as cultural and later legal authority, a trajectory whose origins we can trace back to the long eighteenth century. Indeed it was during this century, in both the British Isles and North America, that a particular species of ethnolinguistic chauvinism organized around "proper" or "standard" linguistic behavior came to dominate anglophone cultural life. It was also during this century that the ideological groundwork was laid for making Standard English pedagogy into a constituent element of imperial rule, a process that Gauri Viswanathan's *Masks of Conquest* (1989) chronicled nearly three decades ago.[4] The eighteenth-century drive to standardization is a decisive chapter in anglophone history. It is one of the preconditions for the educational violence staged in the testimonies above. In this drive one finds an increasingly intrusive set of practices for eliminating certain forms of linguistic diversity, practices that have reverberated throughout anglophone cultural life ever since.

While Chapters 2 and 3 directly address the role of eighteenth-century standardization and translation theories as agents of linguistic homogeneity, in order to pave the way for that discussion this first chapter focuses more broadly on the relationship between linguistic identity and power in the period. I begin with these epigraphs because they are one possible endpoint of eighteenth-century linguistic thought. Specifically, they show normative systems of cultural and linguistic authority taking the extreme measure of adjudicating living human languages as "crimes" befitting "corporal punishment"—"a square bit of timber, called *the score*, suspended from the neck of each new scholar," as in the first epigraph, or, "three to five strokes of the cane on the bare buttocks," as the second has it. How are we to conceive of the cultural history that gives birth to this definition of "crime"? The starting point that I pursue here involves emphasizing the crucial eighteenth-century dialectic between the linguistically normative and nonnormative, conceptual immediacies that acquired fixed meanings over the course of the period.[5] Among other things, these epigraphs show normative linguistic practices brutally harrying the nonnormative. In so doing they indirectly highlight multilingualism's limited but provocative options for refusing its own eradication.

The first epigraph is taken from an 1827 speech delivered in Liverpool by an "Irish Catholic Clergyman" whose name appears in the record only as Reverend Lyons.[6] In his bombastic speech, Lyons addresses an English Catholic organization as an invited guest, a native informant called on to quantify the tentacular reach of anglophony into Irish society. Delivered in Standard English, the speech attacks the "proscription" of "the Irish language and the Irish people" as it was practiced in Irish-run hedge schools before the establishment of the National School system in 1831. As his argument unfolds, Lyons challenges normalizing linguistic intrusions that are—in point of fact—the basic formal preconditions of his speech. After all, he was among the Irish-speaking students disciplined into anglophony by "the square bit of timber, called *the score*," a wooden index of linguistic loyalty that shuttled news of subversive, nonanglophone behavior between the private space of the home and the semipublic space of the hedge school. The fact that this multilingual subject delivers his fierce criticisms of anglophone expansion as it interfaces with Irish culture and religion is interesting enough. More interesting still, however, is that speaking *against* anglophone cultural imperialism *in* Standard English and *in* England is a theoretical problem that Lyons manages in a proleptic way, a point I address later. I present Lyons's words here and elsewhere in this book because his reflections invite scholars in the present to think carefully about multilingualism as a prerequisite for (and an enduring dynamic within) our own moment's rapidly changing linguistic and literary practices.

The second epigraph is taken from Ngũgĩ wa Thiong'o's essay "The Language of African Literature," a masterstroke of postcolonial theory that was published in 1986 as one of the four parts of *Decolonising the Mind: The Politics of Language in African Literature*. As part of Ngũgĩ's discussion of language's role as a carrier of culture, his essay interrogates the destructiveness of anglophone schooling in late-colonial Kenya. The author skewers colonial linguistic intrusions with great energy, and rightly so. For him they produced the "colonial alienation" and "spiritual subjugation" that postcolonial writing must overcome.[7] "In my view," he writes, "language was the most important vehicle through which that power fascinated and held the soul prisoner."[8] In addition to highlighting these metaphors of repression and confinement, I want to suggest that the colonial "politics of language" evoked by Ngũgĩ's title and eviscerated in his text is the intellectual descendant of a more diffuse "monolingual politics of language" that takes shape in colonial as well as noncolonial spaces during the eighteenth century. This form of linguistic politics need not be legally ordained to have massive cultural ramifications.

To recap, both Lyons and Ngũgĩ attack the use of linguistic prohibition so as to "control a people's culture" and thus "control their tools of self-definition in relation to others."[9] These authors' twinned exasperation with these forms of control implies a "transtemporal" and transperipheral connection, one that embeds the cultural logics of Ireland in the 1790s, Liverpool in 1827, and Kenya in the 1950s into the cultural landscape of 2017 while also making space for the yawning gaps separating these unique historical episodes and geocultural spaces.[10] Lyons and Ngũgĩ have both inherited a monolingual politics of language that developed during the eighteenth century. We too are the heirs of this monolingual politics of language in manifold ways, and we would do well to ask ourselves about the long cultural and historical developments required to place nonnormative linguistic identities like theirs under prohibition.

It is important to remember that linguistic situations like Lyons's and Ngũgĩ's are not outliers but instead common.[11] In the words of sociolinguist Rajend Mesthrie, a scholar who has catalogued British imperialism's linguistic dimensions, "In territory after territory, from Wales to the Cape, India to Sri Lanka, a common practice in introducing English in schools was to silence the local languages."[12] The verb "silence" in Mesthrie's sentence is an obvious euphemism that masks more drastic practices.[13] He alludes to but does not spell out these practices, stating simply that "the methods [of linguistic instruction] in territory after territory smacked of raw power."[14] Nor does Mesthrie discuss linguistic impositions in Britain, but it is safe to say that the dialectic of normative and nonnormative functioned similarly in eighteenth-century Britain's constituent kingdoms and provinces, a phenomenon I chart in Chapter 4.[15]

Beyond highlighting the violence that has often accompanied linguistic intrusion, there is a better reason for starting with these two epigraphs. However coercive and dehumanizing, and whether by convention as in Lyons or imperial statute as in Ngũgĩ, the exercise of "raw power" on multilingual subjects at anglophony's threshold has been the engine for startling modes of creative resistance. This is true in politics as well as in aesthetics.[16] In the now long-standing political and aesthetic traditions that have emerged as responses to diverse linguistic intrusions—and which, it must be emphasized, are not the only way of responding to imposed languages—"education" often acts as a byword for linguistic proscriptions, proscriptions that diminish cultural variety by inculcating the "lucrative value of being a traitor to one's immediate community" alongside but also *as part of* anglophone literacy and its itinerant versions of humanism.[17] This rightfully cynical reading of "education" allows nonnormative linguistic subjects to anticipate, critique, manipulate, subvert, and challenge such intrusions—and often brilliantly. In other words, a politics of normative anglophone monolingualism has often naturally generated a counterpolitics of nonnormative multilingualism, a counterpolitics that is spearheaded by those under pressure to adapt their linguistic and community identities to inscrutable flows of capital and external forms of power.[18] Just as we have inherited the monolingual politics of language that developed in conjunction with anglophony's eighteenth-century expansion, so too are we heirs to exciting versions of linguistic counterpolitics, including those visible in Lyons and Ngũgĩ, both of whom choose autobiographical testimony to exorcise cultural violence. The stories told in this book address the mechanisms of linguistic intrusion. However, my primary goal is to describe forms of multiplicity, vitality, and creative productivity that have flourished in spite of linguistic intrusion from the eighteenth century to the present.[19]

Monolingualism as a Politics of Language

Up to this point, I have been using the terms "politics of language" and "counterpolitics of language" without defining them rigorously, which is a problem insofar as these terms can seem unsatisfyingly imprecise.[20] Like others who have considered the dialectic of normative and nonnormative language in culture, I submit here that one way we can start to access and fix the shifting meanings of the terms "politics of language" and "counterpolitics of language" is by way of Jacques Derrida's *The Monolingualism of the Other*, a giant little book whose title has been reformulated as the governing metaphor of this chapter. For Derrida, as for Lyons and Ngũgĩ, colonial language politics are always monolingual in nature. "The monolingualism imposed by the other," Derrida argues, "reduce[s] language to the One, that is, to the hegemony of the homogenous."[21] In response, linguistic counterpolitics resists the "hegemony of the homogeneous" by featuring nonnormative multiplicities as a basic principle. Put another way, whereas a monolingual politics of language seeks to inculcate within varied linguistic subjects the law that "we [the civilized] only ever speak one language"—Standard English, for example—a multilingual counterpolitics of language spawns heterogeneity within the fantasy monolanguage itself.[22]

"Monolingualism" in Derrida is a political construction. It is a discourse of control that is instituted through the purposeful imposition of normative language forms over a population that is perceived to be linguistically inferior, untethered in loyalties, and therefore threateningly mobile, as has regularly been the case in colonial and provincial situations. Following Derrida, Yasemin Yildiz has lucidly historicized the fetishized concepts of monolingualism and the "mother tongue" within the context of European nationalism.[23] Yildiz demonstrates that in Europe the long eighteenth century gave rise to a nation-based and "reified conception of language," one that enabled the very "distinction between monolingualism and multilingualism" in the first place. The difference between monolingualism and multilingualism was not salient before this period, Yildiz argues. Relatedly, Thomas Paul Bonfiglio offers a detailed analysis of the eighteenth-century birth of "ethnolinguistic prejudice," a way of thinking about language in which monolingualism as "modeled on the elite speech of the court and of the best authors" becomes "an organ of the political power of the nation and empire."[24] In these authors, monolingualism is a contingent and historically situated method of centralizing cultural and political power. Under this regime, monolingualism buttresses and reproduces itself through sustained attempts to police or "imprison" the nonnormative and often multilingual linguistic behaviors of the other, to paraphrase Ngũgĩ.[25]

For Derrida, monolingualism metaphorizes authority and "sovereignty" whereas nonnormative linguistic practices trouble both. Monolingualism is thus peddled as a form of linguistic identity toward which the colonized, subaltern, and multilingual are compelled to aspire, a form of identity that will presumably confer cultural capital, career advancement, and full humanity.[26] This fantasy vision of monolingualism is the very heart of the matter. The nonnormative linguistic subject is obliged through rhetoric, education, and "raw power" to see the monolingualism of the "master" as a *terminus ad quem*, a perpetually receding destination where—should they ever arrive—nonnormative linguistic subjects will attain normativity and thus be enfolded into the structures of cultural power. In this way, a politics of monolingualism becomes a tool of control. Monitoring, corralling, and attempting to eradicate nonnormative linguistic identities occurs whenever linguistic difference connotes danger, illegality, arrested development, or inassimilable alterity. In brief, the monolingualism that Lyons, Ngũgĩ, and so many others have faced is all at once political and nomothetic—"political" because it concerns the linguistic norms of the polis and "nomothetic" because it usurps the power to give names and form deliberate linguistic communities.

Derrida conceives of the politics of monolingualism in a way that productively resonates with the work of Mikhail Bakhtin, whose exploration of the "dialogic imagination" provides a capacious idea of multilingualism emphasizing the "peasant's" obligation to move between diverse sociolinguistic registers, especially in dealings with "authority": "An illiterate peasant, miles away from any urban center, naively immersed in an unmoving and for him unshakable everyday world, nevertheless lived in several language systems: he prayed to God in one language (Church Slavonic), sang songs in another, spoke to his family in a third, and, when he began to dictate petitions to the local authorities through a scribe, he tried speaking yet a fourth language (the official-literate, 'paper' language)."[27] This passage encourages one to seek linguistic multiplicities where they do not initially disclose themselves. More generally, Bakhtin's humanizing celebration of the "illiterate [but still multilingual] peasant" opens up new avenues for thinking normative linguistic power as it works to define nonnormative identities. The "illiterate peasant" is "multilingual" in his particular way, an unexpected qualifier, perhaps, but an instructive one. What I mean is that such a form of multilingualism allows the peasant to move from the linguistic registers of local life, family, and religion to the monolanguage of authority when the exigencies of subaltern life so demand. This is different from but comparable to the multilingualism displayed by cosmopolitan writers and translators of the eighteenth-century world republic of letters, people who transfer cultural material between different linguistic system like Samuel Johnson, Robert Lowth, Alexander Tytler, and others who are taken up in later chapters. Indeed, it is under the banner of a nonnormative multilingualism so construed that the "provincial" peasant can be brought together with the most highly educated translator. Monolingualism is, as in Derrida, a political construction. It is the simple idea that the great messy spectrum of human linguistic behavior can be singularized, standardized, and (forcibly) exported to others.

For me, the value of thinking with this binary of normative monolingualism and nonnormative multilingualism is that it brings together seemingly disparate ways of being in language. To be clear, the term "multilingual" as I will use it hereafter gathers in its fold subjects whose multilingualism is as commonly construed: an interlingual ability to communicate in different language systems, like "English" or "French" for example. The term also includes intralingual multilinguals, that is, subjects who choose or are compelled to code switch between differently marked forms of a particular linguistic system (in this case anglophony) irrespective of whether or not they are capable of using another linguistic system like French. The reason I have chosen to use these terms in this novel way is that, during the eighteenth century, these two figures—the multilingual cosmopolitan and the nonnormative, local "peasant"—both came into contact with the politics of anglophone monolingualism's rapid and invasive spread. For me, this is the multilingualism of the other—whether as the interlingual ability to use different linguistic systems or as the intralingual obligation and ability to move from one's local linguistic identity to "the official-literate, 'paper' language." Both of these abilities amount to a counterpolitics of language that productively troubles those fantasies of linguistic homogeneity that have had a narrowing influence on anglophone culture.

In addition, the definitions of monolingualism and multilingualism that I am deriving here are supple in the way they bring together colonial and provincial space. For example, monolingualism has had inestimable implications for rural and nonmetropolitan spaces of England. These spaces cannot rightly be construed as subject to colonization, at least not insofar as we currently define colonization, but nonetheless, the monolingual politics of Standard English has had important cultural effects in these spaces. Katie Wales makes a related point in her book *Northern English: A Cultural and Social History* (2006). Wales points out that "there has also been a strong bias in histories of English towards both a metropolitan bias, and a southern one: what I shall term *metrocentrism and austrocentrism* respectively."[28] With these terms metrocentrism and austrocentrism, Wales registers the geographical origins of the normative vision of Standard English around which the politics of monolingualism grew. While we can trouble this geographical origin by engaging with works staging the multilingualism of the other as well as a counterpolitics of multilingualism in metropolitan and "austral" parts of Britain—works such as Samuel Pegge's *Anecdotes of the English Language* (1803), for example, which I take up in a later chapter—Wales's point is instructive. The incursion of linguistic normativity emanating from the court, bar, and universities of metropolitan southern England had a particular impact on northern England, and this matters immensely during a period when northern England was experiencing rapid (though uneven) economic and demographic growth.

One way of summarizing what I have been arguing so far is to reiterate that a politics of monolingualism chases after linguistic difference wherever it resides. This is a metaphor, of course, but one that has literal manifestations in the historical archive. What follows in the next section is an investigation of the politics of monolingualism as it appears in a particularly naked form: fugitive advertising, a curious genre of eighteenth- and nineteenth-century writing in which nonnormative subjects are literally on the run. I choose fugitive advertising rather than grammars, dictionaries, elocution texts, style guides, and translation manuals at this early moment of my argument because the politics of monolingualism is unconcealed and instructive in these ephemeral documents. In addition, the hot pursuits that these ads index can serve as so many symbols for the progressive policing of linguistic diversity that a politics of monolingualism seeks. In addition to a politics of monolingualism, equally evident in these ads is the multilingualism of the other, by which I mean the diversely formed bodies and identities of nonnormative linguistic subjects, people like Peros, Jack, Neptune, and Cupid, people whose bobs, feints, and flights metaphorize nonnormative models of being resistant, being in language, and being in the world. That a politics of monolingualism became a structural principle of anglophone culture during the eighteenth century—and through a variety of written forms including grammars, dictionaries, elocution texts, style guides, and translation manuals, but also through metalinguistic writing in commonplace organs like newspapers—is evident. And yet, the other's multilingualism—however infelicitous the phrase and however imaginary the "other"—is often underinvestigated.

Sound Opinions: Of Language and the Body

Some instinct induced me to lay my hand upon a newspaper. . . .

I threw a languid glance at the first column that presented itself. The first words which I read, began with the offer of a reward of three hundred guineas for the apprehension of a convict under sentence of death, who had escaped from Newgate prison in Dublin. Good heaven! How every fibre of my frame tingled when I proceeded to read that the name of the criminal was Francis Carwin!

The description of the person and address were minute. His stature, hair, complexion, the extraordinary position and arrangement of his features, his

> awkward and disproportionate form, his gesture and gait, corresponded perfectly with those of our mysterious visitant. He had been found guilty in two indictments. One for the murder of the Lady Jane Conway, and the other for a robbery committed on the person of the honorable Mr. Ludloe.[29]

The eighteenth century was a period when newspapers carried abundant advertisements for fugitive apprentices, servants, slaves, soldiers, and suspected criminals.[30] Anglophone papers disseminated thousands of notices over the course of the century in pages where fugitives were flanked by ads for theatricals, tutors, books, commercial products, and many other commodities.[31] In fact, as Marcus Wood and others have noted, British fugitive ads blazed discursive trails for the nineteenth-century explosion of fugitive slave notices in North America, a genre of writing that became financially critical to the business model of some newspapers, including Benjamin Franklin's.[32] These ads reveal some of the linguistic, racial, gendered, and bodily intersectionalities that constituted public identity for enslaved, indentured, and free people who appeared as outlaws in papers from Britain to North America, from the Caribbean to South Asia.[33] Beyond being the transatlantic archive of the economic entanglement between slavery and the press, fugitive ads should be seen as informative textual products common to anglophone communities around the globe. Irrespective of place, anglophone communities used fugitive ads to invent and propagate ideas of human difference as they related to embodied social interaction. In many cases the politics of monolingualism is in the foreground while the creative productivity of multilingual lives lurks beneath the surface.

If we view fugitive advertising as an important genre—and generator—of descriptive writing throughout the eighteenth and nineteenth centuries and across the diverse spaces of the anglophone world, as I believe we should, then metalinguistic descriptions at work in these ads enable analytical insights about the emergent politics of monolingualism that I have been describing. For one, we can acknowledge that linguistic practices were viewed as an aspect of embodiment, an aspect that the ads' metalinguistic writing must find ways to represent or "capture." This is important because—in spite of the productive attention that has been given to identity as a visual interpretive event—critics have yet to think through what spoken language means in conjunction with identity schemas based on visualizing the body.[34] More generally, appreciating the copresence of visual and auditory descriptors in these ads allows us to see that only by virtue of the patterned interweaving of all these descriptive vocabularies do fugitive identities take shape in text. This is not to say that linguistic qualifications or descriptions are present in all fugitive ads; they are not.[35] Rather, I merely mean to suggest that a subsection of these ads gives us the opportunity to eavesdrop on the linguistic dimensions of public identity. When we seize this opportunity, we come into contact with a wide variety of subjects, all of whom are ordered with respect to one another and with respect to a politics of anglophone monolingualism in complex ways.

Furthermore, it is clear that eighteenth-century fugitive ads register the long development of our own enmeshed and misrepresentative racial, ethnic, sexual, gender, ability, and class (often occupational) categories. These ads refer regularly to these categories, just as they often luridly catalogue visible bodily differences and disabilities. I stress the linguistic components of these ads not because I want to deemphasize more familiar critical dimensions for analyzing the hierarchies of social reality, but rather because I want to build on the work others have done by thinking through linguistic embodiment as it reinforces and in some cases stands in for these other dimensions of public identity. Whereas features of identity like race are grafted onto bodies via an interpretive oscillation between visible somatic features and the discursive environment, an individual's linguistic identity represents the interaction of that same discursive environment with the more ephemeral event of speaking, an event over which the speaker might have a certain control.[36] To reiterate, one theoretical opportunity that I see in these ads is the opportunity to think about linguistic identity in relation to other vectors of interpersonal difference, and more generally, to think about power and identity with and beyond the categories of ability, class, ethnicity, gender, race, and sex.

Consider the following descriptive cues as they intersect with legal and moral prejudgments in a London ad announcing a hefty bounty placed on the head of Elizabeth Baker, a Bristol "spinster" suspected of abetting the forced elopement of a wealthy heiress "for the lucre thereof." In this description of Baker, her linguistic profile is a vital clue. We see its significance in the ad's narration of Baker: "The said Elizabeth Baker is about 22 years old, stout limbed, handsome face, and fresh colour, is rather tall, dark eyes, and has a great deal of the Somersetshire dialect in her speech."[37] Motivated reward seekers would have to keep their ears to the ground for a woman speaking in nonnormative West Country sounds.[38] "Somersetshire dialect" works here in tandem with the term "spinster" in order to cast a gendered suspicion on the suspect, a potentially unmarried woman who, according to the allegations, helped dupe another woman into abduction and marriage.[39] The ad for Baker creates a sprawling mesh of mutually reinforcing censures, including, most obviously, her criminal designs on "lucre." With lucre in mind, it is worth noting that the ad for Baker, like most others in the period, incentivizes the reader's careful internalization of this mesh with the promise of financial windfall, "100 guineas" in Baker's case. A reader would be paid to properly envision, intone, and identify outlaws narrated in the paper.

Reaping the monetary rewards of reading fugitive ads like the one for Baker required readers to be familiar with anglophone life as it was structured around multiple, intersecting dimensions of embodied and vocalized difference. In British papers, language specifications register cultural, educational, and class divisions between province and capital, and it is around these core divisions that other aspects of identity tend to orbit. British ads also stress the linguistic abnormality and insularity of people from English provinces like Baker's native Somerset. Implicit in the logic is the notion that suspects like Baker lack normative linguistic propriety to the same degree that they lack qualities that would permit them to be part of the imagined extension of a national community. In this vein, a 1771 advertisement in the *Gazetteer and New Daily Advertiser* announces a search for John Anderson, a sixteen-year-old apprentice accused of unlawfully absconding from his shipmaster, Captain Robert Elder, a seemingly reputable factor of British maritime trade. Anderson, the ad reveals, "speaks thick and mumbling, and has something of the Yorkshire dialect."[40] This linguistic judgment directly follows the public declaration of the man's deserter status. The "mumbling" fugitive's linguistic deficiencies dovetail with his failures as a sailor, and vice versa. Caught in a related but different state of linguistic exception, Derby jail escapee Anne Williamson "talks in the Yorkshire Dialect and belongs to a notorious Gang of Gamblers, her Father, Mother, and another, being now in Leicester Gaol in order to take their Trial at the next Assizes, for stealing Great Coats at Melton Fair."[41] Williamson appears in this ad as a member of a criminal family existing well beyond the linguistic, bodily, and legal ideals of normative society, a family who resembles an early modern canting crew rather than the fundamental social unit of a society cinched together by a standard language propagated by the literate mother's tongue.[42]

Under a politics of monolingualism, disciplinary coercion is not just thinkable but practicable, especially so on bodies that are not fully (and perhaps *never fully*) enumerated as human owing to their precarious apprenticeships to the language being enforced and the other norms of identity that accompany standard language. At issue in the question of a monolingual politics of language versus a multilingual counterpolitics of language is the humanity of those who maintain ties to unauthorized or nonprestigious linguistic systems. Even in the earlier epigraphs by Lyons and Ngũgĩ, vocabularies of animality eclipse those of humanity as they pertain to multilingualism, a fact that the larger context of these two pieces bears out more fully. Both figures allude to being perceived and treated as multilingual, other, and even animal. In Lyons, the notched "score" is suspended from the "stammering urchin's" neck to keep a damning tally of the speaking animal's uncanny linguistic crimes. In Ngũgĩ, a metal plate reading "I AM A DONKEY" publicly proclaims the bestialization of its wearer to anyone who can read English.

The definition of the human is similarly at issue in advertisements that use a suspect's linguistic embodiment in conjunction with explicitly ableist appraisals of physical structure, as though bodily and linguistic irregularities prefigure legal transgressions. When apprentice Thomas Norris escaped from his Battersea master in May 1747, the ad announcing the ten-shilling reward for his capture described him like this: "He is about Twenty Years of Age, near five Feet six Inches high, full fac'd, his Knees bending inwards, born at Sainsbury, talks the West-Country Dialect."[43] The diagnosis, "knees bending inwards," tries to characterize Norris's exceptional body. The description then moves on to his place of birth and linguistic distinctiveness. The concatenation of these details invites the reading that they are correlative.

Fugitive ads show that central to the eighteenth-century's emergent monolingual politics of language are the processes by which normative linguistic impositions made other linguistic identities into evidence of a speaker's uncorrectable infrahumanity. After all, an infrahuman is capable of neither politics nor art. Another way of stating the principal drama of the last section's two epigraphs—as well as fugitive ads—is that Lyons and Ngũgĩ are forced by a monolingual politics of language into that liminal space between human and animal. They must make the case, through Standard English—and only Standard English—for their humanity as multilingual subjects. This is predictable. For not only is there a long human tendency of relying on the shibboleths of others to determine who is a full-fledged member of one's linguistic and cultural confraternity, there is an equally robust anglophone tradition of demanding that subjects prove their humanity in and through Standard English lest they be classified instead as animals, as in racializing discourse, or as commodities, as in the case of the slave trade.

The depiction of fugitive bank clerk John Carwardine's linguistic embodiment offers a more pointed example. Not only does the ad inscribe a British provincial-metropolitan binary into the understanding of Carwardine, it reads the suspected embezzler's delinquent dialect as indicative of a more general pattern of bodily deviance. Carwardine stands "five feet nine inches high, or thereabouts, very thin made, fair complexion, wide mouth, turned-up-nose, sickly look . . . two small red lumps near his right ear . . . the muscles of his face work very much when spoken to by a stranger; shews his upper teeth; which are large and yellow, and speaks the Herefordshire dialect."[44] The distinctive mouth, teeth, and facial muscles—all elemental organs in the production of speech—seem to explain the suspect's Herefordshire accent, which appears deficient through its disabling adjacency to his nonnormative body. Intensifying this effect, Carwardine, the ad claims, evinces still other elements of a singular physical presence: a "head leaning considerably to the left shoulder" and an asymmetrical gait that causes him to "swing his right arm a good deal." Carwardine's embodiment, Herefordshire linguistic habits, and legal transgressions reinforce and implicate one another, even to the point that they resist parsing. The simultaneous manifestation of crime, body, and language restricts Carwardine's humanity to an insidious degree. His language practices are depicted as immature, badly developed, hyperlocal, or "rustic," as the period's literature would increasingly term it.[45] On the great chain of being, Carwardine occupies a lower rung by virtue of his linguistic embodiment.

Similar interest in the linguistic qualifications of humanity appears in ads that take a body and insist on its "dark" or "black" complexion, an overdetermined symbol in the period of race-based slavery's greatest expansion. An accentuated complexion appears as the visible sign of criminality. Frequently, linguistic idiosyncrasy is the audible analogue to remarkable skin. This is one way of reading the ad for a woman going by the pseudonyms "Mary Webb, Clarke, Gardner, &c." She was held for fraudulent merchandising in 1778 and described in the press as possessing both the

"West Country Dialect" and "a black complexion."[46] A dialect speaker appeared on the front page of a Scottish newspaper in 1789. His name was James Sloveright, a native of Angus, Scotland, "a thick man of black complexion," an escapee from Perth Prison, a speaker of the "East [Scotland] country dialect."[47] "William Lownds or Lowins," who was accused of robbing a mail truck in 1790, was described as having "a dark complexion."[48] It is tempting to see these kinds of examples as a pattern: white, dialect-speaking British criminals are linked via color to disavowed black bodies, bodies that were excluded from the European ethical concept of humanity, bodies on which were elaborated racist antimonies of good and evil. I entertain this interpretation but do not insist on it: the archive is too big and the patterns too tenuous to draw conclusions from the language used to characterize complexion. However, I do want to insist on the fact that in the rhetoric of the four cases above, a remarkable linguistic identity reinforces a remarkable complexion as well as a certain slippage of racializing discourse. So too, a marked complexion encourages the presumption of a strange linguistic identity.

The ad for "William Lownds or Lowins" further maligns the suspect by claiming that he "has been in Ireland lately, and has a little of that Dialect."[49] Here the fugitive's language appears corrupted by multilingual exposure to other linguistic and cultural environments. His tainted language speaks to the corruptibility of his national loyalties in the same way that his visibly "dark" complexion throws his character into a space of typological ambiguity. The linguistic admixtures ascribed to "Lownds or Lowins" capture another important way ads depict linguistic identity. Namely, many ads describe their suspects as evincing not arrested or deficient sublingualism but instead slippery and evasive multilingualism, which, depending on the prestige of the language, was viewed as a nascent "crime" in late eighteenth-century discourse. "Lownds or Lowins" is presented in this way. So too is John Cameron, "a Native of Fort-William, in North Britain [Scotland]," who was wanted in 1793 for "piratically and feloniously serving on board a French Privateer."[50] Cameron's ability to shift between different linguistic contexts was damning. As the ad reports, he speaks "French and English, with a little Scotch Dialect," a set of skills that are called on to explain his "piratical" activities. In addition to fears of deficiency, metalinguistic descriptions register anxieties about how language could be imitated, dissimulated, multiplied, and counterfeited so as to obscure a speaker's origins and loyalties.[51]

In North American, Caribbean, and South Asian contexts, we find many more fugitive ads in which race and multilingualism are central to descriptions of linguistic embodiment. More often than not, these ads imply that nonwhite racial identities carry with them the threat of linguistic subversion made evident by sonic traces of experience in different linguistic settings. In fact, at the intersection of nonwhite racial and linguistic identities, one regularly finds the specter of linguistic superabundance. In 1816, for example, the following apprehensive ad appeared in the *North Carolina Minerva and Raleigh Advertiser*: "TEN DOLLARS REWARD—Ran or absented himself from the subscriber, his black man Tom, well known in this place. He is artful and may procure or forge a pass as he can write—he is about 22 years old, 5 feet 8 or 9 inches high, of slim make and thin visage, an African by birth; speaks badly: from his appearance and dialect might be taken by some for a French negro."[52] "Artful" and "African by birth," "Tom" speaks English, not in "dialect" per se, but "badly," as though his English is erected over the shifting foundations of antecedent grammatical and phonological structures trained into the brain.[53] Whether or not he speaks French is unclear but implied, as the advertiser frets that "Tom" might be confused for a slave who does. Knowing what we do about transatlantic subjects like "Tom," it is probable that French and English were acquired later in life and via exigency, perhaps as his second and third languages, but more likely as his third and fourth, or perhaps fourth and fifth. Complementing his linguistic plenitude is Tom's subversive ability to write, a skill that could enable him to compose the documents authorizing his own free passage. Whereas today "Tom's" description bespeaks the tortured loss of African languages in the Americas, to literate slave owners in the period, "Tom's" linguistic embodiment would have been threatening precisely to the degree that it was unfixed and mobile.

Others have written prolifically about the complexities of fugitive slave advertising in America.[54] Rather than repeat what has been said, it is worth gesturing toward the convergences and divergences of race and multilingual embodiment as they crop up in other anglophone spaces. It was not only slaves in America and the Caribbean who embodied and intoned threatening traces of interwoven racial and linguistic differences. A similarly anxious illustration of linguistic plenitude was published twenty-six years earlier in Calcutta, where in 1790 a newspaper announced the pursuit of "A BLACK MALABAR SLAVE BOY" who spoke English and "good French" (and likely several other languages).[55] The "thin" body, "very dark" skin color, and heterogeneous linguistic practices of this boy unite to form a visible and audible gestalt. As in the ad for "Tom," the multilingualism of the "BLACK MALABAR SLAVE BOY" threatens his pursuer in a palpable way, most obviously because the ability to communicate with diverse parties facilitates the continuation of an escaped slave's liberty.

As previously mentioned, the ad for "Tom" notes the risk of "Tom's" language skills allowing him to pass as a "French Negro." It treats "Tom's" multilingualism as evidence of latent rebelliousness. The ad for the "BLACK MALABAR SLAVE BOY" does the same thing, but it also has an additional effect. It concedes that a South Asian slave's multilingualism is in fact a great financial boon to its owner, because value inhered in the plural language skills of these slaves. Because owners would have used multilingual South Asian slaves as scribes, translators, procurers, and fixers, to name just a few roles, a slave's flight represented a capital loss of several forms. This is more obvious still in an advertisement alerting the public to the search for "a Little Slave Boy about twelve years old [who] can speak, read, and write English very well."[56] Remarkable for his youth, literacy, and multilingualism, the slave's owner laments his loss in a speciously caring way. We can attribute this affect to the fact that the initial investment in the boy had likely not yet been recouped. Put another way, the longer the slave had stayed in subjection, the longer his language skills would have worked for his master, thereby amortizing the slave's cost with every passing day. The master seeks the boy among the servants of other Europeans in South Asia. As he writes, "Any Gentleman discovering such a person amongst his servants, and [who] will give intelligence to the Printer it shall be thankfully received." A crasser reference to the value of multilingualism and literacy among escaped South Asian slaves can be found in an ad for a "slave Boy aged twenty Years, or thereabouts . . . tall and slender . . . and mark'd with the small Pox."[57] Here the "Mistress" from whom the "pretty white" slave escaped tells readers, "It is requested that no one after the publication of this will Employ him, as a Writer, or in any other capacity." Be on the lookout for these nimble practitioners of linguistic plenitude, such ads enjoin. Multilingual escapees like these are capable of securing their own safety. Moreover, if proper attention is not given to their remarkable bodies, these thieves who have stolen valuable linguistic skills might get away.[58]

The final fugitive ad I will mention in this section also comes from South Asia. It captures the dynamics of multilingual linguistic embodiment I have been tracing up to now. Like so many other ads, this one shows that, across the expanding anglophone world, linguistic embodiment was a way to communicate identity in text. Here then is the ad for another one of the legions of victims of forced labor, incidentally, another victim renamed "Tom" by his European master: "ELOPED on Monday last, A SLAVE BOY, about fourteen years old, fallow complexion, broad lips, very knock kneed, walks in a lounging manner, hair behind long and bushey, had on when he eloped the dress of a Kistmutgar, speaks good English, has rather an effeminate voice, went by the name of Tom, it is suspected that he has Stolen many things. Whoever will give information, so that he may be apprehended to Mr. PURKIS, at No. 51, Cossitollah, shall be handsomely rewarded, if required."[59] From a wide and well-known avenue of British Calcutta, Mr. Purkis advertises in order to search for the young slave who had duped him. "Fourteen years old, fallow complexion, broad lips, very knock kneed, walks in a lounging manner, hair behind long and bushey." These visual clues culminate in a reference to the unmistakable dress of a *Khidmutgar*, a servant charged with serving master Purkis his meals.[60] From there, the reader departs the domain of the visible for that of the auditory—"speaks good English, has rather an effeminate voice, went by the name of Tom." Image and sound are conjoined, as are complexion and voice, embodiment and language, conversational interaction and, perhaps, desire. The visual image of a physically exceptional boy redoubles the intoned sounds of an "effeminate" slave speaking English, likely one language among several that "Tom" could speak. Purkis's textualization of the fugitive "Tom" creates a character, one subjected to the politics of monolingualism that underwrites all the ads I have described so far.

Having shown some of the ways language and body intersect in fugitive advertising, my argument now moves toward investigating language, embodiment, and aesthetics. Even while eighteenth- and nineteenth-century multilingual subjects are to some degree hobbled by their attempts to be included in polities organized around Standard English monolingualism, these multilingual subjects are also uniquely able to pursue aesthetic practices in newly multiple ways. Writers committed to forging literature with an aesthetics of linguistic difference are able to subvert monolingualism by putting the plenitude of their multiplicity on display. It is the basic premise of my argument regarding monolingualism, multilingualism, and alterity that normative linguistic impositions have often (and falsely) reconstituted the multilingualism of the other as an incoherent babble of mistakes, threats, subversions, and disloyalties; this process has had incalculable consequences. When monolingualism becomes a powerful political force in Britain after the mid-eighteenth century, and in U.S. America during the first decades of the nineteenth century, it corrals the multilingualism of all others by carving out small, contained, and falsely compensatory spaces for linguistic multiplicity.[61] Often and importantly, these are aesthetic spaces, as I will show, and often and importantly again these are aesthetic spaces of comedy and farce, or criminality and villainy. In this way normative language practices become the precondition for community belonging as well as the obligatory framing mechanism for the contained staging of non-normative languages as objects of aesthetic contemplation.[62]

For subjects like Lyons and Ngũgĩ who experienced firsthand the ramifications of the politics of monolingualism that treated their multilingualism as a dangerous and dehumanizing signifier, the effects are indelible. At worst, the silencing of voices this politics demands results in linguicide. At best, attempts to silence language become the engine for the formation of a counterpolitics of multilingualism, a counterpolitics that holds on to and generates in suppressed counterlanguages even as those languages are maligned, attacked, and damaged. Eighteenth-century multilinguals in the British Isles and anglicizing spaces beyond the seas faced the same stark linguistico-political dilemma: either submit to the aesthetic appropriation, ghettoization, and slow death of local languages, or generate forms, genres, and aesthetic tactics for preserving them, however experimental. It happens that this paradigm links the eighteenth century to the present in ways that exceed political and aesthetic questions. It is impossible to ignore, for example, that ours is an era of unprecedented language death. This is a cultural catastrophe that no remediated politics of language will be able to solve. However, against the gloom of language loss, it must be said that linguistic multiplicity is still obviously and thankfully alive, which everyone should celebrate. This is true in spaces all over the globe just as it is true in contemporary anglophone aesthetic practice, the roots of which grow out of the long eighteenth century.

Anglophony's Fringe: The Multilingualism of Phillis Wheatley and Robert Burns

Even in Scotland, the provincial dialect which Ramsay and he [Burns] have used is now read with a difficulty which greatly damps the pleasure of the

> reader: in England it cannot be read at all, without such constant reference to a glossary as nearly to destroy that pleasure.[63]

Tracking anglophone linguistic multiplicity in ephemeral forms like fugitive advertising demonstrates its visibility in eighteenth-century culture. Similarly, tracing linguistic multiplicity opens up texts, authors, and poets in vibrant new ways. Furthermore, attending to linguistic multiplicity can provide students in the globalizing present with familiar dynamics from the cultural past. Consider, for example, the well-known case of Robert Burns. It is fascinating to examine with contemporary students the role of language difference in eighteenth-century aesthetic evaluation. Students approach with curiosity the fact that in early reviews, Henry MacKenzie and Tobias Smollett both question Burns's use of Scots even while endorsing his poetic "genius." MacKenzie writes, as above, that Scots is read by literate anglophones "with great difficulty" while Smollett, for his part, asserts, "It is to be regretted, that the Scottish dialect, in which these poems are written, must obscure the native beauties with which they appear to abound . . . render[ing] the sense often unintelligible to an English reader."[64] In both MacKenzie and Smollett, Burns's language is figured as a scrim that "obscures" rather than reveals "native beauties" for Standard English readers. But poetic "beauties" are still assumed to exist somewhere behind the unfamiliar linguistic forms. This is a generous assumption, an assumption that was perhaps borne out of Scottish solidarity for a native son. It is an assumption that clashes dramatically with those made in the reception history of Phillis Wheatley, Burns's contemporary, a woman whose entire poetic career was organized around proving herself to be a capable user of Standard English.[65]

Burns's meteoric career can be explained in now-outmoded terms by citing the "heaven-taught Plowman's" transcendental genius for capturing the spirit of his people, although non-Scottish students who are unfamiliar with Scots and who are struggling to read Burns's actual language might not necessarily feel the weight of this genius. In a different vein, Burns's canonicity can be explained as part of a much longer tradition of Scots-language writing, a tradition that happened to be experiencing its own cultural renaissance when Burns first brought *Poems, Chiefly in the Scottish Dialect* into the world in 1786. In this explanation, Burns's status as contemporary icon of Scottishness derives from his ability to gather the linguistic and cultural practices of vernacular tradition—the ballad, for example—

and then project those practices into the future as a prophylactic against anglophone encroachments. Students might digest this more easily, although the explanation implicitly places "Scots" and "English" writing in separate and noninteractive lineages.

Another way to see and teach Burns's career, which many scholars have touched on, involves situating the poet's work within the imperial linguistic dynamics of his era, an era in which the Scots world and the anglophone world intermingled at various levels. The geographic itinerary traced by the publication locations of the first three editions of *Poems, Chiefly in the Scottish Dialect*—Kilmarnock, Scotland (1786); Edinburgh, Scotland (1787); London, England (1787)—speaks to the hierarchically organized linguistic and cultural matrix within which Burns's reception occurred. Extending these observations, one might account for his past and present popularity, especially as that popularity is affixed to stock images of Scottish national identity, by noting that Burns was keenly confluent with the linguistico-cultural pressures of his period. He knew what it meant to pitch and sell his particular brand of Scots literature in Kilmarnock, Edinburgh, and London. His dedications and expanded glossaries in these various editions show this clearly.[66] As a multilingual writer whose prefaces and poems are themselves multilingual, Burns was attuned to the promise and limitations of cultural interest in linguistic difference—it helped too that his race and gender were unproblematic for readers of the period. Still, his poetry makes linguistic difference into an aesthetic object as well as a framework for dissent against existing aesthetic criteria. In a period of tremendous linguistico-cultural ferment, Burns gave readers what some were seeking: ethnolinguistic performance in which a Scots counterpolitics of language was embedded.[67]

The specific form of Burns's counterpolitics of multilingualism is thrown into relief when compared to Phillis Wheatley's. Indeed, it is under the banner of anglophone multiplicity that figures like Burns and Wheatley can come together most felicitously. Both are poets, but more specifically, both are also multilingual anglophone poets. One need only rehearse well-known facts a bit differently to stress the importance of this multilingual dimension to Wheatley's life. As the *Oxford Dictionary of National Biography* reports, Phillis Wheatley was born somewhere along the banks of the Gambia River, exact place and date unknown.[68] She was forcibly brought to North America in 1761 on the slave ship *Phillis*, a boat whose name would soon become her own.[69] She was purchased by a well-to-do Boston family called the Wheatleys, a family whose name would soon become her own. Based on the invasive observation that she had adult front teeth at the moment she was sold, it is believed that she was roughly seven or eight years old, an age when one's language skills are already well formed. Appraising her intellectual formation at her moment of sale, scholar John Shields speculates, "At this age she had doubtless already been influenced by a syncretistic amalgam of animism, hierophantic solar worship, and Islam practised in that region of the Gambia at the time of her birth." Unfortunately he says nothing about her linguistic biography—but of course he can say very little, for nothing is recorded.[70] The child who was to be renamed "Phillis Wheatley" certainly spoke and thought in language when she arrived in Boston. Perhaps she spoke and thought in several.

Though these linguistic details are unknown, the determining fact in Wheatley's life and subsequent career was that she was purchased by a family whose language and worldview would soon reformulate her existence entirely. The Wheatleys' goal was to provide a proper religious education, and, for Phillis, the initial means to this proper religious education was Standard English. Against all trends of this barbarous period in transatlantic history, then, Phillis Wheatley was taught by this family to read Standard English and probably by an outside tutor to read Latin during her time as an unpaid servant in her owner's house. Indeed, John Wheatley's brief summary of Phillis Wheatley's education triumphantly claims that, "without any Assistance from School Education, and by only what she was taught in the Family, she, in sixteen Months Time from her Arrival, attained the English Language, to which she was an utter Stranger before, to such a Degree, as to read any, the most difficult Parts of the Sacred Writings, to the great Astonishment of all who heard her."[71] Like Peros, who became "sensible" and "judicious" once in anglophony, Phillis Wheatley's earlier language or languages must go unmentioned. Phillis Wheatley's having "attained" English obviates their being mentioned. However, it does not mean that there was not suspicion surrounding her abilities in English. This is one reason why an attestation signed by eighteen of "the most respectable Characters in Boston" precedes her volume with the words, "We whose names are underwritten, do assure the World that the POEMS specified in the following Page, were (as we verily believe) written by *Phillis*, a young Negro Girl, who was but a few Years since, brought an uncultivated Barbarian from Africa."[72] Lest someone still suspect this multilingual subject of being incapable of writing anglophone poems of such a high caliber, the publisher also sees fit to note at the bottom of the attestation, "The original Attestation, signed by the above Gentleman, may be seen by applying to *Archibald Bell*, Bookseller, No. 8, *Aldgate-Street*."[73]

For me, it is crucial to reread these tantalizing biographical and paratextual details in order to emphasize that Wheatley's education was primarily organized around mastering Standard English—"to which she was an utter stranger before"—as a conduit to biblical and classical knowledge. As Vincent Carretta notes, "The education that Phillis Wheatley received from Susanna and/or Mary Wheatley would have been very impressive for a white man of high social standing at the time."[74] He also speculates that Phillis's transgressive educational achievements might have been partially a result of John and Susanna Wheatley's perverse desire to experiment with the education of an African-born woman: "Phillis Wheatley's writings demonstrate that she was granted an education that went well beyond what was needed in order to be catechized on Christianity. . . . The Wheatleys offered her an extraordinary opportunity to develop her talents and interests. They may have done so as a kind of social experiment to discover what effect education might have on an African."[75] As Carretta has it, this education represents an unusual contravention of racial, class, and social categories organized around educational and especially literate attainments. Whether her education was the product of a strange experiment or simply the Wheatleys' avowedly Christian commitment to a form of literate anglophone religiosity that was spawned in the wake of the First Great Awakening, Wheatley's natural aptitude and anglophone education enabled transformations in her subjectivity, as all linguistic education must. There is another wrinkle to recollect. The education the Wheatleys gave her was not her first. Phillis Wheatley's natural aptitudes might have been complimented by her once and perhaps still multilingual mind. Her transatlantic transit meant that she was the kind of person forced to think about linguistic protocol, translation, and especially survival *outside of* and *before* her anglophone education. These earlier experiences would have informed the poetic projects she later undertook.

Wheatley is now widely known and taught as the first African American woman to publish an anglophone book in Britain, entitled *Poems on Various Subjects, Religious and Moral* (1773). This quality of being "first" coupled with the importance of the transatlantic slave trade to eighteenth-century anglophone culture frequently means that the brief poem "On Being Brought from Africa to America," one of the thirty-nine poems included in her first volume, is Wheatley's most regularly taught and anthologized work. The assumed exemplarity of this poem derives from the fact that it speaks generally to the situation of enslaved transatlantic subjects as well as to Wheatley's poetic disposition, which is frequently devotional, and not without irony:

'TWAS mercy brought me from my *Pagan* land,
Taught my benighted soul to understand
That there's a God, that there's a *Saviour* too:
Once I redemption neither sought nor knew.
Some view our sable race with scornful eye,
"Their colour is a diabolic die."
Remember, *Christians*, *Negros*, black as *Cain*,
May be refin'd, and join th'angelic train.[76]

The first four lines of this poem can be read as a Christian redemption story but also as an educational autobiography—a different version of what Lyons and Ngũgĩ provide. Wheatley's past here is not an idyll ("Once I redemption neither sought nor knew") but instead a spiritual state that the poetic persona has thankfully left behind. Her anglophone education, which was embedded in her Christian education, and vice versa, is figured as the happy result of her journey from Africa to America. The success of her education even allows her to reach across racial lines, as she also did in her correspondence with famous figures like George Washington and Samson Occom. In this poem, Wheatley reminds (white) Christians that devotion means more to one's spiritual state than race, especially when it comes to entering into a state of grace believed to be the exclusive purview of a dominant racial group: "Remember, *Christians, Negros, black as Cain*, / May be refin'd, and join th'angelic train."

The fact that this poem evinces thankfulness for anglophone and thus Christian education is most fascinating when set against the other poems in the book. If any one poem or poetic form predominates in this volume, it is the elegy—which is fitting, as it was her elegy on the death of George Whitefield that first brought her work into the public eye in October 1770. Fourteen of the volume's thirty-nine poems are straightforwardly elegies or funeral poems.[77] Several others engage the question of death and mourning more obliquely.[78] Wheatley seems instinctively drawn to the elegy in the sense of requiem, a tendency critics have read in various ways.[79] One critic reads Wheatley's use of the elegy in conjunction with the importance of elegy to the classical literature that Wheatley would have studied. In this reading, Wheatley's translation of the form takes on a political function as an attempt to form community, "The elegy functioned as more than a funeral poem for classical writers, and it routinely expressed political positions. . . . Wheatley's elegies created community by drawing local Boston together in corporate mourning for admirable or pitiable members of the community."[80] Another critic, Mary Balkun, finds in Wheatley's elegies an attempt to explore the spiritual doctrine of the transcendent soul's independence from the material body: "The fourteen elegies that constitute a large portion of Wheatley's book may thus be read . . . as a way to insist on the essential unimportance of the body."[81] Wheatley uses the elegy, in this reading, not to mourn the body but to adulate the saved Christian soul.

Balkun's reading of the elegy moves me toward my own reading of how exactly the elegy functions in this multilingual writer's work. Devona Mallory writes, "In Wheatley's case, the recently departed may not be merely references to the deceased; they may be an attempt by the African American artist to console parents who have been separated, beyond their control, from their children."[82] This useful and sensitive reading calls on the biographical details of Wheatley's forced removal from Africa in order to suggest that she possessed a heightened sensitivity—visible in her poetry—to empathize with those who had recently lost loved ones, especially parents, who in the normal order of things are not supposed to be predeceased by their children. Wheatley, having lost her ancestral home and gained another, uses the elegy in the sense of requiem because she knows intimately that this form's plaintive properties come close to capturing the inexorability of loss.

I would add here only that the texture of the question changes if we imagine that Wheatley might also be writing about her lost language or languages, that swirling collection of sounds and meanings she would have learned in childhood and then never heard again after her arrival in Boston harbor, 1761. Several of her elegies invite this reading. For example, the middles stanza of "On the Death of a Young Lady of Five Years of Age," implores mourners to "hear in heav'n's blest bow'rs your *Nancy* fair, / And learn to imitate her language there."[83] The titular character, who has undergone death's passage from "dark abodes to fair etherial light" echoes Wheatley's self-described exodus "from my *Pagan* land" at the hands of "mercy." Just as Nancy has learned a new celestial language that her earth-bound relatives must attempt to divine, Wheatley too has entered a spiritual, cultural, and linguistic environment by leaving others—unnamed and perhaps only hazily remembered—behind.[84]

This section's juxtaposition of Burns and Wheatley is intended as a stark first example of the polarities engendered by the eighteenth-century experience of anglophone linguistic multiplicity. Whereas Burns chooses Scots as his poetic medium, thereby defending local culture as it is attached to a particular linguistic heritage, for Wheatley this is impossible because her language is in effect lost or forgotten. In both cases, educational history is essential to the story that is told about the poet in the paratexts that surround his or her work. Just as it is necessary for John Wheatley to authorize Phillis Wheatley's poetic achievements by overtly stressing her remarkable and precocious education into anglophony, early reviewers of Burns's work stress his authenticity and autodidacticism even as they critique his language. Because of her race and gender, Wheatley's anglophone education must aspire to perfection, but Burns's education is described by his reviewers as happily incomplete. As a case in point, Tobias Smollett's review of *Poems* includes these lines: "We have had occasion to examine a number of poetical productions, written by persons in the lower rank of life, and who had hardly received any education; but we do not recollect to have ever met with a more signal instance of true and uncultivated genius, than in the author of these Poems."[85] Burns has an "uncultivated genius" that has been touched but unspoiled by anglophone education. By contrast, Wheatley's subject position as an African American slave of uncertain linguistic background requires that her genius be cultivated in a way anglophones understand. These are the extremes within which the multilingualism of the other is cognizable in the eighteenth century, either as terrific boon or horrific burden.

By evoking the complexities surrounding differently embodied multilingual figures like Wheatley and Burns alongside the homogenizing systems of commercial, cultural, and coercive power within which multilingualism has long been caught—and against which it has had to fight over the course of the last three centuries—I want to advance here the more general claim that attempts to capture, celebrate, and advance linguistic diversity have been the starting point for several important developments in the history of anglophone literature, in the present, yes, but in the eighteenth-century and Romantic-era pasts as well. Put more explicitly, I argue going forward that linguistic exchange, translation, subjugation, and resistance have long been generative elements in literary practice and aesthetic reception. Can we understand the linguistic interventions of known figures like Robert Burns, and Phillis Wheatley, and others as part of the prehistory of the linguistic aesthetics of the present? Indeed we can. Burns is the male multilingual poet who is able to play on the sonic and written traditions of his minority lect; Wheatley is the multilingual poet with no such recourse, a woman who can only channel the energy of linguistic loss into the necessity of poetry as a form of succor to all who can hear (or read) its strains. In this respect, Burns and Wheatley occupy polar ends of a spectrum of possible aesthetic responses to linguistic imposition, a spectrum that coming chapters flesh out more fully.

Since the standardization and imperial deterritorialization of English during the eighteenth century, disciplinary structures stressing national histories have not always made the investigation of topics like anglophony or anglophone multilingualism into a relevant optics for engaging with the literary object. This has resulted in the fact that broad scholarly methodologies for discussing multilingualism and linguistic difference in conjunction with literary products of the eighteenth century and Romantic era need work. Thankfully, contemporary scholars from various periods have provided good models to project forward and backward.[86] Even with these models, however, the problem remains difficult. Multilingualism's extranational dimensions disrupt the coherence of national formations, and this is problematic if we consider the eighteenth-century and Romantic periods to be nationalism's formative epochs. In general, the consideration of linguistic multiplicity within scholarship threatens to undo intellectual projects organized under the rubric of national history and national thought. Nor has it seemed relevant to think of mainstream cultural phenomena as conditioned by multilingual exchanges transacted at the fringes of national literary culture.[87] In the present, however, the economic processes of globalization, which seek both homogeneity as well as the marketability of tolerable differences, demand the further investigation of these phenomena. In a time like our own, scholarship that attends to linguistic multiplicity and what it indexes culturally is both imperative and overdue.

MULTILINGUAL LIVES

Reverend Lyons

There is more to say about the predicament of the multilingual subject Reverend Lyons. In particular, Lyons's description of the "Irish language and Irish people's" proscription reaches across the centuries as a foreign and yet familiar discourse of linguistic imposition. Just as Peros, Jack, Neptune, and Cupid are caught in the mesh of a monolingual politics of language (as well as other forms of institutional violence) and have little agency in defining their own identities—much less linguistic identities—which are always preceded and delimited by the textual discourses in which they appear, Lyons's life speaks to a different but equally important question: the fusion of linguistic and cultural loss.[1]

Unlike Ngũgĩ's *Decolonising the Mind*, which has rightly become canonical reading in numerous disciplines because of its vigorous interrogation of colonial ideology as it has outlasted colonialism, Lyons's speech is recorded in only a few collections of ephemeral pamphlets that are housed at the British Library and the National Library of Ireland. Brief but pithy, the speech is worth reading in detail for the following points: (1) like Ngũgĩ, Lyons argues that the imposition of Standard English has occasioned a cultural disaster for nonanglophones in Ireland; (2) he resigns himself to the impossibility of reversing the force of anglophony in Ireland; and (3) he picks a pragmatic way forward in anglophony while eulogizing his community's linguistico-cultural past. His lament for the Irish language as a vehicle of cultural continuity is similar to that which I have imputed to Wheatley's poetry, but Lyons is far more explicit. Not only does he tabulate the destructive effects of the monolingual politics of language I have been describing; he ties this monolingual politics to national, imperial, and religious issues. He also blames it for producing a special kind of literacy problem.

The occasion for Reverend Lyons's speech is a fund-raising dinner for the Benevolent Society of St. Patrick, a Catholic charitable organization that worked among Liverpool's poor.[2] After praising the society's ecumenical work, Lyons launches a vitriolic attack on Protestant charitable societies operating in Ireland. Specifically, he berates Irish-language Bible publishers like the Hibernian Bible Society (est. 1806), a group that aimed to bring inexpensive Christian scriptures to people in their own languages, thus making it akin to the better-known British and Foreign Bible Society, an organization established by abolitionist William Wilberforce in 1803.[3] As Lyons frames it, British-based Bible publishers are associated with "illiberality, [Protestant] proselytism, and persecution" in Ireland even though their primary and seemingly laudable goal is to circulate Irish-language Bibles. Far from celebrating these organizations for making the scriptures accessible to Irish people in their own language, however, Lyons characterizes them as little more than the covert "money-making" vehicles of Protestant evangelism.[4]

Lyons alleges that the fundraising mechanisms of Irish-language Bible producers in England are a "complete hoax upon the English people."[5] They should therefore be exposed as fraudulent. "From Erris to Howth, and from Dingle to Donaghadee," he proclaims, "these societies have left lasting proofs of their bigotry and intolerance."[6] Lyons's sympathies are unambiguous: Irish-language Bible publishers from Britain pursue conversionary ends by manipulating Irish people through appeals to the cultural resonance of the Irish language they are rapidly losing.[7] That Lyons should go so far as decidedly rejecting the value of Irish-language Bibles is revealing, for this is a man who in the same speech will also furiously denounce Standard English's intrusiveness in Ireland. Not at all a contradiction, his move has everything to do with a pragmatic sense that Irish linguistic ground has already been swept out from under his feet. By endorsing English-language Bibles that properly hew to Catholic orthodoxy, Lyons drives home the point that British imperialism has already set in motion the Irish language's death; only religion can be preserved as a cultural testament to the Irish past. In 1755, Samuel Johnson famously ended the preface to his dictionary by claiming that tongues, like governments, have a natural tendency to degeneration. "We have long preserved our constitution, let us make some struggles for our language."[8] Several generations later, and from across the Irish Sea, Lyons inverts this idea by insinuating that the struggle for the Irish language is over. Irish people should therefore fight a battle they are capable of winning: the preservation of a traditional religious culture now that traditional linguistic culture is under such threat.

In the present, the politics of self-determination are commonly linked to native language rights. This is also the case in Lyons's speech, except that he views the Irish language as a natural right that can no longer be reinstituted. Put another way, at the same time that Lyons asserts the value of an indigenous Irish culture rooted in the Irish language, he also claims that the latter is doomed to disappearance—a fait accompli previously settled by the anglophone "score."[9] In order to make the claim that Irish-language Bibles are superfluous in Ireland because anglophony penetrated that country so deeply, Lyons delves into questions surrounding Irish- and English-language literacy.[10] He declares that Irish-language Bibles are incapable of cultivating both biblical and linguistic knowledge.[11] Standard English language's pedagogical primacy in Ireland has produced a literacy problem in which anyone who can read Irish must already be able to read English. Lyons's point is that Standard English literacy has become the formal precondition for Irish-language literacy. In Lyons's era, like today, lack of literacy in a language deeply affects its potential for survival.

Relating his recent journey through Ireland, the kind of journey that regularly crops up in eighteenth-century studies of regional languages, Lyons notes, "All the proficients in Iberno-Celtic (and they were few) were proficients in English also; their grammatical knowledge of the former ['Iberno-Celtic'] was attained through the medium of the latter [English]."[12] Straight to the point: "Every one of them [literate Irish people], without a single exception, could read and write English before they ventured to learn the letters of the Irish alphabet."[13] In 1827, only a generation after the full political union of Ireland with the Kingdom of Great Britain, Lyons's anecdotal experience testifies to the fact that Irish-language literacy was fully contingent on English-language literacy. A reader of Irish was by definition already a multiliterate anglophone. Regarding the question of Irish-language Bibles, Lyons concludes that monolingual speakers of Irish still existed, but certainly no monoliterate Irish readers.

Advice follows Lyons's grim assessment of Irish-language literacy existing only as the aftereffect of Standard English literacy: no Christian should give money to British organizations claiming to produce and distribute Irish-language scriptures. Such organizations, Lyons argues, fill their coffers by providing "unreadable volumes" of Irish-language scripture to the Irish. Next they attempt to convert the population to Protestantism by virtue of the goodwill their translations have engendered. In Lyons's eyes, the mendacity of this process is self-evident. "With regard to the translation of the Pentateuch, lately foisted on the public," he writes, "it is a burlesque upon the language, and replete with the most glaring errors in grammar and in rendering."[14] The Irish-language reading materials these organizations produce are terrible, in other words, a fact that Lyons claims Irish "readers" can no longer even register. Lyons feels compelled to testify to these dubious translation practices. He even alleges that producers of Irish-language Bibles are actively manipulating spotty Irish-language literacy in order to inject Protestantism into a population that would otherwise resist such injections. In other words, unreadable and doctrinally suspicious Irish-language translations are put before an Irish audience that can read English much more fluidly, if they can read at all. These translations are worthless except as "wrapper for the snuff-seller and the tobacconist," he claims.[15] This is the lamentable situation linguistic imperialism has produced.[16]

Lyons's emphasis on English-language literacy as a precondition to Irish-language literacy does not mean that he has given up on the Irish language wholesale. In a nostalgic vein, he points out that Irish remains a bearer of cultural patrimony in certain communities, like those of County Mayo, which he references saying, "There is no part of Ireland in which our sweet, expressive, and beautiful language is better known and spoken than in the county of Mayo, of which I am a native."[17] But even in the linguistic counterpublic of County Mayo "there is not one *mere Irish scholar*."[18] Context suggests that "*mere*" in this sentence means monoliterate, a person trained in reading and writing only Irish. Elsewhere in Lyons the word "mere" means monolingual, as when the speaker, evoking the hierarchies governing Irish linguistic life, recalls, "I remember when a mere Irish servant would not be employed in my father's house, for fear his children should learn this (to him) vulgar tongue."[19] The expressions "mere Irish servant" and "*mere Irish scholar*" produce a powerful tension. The "mere Irish servant" is a figure of monolingual lack or absence, a servant who cannot be hired because he can speak *only* Irish.[20] The "*mere Irish scholar*," on the other hand, is an impossible fantasy of monoliterate purity, a reader who reads *only* the Irish language, and can do so unaffected by English-language mediation.

Given that no "*mere Irish scholar*" exists, Irish-language literacy must always be undercut by Standard English literacy. As part of his linguistic biography, Lyons reports that he was kept isolated from his native Irish for the first nine years of his life, in "perfect ignorance of the finest medium of communication with which I happen to be acquainted."[21] Lyons, like Wheatley, was primarily educated in an anglophone home, one that eschewed languages other than Standard English as a matter of social, cultural, and occupational necessity. With a childhood like the one he describes, an adulthood beyond anglophony is almost unthinkable. Lyons relates his autobiography in a tone that anticipates what Derrida, in a melancholic phrase, refers to as the "strangely bottomless alienation of the soul" that an imposed language produces.[22]

These dynamics account for the counterintuitive way in which, for Lyons, Irish-language biblical materials come to represent an encroachment on Irish society, a duplicitous form of lip service that cannot slow the pace of Irish-language erosion that is already underway. Toward the end of his speech, Lyons asks the audience to consider the following hypothetical scenario: imagine that a group of Irish Catholics were to establish schools throughout England for the purpose of "educating the Protestant poor."[23] Then imagine, he enjoins, that they were to raise money to print Catholic-tinged anglophone Bibles to foist on the people. Imagine further that they were to hold fund-raising meetings in Ireland where they "malign the Protestants of England, caricature their religion," and in so doing, "enlist the popular feelings of the Irish in favour of their [evangelical] society."[24] As the inverted scenario becomes more elaborate, the anti-imperial subtext of Lyons's attack on the Bible-producing societies erupts. Imagine, Lyons suggests, that "Irish Papists, who hold meetings in every town in England; insult the people; outrage their religious feelings; assault their persons; and madden round the land."[25] Obviously, English Protestants would be outraged; they would justly feel their language and culture under assault. They might opt for Irish-language Bibles (as Lyons opts for Standard English ones) so that the foreign-language Bible societies would dissolve or be discredited. They might choose the linguistic imposition of a Bible in another tongue, in other words, in order to fight off a larger assault on culture and religion.

Reverend Lyons is one multilingual anglophone who uses pointed rhetorical and narrative strategies for characterizing his identity vis-à-vis language and culture. For him, educational memories are told as tragedy. Adjoined to this, his counterhistory in which Ireland conquers England and spreads its language there becomes a way to argue that the Irish language cannot be saved, and so Irish Catholicism must be. That a person should have to choose religious identity over linguistic identity speaks to the enormous pressures of anglophone imperialism in Ireland in a way that few other choices can. Though Lyons does not push the scenario any further, his counterhistory is worth considering within the context in which it was elaborated: if the vectors of British imperialism in colonial Ireland were reversed and the thoroughgoing anglicization of Ireland undone, would the Irish language experience a meaningful revival? In such circumstances, could a "*mere Irish scholar*" come into being? Lyons is all too aware that most "*mere*" English scholars felt no need to learn his language except in the interests of evangelism, which he sees as culturally invasive. His imagined scenario captures one particularly negative view of the future of the Irish language. It also reflects an uneasy awareness of anglophony's growing textual heft—its grammar texts, style guides, literacy manuals, and translation treatises.

In short, the fantasy of a "*mere Irish scholar*" is as much about the word "*mere*" as it is about the meaning of a linguistic "*scholar*." The next two chapters examine mid- to late eighteenth-century anglophone linguistic scholarship as it relates to culture and literature. In these chapters I unpack the theories of standardization and translation that make possible the invasion Lyons excoriates. The goal is to reveal the development of the monolingual politics of language I described in the first chapter, but also to reveal points of discontinuity within that politics in which narrow forms of multiplicity were allowed and even encouraged to flourish, albeit in limited ways. Beyond anglophony's ubiquity, Lyons envisions purity in the form of an unmediated Irish-language reader. However, as we will see in the next chapter, anglophony's metalinguistic armature in this period meticulously inoculates itself against the idea of monolingual purity by embracing certain forms of mixture. Standard English is by nature mixed and "copious," the standardizers repeat, an idea that leads toward further justification of English's ongoing and intrusive impositions into colonial and provincial spaces.

CHAPTER 2

De Copia

Language, Politics, and Aesthetics

Multiplicity and Aesthetics

> He's still critical at the moment, but he might be stable in a few days. In the meantime we'll have to run some more tests—
> —More test? Test fi what? You must think him inna school the way unu ah run test. And none of unu test can give me no result.
> . . .
> —Millicent . . . ah . . . how do I put this? I'm not exactly following what she's saying. I mean, I think I have the gist but wouldn't want to put one's foot in one's mouth, if you catch my drift. Can you speak to her?
> —Ah . . . sure.
> —Maybe in your native tongue.
> —What?
> —You know, that Jamaican lingo. It's so musical it's like listening to Burning Spear and drinking coconut juice.
> —Coconut water.
> —Whatever. It's so beautiful, good God, I don't have a damn clue what you're all saying.[1]

This snippet of dialogue from Marlon James's *A Brief History of Seven Killings* (2014) exemplifies the book's swift movements between diverse registers of contemporary anglophony, movements that foreground the way that power imbalances glom onto these different linguistic forms. James's sprawling realist novel encompasses the last fifty years of Jamaican and Jamaican diasporic history. In his fictional account, the Caribbean, North

America, and Europe are stitched together by Cold War geopolitics, drug trafficking, and popular culture, specifically, the global phenomenon of Jamaican music. Formally, this means that each of the novel's chapters is told in a different narrator's unique voice.[2] James masterfully crafts and situates the idiolects of his diverse speakers. This is perhaps one of the reasons why his novel has won the Booker Prize for Fiction, arguably the most prestigious award in anglophone literature.[3] In fact, James excels at a writing technique that many consumers of literary fiction have come to expect. Characters are authenticated through forms of spelling, vocabulary, and syntax that translate living forms of anglophone orality into print in explicit juxtaposition to Standard English. Representing one's unique perception of orality in nonnormative writing is a celebrated way of aestheticizing both local identity and anglophone linguistic diversity.

My invocation of a contemporary novelist in this book about the long eighteenth century is meant less to praise James's work (engaging as it is) than to draw attention to a lineage between an earlier moment in aesthetic history and our own. James's novel, which is sewn together from a diverse array of standard and nonnormative anglophone forms, makes literary "art" via the spectacle of linguistic difference on the page. More capacious than Burns's 1786 volume of poetry, James's novel draws the reader into aesthetic contemplation of an entire ecology of intermingling anglophone "dialects," a term I use here with caution.[4] In this respect, the novel joins a long and exciting tradition, but not a tradition that has always been seen as literary. This is because nonnormative language has traditionally had limited avenues for being perceived in aesthetic terms. To access revealing aspects of this tradition, as well as its contemporary visibility, one can start by examining the shifting aesthetic horizons of the long eighteenth century, a period when the reading public was coming into increased contact with nonnormative anglophone forms in text. Reviewers in this earlier moment of aesthetic history frequently met linguistic difference with skepticism, often concluding that a given work had literary merit *in spite of* its linguistic diversity rather than *because of* it, another reason why Burns's quick and sustained popularity is a landmark aesthetic event.[5] Most examples of nonnormative writing, especially nonnormative writing authored by women, were never treated in aesthetic terms at all. As I argue here and later, the disciplines of philology, dialectology, and ethnography grew up as discursive catchments for forms of anglophone writing like these that fell beyond the horizons of aesthetic evaluation.

This is because the monolingual politics of language described in the last chapter delimited the eighteenth-century aesthetic realm such that it was difficult if not impossible to perceive certain types of anglophone writing in aesthetic terms. This politics of language also made it impossible to see certain embodied anglophone subjects as origins of original aesthetic practice—Phillis Wheatley's state of exception. These are the two primary ways in which linguistic politics acted on aesthetic judgment in the period: the dismissal of nonnormative writing as aberrant and therefore nonliterary; and the dismissal of certain subjects as incapable of literary art. To understand our own aesthetic moment, which prizes linguistic difference mainly when it skillfully embellishes depictions of character, interiority, and place, it is necessary to consider why eighteenth-century texts featuring linguistic difference were not generally read in aesthetic terms, even if some signal works like Burns's were. In other words, why does some eighteenth-century anglophone writing rise to the level of aesthetic contemplation while a great deal of similarly innovative writing does not? Relatedly, how can contemporary scholars project value backward onto texts that today look like points of origin even though they may have struck their contemporary readers as aesthetically inert?

Jacques Rancière's *Aisthesis: Scenes from the Aesthetic Regime of Art* (2013) tries to chart the processes by which practices of representation come to qualify as aesthetic when previously they were invisible as such.[6] For Rancière, "aisthesis" names "the mode of experience according to which . . . we perceive very diverse things . . . as all belonging to art."[7] In other words, "aisthesis" refers to a beholder's engagement with the "sensible fabric" or "sensorium" within which diverse representative practices—theater, sculpture, architecture, dance, mixed media, the novel, et cetera—are all discernible as aesthetic rather than anaesthetic, a term that I use here to mean, "not rising to the level of aesthetic evaluation." As a dynamic mode of experience and interpretation, "aisthesis" updates and alters the sensible fabric within which diverse representative practices are gathered. In this way, Rancière's intervention posits aesthetic categories as flexible and historical, always changing in order to match complementary changes in technology, media, and especially politics.

According to Rancière's argument, "Art as a notion designating a form of specific experience has only existed in the West since the end of the eighteenth century," a period that witnessed the gradual collapse of a longstanding distinction between the fine arts, which were reserved for leisured gentlemen, and the mechanical arts, "those material performances that an artisan or a slave could accomplish"—nonnormative language, for example.[8] Dating contemporary definitions of art to the late eighteenth century's social and political revolutions in this way, Rancière proceeds by describing fourteen moments of rupture in aesthetic history, from Winkelmann's celebration of the fractured Belvedere Torso in *Geschichte der Kunst des Alterthums* (1764) to James Agee's inventories of ordinary objects in impoverished homes of the American South during the Great Depression. Rancière's goal is to demonstrate ways in which "a regime of perception, sensation, and interpretation of art is constituted and transformed by welcoming images, objects and performances that seemed most opposed to the very idea of fine art."[9] Under what conditions does a broken sculpture become more artful than an unbroken one? Under what circumstances can mundane household objects become artful assemblages? Rancière does not discuss representations of linguistic diversity, though his methodology is adaptable. "Dialect" or nonnormative writing—taken here to mean a technology of representing anglophone linguistic difference rather than actual anglophone speech—begins demanding "welcome" into "a regime of perception, sensation, and interpretation" during the eighteenth century. But how does it do so?

Rancière's claim that a culture's aesthetic fabric or sensorium "ceaselessly redefines itself," admitting certain practices while others remain invisible, begs an important question: what produces these "ceaseless redefinitions"? Rancière names this process "dissensus," the operation by which political and aesthetic categories are made to change. Dissensus formulates new aesthetic criteria in just the same way that new political subjects come into being.[10] In politics, dissensus refers to the process by which a group emerges by differentiating itself from (and thus reordering) existing constituencies, thereby bringing into being new forms of political subjectivation.[11] In aesthetics, dissensus is the process by which objects of contemplation are suddenly taken to represent things that otherwise cannot and perhaps should not be seen. To provide an example of dissensual aesthetics in action, consider the slow but dramatic expansion of anglophone literacy over the mid- to late eighteenth century. Before its wider accessibility, literacy had been confined to a small group that was constituted by its exclusivity. Nonnormative anglophone writing cannot be seen as literary when Standard English literacy belongs to a small few. Only when nonnormative anglophone writing is viewed as constellating new but necessary representative and aesthetic possibilities can it become recognizable in aesthetic terms.

Over the past two centuries, nonnormative writing has gradually appeared to anglophone readers as a representative technique that reorders and makes sense of lived reality. In this way, nonnormative writing has become cognizable and evaluable in aesthetic terms not *in spite of* but instead *because of* the ways it depicts linguistic difference.

In the present one can look at the multilingual forms of writing assembled by Dohra Ahmad's fascinating anthology *Rotten English* (2007) and call them aesthetic practices without equivocation, a denomination that would have been unthinkable or at least avant-gardist until recently.[12] Troubling unthinking use of the term "dialect," as I do, because it is a disparaging bequest from eighteenth-century monolingual politics, Ahmad notes that the authors assembled in her volume "each challenge the hierarchy implied by 'dialect' versus 'language.' . . . The codes they practice [must] be recognized for their strength coherence, and communicative capacity."[13] The anthology includes poets, short story writers, novelists, and essayists like Paul Laurence Dunbar, Louise Bennett, Zora Neal Hurston, Irvine Welsh, Junot Díaz, and Amy Tan, among others. From one perspective, the sensible fabric of aesthetic experience has altered in such a way as to permit the assemblage of these multilingual anglophone authors into one anthology. The criteria of inclusion are that these authors challenge monolingual normativity in anglophone writing.

The pedagogical aspirations of this anthology confirm that the anglophone languages of Ahmad's authors are recognized to be aesthetically valid, vibrant, timely, and needed. Ahmad herself convincingly argues that "rotten English" has become sensible and significant, politically as well as aesthetically. As she puts it, "These authors write in direct opposition to all socially accepted institutions, whether school, church, various forms of the welfare state, or Standard English itself."[14] In other words, Ahmad sees a homology—visible from the present—between her authors' subversions of linguistic normativity and their resistance to "socially accepted institutions" and modalities of institutional power. Aesthetic resistance to the politics of monolingualism is, in Ahmad, a political endorsement of multiplicity in all social forms. The editor's focus on linguistic subversion paints anglophone writing as the aesthetic analogue of widespread resistance to contemporary forms of inherited normativity.

If in the present these "anti-institutional" anglophone forms of writing are acknowledged to have both aesthetic and political valences, I posit that there is a longer history subtending this collation. Certainly, the present has witnessed a dissensual change in aesthetic criteria that allows for and even actively desires the assembly of Ahmad's "rotten English" writers into a coherent and meaningful category. The process has not been sudden. Ahmad herself acknowledges that a long history of aesthetic and political change is at work as she sketches the process of British and American colonial (and linguistic) expansion. In this respect it is instructive that the earliest figure appearing in the anthology is Robert Burns, whose "Auld Lang Syne," "Highland Marry," and "Bonnie Leslie" are included. Ahmad styles Burns anachronistically as an "ethnomusicologist," one whose attention to the ballad form produced subversive works analogous to the anticolonial poetry of W. B. Yeats and Rabindranath Tagore. Burns's predecessors and contemporaries—those who made his aesthetic coup possible—are noticeably absent from this anthology, however, as most of the figures are drawn from the twentieth and twenty-first centuries.

In Rancière's model, "the degrees of importance retrospectively granted to artistic events erase the genealogy of forms of perception and thought that were able to make them events in the first place."[15] In other words, the ways in which aesthetic events like Burns's dialect poetry are remembered, commemorated, and reinscribed into aesthetic history through the processes of canonicity efface prior, contiguous, and adjacent practices that enabled the aesthetic event in question to be perceptible as aesthetic in the first place. The fact that Burns represents both a precursor to "anticolonial poetry" and an origin for the aesthetics of "rotten English" suggests that Burns's work constellates and makes coherent a series of developments relating to language and identity.[16] Burns's larger linguistic environment makes additional lineages of nonnormative anglophone writing visible.

By way of transition, it is important to gesture toward the ways that writers can act on aesthetic criteria and political horizons through their work. Derrida includes a charged injunction to action regarding the politics (and aesthetics) of monolingualism, one that helps make sense of eighteenth-century anglophony. The injunction comes when Derrida is suggesting that one can defend a language while also attacking the language politics that accompany it. How, in other words, can one disable the politics of monolingualism in order to produce a counterpolitics of multilingualism and an altered set of aesthetic practices and criteria? For Derrida, the counterpolitical (dissensual) solution is as follows: "That jealous guard that one mounts in proximity to one's language, even as one is denouncing the nationalist politics of language (I do the one and the other), demands the multiplication of shibboleths as so many challenges to translations, so many taxes levied on the frontier of languages, so many alliances assigned to the ambassadors of the idiom, so many inventions ordered for translators: therefore invent in *your* language if you can or want to hear mine."[17] A writer or "translator-poet" must "invent" and engage in the "multiplication of shibboleths" in order to arrest a politics of monolingualism, which Derrida later refers to semi-ironically as "patriotism."

The thinking here is subtle. Derrida advocates for multiplying shibboleths, or markers of linguistic otherness, in order to "disturb" his "fellow [linguistic] citizens" with the alterity that is always already present in their seemingly unitary "national" language. Derrida seeks to multiply shibboleths as "so many challenges to translation" as "taxes levied on the frontier of languages." One effect is to destandardize the "national" language in order to trouble the notion that language and nation are coterminous. Another effect is to "levy taxes" at a language's borders in order to encourage translation practices that enrich a language's health and expressive range. I take this to mean that Derrida desires translations that will stage a language's unique capacity for being altered. Derrida's challenge that translators multiply differences in language is not an argument for untranslatability or an argument in favor of the irreducible singularity of different linguistic systems. Rather, Derrida enjoins translators to "invent in *your* language if you can or want to hear mine." Translators must be equipped to "invent" analogous linguistic forms that upset but also improve the target language.

On the one hand, this is an argument in favor of cultivating linguistic difference so that language is always different from itself and from what commonsense users think it is. Cherish language by inventing new and copious capabilities. Cherish language's permanence by requiring it to evolve constantly, such that it is always different from itself. This is what Burns does, and what Marlon James does. It is also what Ahmad's "rotten English" writers do. These forms of cherishing are political possibilities that open any language to its heterogeneous community of speakers. On the other hand, this is also an argument in favor of forcefully acting on the criteria of aesthetic reception. Seeming "nonsense" cannot be processed within an aesthetic sensorium unless one makes space for "nonsense" to take on sense and to be seen as aesthetically meaningful. Another critic, Evelyn Nien-Ming Ch'ien, is exactly correct when she points out that reading contemporary multilingual writers as inscrutable or resistant to interpretation is exactly the wrong way to read them. "These writers know that being on the margin of communities starts when they are considered inscrutable or untranslatable. They also know that those who call them untranslatable are excusing themselves from engaging in acts of interpretation."[18] So too eighteenth-century anglophones. Reading them as inscrutable is no reading at all. Reading them in Derridean terms as always estranging language from itself in the interest of the linguistic community is more useful.

This is the interpretive attitude that I bring to the wonderfully "rotten" and "weird" works of long eighteenth-century anglophone writing. I believe it is incumbent on us, as scholars and students of Standard English literature as well as anglophone literatures and histories, to rethink the history of our aesthetic sensorium so that it is truer to aesthetic creations of the past and the present. It is in this spirit of expanding our sense of the historical multiplicity, incommensurability, and aesthetic importance of linguistic difference and diversity that my critical intervention seeks to dephilologize, dedialectologize, deethnographize, and depathologize texts and subjects that literary posterity has relegated to anaesthetic discursive traditions that cast little light on contemporary linguistic, political, and aesthetic issues.

Anglophony and Standardization

> Dictionaries have in all Languages been compiled, to which, as to Storehouses, such Persons may have Recourse, as often as any thing occurs in Conversation or Reading, with which they are unacquainted, or when they themselves would speak or write properly and intelligibly.
>
> And as such Helps have been thought useful in all civilized nations, they appear more eminently necessary in the English Tongue; not only because it is, perhaps, the most copious Language of any in Europe, but is likewise made up of so great a variety of other languages, both ancient and modern, as will plainly appear to any one who shall peruse the following Dictionary. Of the Reason of which Mixture, and by what Accidents it was brought about, I shall give the following Account.[19]

The eighteenth century, and in particular the second half of the eighteenth century, is unprecedentedly generative for the production of discourses about anglophony, almost all of which allude to the language's "Mixture," as in lexicographer Nathan Bailey's description of dictionaries included above. For the rest of this chapter and the next, I describe the production of two of these metalinguistic discourses, standardization and translation theory, in terms of how they relate to the evolution of aesthetic criteria in the period. I emphasize how standardization and translation theories arise out of and interact with their eighteenth-century linguistic environment. Central to standardization is a concern with remediating anglophone multiplicity. Central to translation theory of the period is controlling the effects global linguistic multiplicity has on Standard English. The discursive ferment surrounding anglophony was—especially as it relates to standardization and translation—crucially conditioned by a pronounced interest in internal and external linguistic multiplicities. An example of this can be seen in the coupling of local and global that Bailey performs when he ratchets up his initial description of Standard English as "the most copious Language of any in Europe" toward the more bombastic claim that Standard English has "become the most Copious and Significant Language in *Europe*, if not the World."[20]

In concrete terms, the standardization movement produced dictionaries, grammar books, style manuals, and elocutionary tracts that all take on recognizably modern shapes in this period. Of importance is that these were produced not as a result of autochthonous anglophone invention, but instead as a result of the deliberate translation of textual protocol from other linguistic contexts. Other scholars have ably catalogued the forms and historical contexts of these standardizing texts, especially their classical substrates. My intention is not to repeat their work here but instead to emphasize the tremendous multiplicities at the heart of their supposed normativity. In fact, I argue that even as these metalinguistic texts argue for linguistic homogeneity, their patterns of argument, exemplification, and proof are multiply constituted, in language as in thought. Their rhetoric is artistic in a manner that only linguistic multiplicity can generate. They provide insight into the aesthetic sensorium of the period that is illuminating. We can think of them as filling in part of Rancière's forgotten "genealogy of forms."

Crucially, the standardization movement is ambivalent about linguistic multiplicity through and through. Even as it argues at times for multiplicity's eradication, at other times standardization acts to preserve limited versions of linguistic multiplicity. Consider again Bailey's epigraph. By pointing out that "Dictionaries have in all Languages been compiled" so that people will have "Helps" when they seek to "speak or write properly and intelligently," Bailey implicitly but clearly frames his own work within translocal, transnational, and translational traditions.[21] What all other languages have done, those desiring a Standard English should also do. The "universal Practice of all polite Nations" must necessarily be repeated and done better for Standard English, Bailey argues, because a well-organized language contributes to "a learned Education." Standardized linguistic education in the canons of useful knowledge and the protocols of polite interaction is essential to national and imperial progress.

However, as in most texts of its kind, an unavoidable ambivalence arises surrounding multiplicity. Even as Bailey asserts that a standard form of English must adapt and then improve on the metalinguistic texts surrounding other languages, in particular the lexicographic and grammatical apparatuses of French, Greek, and Latin, he also makes space for the multiple relationality of all languages. "All languages . . . do interchangeably participate each with other," he writes. This notion is crystallized in the simultaneously local and cosmopolitan list of abbreviations that Bailey's text uses to name the component languages of the "mixture" that his dictionary's pages chart: "*A* for Arabick. *B.* British. *C.* Country Word. *Cant.* Canting Word. *C. Br.* Welsh. *Ch.* Chaldee," and so forth.[22] Etymology, the project of which is to name and catalogue language's multiple origins, becomes for Bailey a way to group together nonanglophone linguistic sources, "Greek," "Hebrew," "Spanish," and "Syriac," et cetera, with anglophone analogues, "North Country," "South Country," and "West Country," to name a few. In this respect, multiplicity is not overcome but instead laid bare and preserved, not in a living or vibrant way, but in a textual one, one that presupposes continual contact between emerging and residual linguistic groups.

Grammarians, rhetoricians, and elocutionists like Bailey generally display a similarly marked awareness of interlinguistic "participation."[23] In another example, theologian Anselm Bayly's *A Plain and Complete Grammar of the English Language* (1772) states plainly that "English is not self-originated." This claim exercises the same species of interlinguistic thinking that marks an earlier work of Bayly's, namely, his four-fold philosophical grammar, *An Introduction to Languages Literary and Philosophical; Especially to the English, Latin, Greek and Hebrew* (1758), the visual form of which carries on the long tradition of the polyglot Bible.[24] Crucial too, both of Bayly's works are oriented toward teaching Standard English for a foreign audience. Rather than just focusing on Standard English as a pillar of English nationhood and British imperial practice, as some readings of standardization might suggest, Bayly's grammatical theories demonstrate a reciprocal set of invitations to anglophones and nonanglophones alike. He states the goals of his grammar like this: "*English* might be learned much sooner than it commonly is both by Children and *Foreigners*; and again, *Foreign Languages* by *Englishmen*, if taught by some such ALPHABET as the following."[25] While it is a critical commonplace that eighteenth-century metalinguistic discourses such as standardization draw heavily from classical Greek and Latin models, in terms of linguistic influences, however, they draw from far more models than just these.[26]

One traditional reading of the eighteenth-century standardization movement emphasizes the emerging nationalist and prescriptivist tendencies that preoccupy dictionaries, grammars, style manuals, and elocutionary tracts after midcentury. This is understandable, for prescriptivism in the service of the idea of national coherence is one of the preoccupations of the best-known proponents of standardization during the period. Samuel Johnson's "Preface," which I discuss at length below, at times censures what I have been calling the multilingualism of the other by claiming that anglophony "has itself been hitherto neglected, suffered to spread, under the direction of chance, into wild exuberance, resigned to the tyranny of time and fashion, and exposed to the corruptions of ignorance, and caprices of innovation."[27] Johnson's polemical solution to anglophony's "exuberance" and "corruption" is to eliminate this sort of neglect by imposing order and regulation. Similarly, Robert Lowth writes in the introduction of his important 1762 grammar, "The truth is, Grammar is very much neglected among us," a statement in which "us" is clearly meant to include anglophones alone.[28] In the same period, Thomas Sheridan declares in his popular elocutionary lectures that there prevails in Britain "a general deficiency in point of public reading and speaking."[29] He then continues by threatening the national public that they will be classed "amongst the Barbarians" if they continue to forget to master proper elocution, a skill that will give "ocular proof of your being a people perfectly civilized."[30]

As a motley movement concerned with linguistic neglect and deficiency, standardization's emphasis on linguistic propriety was successful, inasmuch as the prizing of aspirations toward normativity can be counted as success. As a case in point, Jim Milroy describes anglophony in an earlier period as being organized around unchangeable linguistic hierarchy. "It is quite unlikely that there was a general consciousness of a *standard* pronunciation [of English] in 1600: what people did know about were socially marked pronunciations that were indexical of social status, regional origin, and belongingness."[31] In contradistinction to this earlier moment, the editors of the most recent edition of *The Cambridge History of the English Language* (1999) argue that by the end of the eighteenth century and as a result of texts like those cited above, "there existed something more than ever before like an institutionalized standard [English]," in grammar, style, and in pronunciation.[32] This is not to say that the indexicality of "marked pronunciations" relative to "social status, regional origin, and belongingness" had collapsed. Far from it: what changed was the sense that people could and should conform themselves to the "institutional standard." Like other standardizers, Sheridan valorizes such conformity: "It can not be denied that an uniformity of pronunciation throughout Scotland, Wales, and Ireland, as well as through the several counties of England, would be a point much to be wished," not least because such an achievement would "destroy those odious distinctions between subjects of the same king."[33]

As Tieken-Boon van Ostade has argued, it is important to counter the commonplace notion that all of the standardization movement was rigidly prescriptivist.[34] It certainly was not, and this has important ramifications relating to the long lineage of multilingual writing that I am positing. Tieken-Boon van Ostade's point comes from the domain of the history of linguistics, but for me it is applicable as a way to grasp those parts of the standardization movement that were never uniformly prescriptivist, parts of the movement that always allowed limited aesthetic recognition of certain forms of nonnormative writing. If prescriptivism refers to writing about English that directly advocates for uniform public linguistic practices as a regulatory corrective for the diversity of the anglophone linguistic environment, then the discourse of prescriptivism is narrower and less capacious than the discourse of standardization even if in broad strokes these two gestures are largely similar. This distinction is valuable. In the space between standardization and prescriptivism reside cultural and historical insights as well as aesthetic potentialities for linguistic multiplicity. What I will here be referring to as standardization—represented in my discussion below with texts by Defoe, Johnson, and Blair—often cautiously values anglophone multiplicity whereas prescriptivism generally does not. Standardization's cautious endorsement of certain, narrow forms of multiplicity, in other words, allows us to track the aesthetic alterations that eventually give rise to the present's much more capacious aesthetic interest in carefully curated representations of linguistic difference. Certainly, standardization seeks uniform public linguistic practices but does so in a way that concedes to and in some cases celebrates the impossibility of expelling all forms of multiplicity from anglophony.

When we focus on standardization, we see ways in which standardizing writers try to recuperate and positively valorize aspects of anglophone multiplicity, the kind of multiplicity that Bailey alludes to when he writes that the "*English* Tongue" is "made up of so great a variety of other languages, both ancient and modern, as will plainly appear to any one who shall peruse the following *Dictionary*." Other writers, Johnson especially, might actually be best understood as more interested in anglophone multiplicity than is traditionally thought, an argument I make below by way of Johnson's theoretical wrestling match with the loaded and frequently occurring terms "copious" and "copiousness." Like "mixture," these related terms are crucial to linguistic thought in the period. By pointing this out, my overarching claim is that, faced with anglophone multiplicity, the standardization movement's true concern is both imperial and aesthetic: Standard English must defuse while still cultivating copiousness. Rarely do authors claim that copiousness should be eliminated outright. Instead, copiousness—as code word for a manageable and unthreatening variety of multiplicity—is regularly bandied about as anglophony's chief vice *and* virtue.

De Copia

Wolfram Schmidgen's *Exquisite Mixture: The Virtues of Impurity in Early Modern England* (2013) asks scholars to examine strains of seventeenth- and eighteenth-century thought that valorized hybridity.[35] He shows that scientific, political, and linguistic debates often characterized mixture as a "maker of forms, an agent of improvement, [and] a guarantor of liberty and unity" rather than a cause of "impurity, degeneration, instability, and formlessness."[36] Schmidgen's observations are particularly germane to anglophone aesthetics during the eighteenth century. He is right to note that many eighteenth-century accounts find unexpected ways to celebrate the language system's heterogeneity. He is also right to note that the era's recuperation of linguistic heterogeneity echoes ongoing debates about social, political, and economic life. Other critics have advanced this thesis before, most notably Tony Crowley and John Barrell, both of whom link language theory to burgeoning theories of democracy, common law, and constitutionalism.[37] Schmidgen usefully takes the conversation further by suggesting that recuperations of the English language's heterogeneity generated aesthetic ideas that praised mixture as a "maker of forms" rather than just a condition. Schmidgen's movement from mixture in language theory to mixture as aesthetic practice is an important point of departure for thinking about forms of heterogeneity that were palatable and indeed laudable in the period, as well as those that were neither.

In order to adapt Schmidgen's thinking to the present inquiry, it is necessary to point out first that from the Renaissance well into the nineteenth century, the most common way of describing anglophony was to invoke the system's "copiousness" rather than its "mixture." Of course, "mixture" also appears frequently, as in Bailey. But the terminological difference can be useful. Copiousness is a rhetorical concept with a long history in classical and Renaissance writing. In using this term rather than "mixture," anglophone theorists of the vernacular took their cues from Erasmus's *De duplici copia verborum ac rerum commentarii duo* (1512), a treatise that figures *copia*, or abundance, as the precondition for "richness of expression" and "richness of subject matter."[38] The exercises Erasmus lays out in his book are meant to give the reader the rhetorical resources to adopt any style of writing, the three main varieties of which Erasmus orders as "the Laconic style," "the intermediate style of Rhodes," and "the exuberance of Asianism."[39] Anticipating the criticisms of those who prefer expressive concision to "exuberant" styles, Erasmus argues that copia need not lead to unnecessary ornamentation. As proof he asks, "who will speak more succinctly than the man who can readily and without hesitation pick out from a huge army of words, from the whole range of figures of speech, the feature that contributes most effectively to brevity?"[40] With this question, Erasmus implies that copia enables the kind of specificity that only a "huge army of words" can produce. When eighteenth-century anglophone theorists of the vernacular use the term "copiousness" to describe English, they are translating Erasmian vocabulary in order to make their language seem worthy of prestige beyond Britain.[41] Given that most of the period's theorists of language were trained in the classics, the term "copiousness" links anglophony to the literate empires of Greece and Rome by recoding "mixture" in a venerable way.

For the investigators of anglophone copiousness that I detail in this section, copiousness as linguistic quality is more than just the potential for Erasmian specificity. Anglophony's unique variety of copiousness is read by turns as an aesthetic advantage, defect, opportunity, and obstacle. Given that anglophone lects were the primary medium for linking the increasingly far-flung empire, copiousness also often serves as a metaphor for the linguistic pluralism of Britain's heterogeneous imperial publics. The term registers the shared idea that anglophony and the British imperial polity were singular *because* plural. Copiousness was the language's expressive quiddity just as it was the British empire's fundamental geocultural condition. Though these writers share the notion that language's present forms have something to do with the future of British society, they differ in opinion about how to manage copiousness in language just as they differ in opinion about how to handle copiousness in society. Some evoke anglophone copiousness alongside fantasies of imperial progress through trade, incorporation, and the spread of liberty. A less sanguine approach reads copiousness as a cultural illness rooted in the fact that British people have not "been formed in a manner within themselves" and therefore suffer from social fragmentation and imperial belatedness.[42] A more radical approach repurposes linguistic copiousness as a way to resist metropolitan cultural domination while still another approach thinks of copiousness as a way to balance metropolitan favor with local identity. In short, descriptions of anglophone copiousness communicate diverse hopes, fears, and imperial fantasies—and sometimes all of these at once.

To understand the rhetoric of copiousness and its astonishing frequency in eighteenth-century discussions of the Standard English to come, one must also consider earlier periods in which copiousness as a linguistic quality echoes broader public discussions. Emphasizing the importance of commerce, for example, Richard Carew's "The Excellencie of the English Tongue" (1595) associates "Copiousnesse" with English entrepreneurship.[43] Carew figures "the English tongue" as a tattered fabric that has been resourcefully patched over with material salvaged from other languages. For Carew, this fact redounds positively on the language's speakers. Their industriousness supplements the language with importations just as their overseas trade provides goods that cannot be made at home. "For our owne parts," he writes, "we employ the borrowed ware so farre to our advantage that we raise a profit of new words from the same stocke, which yet in their owne countrey are not merchantable."[44] Borrowed words resemble traded goods in that both "raise a profit" from "wares" that remain valueless where they are originally produced. Carew's metaphors treat anglophone "copiousnesse" as a positive reflection of England's history as a commercial crossroads.

William Camden, writing in 1605, also emphasizes England's position as a crossroads. England's uniqueness "hath beene brought in by entrance of Strangers, as *Danes, Normans*, and others which have swarmed hither," Camden writes.[45] Explorers, invaders, and immigrants came into productive contact in Britain, blending their languages into a flexible medium. By "enfranchising and endenizing strange words," emergent Standard English became a formidable language, one "as copious, pithie, and significative, as any other tongue in Europe."[46] Peter Heylyn, adding his voice to the issue in 1652, sees anglophony as the product of happy decomposition: "The *English* Language is a De-compound of *Dutch, French* and *Latine*, which I conceive rather to adde to its perfection, than to detract any thing from the worth thereof; since out of every Language we have culled the most significant Words, and equally participate of what is excellent in them, their Imperfections being rejected."[47] Writing at the beginning of the seventeenth century, Camden locates copiousness in the naturalization of "strangers" and their words; Heylyn sees copiousness in terms of "culling" and "participation," ideas that are both later projected beyond Britain during the eighteenth century's robust imperial expansion. During this later period, Britain's ocean-spanning anglophone empire becomes a commercial and cultural crossroads that is no longer geographically coterminous with the British Isles, which leads to a global scope for "culling" and linguistic "participation." Deterritorialization, which is one of anglophony's defining eighteenth-century characteristics, brings into being new paradigms for negotiating linguistic copiousness.

As Latinity's transnational currency dwindled over the course of the seventeenth and eighteenth centuries, attention to the expressivity of anglophone forms intensified. Attention became even more urgent when John Locke, whom Schmidgen discusses in detail, published his comprehensive vernacular account of hypothetical filiations between language and mind.[48] Locke's interest in the reciprocity between arbitrary linguistic signs and the contours of human thought stimulated an unprecedented amount of writing about language. Indeed, by some measures, the need to process Locke's theories was one factor in the production of the slew of eighteenth-century pedagogical texts that critics now group as the standardization movement.[49] Through Locke, standardizers believed that they could act on and improve linguistic culture by producing pedagogical texts that concretized "proper" linguistico-cultural standards while managing literacy's revolutionary potential.

Less commonly recognized is the way that empire also stimulated efforts to fix and police anglophony's excesses in the interest of molding a reputable Standard English. Appreciating the contentious debates about empire that mark the period, attempts at what Jonathan Swift called "correcting, improving, and ascertaining the English tongue" must be seen in conjunction with two imperial problems: (1) how Standard English might serve as the foundation for cohesion between subjects hailing from different nations, ethnicities, classes, and continents; and (2) how cultural cohesion in language might be projected outwardly as a badge of imperial strength.[50] As an imperial medium, emergent Standard English came up short when compared to historical models and contemporary competitors. Classical Greek's "pregnant brevity"[51] had fostered humanistic progress to the tune of Herodotus, Sophocles, Socrates, and Plato.[52] In addition to generating its own archive of humanistic achievements, classical Latin had sutured together the entropic Roman Empire at its most bloated extent. Likewise, language theorists fretted over anglophony's inferiority relative to other transnational networks like the *Respublica literaria* and the *République des belles lettres*—both of which were lauded as "elegant" and "refined" but less frequently as "copious" models.[53] Anglophony's prima facie multiplicity seemed disreputable by comparison, a condition Peter Burke aptly calls the "anxiety of deficit."[54] Insofar as it was possible, the standardization movement set about crafting a copious Standard English to come in conjunction with Britain's domestic and imperial dynamics.

For these reasons, eighteenth-century attempts to form Standard English pull in multiple directions. Some theorists praise the language for its copiousness even while advocating for the limitation of copiousness in the interest of domestic unity and overseas publicity. James Greenwood's *An Essay Towards a Practical Grammar*, which was published numerous times from the 1720s through the 1750s, renders this tension clearly: "A vast Medley of foreign Words has been receiv'd into our Language; not that the *English* is of it self poor and barren, but is [now] sufficiently enrich'd with Words and Elegancies; and, if I may so speak, is copious to an Excess."[55] Though it was useful at first, Greenwood suggests that the language's copious enrichment now tends toward decadence. Without moderating efforts, copiousness accelerates change and risks engendering instability. Scottish rhetorician and translator George Campbell tacks the opposite direction, warning that linguistic regulation will hamstring British power. Campbell chides grammarians and lexicographers who attack copiousness, observing that "our mother-tongue, by being too much impaired, may be impoverished, and so more injured in copiousness and nerves, than all our refinements will ever be able to compensate."[56] Greenwood tries to stanch copiousness; Campbell defends its value. Their accounts can be read as competing allegories of ongoing social debates. In such a reading, Greenwood can be said to argue against the kinds of diverse human imbrications produced by commerce, trade, travel, and empire while Campbell appears in favor of them. Herein it is obvious that the social debates of the eighteenth century are inscribed in metalinguistic discourse. Additionally, it is possible to see metalinguistic discourse formulating the terms of these very debates.

It is important to repeat that language theorists in the period use debates over anglophone copiousness as a way to frame domestic and imperial concerns. Consider how Standard English's abundance is put forth as a compensation for some missing cultural quality in James Harris's peroration on the "Genius of the English Language." Harris touts the "elegance" of Greek, Latin, and French before continuing: "We have this advantage to compensate our defect, that what we want in *Elegance*, we gain in *Copiousness*, in which last respect few Languages will be found superior to our own."[57] Admitting that Standard English lacks French's "elegance," he assures readers it still possesses rewards that counteract these "defects." As he puts it, "Our Terms in *polite Literature* prove, that this came from *Greece*; our Terms in *Music* and *Painting*, that these came from *Italy*; our Phrase of *Cookery* and *War*, that we learnt these from the *French*; and our Phrases in *Navigation*, that we were taught by the *Flemings* and *Low Dutch*."[58] Copiousness sets anglophones apart and makes their language exceptional in its expressive range. The language's ability to adapt and domesticate other languages' words makes it uniquely qualified to unify the empire's constituent peoples, now newly yoked together in an imperial project with global aspirations.

The rest of this section offers close readings of important (but not exhaustive) evocations of copiousness as a constituent feature of what I have been calling eighteenth-century anglophony. Each of the writers I discuss treats anglophony's internal variety as a historical and political signifier, and each recuperates a particular definition of copiousness as compensation for some perceived cultural lack. Far from uniformly advantageous, copiousness is figured by all these writers as simultaneously an aesthetic promise and a political threat. Taken together, they provide a cross-section of imperially inflected views of linguistic copiousness that circulated during the eighteenth century. Moreover, they attest to the fact that the metaphor of copiousness is no mere curio in the history of writing about language. Far from it, it is a regularly deployed qualifier with cultural referents that were known to people of the period. As seen through these writers, the problem of copiousness gets at the most contentious aspects of British imperial society's eighteenth-century self-image, overseas activity, and domestic concerns. Writing about anglophone copiousness becomes a way to explore tensions between unity and multiplicity, order and disorder, law and lawlessness, tradition and revolution, and identity and community.[59]

Daniel Defoe believed a standard form of English would do better on the world stage if its unique qualities were properly managed and widely broadcast. Toward this end, his "Essay Upon Projects" (1697) advocates for a regulatory institution modeled on Richelieu's *Académie Française* and charged with defining the language's "true glory."[60] The projected institution would produce "the noblest and most comprehensive of all the vulgar languages in the world," thereby staking a claim to Britain's world historical significance. Locating nobility in vulgarity, Defoe stresses the homology between the Standard English to come and Britain's empirical, commercial, and democratic values. He calls for a committee of "learned men" to improve the language. Yet, he seeks "very few, whose business or trade was learning" because to his mind scholarly language was stilted and lifeless, "full of stiffness and affectation, hard words, and long unusual coupling of syllables and sentences."[61] Defoe's committee would have to be socially mixed and publicly aware, not cloistered in libraries like the arbiters of the "literate" tongues.[62] This fantasy committee would enshrine limited social mixing by bringing together thirty-six men, "twelve to be of the nobility, if possible, and twelve private gentlemen, and a class of twelve to be left open for mere merit."[63] Lacking female voices,[64] the semidemocratic committee would quash subversive "coinages"[65] while fine-tuning English's natural vitality.

A vision of that copious vitality occurs in Defoe's "The True-Born Englishman" (1700), a poem in which English is described as unruly and deracinated, the aberrant offspring of promiscuous breeding between unlike groups:

From this Amphibious ill-born Mob began
That vain ill-natur'd thing, an Englishman.

> The Customs, Sirnames, Languages, and Manners,
> Of all these Nations are their own explainers:
> Whose Relicks are so lasting and so strong,
> They've left a *Shiboleth* upon our tongue;
> By which with easy search you may distinguish
> *Your Roman-Saxon-Danish-Norman* English![66]

Here as elsewhere in his satire, Defoe exposes the syncretism at the heart of "amphibious" English identity through an appeal to history's *longue durée.* Look back far enough, he implores, and "the well-extracted blood of Englishmen" is seen to descend from a "nauseous brood" rather than ancestors of distinction. By reversing "vain" fantasies of hereditary purity, the poem leaves the "wells of English undefiled," looking mixed, multiple, and far better for it.[67] Featuring violent and promiscuous breeding of unlike groups as an engine of cultural genesis, Defoe's counterhistory highlights anglophony's composite nature: impure from its very origins, begotten by the "furious lusts" of intersecting tribes, and permanently littered with intercultural "relicks." Moreover, by using the mixed tongue as a metonym for its speakers' historical and political characteristics, Defoe emphasizes the constitutional untenability of exclusionary definitions of national identity. Irrespective of the fact that the poet might well have appended "Celtic-" to the list's beginning, or, if it were metrically permissible, infixed "-Hebrew-Greek-" somewhere in the chain, "*Roman-Saxon-Danish-Norman* English" states the case of fundamental anglophone linguistic and cultural multiplicity in clear and unequivocal terms.[68]

Defoe recuperates English's mixed heritage to make a political statement: Englishness is a hybrid category by historical necessity. Any attempt to overwrite that hybridity should be checked. Lingering within this passage too is an aesthetic recuperation that revels in poetic possibilities latent in anglophone copiousness. Defoe names and enacts copiousness as aesthetic strategy. The formulation, "They've left a *Shiboleth* upon our tongue," is a verbal recursion that is clever and instructive. The punch line is that "*Shiboleth*" is a shibboleth, that is, an exemplification of its own definition. It is a word transported from another linguistic context, a word that calls to mind both its own alterity and anglophony's spongiform copiousness.[69] At the level of meaning, Defoe asserts English's lexical hybridity, and at the level of form he deploys a curious example of that hybridity. The odd word's formal merits are undeniable. Even while indexing its own alien etymology, shibboleth fits snugly into the poem's unbroken meter, thus redoubling the satirist's point. Through such poetic calisthenics, Defoe affirms both Englishness and the English language as singular *because* plural, absorbent, multiply formed, and adaptable. There is "a *Shiboleth* upon our tongue," he asserts, which is a fine metaphor for the teeming linguistic plenitude that must always exceed narrow national designators. English is irrevocably copious, Defoe suggests, so let it be copious in a way that flatters Britain's domestic and imperial self-interest.

Lest we read too much into this use of "shibboleth," it is worth recalling the conservative idealization of unblemished heredity against which Britain's tawdry linguistic history is sometimes implicitly posed in Defoe. Think of the topsy-turvy social spectacle depicted in these blunt lines, also from the satire: "Wealth, however got, in *England* makes / Lords of Mechanicks, Gentlemen of Rakes. / Antiquity and Birth are needless here / 'Tis Impudence and Money makes a Peer."[70] This fearful depiction of social anarchy meshes most neatly with Defoe's conservative approach to language regulation in "An Essay Upon Projects," a text whose comments on language can at certain moments be characterized as definitively against unsanctioned linguistic innovation. In other words, though we might read the "shibboleth on our tongue" as a positive endorsement of linguistico-cultural copiousness, Defoe is quite normative elsewhere. His linguistic normativity is clear in his linguistic depiction of Friday in *Robinson Crusoe* (1719) and most of the nonwhite characters in *Colonel Jack* (1722). Among other examples, we might point to his purposeful linguistic othering of the North English in *A Tour Through the Whole Island of Great Britain* (1724–27), wherein Defoe writes, "I must not quit *Northumberland* without taking notice, that the Natives of this Country . . . are distinguished by a *Shibboleth* upon their Tongues in pronouncing the Letter R, which they cannot utter without a hollow Jarring in the Throat, by which they are as plainly known, as a Foreigner is in pronouncing the *Th*: this they call the *Northumberland R*, or *Wharle*.[71]

Thinking about these lines from the *Tour*, I suggest that it is worthwhile to contemplate the maneuver by which Defoe's satire identifies a shibboleth on "our" first-person-plural tongue to begin with. One way of reading the satire is to say that Defoe uses the concept of the "shibboleth" as a self-foreignizing trope *and* self-identificatory device. This rhetorical trick works in the context of an exaggerative satire because "our" shibboleths should, according to normal usage, be inaudible or at least unremarkable to "ourselves." By contrast, Defoe's interest in "their" shibboleths posits the existence of a phonological feature that not only rings in the ear but also alerts "us" to the boundaries of what is construed, rightly or wrongly, to be "our" category. A shibboleth on "our" tongue acknowledges distinctions that unite; a shibboleth on "their" tongue, as in this passage from the *Tour*, provides an index of just how much "our" tongue is not "their" tongue. To the degree that the shibboleth of "The True-Born Englishman" surprises, the shibboleth of *A Tour Through the Whole Island of Great Britain* is a conventional reading of diverse language forms as an index of human difference and cultural dissimilarity.

It is no surprise that Defoe should deploy countervalent uses of the same word, but it is revealing. My goal is to suggest that these two usages indicate emerging assumptions about literary language as it interfaces with cultural difference. My point is that the bifurcation visible in "a Shibboleth on our tongue" (inclusive) and "a Shibboleth on their tongue" (exclusive) can usefully contribute to our understanding of what counts as literary or aesthetic language. This inclusive and exclusive bifurcation is effectively an aesthetic demarcation, one that sets parameters for what can and cannot be construed within the aesthetic frameworks of Standard English as such. Whereas "their" shibboleths are signifiers of cultural difference, our "shibboleths" are indicative of English's multiform copiousness. This bifurcation splits the eighteenth-century archive. As previously mentioned, there is a large amount of published writing from this period that is banished outside literary consideration because of the perception that its language is outside or beyond Standard English and therefore anaesthetic in the sense of not rising to the level of aesthetic contemplation.

In Defoe, we see the gathering of a wave of ambivalent linguistic standardization ideas that characterizes the latter part of the eighteenth and much of the first half of the nineteenth centuries. If Defoe is an early harbinger of this development, other well-known writers on language contribute to the question in more forceful ways. The "Preface" of Samuel Johnson's *Dictionary* (1755), for example, is one such text. Johnson announces from the outset the dictionary will strive to display English's unique history and genius in every word. By way of describing this history and genius, he asserts that anglophony as it exists is naturally "copious without order" and "energetick without rules," ambivalent conjunctions that reflect the language's unfortunate descent from a "wild and barbarous jargon."[72] As a lexicographer, Johnson tasks himself with balancing "order" and "rules" with fidelity to English's "copious" and "energetick" genius. Because Johnson believes that the Standard English to come must conform to Britain's customary constitution, maintaining the language's genius requires that some speakers have rights in the determination of standard forms while others do not. This political subtext is visible in his description of the dictionary's inclusions and omissions. When only one or two authors attest words, Johnson calls them "probationers" and concludes that they "must depend for their adoption on the suffrage of futurity."[73] By thinking of neologisms as auditions subject to public approval, Johnson reinforces the notion that language is a copious and semidemocratic assembly staffed by lexicographers charged with monitoring English's subtle changes. A word's obsolescence is the product of "suffrage," he tells us. To borrow the impoverished vocabulary of contemporary discussions surrounding nationality, language, and citizenship as a way of showing how deeply rooted in the past those discussions are, Johnson's mode of thinking about language implies the existence of "alien," "nonnaturalized," or "inassimilable" words, categories of language that are roughly analogous to what Defoe refers to as the language produced by those with a "shibboleth on their tongue."

Johnson's preface attacks any and all infringements on his paternalistic vision of sanctioned language change. As a case in point, he reprimands those who illegitimately alter English "by their knowledge of foreign languages, or ignorance of their own, by vanity, or wantonness, by compliance with fashion, or lust for innovation."[74] Thus begins his criticism of agents disloyal to Standard English and seditious to Britain, criticisms that move in surprising directions. "Commerce," so essential to British self-understanding, "depraves the manners and corrupts the language," and it also creates the conditions of possibility for treasonous traders who "have frequent intercourse with strangers, to whom they endeavor to accommodate themselves."[75] Relatedly, philosophy causes fluctuations in language because philosophers are dissolute, "sustained and supported by the labour of the other."[76] Worse still, the "most mischievous" cause of change is translation, that "great pest of speech" on which British imperial ventures and literary aesthetics would increasingly rely in the late eighteenth and nineteenth centuries.[77] Johnson takes issue with the way translation upsets historically sanctioned forms of grammar, syntax, and thought. Translation's most threatening aspect is that it "alters not the single stones of the building, but the order of the columns."[78] That is to say, it acts on linguistic, political, and aesthetic standards. I return to the question of translation and anglophony in the next chapter, but for the time being, it suffices to say that in Johnson, translation attenuates Britain's relationship to its own cultural history.

Reading Johnson only in this way, one would be justified in thinking of him as inhibiting linguistic copiousness in spite of the lip service he pays to language as a democratic creation. However, the "Preface" also contains a series of brilliant and beautiful concessions to the dynamic, inexorable, and necessary increase of linguistic variety. For example, one key moment addresses the various ways vowels are enunciated, saying, "Such defects are not errours in orthography, but spots of barbarity impressed so deep in the *English* language, that criticism can never wash them away."[79] Here Johnson executes a verbal recursion similar to Defoe's use of "shibboleth." That "barbarity" derived from a Greek onomatopoeia signifying "of another speech" or "incomprehensible" would have been obvious to many of Johnson's readers, even if only as the opposite of "civilization." "Barbarity," "barbarism," "barbarous," and the like are naturalized words that signify otherness and foreign extraction by way of etymology. And yet if one wants to write in terms that reflect anglophony's composite history and genius, Johnson's use of the term suggests that "barbarity" must be accepted as a natural feature of the language's historical layering.

Johnson unfurls several other revealing and also aesthetically appealing concessions to copiousness. In one, he acknowledges that individual aspirations to jurisdiction over communal property are vain: "When we see men grow old and die at a certain time one after another, from century to century, we laugh at the elixir that promises to prolong life to a thousand years; and with equal justice may the lexicographer be derided, who being able to produce no example of a nation that has preserved their words and phrases from mutability, shall imagine that his dictionary can embalm his language, and secure it from corruption and decay."[80] Language outpaces attempts to arrest its "corruption and decay." This sublime sense of the individual's insignificance in the face of linguistic history dovetails into a series of metaphors for the fool's task of fixing language once and for all. "To enchain syllables, and to lash the wind are equally undertakings of pride," he remarks.[81] He continues by pointing out that change in language is "as much superior to human resistance as the revolutions of the sky, or the intumescence of the tide."[82] Ineffable cycles of life, death, and decay, the wind's invisible force, planetary revolutions, the ocean's ceaseless ebb and flow: not only is the kernel of the Romantic natural sublime here, there is also a sense that linguistic copiousness is inevitable because language is the shared creation of a public whose historical origins and ends are "superior" to individual will. In another metaphor, Johnson likens lexicography's challenges to artistic representation: freezing words on paper is like sketching "a grove [of trees] in the agitation of a storm . . . from its picture in the water."[83] If language's natural dynamism will forever escape attempts to capture it, then why does the dictionary try? Johnson answers the question with reference to politics, tradition, Britain. Lexicography stands in for the permanent project of achieving political unity: "We have long preserved our constitution, let us make some struggles for our language."[84] English may reject a fixed and final constitution, but it still demands one, one that is subject in perpetuity to emendation, evolution, and "suffrage."

Johnson styles himself as language's superintendent and wields his sanction to ensure that copiousness is maintained but checked by rules and standards. As noted, he objects to the risk of linguistic disorder. "Traders," "translators," and "philosophers" all "obtrude borrowed terms and exotick expressions" into the public sphere.[85] In addition, the "vulgar" spread "colloquial licentiousness," another threat to British cultural coherence that can be understood through the slippery term "copiousness." At times, Johnson's rhetoric conjures up a savage invasion from language's peripheries, one led by mobs of "illiterate writers"[86] composing books without proper education and desecrating language with unauthorized attempts at public speech. In 1595, Richard Carew had been much more cheerful about anglophone variety. For Carew, "the copiousnesse of our language appeareth in the diversitie of our Dialects, for we have Court and we have Countrey English, we have Northerne, & Southerne, grosse and ordinarie, which differ each from other . . . yet all right English alike."[87] Though he abstractly characterizes the language as the unfolding of a democratic process, Johnson would object to this last leveling idea—"yet all right English alike"—for public will and lexicography determine what forms shall rise and fall in the movement toward linguistic unity.

In this nonexhaustive accounting of debates over copiousness, it is necessary to also give voice to outsider thought. Twenty years after the *Dictionary*, radical pamphleteer, lexicographer, and language theorist Thomas Spence attacked Johnson's prioritization of a singular linguistic standard over copious linguistic increase.[88] Spence's work pursues the idea that nonnormative anglophone forms must oppose the standard for the sake of their survival. Spence points out that in dictionaries like Johnson's, "the standard of pronunciation is affixed to the custom which prevails amongst people of education at court, so that none but such as are bred up amongst them, or have constant opportunities of conversing with them."[89] In his view, dictionaries are instruments for solidifying the domination of a single privileged group over others. Dictionaries forcibly exile large sections of the language community outside the limits of polite public discourse, not to mention the limits of aesthetic contemplation. In Spence, copiousness is anglophony's historical and contemporary reality. It is a feature of language that proves there are multiple possible standards because there is a radical equivalence of anglophone varieties throughout the empire.

Toward the goal of decentralizing anglophony further, Spence writes his own dictionary, *The Grand Repository of the English Language* (1775). He also invents a schismatic alphabet for spelling the sounds of his native North English speech. *A S'upl'im'int Too thĭ Hĭstĭre ŏv Rŏbĭnsĭn Kruzo* (*A Supplement to the History of Robinson Crusoe*) (1782) uses this invented alphabet to tell its antiestablishment story, a move that is analogous to the fusions of form and content in Defoe's defense of the "*Shiboleth* upon our tongue" and Johnson's preface's gloss of "barbarity." The *Supplement* imagines Crusoe's island in the not-too-distant future. Prosperity has overpopulated the land and produced a caste of profligate landlords who dominate society while living as absentees in England. At the level of plot, the disenfranchised residents revolt and collectivize the land, a story we are told through the liberatory glyphs of the Spensonian alphabet.[90] At the level of meaning, the reader is to glean that privately owning land is as illegitimate as trying to own language. This interpretation is buttressed by Spence's direct and incendiary riposte to Johnson in *The Grand Repository*'s definition of "Property," which, just as Johnson's dictionary does, redirects one to the definitions of "possession" and "to possess." Whereas Johnson denotes "to possess" as "to have as an owner, to obtain," Spence defines the verb as, "to enjoy as a master, to seize." Spence's railing against the tyranny of property is inseparable from his purposeful subversion of alphabetic convention.

Spence's radical repurposing of linguistic copiousness might seem crankish, but it is important to note that others shared his sense that the decentralizing pursuit of copiousness was a revolutionary opportunity. Scottish-born writer James Elphinston, for example (Figure 1), uses orthographic copiousness against forms of power accreting around Standard English: "Such members ov dhe Metroppolis, az hav had dhe goodfortune (hweddher from dellicate edducation, or from incorruptibel taste) ov keeping equally free from grocenes, and from affectation: have doutles a chance, if still but a chance for purity. But the distant have no possibel chance, unless from repprezentacion."[91] Like Spence, Elphinston acts on the technology of "repprezentacion" to empower those who are "distant" from "dhe Metroppolis," a metonym for power and influence. The British periphery's linguistic subjugation goads both Elphinston and Spence, and each uses linguistic copiousness as an instrument that facilitates local self-determination. Making language typographically copious becomes a way to obstruct the tyranny of those with cultural and economic capital.

In this same vein, John Horne Tooke's linguistic work evinces a celebration of multilingualism, visual heterogeneity, and revolutionary populism in linguistic matters. Like Spence and Elphinston before him, Tooke's texts juxtapose normative and nonnormative anglophone forms in order to counter the political domination and corruption that he sees as implicitly embedded in Standard English's partiality. It is important to note that Tooke shares Spence's resistance to rigid metropolitan definitions of linguistic propriety in Standard English just as he shares his critique of economic and political power. I will not dwell here on the well-known details of his prosecutions in 1777 and 1794, but suffice it to say, Tooke already had a radical pedigree when he published the first volume of *The Diversions of Purley* in 1786. By 1806, when the second volume of *The Diversions* came out, he had motivation enough for intensifying his leveling theory of language.[92] Where "Gentleman Radical" Tooke supersedes Spence, however, is in his masterful (albeit often inaccurate) multilingualism and sophisticated ability to weave this linguistic mastery into an argument for the everyday anglophone's natural intelligence and ability. Not only does he aestheticize common and rustic expressions, but he also argues for their superiority over the refined abstractions found in legal and political discourse. As he writes, "Truth, in my opinion, has been imagined at the bottom of a well: it lies much nearer to the surface: though buried indeed at present under a mountain of learned rubbish."[93] Tooke's work is an important culmination of the texts and theorists discussed so far in this chapter, especially insofar as he challenges prevailing theories of Standard English by equipping common people with the skills for pulling Standard English apart into its copious elements.

Language, Tooke says, develops over time through creative abbreviation of elemental words, which he calls "dispatch."[94] By this logic, linguistic

Figure 1. By emphasizing the book in his hands, this early nineteenth-century portrait of James Elphinston by James Caldwell highlights the educationalist and translator's interventions into technologies of "repprezentacion." © National Portrait Gallery, London.

abstraction is the oppressive product of language's tendency to collapse into itself, ever fusing and shortening such that a common person can never tell where an abstract legal or political term comes from. However, given the correct tools for digging—which Tooke claims he can supply—anyone can excavate the primitive terms that combined to produce the appearance of abstraction. As an example, the abstract word "right" as it is variously used in expressions like "right conduct," "to be in the right," or, what was timely, "the rights of man" can be defined concretely and unambiguously such that the semantic core linking all such seemingly disparate uses is clear. Tooke arrives at the semantic core "ordered" for "right" in the following way: "RIGHT is no other than RECT-*um* (*Regitum*), the past participle of the Latin verb *Regere*. Whence in Italian you have RITTO; and from *Dirigere*, DIRITTO, DRITTO: whence the French have their antient DROICT, and their modern DROIT."[95] The "right" is what is ordered. Speakers aiming for communicative dispatch pare down words into unrecognizable husks of their former selves. To get to the heart of meaning, in other words, a common individual need only learn to decoct learned abstractions. That individual must also engage linguistic multiplicity

Historian of linguistics Hans Aarsleff, the reference point for a number of critics of eighteenth-century linguistic politics, has few positive words for Tooke.[96] Reading the history of eighteenth-century philosophy of language as a teleological process climaxing in the scientific methods of philology pioneered by Wilhelm von Humboldt, August Schlegel, and Franz Bopp, Aarsleff can only describe Tooke as having derailed more meaningful philological trends. He criticizes Tooke's flawed etymologies and deficient understanding of linguistic processes.[97] For my purposes, however, Tooke's etymological inaccuracy is immaterial. What is important is the way he weaves together multilingualism, radicalism, history, and aesthetics into one popular and politically incendiary celebration of anglophony as a copious language to which all should have access. Fittingly, he chooses spoken dialogue as the most appropriate form for the presentation of his material—both in reference to the philosophical tradition of the Socratic dialogue and as a way to highlight colloquy between anglophones. The visual work done by long swaths of etymologies and competing alphabets shatters any semblance that the discourse he narrates actually happens as embodied speech between conversants. However, the idea of dialogue is still indispensable. Tooke's extended dialogue foregrounds the notion that, at best, language happens democratically between people. When the democracy is imperfect, abstraction reigns, and the politically powerful consolidate even more privileges through obfuscatory language.

Edinburgh theologian Hugh Blair, one of the towering figures of the Scottish Enlightenment and one of the primary originators of the discipline of English literature, offers the last figuration of copiousness that I will mention in this chapter. And rightly so, for Blair's vision of anglophone copiousness poses conceptual problems related to politics and aesthetics while also opening up opportunities for the justification of imperial expansion. His *Lectures on Rhetoric and Belles Lettres* (1783) features the following architecture of anglophone copiousness:

> From the influx of so many streams, from the junction of so many dissimilar parts, it naturally follows, that the English, like every compounded Language, must needs be somewhat irregular. We cannot expect from it that correspondence of parts, that complete analogy in structure, which may be found in those simpler Languages, which have been formed in a manner within themselves, and built on one foundation. . . . Our words having been brought to us from several different regions, straggle, if we may so speak, asunder from each other; and do not coalesce so naturally in the structure of a sentence, as the words in Greek and Roman Tongues.
>
> But these disadvantages, if they be such, of a compound Language, are balanced by other advantages that attend it; particularly by the number and variety of words with which such a Language is likely to be enriched. Few Languages are, in fact, more copious than the English.[98]

In this tense and metaphorically complex passage, Blair explores the idea that the "compounded" English language's strengths "balance" its potential weaknesses—"irregularity," "narrow" syntax, dearth of "concordance," skeletal paradigms of "conjugation" and "declension." With hesitation, he figures English's mixed ancestry as an expressive boon, a gesture we might see as his reflection on the uneasy but productive yoking of Scotland to England.

If we understand the Scottish Enlightenment as one possible result of the absence of political culture in Edinburgh following the union of 1707, then Blair's work on literature and language can be read in part as a set of political gestures by proxy. Like Adam Smith, who wrote a tract comparing English to the classical languages, Blair's work on English both resists and endorses empire.[99] More specifically, it endorses a polycentric anglophone empire that is responsive to cultural developments in its constituent kingdoms, a view that might account for Blair's enthusiastic endorsement of MacPherson's Ossian poems. The fact that Blair was both part of and peripheral to dominant cultural powers of the period allows us to read the strong first-person plural possessive in the sentence "our words . . . straggle . . . asunder from each other" as a comment that pertains literally to language and metaphorically to British society. Though anglophony's parts (like Britain's) "straggle" away from one another, this first great (Scottish) theorist of Standard English credits the language with a vital "advantage": in his words, "Few Languages are, in fact, more copious than the English."[100] Blair's twin career as a Presbyterian theologian and scholar of English rhetoric formed the shifting ground for his scholarly prestige in an imperial environment where Scotland's fortunes were wedded to but subordinate to England's.

Against the ambivalent reading above, there are other ways in which this passage forcefully endorses British imperial expansion by ruminating on language. Blair describes the English language as an assemblage of "dissimilar parts" that are not "built on one foundation," an idea that would have had obvious political resonances given Scotland and England's uneasy union. The streams draining into English do not always "coalesce so naturally," and yet their combined flows "enrich" the tongue, vivify its ancient "barrenness," and generate variety in poetry and prose.[101] Layering economic metaphors over ecological and architectural ones, Blair goes on to say English's "great store" is sourced "from every quarter," a statement that is difficult to interpret outside of the contexts of empire and commerce. Moreover, the language's ample "stock and compass" flatters British literary culture, the very groundwork for a unified imperial culture that can work in conjunction with local identities and attachments. Blair even proposes a causal link between culture and language by stating that English "receives its predominant tincture from the national character of the people who speak it."[102] His evocations of wealth, migration, resources, progress, and copiousness capture this "tincture" by rehearsing in metaphor emerging notions about the distinctiveness of eighteenth-century British culture.

In these important writers, anglophony's "copious" internal diversity is a basal fact that comes to be aesthetic in limited ways. What copiousness signifies and what, if anything, should be done about it varies, but it is important to my argument to point out that they all identify linguistic difference as a constituent and animating feature of anglophone life. Each also uses a specific set of aesthetic strategies for valuing while also defusing the copious multilingualism of the other, which is representative of my claim that linguistic diversity produced narrative, poetic, and aesthetic conventions rather than running counter to them. Defoe, for instance, enacts copiousness in verbal recursions surrounding the word "shibboleth" as a way to think through multilingualism as a historical inheritance. Johnson praises recuperable strains of multilingual copiousness and concedes the impossibility of halting others in metaphors that anticipate the Burkean sublime, a theory sketched out two years later in *A Philosophical Enquiry into the Origin of Our Ideas of the Sublime and Beautiful* (1757). Spence and Tooke think of how to make copiousness accessible to common people. Finally, for his part, Blair thinks through the seeming undesirability of copiousness in positively valorized ecological, social, and imperial metaphors, all of which would have seemed timely and flattering to nationalistic readers in the period. The metalinguistic discourses of English standardization, in other words, evince a range of ways of thinking about and writing about the potentially threatening but always negotiable copiousness of anglophone life. Translation theory, which is the companion discourse to English standardization in the period, has its own recurring sense of anglophone diversity's threats, rewards, and possible aesthetic forms. I turn to this question in the next chapter.

MULTILINGUAL LIVES

Dorothy Pentreath and William Bodener

Revealing ambiguities surround the life of an eighteenth-century Cornish woman named Dorothy or "Dolly" Pentreath (Figure 2), a woman who has been hailed as the last speaker of the Cornish language in spite of the fact that this designation is misleading.[1] Nonetheless, by being identified with Cornish's disappearance, Pentreath has become a metonym for cultural death—as well as the possibilities and challenges of linguistic revival—and so it is worth investigating her legacy for what it reveals about the period's language practices and politics.

From the facts of the case, one can deduce that in speech Pentreath understood two languages, Cornish and English.[2] She was likely illiterate in both. To be more precise, she wrote nothing in her own name that has been preserved in either language; everything we know about her is mediated through the discourses of eighteenth-century antiquarianism and nineteenth-century philology. Though she left no signed documents, Pentreath can be treated as a limit-case origin of discourse in the sense that she was copiously written about by two men with a common interest in Cornish history and the embodied life of living languages. In the present, critics can access only these narrow, secondhand accounts of Pentreath's life, her own narratives and opinions having evaporated at the moment of their production, thus remaining forever in the gap between cultural history and myth. One of the only direct quotations attributed to Pentreath is a curse directed at one Mr. Price, a man who knocked over her basket of fish in the marketplace. Nineteenth-century writer on Cornwall William Bottrell transliterates the curse as, "*Cronnack an hagar dhu!*" ("ugly black toad!").[3]

What we learn from secondary accounts of Pentreath's life is that she was a residual linguistic subject whose life story foregrounds anglophony's

FIGURE 2. This unattributed engraving of Dorothy Pentreath from 1781 identifies her as "the last Person who could converse in the Cornish language" and visually underscores her occupation as a fishmonger. © National Portrait Gallery, London.

rapid eighteenth-century expansion. Subjected to this spread, Pentreath's linguistic identity was under siege for her entire life—which might account for why most testaments to her stress her irascible penchant for cursing outsiders in language they did not know.[4] Her form of multilingual embodiment opens up different avenues for further understanding non-normative language communities in conjunction with anglophony, and in particular, in conjunction with anglophone antiquarianism's zeal for documenting the ebb of indigenous British cultures. Pentreath thus helps us chart the period's aesthetic and political interest in linguistic and cultural supersession—a concern that has already cropped up in Reverend Lyons's fatalistic invocation of the impossibility of "one *mere Irish scholar*." The tropes at the heart of Pentreath's obscure story are, in some respects, master tropes of the eighteenth-century origins of the Romantic aesthetic mode.[5] What I mean is that Pentreath can be understood in relation to the trope of the vanishing bard as poetic origin, a woman whose spirited refusals to speak English stoked interest in the historical dimensions of local culture's displacement throughout the British Isles.[6]

Verifiable details surrounding Pentreath's life are scant. The primary materials indicate that she was born and baptized in 1692 at Mousehole, a fishing village on the Cornish coast just southwest of Penzance. She lived in several nearby places and gave birth to a son in 1729. With few other details of her life etched into the historical record, she died and was buried in the place of her birth in 1777.[7] On the basis of this information, the late nineteenth century saw Pentreath transformed into such a loaded symbol of Cornish history and identity in Britain that her body was exhumed from its unmarked grave, "exposed," "examined," and then reburied in a new grave that, far from unmarked, has since become a site of cultural pilgrimage.[8] Pentreath's first step toward elevation to cultural iconicity occurred when her linguistic insularity attracted the attention of Daines Barrington, a fellow of the Society of Antiquaries of London as well as the Royal Society. In an era increasingly intrigued by antiquarian research into the seemingly occluded cultural practices of bygone days—as seen in the zeal for Macpherson's Ossian poems (1760) as well as the publication of texts like Percy's *Reliques of Ancient English Poetry* (1765)—the perception that Pentreath might be the last speaker of a once-widespread British language was tantalizing.[9]

For his part, Barrington was an eclectic scholar of antiquarian miscellany who researched "topics as varied as the history of archery, gardening, and card-playing in England, Caesar's invasion of Britain, and the history of the Cornish language."[10] He "discovered" Pentreath during his attempts to investigate the state of the Cornish language in the 1760s and 1770s.[11] The two essays on the Cornish language that Barrington published with the Society of Antiquaries depict Dolly Pentreath as a cultural curio on death's door, a multilingual subject whose linguistic insularity and imminent death evoked the notion of a yet living (but rapidly dying) relic of the mythic past. In tone, Barrington's accounts of Pentreath register the sense of a closing and homogenizing world, a shifting cultural landscape in which new practices were rubbing out the old with great speed. It is meaningful in this context that Pentreath's subjectivity remains entirely inaccessible in Barrington's accounts. For Barrington, who spoke no Cornish, Pentreath was "less entirely a person" than she was an object lesson for exploring linguistico-cultural extinction.[12]

Barrington's first essay, the sensationally titled "*On the Expiration of the Cornish Language*," recounts his 1768 journey to locate speakers of Cornish.[13] He describes how, over the course of his "very complete tour," he repeatedly queries natives about where one could still hear the Cornish tongue spoken.[14] Despite the fact that several locals "considered it as entirely lost," Barrington keeps on, eventually hearing rumor of the existence of an elderly, Cornish-speaking woman in the village of Mousehole three miles southwest of Penzance.[15] There in a market stall Barrington observes the Cornish-speaking fishmonger, a woman whom he twice refers to as "the last spark of the Cornish tongue."[16]

Seeking an introduction, Barrington perpetrates a ruse in which he is presented to Pentreath "as a person who had laid a wager that there was no one who could converse in Cornish."[17] Predictably, this strange wager provokes Pentreath. Barrington reports that she "spoke in an angry tone of voice for two or three minutes, and in a language which sounded very like Welsh."[18] These "two or three minutes" of unrecorded and thus untranslatable self-assertion are of tremendous interest to me, but for different reasons than they were to Barrington and have been to other scholars. Whereas Barrington reads Pentreath's speech as the uncouth outburst of an expiring tongue, and whereas others have read it as a heroic statement of linguistic resistance, I want to draw attention to the way these aporetic "two or three minutes" are impossible for Barrington or his readers to gloss or comprehend.[19] From the antiquarian's perspective, the speech itself is senseless sound. To inscribe it into some legible form, Barrington reaches for meaning via cultural analogism. All he can come up with is that the stream of syllables "sounded very like Welsh," an interlinguistic perception that Barrington might have gleaned from reading the work of Edward Lhuyd (Lhwyd), a Welsh antiquarian who undertook his own four-month expedition to find and record Cornish in 1700.[20] As she speaks, Pentreath's mind stands before Barrington in asymmetrical suspension. Whereas she understands and reacts to his anglophone questions, he remains perpetually banished from any mutual exchange in his interlocutor's tongue, a banishment that corresponds to the basic condition of monolingualism in a multilingual environment like eighteenth-century Britain. And even though she still lives and speaks, Barrington's descriptions transform Pentreath into a linguistic anachronism, a narrative spun from his own inability to translate her mode of self-assertion.

During his unsuccessful interview, Barrington becomes curious about the onlookers, whose linguistic aptitudes he describes in the following terms: "These neighbours could not speak the language," but "they comprehended her abuse upon me, which implies a certain knowledge of the Cornish tongue."[21] He asks the "neighbouring" women if "she [Pentreath] had not been abusing me," and they answer, "very heartily, and because [you] had supposed she could not speak Cornish."[22] This multilingual gathering of explicitly gendered Cornish women is configured through the exoticizing discourses of linguistic and gender alterity. It brings Barrington face-to-face with a yet living linguistic community, dying perhaps—or being killed—but still a community. Pentreath may be the most fluent Cornish-speaking individual in the community, and perhaps the only one who had spoken the language from birth, but there are certainly others with varying degrees of facility. This means that on the point of what Barrington extravagantly calls Cornish's "expiration," the Cornish language and thus the multilingual composition of anglophony endure in several forms. Cornish's surprising endurance in Mousehole contributes to Barrington's claustrophobic sense of being a foreigner in place as well as time—trapped in a provincial chronotope wherein his anglophone speech is met with a Cornish woman's refusal to engage. These facts might account for the discomfiting eagerness with which the antiquarian seems to desire the language's imminent death even while putatively engaged in arguing for its preservation.

Toward the end of this first essay, Barrington suggests that a capable scholar must travel to Cornwall to preserve the Cornish language by using

Pentreath as a native informant. Just as it would be easy, Barrington claims, to "form a Latin vocabulary" by querying "the most learned men of this country," it would be easy to form the same for Cornish by treating Pentreath as a cultural repository.[23] Here, a chain of Celtic filiation is pulled into operation.[24] A Welsh-speaker who records what remains of Cornish is working for the benefit of Cornish people, of course, but perhaps mostly for the benefit of anglophone antiquarians like Barrington who want the incomprehensible to be made comprehensible. In a moment of antiquarian free association, Barrington departs on a tangent relating to the Welsh language's survival, opining, "As for the Welsh, I do not see the least possibility of its being lost in the more mountainous parts; for there are no valuable mines in several of the parishes thus situated, I do not conceive that it is possible to introduce the use of English."[25] Welsh may be secure from anglophone capital's incursions in its mountainous redoubts, but peninsular Cornish is imperiled. The advancing shadows of Pentreath's death and Cornish's vanishing become parables of commerce and loss. As anglophone trade and industry spread so too will women like Pentreath and languages like Cornish fade away. Antiquarianism's desire to uncover, elucidate, and preserve the past must race against anglophone commercial expansion, a far speedier rival, and one just as capable of exploiting "valuable mines" as marching inland from the small ports along Cornwall's long coast.

A later volume of *Archaeologia*, the journal of the Society of Antiquaries, contains a second and updated essay from Barrington in which Cornish is at issue. In a letter dated March 20, 1776, and read before the society on March 21, 1776, Barrington reports that "Dolly Pentreath . . . is still alive, being supposed to be ninety years of age, and is now grown excessively deaf."[26] Neither Barrington nor the society had any way of knowing that Pentreath would be dead by the end of 1777, roughly a year and a half later. But after Barrington's update regarding Pentreath's endangered life and health—her deafness pitched here as a signifier of Cornish's coming demise—the antiquarian presents new evidence pertaining to the case of Cornish in Britain. Specifically, he discusses a multilingual letter that he received from William Bodener (Bodinar in the Cornish spelling), a sixty-five-year-old fisherman who lived his life, like Pentreath, in Cornish and English worlds. In Bodener's letter, Barrington has at his disposal a communicative accessibility that neither Pentreath nor Pentreath's female onlookers would grant.[27]

Bodener's letter informs Barrington that, contrary to his assumptions, "there are four or five persons still living in the village of Mousehole, who can converse in Cornish."[28] What interests me in this letter is the unwittingly poetic and also mournful tone of Bodener's communiqué. As the letter's multilingual form is more interesting than its summary, the Society of Antiquaries reproduces part of it in print, some of which can be seen below:

me rig deskey Cornoack termen me vee mawe
I learnt Cornish when I was a boy
me vee demore gen cara vee a pemp dean moy en cock
I have been to sea with my father and five other men in the boat
me rig scantlower clowes Edenger sowsnack Cowes en cock
and have not heard one word of English spoke in the boat
rag sythen ware bar
for a week together
. . . .
na ges moye vel pager pe pemp endreau nye
there is not more then four or five in our town
Ell classia Cornish leben
can talk Cornish now
poble coath pager eyance blouth
old people four score years old
Cornoack ewe all ne cea ves yen poble younk
Cornish is all forgot with young people[29]

The letter, which alternates a Cornish line with its Standard English translation, enables a reader who is familiar with contemporary multilingual poetry to extract a feeling of poetic expressivity even though the letter was not intended as such. Generally taken as a factual statement from a local person who had heard of Barrington and wanted to aid his antiquarian research, Bodener's letter contains artful binaries that allow us to explore the doubledness of his two tongues and their respective futures. These binaries produce and trouble fixed meanings just as the alternating lines of the multilingual text generate an aesthetic experience in which alterity is deeply embedded—indeed interlaced—with the familiar. First, there is the obvious topological binary: only on a mobile boat at sea can Cornish be cultivated for days at a time without a word of English being spoken. This image of movement is juxtaposed to the fixed anglophone space of "our town" where "Cornish is all forgot with young people" and, by implication, English reigns. There is also a chronological binary. The "old people" speak Cornish whereas the young cannot. As in Barrington's depiction of the differential space of Cornish comprehension surrounding Pentreath, the multilingual and changing community Bodener describes intersects dramatically with the history of anglophony, shown here in its expansive youth.

In addition to these, Bodener's letter features a provocative linguistic binary as well. Namely, the semantic content of his interwoven lines carries a different affective charge depending on the language one is reading. Though I neither read nor speak any Cornish, I have to speculate that the lines "there is not more then four or five in our town / can talk Cornish now" signify differently in each of the text's languages. Articulating the wane of Cornish in Cornish must be differently evocative than articulating it in some anglophone form. If that is the case, then this document unintentionally demonstrates the dramatic capacities of multilingual anglophone writing in its most elemental form. Bodener's letter indexes the existence of a linguistic counterpublic even while narrating, in stunning multilingual form, its senescence and extinction. The linguistic practices that I have been calling anglophony intersect with spaces of imperiled linguistic alterity, spaces related to Anzaldúa's borderlands and Pratt's contact zones, spaces that can be celebrated, analyzed, and taught alongside these other models.[30] This is not at all to say that Cornish linguistic history ought to be subsumed into a teleological history of English as a "Global Language" or approached merely as a handmaiden to anglophone self-understanding. Far from it, my claim is that scholars of anglophone writing would do well to recall and make central to research purposeful assertions of linguistic identity by multilingual people who have been and will remain elemental parts of anglophony, people who have had a part in formulating the aesthetic and expressive capacities of anglophone writing even if they are often seen as marginal and always almost extinct. Like Pentreath and Bodener, multilingual subjects of the past equip scholarship with renewed resources for grasping multilingual aesthetics in the anglophone present.

CHAPTER 3

De Libertate

Anglophony and the Idea of "Free" Translation

Standardization and Translation

> The great pest of speech is frequency of translation. No book was ever turned from one language into another, without imparting something of its native idiom; this is the most mischievous and comprehensive innovation; single words may enter by thousands, and the fabrick of the tongue continue the same, but new phraseology changes much at once; it alters not the single stones of the building, but the order of the columns. If an academy should be established for the cultivation of our stile, which I, who can never wish to see dependance multiplied, hope the spirit of *English* liberty will hinder or destroy, let them, instead of compiling grammars and dictionaries, endeavour, with all their influence, to stop the licence of translatours, whose idleness and ignorance, if it be suffered to proceed, will reduce us to babble a dialect of *France*.[1]

Interwoven rather than separate—dialectically formulated rather than distinct—standardization and translation theory are the two most prolific tranches of the eighteenth-century archive surrounding language. Even though scholars have historically treated standardization and translation within separate disciplines and as discrete activities, these ways of analyzing and narrativizing language are intimately related. They enable a set of important insights into the period when seen as mutually implicative practices. For this reason, they ought to be understood in conjunction, and they ought to be understood as the primary mediators of the aesthetic assemblages into which the period's writing practices are ordered.

The additional quotation above from Johnson's "Preface" captures some of the tense ways in which anglophone discourses of standardization and translation are conceptually intertwined during the eighteenth century.[2] Johnson's anxious depiction of translation as a pestilent disruption of standardization offers a way to begin contextualizing this close relationship. Pitching these ways of writing about anglophony as separate and antagonistic, Johnson asserts that certain forms of translation dismantle standardization's efforts toward an orderly and regular linguistic system, which is what he means when he calls translation a "great pest of speech." Yet it is important to note that this is not a blanket denunciation of translation as such. In Johnson there are innocuous forms of translation—those that act only on the "fabrick of the tongue"—and there are more noxious forms of translation—those that act on the "order of the columns." Johnson claims that translational importations of the first variety improve the language's expressive copiousness while those of the second derange the language and upset efforts toward standardization. This is why "single words may enter by the thousands," thus increasing specificity while leaving the language's syntactic and grammatical weft intact. At the same time, more virulent forms of translation calque "new phraseology" from a source language so as to alter the language fundamentally.[3] The destabilizing shock of the new that is symptomatic of these more virulent forms of translation is generalized in Johnson as the "mischievous and comprehensive innovation" of "imparting something of its native idiom" into Standard English. According to Johnson, the worst forms of translation deform syntax with new and perverse multiplicities rather than containing existing copia in proper forms.[4]

The relationship between standardization and translation is myriad. This chapter traces five important intersections of these two ways of writing about language in order to argue for the importance of the standardization-translation nexus in the production and alteration of literary aesthetics. The first three intersections pertain to local imbrications of these discourses. (1) As modes of writing about language, standardization and translation take shape with constant reference to the other, a local example of which is Johnson's epigraph and a more general example of which are the singular careers of standardizer-translators like Robert Lowth and George Campbell.[5] (2) Standardization and translation theories are both adapted from other linguistic contexts and retrofitted to apply to anglophony's unique (and always-changing) conditions by multilingual and/or multiliterate writers. This means that both of these discourses are the products of translation and bear with them the traces of the linguistic contexts from which they were carried over. (3) Both standardization and translation theories are sold in the period as known textual commodities, and briskly selling ones at that.[6] These metalinguistic discourses, in other words, solicit overlapping markets of the literate public sphere even as they undergird the market for literary texts.

The fourth and fifth intersections that I will describe have to do with the larger linguistic, cultural, and historical matrices in which eighteenth-century standardization and translation flourish. (4) Both discourses directly articulate themselves as regulatory agents within a field of linguistic multiplicity; this means that both strategically embrace parts of anglophone copiousness while antagonizing the rest, sometimes with great rhetorical force. A related point is that both discourses take as axiomatic the assumption that varieties of linguistic difference—internal and external to anglophony—are relevant optics for reading, judging, and aesthetically evaluating the world at large. (5) Finally, insofar as standardization and translation theories are profoundly concerned with elaborating rules for how any one individual can act on the public substance of language, these discourses are precursors to fully elaborated nationalist thought in that they share a common concern for defining the limits of Standard English, an essential element of which is the admissibility of certain forms of language into the realm of aesthetic practice. Given these five relational dimensions, it is singular that an incisive linguistic thinker like Johnson should paint the goals of standardization and the effects of translation in largely antagonistic terms, portraying them as though one were antithetical to the other rather than its fellow traveler. When Johnson charges any potential "academy . . . for the cultivation of our stile" with endeavoring "to stop the licence of translatours," he is obscuring standardization's debts to translation practice and vice versa.

Taken in context, Johnson's antagonism toward translation echoes a common refrain against the perception of French's outsized influence within anglophony during the period.[7] A survey of contemporaneous translation theory and practice, however, reveals that eighteenth-century translators—even translators from French—are more interested in preserving and stewarding anglophony's "order of columns" than Johnson acknowledges.[8] Translators simply posit a different set of ideas regarding the form that acts of linguistic preservation and stewardship should take. Johnson's image of the "spirit of *English* liberty" as a consensual force that resists governmental centralization of language while enforcing common norms is also visible in many translation theories. As a case in point, translators and translation theorists enshrine an analogous form of regulated "liberty" (as opposed to "servility") as the gold standard for anglophone translation practice in the period. They do this by claiming that a successful translator should be "liberated," "liberal," and "free"—although never too "free" or "licentious." "Licentious" is used in evaluations of translation as the adjective form of "licence." When Johnson accuses translators of "excessive licence," he is using evaluative vocabulary that comes directly out of the context of translation theory. He is unintentionally echoing criticisms that translators had already expressed about their own practices as a way of moving toward a theory of translation that would preserve rather than distort anglophony's perceived linguistic architecture.

Alexander Fraser Tytler, one of the translation theorists and translators under examination in this book, echoes Johnson's interest in tempered linguistic liberty throughout his important work *Essay on the Principles of Translation* (1791; 1797; 1813).[9] Examining the relative translatability of various forms, Tytler writes "the lyric is that which allows of the greatest liberty in translation. . . . Yet even in this, which is the freest of all species of translation, we must guard against licentiousness."[10] Like Johnson, Tytler fears that "licentiousness," or excessive "freedom," leads to centrifugal linguistic deviance. These and other discussions of translation indicate that some translators regularly agreed with Johnson that bad translation displayed "idleness and ignorance," which, as the eighteenth century progressed, they recurrently discussed in terms of "servility" or "slavishness," concepts that are particularly loaded when set against the transatlantic slave trade and other systems of contemporaneous global labor exploitation. Far from seeking to revise anglophony's "order of columns," translators of the period actually sought to strengthen them with their own version of the "spirit of *English* liberty" that Johnson extols, a spirit that would never countenance translational "servitude." "An ordinary translator sinks under the energy of his original," Tytler writes, but "the man of genius frequently rises above it."[11] Tytler's way of emphasizing anglophone liberty is to define the translator as a literary figure whose sovereignty over the source text is permanently in question and must continually be asserted. In this context, translation represents an ambiguous act of literary creation. The translator vacillates constantly between submission to a supervening source text and the creative refusal of direct submission.

By approaching translation theory of the period through its most prevalent metaphor—"freedom" versus "servility"—I do not mean to make the claim that there were not major and sometimes antithetical developments in the theory and practice of translation across the period. There absolutely were. I track these developments in this chapter with reference to scholars who have already made impressive work of them, scholars like Frederick Burwick, Mary Helen McMurran, Padma Rangarajan, Lawrence Venuti, and others. Taken together, these scholars have outlined—and critiqued—a model of translation over the long eighteenth century that generally moves from domesticating to foreignizing practice.[12] As Louis Kelly summarizes this tendency, "After a mid-century redefinition of originality, the source author was increasingly respected, and the translator's discretion was consequently curtailed in the search for greater textual accuracy."[13] This transition from a period when translators were valued as original creators or re-creators (domesticating) toward one when translators were seen more as agents of the exacting reproduction of a source text's style and content in the target language (foreignizing) is apt.[14] It meshes well with Venuti's now classic description of the way a translator's creative labor has been made "invisible" in the anglophone literary marketplace.[15] To paraphrase Venuti, after the eighteenth century, the translator ceases to be cognizable as a creative origin because translators are increasingly viewed as conduits through which cultural material is transmitted from a source culture and language to a target culture and language.

The point I want to bring out here is that even though there are these large changes in translation protocol over the period (including a "redefinition of originality," as Kelly has it), the vocabulary for evaluating translation does not change in complementary ways. By charting the stability of an evaluative vocabulary whereby translators are judged based on the "liberty" and "freedom" or "servility" and "slavishness" they show in relation to the source texts even amid these larger practical shifts, I want to show that this vocabulary functions in a similar way to "copiousness," standardization's recurring metaphor. Less a means of evaluating translation than it is a floating concept for what is culturally sanitary in terms of language practice, the spectrum from "free" to "servile" translation gestures to a larger cultural context regarding ideas of what must be cultivated (freedom) and what must be guarded against (servility).[16] Except for the fact that the eighteenth-century transatlantic slave system ruthlessly dislocated people from familiar linguistic contexts—forcing them into translational settings, in other words—there is no self-evident or simple reason why translation should be coded in slavery's metaphors.[17] As I argue, by using metaphors like "copiousness" to describe anglophony and "freedom" and "servility" to describe ideals of translation, writers elaborate ways in which individual creative agents can act on that system through their works, whether invented, translated, or indeed, transcreated.[18]

Eighteenth-century studies and translation studies are growing rapidly, but scholars have not yet taken up the implications—political or aesthetic—of the relationship between standardization and translation theory that I am describing. The interpenetration of these ways of discussing language shows that, like standardizers, translators were all at once wary and appreciative of anglophone multiplicity in complementary ways. In addition, they were equally wary and appreciative of global linguistic multiplicity. Bracketing for the moment the basic occupational reality that most eighteenth-century standardizers were also translators, and vice versa, their shared but narrow appreciation of a specific form of anglophone multiplicity—its copiousness—is crucial. Whereas standardizers can generally be said to have engaged anglophony's internal hierarchies by subordinating living linguistic multiplicity to a copious vision of Standard English, which became the form against which all others were evaluated, translation theory negotiated anglophone difference by serving as a mechanism of interlinguistic border patrol, a custodial role that allowed translators to pass judgment on linguistic forms that they believed could not be permitted to cross into anglophony's aesthetic structures as well as those that could. Adding one more dimension of similarity, standardizers and translators alike lived their lives against the backdrop of an expanding British Empire and a flourishing transatlantic slave trade, related historical developments that represent the intersecting horizons of two of the most dramatic developments in human linguistic culture ever recorded.

Some definitions are in order, especially given that translation has too frequently been treated as peripheral to the main trends of eighteenth-century research despite the fact that it is central to many forms of cultural exchange during the period, from the vernacular cosmopolitanisms of slave life to the hieratic cosmopolitanisms of interimperial diplomacy. My general definition is derived from a passage in Venuti: translation recodes a chain of signifiers according to another set of signifying conventions; by necessity, this recoding has linguistic, political, and therefore aesthetic effects.[19] In essence, translation recodes one linguistic system in another by first assuming that the systems fundamentally differ.[20] Thus, when I discuss translation going forward, I use the term to indicate both intralingual translation and interlingual translation, the more common construal.[21] One can translate from the anglophone languages of North Britain into Standard English just as one can translate classical Arabic into Standard English, among others.[22]

Acknowledging that intralingual translation and interlingual translation differ in both theory and practice, I will explicitly differentiate between these two when the context so requires, as in the fourth and fifth chapters of this book. The risk of flattening these two terms together for the time being is countered by the benefit that when one uses translation as a term that calls forth both intralingual and interlingual varieties, standardization and translation are always already conceptually paired. Eighteenth-century intralingual translation, which typically recodes a nonnormative form of anglophony into Standard English, is a species of standardizing practice that consolidates normativity.[23] Likewise, interlingual translation in the period, which recodes nonanglophone languages in anglophony, reproduces Standard English norms as it reproduces source content in a target language, thus regularly delimiting the radical potential for anglophone multiplicity in a way that is similar to standardization.[24] Adding another dimension, standardization itself is a form of translation, a notion that the suite of equivalences accompanying any dictionary or thesaurus heading confirms. This broad view that takes standardization and translation together—and that takes translation as composed of both intralingual and interlingual varieties—has the virtue of shedding light on the cultural ordering of anglophony's internal hierarchies while also mobilizing longstanding insights of translation studies that have not yet been fully integrated into the routines of literary and cultural studies.[25]

Integrating translation studies into eighteenth-century studies more comprehensively could take many forms. Across the next two chapters, for example, I pose a version of a question that Venuti has recently asked in the following terms: "If translation contributes so materially to economic exchange," which it does, then to what degree can translation "constitute a cultural means of resistance [or dissensus] that challenges multinational capitalism and the political institutions to which the global economy is allied?"[26] The eighteenth-century versions of this question, which I want to ask going forward, are: what is the position of translation in the eighteenth-century literary market, and how does this affect how we think about the present? I address these questions head on in the fourth and fifth chapters of this book, but for now I want to point out the following: taken as a meaningful set of mediating practices rather than as a set of intercultural transmission conduits, translation studies can help scholars of the eighteenth century gain a better sense of the textured complexities of the period they study and its meaning to the present. So too, translation studies can continue assisting contemporary scholars of postcolonial anglophone literature in historicizing the longue durée of their field, a field whose proper historicization is in every anglophone humanist's interest.

Dialectical Discourses

> We must introduce into our schools *English grammar*, *English compositions*, and frequent *English translations* from authors in other languages.[27]

Writing just one generation after Johnson, Joseph Priestley brings standardization and translation together in a way that is different from his predecessor. Because the first intersection between standardization and translation that I want to trace here is their mutual development, Priestley's yoking of grammar, composition, and translation is an appropriate place to start. Priestley suggests that "stopping the licence of translators" requires that students study Standard English grammar (rather than Greek and Latin grammar), perform Standard English compositions (rather than Greek and Latin ones), and either study or perform translations from other languages into Standard English. The third element of Priestley's pedagogical program obliges students to contemplate textual objects that are self-consciously identified as translations. Exposure to texts that have been translated into an appropriate version of Standard English is designed to ensure that anglophone students respect (Priestley's idea of) their language's expressive capacities. Proper translations—those that are respectful of Standard English's "order of columns"—have an important role to play in standardization because they communicate to students those types of linguistic deviance that are and are not permissible. Priestley's assumption that the full project of anglophone standardization demands exposure to translation is, like Johnson's earlier epigraph, evidence of the intercourse between these two discourses. Both writers reference translation as an activity that can build and dismantle linguistic knowledge. Priestley also holds out anglophone translations from other languages as a type of text that students should be required to study.[28]

Priestley's precursors in both standardization and translation theory had long built these two fields relationally. For example, Robert Lowth's *A Short Introduction to English Grammar* (1762) points out several times that translation has played a constituent role in the creation of Standard English, especially as it has come down to anglophones through the King James Version of the Bible.[29] One of the most celebrated grammarians and translators of the period, Lowth argues that certain locutions are justifiable only on the basis of their history in usage. As a case in point, his discussion of the "double superlative" suggests that such expressions are admissible if and only if they have a long pedigree in "common discourse," which for him includes the history of translation.[30] He writes, "The double superlative, *most highest*, is a phrase peculiar to the old vulgar translation of the Psalms; where it acquires a singular propriety from the subject to which it is applied, the Supreme Being, who is *higher than the highest.*"[31] In this reevaluation, "*most highest*" and "*higher than the highest*" are forms of language that act on anglophony's "order of columns." To Lowth they represent examples of exacting semantic precision. Lowth calls these expressions a "singular propriety," but Priestley later calls them "greater impropriet[ies]," justifying his condemnation in sectarian and translational terms. "But I own it offends my ears, which may, perhaps, be owing to my not having been accustomed to that translation."[32] While Lowth and Priestley disagree on the propriety of the double superlative, both imply that Standard English takes shape from translational interventions past and present.

In complementary fashion, translation theorists reconstituted the concerns of standardizers in their anglophone versions of foreign texts. For example, Tytler's translation treatise fully reproduces his standardizing contemporaries' concern with "dialect" as a signifier for impropriety. In a passage condemning deviant registers in translations of the classics, he asks, "What must we think of the translator who makes the solemn and sententious Tacitus express himself in the low cant of the streets or in the dialect of the waiter of a tavern."[33] Similarly, he criticizes historian and Latin-to-English translator Laurence Echard, "who saw no distinction between the familiar and the vulgar, [and] has translated [Plautus] in the true dialect of the streets."[34] Censuring translation into nonnormative anglophone registers, Tytler notes, "The most licentious of all translators was Mr. Thomas Brown, of facetious memory, in whose translations from Lucian we have the most perfect ease; but it is the ease of Billingsgate and Wapping."[35] Tytler's down-the-nose evaluation of East London anglophone speech indicates that just as standardizers recognized a need for regulated translation, translators borrowed from standardization's normative premises. In so doing, they developed frameworks for thinking about translation as a way to regulate the "proper" or appropriate processes by which new words, locutions, and syntaxes could enter into the scalable but increasingly rigid system of appropriate expression in Standard English

Beyond the fact that eighteenth-century standardization and translation theory constantly reference one another, the second main point I want to make here is that these two ways of writing about anglophony are adapted rather than self-generating. Even as they try to carve out a space for anglophone uniqueness, early standardizers draw from other linguistic contexts in formulating ideas of proper English just as translation theorists draw on treatises from the classical world and the European continent in formulating what counts as elegant translation, a point to which I will return in the next section's discussion of anglophone translations of Horace. Suffice it to say now that, in addition to classical translation theory, French translation theory was tremendously influential in the anglophone context. Theorists like Huet, D'Alembert, and Batteux are referenced as precursors and foes in the same way that anglophone grammarians continually invoke the *Port-Royal Grammar* of 1660, a book whose centralizing aspirations inspired both admiration and anxiety.[36]

As in translation theory, the borrowedness of standardizing discourse is obvious in the earliest texts that advocate for anglophone standardization. John Wallis's highly influential *Grammatica Linguae Anglicanae* (1652), for example, is a Latin-language grammar published and sold in England. In this book, Wallis's ideas of Standard English phonology and grammar are described in Latin and via Greek and Latin comparisons.[37] Using this adapted form, Wallis makes an effort to expand on anglophone particularities, and so his standardizing gesture is both borrowed and differentiated. Schoolmaster and grammarian James Greenwood later describes Wallis's uniqueness: "Dr. Wallis justly finds fault with our *English* Grammarians, where he says, All of them forcing our *English Tongue* too much to the *Latin Method*, have delivered many useless Precepts . . . which our Language hath nothing at all to do with."[38] Further differentiated, but still borrowed as a discourse of standardization, Joseph Aickin's 1693 grammar invites readers who want to "attain the Perfection of his Mother Tongue, without the assistance of Latine."[39] Departing from the Latin tradition, the document is still highly indebted to the structural principles of Latin grammars as they circulated at the time as commodities.

Later writers also regularly buck against the influence of substrates from the Greek and Latin traditions. Priestley, for instance, is "surprised to see so much of the distribution, and technical terms of the Latin grammar, retained in the grammar of our tongue; where they are exceedingly aukward and absolutely superfluous."[40] His surprise notwithstanding, he also briefly worries he has gone too far in excising Latin from his Standard English grammar. "It is possible I may be thought to have leaned too much from the Latin idiom . . . but I think it is evident, that all other grammarians have leaned too much to the analogies of that language contrary to our modes of speaking, and to the analogies of other languages more like our own."[41] Priestley is not saying that the anglophony should be analyzed only in reference to itself, but instead that there are better and more revealing languages with which to compare it. Internalizing while also departing from previous linguistic discourses is what one would expect given the movement toward vernacularization that one sees across Europe during the seventeenth and eighteenth centuries. However, the surrounding cultural subtext of pervasive multilingualism is often deemphasized.

One factor proves clearly that anglophone standardization and translation discourses were adapted rather than invented during the eighteenth century. None of the best-known or best-selling standardizers of this period were monolingual or monoliterate. The thinkers who produced the array of grammars, dictionaries, style manuals, and theoretical treatises that forged Standard English into a political tool and aesthetic medium were more often than not, and to differing degrees, multilingual, and almost always multiliterate, whether educated in authorized or dissenting traditions. Many were actively translators by training, not least because translation was considered to be absolutely central to any conception of a literary vocation. The nature of male education in the period made it so, with the most commonly learned languages and literacies being Greek, Latin, French, and sometimes Hebrew, although the dissenting tradition often demanded additional linguistic accomplishments.[42] Women writers who traversed the segregated itineraries of gender-differentiated education were expected to master and internalize their own nonanglophone linguistic multiplicities, in particular, French.[43] Many important women grammarians learned far more languages than this, however.[44] Irrespective of gender, the fact that these scholars lived in the rich and polyphonic environment of eighteenth-century anglophony means that their exposure to anglophone multiplicity can be assumed. Standardization and translation theory might appear distinct from the present, but this is not how eighteenth-century figures would have understood them. Instead, they would have understood them as two integrated parts of a literary vocation with multilingual roots.

The perception of the separation between these two "fields" is partially attributable to our own contemporary disciplinary formations. This is perhaps because we no longer work and study language in ways that are obvious continuations of eighteenth-century linguistic culture, and rightly so. Considering the differences between education today and during the eighteenth century, Don Chapman advances the notion that "eighteenth-century grammarians were not language experts, at least not the way we think of them today."[45] Chapman goes on to suggest that eighteenth-century grammarians might even appear "amateurish" from a contemporary vantage point, in which public "experts" on language are frequently credentialed members of departments like linguistics, rhetoric, composition, literature, and English, disciplines that all have relatively long institutional histories even if their futures seem less certain.[46] Given that most "amateurish" eighteenth-century standardizers and translators predate the institutional frameworks for the kind of work they set out to do, and given the fact that that most were multiliterate and multilingual, Chapman's emphasis on "amateurishness" registers something crucial about our own era's view of these earlier disciplinary formations. One can read his invocation of amateurishness as a code word for multiplicities of learning that are irreducible to contemporary Euro-American formations of institutional knowledge.[47]

Chapman's reading of "amateurishness" does not insist, as I do, that—then as now—studying non-English languages is an elemental ingredient in any attribution of linguistic expertise. However, he does provide important details that encourage my reading of the word "amateur" as code for the irreducibility of multilingualism to the institutional frameworks we have inherited. Chapman notes, "The language expertise of those who were sufficiently educated to enroll in a university would largely have been their reasonably good command of Latin and perhaps Greek."[48] While he is specifically questioning the "expertise" of eighteenth-century grammarians and lexicographers relative to present models of institutional education, he also makes a point to say that a "university degree from Oxford and Cambridge did not necessarily mean that the holder was intelligent or even knowledgeable, beyond having a proficiency of Latin, maybe Greek and perhaps Hebrew."[49] Chapman's point is that having a reading knowledge of ancient languages does not confirm that a particular person is intelligent. For me, the unfamiliar copiousness of the linguistic achievements he mentions points to the way that linguistic multiplicity should be said to underwrite both standardization and translation practice in the period. Today, however, there is a dwindling range of global prestige languages (and these are almost always European) that anglophone institutional frameworks evaluate as meaningful in the scholars they employ and the students they teach.[50]

The third point of similarity between standardization and translation that I want to discuss here is the fact that both discourses were important parts of the literary economy. Standardizers produced textual commodities like grammars, dictionaries, and style manuals, most of which were sold with accompanying paratextual writings, including dedications, prefaces, and appendices. For their part, translators also sold their work with accompanying paratextual writings, including dedications, prefaces, and appendices. In quantitative terms, the uptick in grammars, dictionaries, and style manuals that is visible in the period is matched by a comparable growth in translation treatises and translations.[51] Especially toward the end of the century, there is a veritable rush of new translations of well-known texts from proximate cultural regions in addition to totally new translations from languages that had never before been brought into anglophony. Translational commodities competed with one another in the marketplace and contributed to each other's commercial momentum.[52]

The market for these products was healthy, and competition was fierce, leading to a constant will toward product differentiation on the part of authors. For instance, Brightland rigorously differentiates his early-century grammar from two competing commodities. "The *first Essayist* has indeed, partly quitted the old Track, but could not prevail with himself to quit it intirely. *The Second* is so far from parting with a little of the old *Greek and Latin Terms* that he puts in a new *Posse* upon us. The *first* is so full of Obscurity and Confusion, for want of Method, that his Book can be of little Use to the Instruction of the Ignorant; and the latter has so little Regard to the *English* Tongue, that in the Title of his Book he is guilty of an evident Misnomer, it being no more an *English Grammar*, than a Chinese."[53] Not only does he stress anglophone nativism against the classical styles and terminologies of the "old Track"; he also informs potential buyers that, unlike the others, his book has a teachable method that will be useful for "the Instruction of the Ignorant." Later in the century, the grammarian Anselm Bayly faults existing grammars and recommends his own in the following terms: "Every master of every petty school thinks himself qualified to write one . . . but the difficulty is manifest from the imperfection of each."[54] Referencing the commodification of his own work, Bayly goes on to say, "The original title was an Introduction to languages, or a grammar literary and philosophical, especially to English, Latin, Greek, and Hebrew; but it was thought too complex, and the present as more simple was preferred by the Publisher."[55] Bayly was aiming more for an audience from an earlier period, an audience made up of people interested in grammar in the sense of universal grammar. His publisher thought better of it, perhaps intuiting the ongoing spread of anglophone mass literacy, as described in chapter four.[56] A grammarian named Alexander Adam, the "Rector of the High School of Edinburgh," pitches to this anglophone market directly. Adam pursues the complex strategy of selling parts of his grammar separately in order to reach a set of consumers with less disposable income. "To render the size of the book more commodious for beginners, a number of copies are printed, containing only the Etymology, with an abridgement of Syntax and Prosody. This part may be had separately."[57] Related dynamics of commodity differentiation are at work in marketing strategies for the period's translations, a point I take up in detail in the next section.

Two additional linkages between standardization and translation are important in the period. In addition to the fact that these discourses are mutually reinforcing, they are also both normative, and therefore central to eighteenth-century aesthetic developments. The fourth of the five main points I enumerated above is that standardization and translation both articulate themselves as regulatory agents within a field of linguistic multiplicity internal and external to anglophony. As discourses, they equally assume that the politics of linguistic diversity are part of the public consciousness. Put another way, both standardization and translation take up the charge of claiming or refuting the aesthetic value of diverse linguistic forms. The fifth and perhaps most important of my five main points is that both discourses investigate the role of any individual in relation to anglophone community. How can any one practitioner of language, whether a standardizer, translator, poet, dramatist, novelist, or all of the above, work within the parameters of anglophone acceptability while also acting on them? These questions animate the rest of the chapter.

Anglophones who wrote about anglophony or translated nonanglophone works during the eighteenth century did so by drawing on experiences with the written traditions, pedagogical apparatuses, and translation practices of other languages to which they had exposure—far more than we typically imagine. They operated comparatively, multilingually, and with a variety of linguistic humility regarding the extra-anglophone world that is often absent from popular accounts of the language system today. This is why Lowth's grammar does readers the courtesy of defining the nature of anglophony by way of a comparison with biblical Hebrew: "Of all the ancient Languages extant that is the most simple, which is undoubtedly the most ancient: but even that Language [Hebrew] itself does not equal the *English* in Simplicity."[58] This is also why Lowth, a standardizer and translator who aims for the widest possible audience, defines the English noun in comparative and multilingual terms: "The Greek and Latin among ancient, and some too among the modern languages, as the German, vary the termination or ending of the substantive. . . . And the English being derived from the same origin as the German, that is, from the Teutonic, is not wholly without them."[59] Just as English must be grasped as one of many language systems, it is impossible for Lowth to describe even a part of speech without recourse to multilingual examples. So it comes as no surprise that the footnotes of this grammar presuppose a reader fluent in the several languages of the eighteenth-century amateur-expert. Writers like Lowth brought their educational histories to bear on the futures they set out for English, which were often deliberately modeled on their knowledge of languages perceived to be particularly venerable or worthy of emulation.[60] These writers did not invent the idea of Standard English whole cloth, in other words. Because of this, they put our contemporary aesthetics of linguistic difference into an exciting new light while also showing that the cultural and aesthetic lineages of linguistic difference are longer, more complex, and more embedded within anglophony than most have assumed.

Translation and Sovereignty

> That servile path thou nobly dost decline,
> Of tracing word by word, and line by line.

Those are the labour'd births of slavish brains,
Not the effects of Poetry, but pains;
Cheap vulgar arts, whose narrowness affords
No flight for thoughts, but poorly strikes at words.
A new and nobler way thou dost pursue,
To make Translations and Translators too.
They but preserve the Ashes, Thou the Flame,
True to his sense, but truer to his fame.
Foording his current, where thou find'st it low
Let'st in thine own to make it rise and flow;
Wisely restoring whatsoever grace
It lost by change of Times, or Tongues, or Place,
Nor fetter'd to his Numbers, and his Times,
Betray'st his Musick to unhappy Rimes
. . . .
He could have made those like, who made the rest,
But that he knew his own designe was best.[61]

First bundled with the poem "Cooper's Hill" in 1650, and reprinted frequently thereafter, the lines above come from a forty-four-line encomium to Sir Richard Fanshawe by poet and translator Sir John Denham.[62] As the lines show, Denham deeply admired Fanshawe's "noble" work of translation entitled *The Faithful Shepherd* (1647), an anglophone rendition of Giovanni Battista Guarani's *Il Pastor Fido* (1590).[63] Translation studies scholars—in the eighteenth century and today—have often seized on this passage because of its celebration of the translator as transformative creative agent. Essentially, it has been read as an inaugural and influential description of adaptive or naturalizing translation practice. The way these lines emphasize the translator's power to remake a text so that it reads fluently has been taken to reveal a great deal about the patterns of anglophone translation practice during the eighteenth century. A vital chapter of Venuti's *The Translator's Invisibility* (1995) spells this out. Venuti foregrounds Denham's celebration of Fanshawe's translation as an origin for the "ethnocentric violence of domestication" that seventeenth-century ideologies of translation engender for later generations.[64] For Venuti, Denham heralds an aristocratic ideology of fluency in which the "illusion of transparency . . . masks the manifold conditions of the translated text," conceals "its exclusionary impact on foreign cultural values," and covers over its own tendency to sideline "translation strategies that resist transparent discourse."[65] This is because Denham suggests that a translator is justified in departing significantly from the source text in order to "preserve . . . the Flame" in a new form. In other words, this oft-quoted poem celebrates translators who translate source texts such that they appear to have originally been composed in the target language.

Put differently, Denham's poem summarizes a particularly anglophone model of translation as linguistic domestication, a difference-effacing model that fits a source text within already existing linguistic and aesthetic conventions. The opposite tactic—reproducing the texture of the source text in anglophony—is a process called foreignizing translation and associated with translators like Antoine Berman and Venuti himself. Domesticating translation, on the other hand, is a mode of translation that is akin to standardization in that it prioritizes adherence to known anglophone standards of propriety or fluency over fidelity to any source.[66] Tracing Denham's afterlives in the eighteenth century, Venuti points to Dryden and Johnson, both of whom "saw Denham as an innovator in translation," a man who was "canonized by later writers because . . . his poetry and poetry translations read 'naturally and easily' and therefore seem . . . more accurate or faithful as translation."[67] In other words, Denham's translations exhibit few linguistic peculiarities that might be attributable to the residue of translation, which both Dryden and Johnson appreciated. In Venuti's view, it was during the seventeenth and early eighteenth centuries that "domestication dominated the theory and practice of English-language translation," a fact with important cultural ramifications, not least the polar system in which translators were left with two options: "ethnocentric reduction of the foreign text to dominant cultural values" (domesticating translation) or "ethnodeviant pressure on those [dominant cultural] values to register the linguistic and cultural differences of the foreign text" (foreignizing translation). We can read "ethnodeviant pressure" as something like what Johnson means when he accuses translators of "imparting something of [the source language's] native idiom" into anglophony.[68]

Mary Helen McMurran offers a discerning new reading of eighteenth-century translation practices. Reading translations between English and French as they relate to the formation of the novel, McMurran critiques the rigidity of Venuti's use of the terms "domesticating" and "foreignizing." As she points out, these terms rely on overly fixed notions of culture. The reason is that the eighteenth century was a period in which ideas of culture, language, and affiliation were far more porous than they would later become. McMurran suggests that unthinking use of the terms "domesticating" and "foreignizing" risks "anachronistically impos[ing] culture on eighteenth-century fiction translating."[69] This is because "Schleiermacher's separation between foreign author and domestic reader is conditioned . . . by the advent of culture in the romantic period which denotes a new integration of language, customs, and other factors into the totality of national identity."[70] For this reason, going forward I am using these terms only as they relate to the hardening standards of literate communities. If eighteenth-century standardization texts demonstrate anything, it is that there were indeed nascent norms for the forms of linguistic practice that communities could be organized around, in which case a restricted use of the terms "domesticating" and "foreignizing" in relation to those norms is justifiable. Because I agree largely with McMurran's analysis, here I will point to a different binary of translation practice altogether, one that complicates our sense of "domesticating" versus "foreignizing" translation.

Returning to Denham's encomium, the view of translation he espouses casts a long shadow over the eighteenth century. An anglophone convention arises around Denham's patterned use of negative descriptors like "servile," "slavish," "vulgar," and "fetter'd" as ways of evaluating translation strategies that are less fluent, that is, less adherent to known anglophone standards of propriety. The evaluative vocabulary Denham uses is crucial to grasping translation's function in anglophone aesthetics in the tradition subsequent to his work, not least because this vocabulary configures the creative act of translation—what Spivak calls "the most intimate act of reading"—as an act not of intimacy but of self-emancipation from the strictures of the original language such that one can appear fluidly and fluently anglophone.[71] Given the historical context of the eighteenth century, figuring translation in a vocabulary adjacent to the vocabulary of slavery additionally positions the act and products of translation in relation to labor and property in startling ways.

The curious ambivalence that characterizes standardization's negotiation of multiplicity also marks the period's translation theory, which, like standardization, is a metalinguistic mode of writing about anglophony rather than a uniform or consistent set of widely agreed on practices. I argue here that eighteenth-century translation theory registers ambivalence about linguistic multiplicity that is comparable to the idea of copiousness in conversations about standardization. This claim is borne out by the fact that, following Denham, anglophone translation theorists gravitated toward one specific set of metaphors in order to advocate for protocols of linguistic inclusion and exclusion that would improve anglophone literary aesthetics within the space of global linguistic multiplicity. Translation theorists' concern with stewarding anglophony through "free" rather than "servile" translation reveals that definitions of these terms shift across the century. In so doing, they intervene into questions surrounding the ways that aesthetic sovereignty can be the result of creative linguistic labor, as well as the ways it cannot. While this book has not and will not offer a comprehensive account of either standardization or translation—others whom I draw on have done this admirably—my analyses of the metaphors of copiousness as well as "free" and "servile" translation disclose literary aesthetics as they grow out of eighteenth-century reflections on anglophony and the other language systems with which it was increasingly interacting.

Using language repurposed from texts like Cicero's *De Finibus* (45 B.C.E.) as well as Horace's *Epistles* (20 B.C.E.) and *Ars Poetica* (14 B.C.E.), eighteenth-century anglophone translation theorists regularly call on the counterpoised vocabularies of freedom and bondage, power and subjection, as well as liberty and confinement in order to figure the varied relationships of source to translation, author to translator, and individual creative agent to linguistic system, in this case anglophony.[72] As in Denham's praise of Fanshawe, translation theorists in the first several decades of the century engage with linguistic multiplicity internal and external to anglophony by focusing on the translator's imperative to eschew "the servile path" so as not to fall under the control of the source language's characteristics. During this period, interest in the "liberty" or "freedom" of translation amounts to a roundabout way of warning against the undiluted and therefore unauthorized transportation of cultural material from other linguistic realms into anglophony. Translators working in this model anglicize foreign texts as acts of creative "freedom." As the century progressed, however, new forms of "free" translation become desirable, many of which directly oppose the earlier definition's resistance to foreignizing translation practice.[73]

Across the century, warnings against translational "servility" or "slavishness" can be read as anxiety about unsanctioned cultural pollution just as they can and should be read in conjunction with the historical matrix of transatlantic slavery, which, as Susan Buck-Morss notes, "had become the root metaphor of Western political philosophy, connoting everything that was evil about power relations."[74] Buck-Morss's insight extends well beyond political philosophy.[75] Seeing anglophone translation discussed in the vocabulary of slavery is less surprising than expected. It is not just that slavery is a vivid metaphor that assists eighteenth-century translation theorists in describing translation as a process. Translation brings different linguistic systems into contact and implicates actual multilingual subjects with material biographies. Metaphors relating to slavery extend beyond discussions of translation, in other words. Their invocation actually works to configure power relations between anglophones and speakers of other languages, and does so in exclusively hierarchical terms as slavery itself would suggest. Put another way, eighteenth-century translation theory's invocations of slavery also work to condition how the multilingualism of the other was construed and managed in the centuries that follow. Equally important, the judgment of whether a translation is "free" or "servile" has to do with the state of translation as a commodity during the period. Because translations were marketed and sold in response to changing consumer demands, the signifying power of these terms matters materially in the same way that it matters historically and linguistically.

The anglophone history of eighteenth-century renderings of Horace's *Ars Poetica* is an instructive place to begin interrogating the evaluative vocabularies of freedom and servility as they relate to translation. These translations are also an ideal place for seeing what this vocabulary means with regard to how translation practices were affected by the systems of transatlantic slavery and global imperialism. Horace's oft-quoted and diversely translated admonition that a poet-translator should avoid translating word for word speaks to the enduring way in which the practice of translation can be seen to enact problems of aesthetic sovereignty, individual sovereignty, and anglophone community all at once. The original lines are worth reproducing alongside my own translation, for what is made of them is remarkable, especially because they do not directly employ any of the common Latin words for servility, servitude, or slavery. Instead, they read as follows,

publica materies privati iuris erit, si
non circa vilem patulumque moraberis orbem,
nec verbo verbum curabis reddere fidus
interpres, nec desilies imitator in artum,
unde pedem proferre pudor vetet aut operis lex.

Public material will be private property, if only
You will not hew to the broad and common circle,
And not undertake to translate word for word, as a faithful
Translator, and not jump headlong, like an imitator, into a narrow space,
Where shame or the work's law may forbid you to advance.[76]

In this passage, Horace describes what a translator should do to assert aesthetic sovereignty over stories that are perhaps already widely known, a process he phrases as making "public material" into "private property" (*publica materia privati iuris erit*). Horace uses negative, second-person singular verbs in the indicative mood and future tense—the same verbal form as in the Vulgate's translation of Exodus 20's "Ten Commandments"—in order to enumerate three practices that the translator should avoid. Namely, a translator should not "hew to the broad and common circle" (*non circa vilem patulumque moraberis orbem*); a translator should not "undertake to translate word for word (*nec verbo verbum curabis reddere*); and a translator should not "jump headlong into a narrow space" whose confining restrictions inhibit progress in the translation (*nec desilies . . . in artum*). Eighteenth-century translators seize on these moments as a way of characterizing their own translations' interventions into anglophone aesthetic practice.

Grasping the afterlives of this passage requires knowing that the point of *Ars Poetica* is to provide advice to poets on generating material for their work. This is a poem about asserting the self as a maker of poetry, an agent who can frame an object worthy of aesthetic attention out of common cultural material. Saying that *Ars Poetica* is deeply concerned with developing a rich theory of translation is false, even if the repeated translations of this passage during the eighteenth century might suggest otherwise. The anonymous translator of *Horace Of the Art of Poetry, In English Numbers* (1735) accurately contextualizes the restricted place of translation within the poetic investments of the work as a whole. "The intention of our Author in that Passage plainly seems no other than to shew the Poet a more practicable easy way of Composition than that of mere Invention, or of composing Characters and *Actions* altogether new."[77] Horace's thoughts are directed "not to the Interpreter . . . but to the Poet in due form," for it is the poet "who designs a true original Performance."[78] I mention this because it is worth remembering that, even in the *Ars Poetica*, translation is explicitly taken to be a type of aesthetic labor that is subordinate to poetic creation.

This assumption is carried over into anglophone practice. Because eighteenth-century translations circulate in a market environment in which the originality of a translation's "Performance" is crucial to its profitability, translation is a form of work that allows the translator to assert anglophone creativity and skill (rather than meticulously reproducing the creativity and skill of the original author).

There are many possible readings of Horace's first and third metaphors, some of which may indeed have tangential relationships to concepts like servility and slavery, depending on how they are interpreted. These may explain the translational interpolations that are visible in the text's anglophone history—and present, for that matter.[79] For example, the first metaphor's invocation of circularity advises against pursuing the exact path as the source language. One possible reading is that Horace has in mind a mill, that animal engine in which a "fetter'd" beast of burden is bound to a shaft and driven in circles around a gear wheel in order to turn a grinding mechanism. The third directive's metaphor is more nebulous. It seems to invoke war by pairing a verb that can mean "to dismount from a chariot" (*desilio, desilire*) with a verb phrase that signifies "to advance" (*pedem proferre*).[80] It would be conceivable to imagine this as an unfocused reference to actual combat, but the link is conjectural.

In contrast to these, the second instruction advises against word-for-word translation, an instruction that is all the more lucid given that it is sandwiched between the other two. In anglophone translations of the eighteenth century, the second instruction's suggestion that one should not be so "faithful" as to translate word for word like a "fidus interpres" is rendered in a variety of ways. I am most interested here in the way "fidus interpres" appears frequently as "servile translator" or "slavish translator," a fact that registers Denham's mediating influence. Indeed, one can even read Denham's poem to Fanshawe as a "free" rendering or anglophone imitation of the *Ars Poetica*. Denham fawns that Fanshawe rejected the "servile path" of "tracing word by word, and line by line" (Horace's *verbo verbum*) and also that Fanshawe "could have made those like, who made the rest / But that he knew his own designe was best" an artful, free, and fluent anglophone transcreation of Horace's *publica materies privati iuris erit*. Later anglophone translations of the Horatian text perpetuate Denham's interventions.

The absence of Denham's mediation in translations before 1650 and its presence in later ones bear this out. Thomas Drant published the first anglophone translation of *Ars Poetica* in 1567, a work that displays the same will toward commodity differentiation as the grammars described in the previous section.[81] Calling his translation "welnye worde for word and lyne for lyne," Drant renders Horace's five lines in three rhyming couplets without ever explicitly calling on semantic realms that include ideas like "servile" or "slavish."[82] Instead, the noun phrase "fidus interpres" shows up as the verb phrase "turne things faythfullye." While it might be argued that "faithfully" carries the same sense of total loyalty and adherence to an original text as "servile" or "slavish" does, the truth is that "faithfully" is drawn from the register of devotional practices, not labor practices, and the difference is crucial. Ben Jonson, whom Tytler later accuses of "the most servile adherence to words," likewise never uses Denham's vocabulary in his 1640 version.[83]

Yet, common matter thou thine own maist make,
If thou the vile, broad-troden ring forsake.
For, being a Poet, thou maist feigne, create,
Not care, as though wouldst faithfully translate,
To render word for word: nor with thy sleight
Of imitation, leape into a straight
From whence thy modesty, or Poëms Law
Forbids thee forth againe thy foot to draw.[84]

Similar to Drant, Jonson opts for the devotional "faithfully translate" as his rendition of "fidus interpres."[85] He also accentuates the fact that *Ars Poetica* is about becoming a poet by explicitly referencing poetry in two phrases—"being a Poet" and "Poëms Law."

Denham's influence becomes more observable in 1680 when Wentworth Dillon, the Earl of Roscommon (Figure 3), issued an influential translation of the *Ars Poetica* that was frequently reprinted throughout the eighteenth century.[86] Unlike Drant and Jonson's versions, Roscommon weaves in both of Denham's keywords and slightly modifies the translation of "fidus interpres" to "too faithfully translate":

For what originally others writ,
May be so well disguis'd, and so improv'd,
That with some Justice it may pass for yours
But then you must not Copy trivial things,

Figure 3. In 1680, Wentworth Dillon, the Earl of Roscommon, published a translation of the *Ars Poetica* that would prove rhetorically influential throughout the eighteenth century. George Perfect Harding painted this miniature watercolor portrait during the early nineteenth century. © National Portrait Gallery, London.

Nor word for word too faithfully Translate,
Nor (as some servile Imitators do)
Prescribe at first such strict uneasie rules
As they must ever slavishly observe.[87]

More than the two versions quoted so far, Roscommon's insists that a translator assert aesthetic sovereignty by working with the source text as one would work to "disguise" and "improve" property. In this version, disguise and improvement are ways of taking "what others originally writ" and gaining aesthetic equity over those writings such that "Justice" will acknowledge the translation of them as a rightful creation by the translator rather than a trivial "Copy" of the original. For a translation to become a commodity, in other words, it must represent the creation of new property through a particular type of free or unbound labor.

Roscommon's use of "servile Imitators" and "slavishly observe" stand out both formally and conceptually in this context. Certainly, these words complete the poem's iambic pentameter and thus bear poetic properties. However, they share the additional feature of being strangely unmotivated by the source text and absolutely resonant with the period's systems of forced labor. He freely supplements Horace's text with his own context, thereby adding value to the original such that it becomes his property and can be sold based on its originality. By contrast, "servile Imitators" cannot take ownership over source texts and cannot make them into salable commodities. This is because they set difficult ("uneasie") rules that foreclose the possibility of improvement or fluency. In other words, "strict" rules that are "slavishly" followed make aesthetic sovereignty impossible in just the same way that unimproved territory cannot justify property rights, as imperial thought of the time held.

Others followed Roscommon's model. Samuel Dunster's *Horace's Satires, Epistles, and Art of Poetry, Done into English, with Notes* (1729) is one example. Though Dunster too makes the common claim that he is being more faithful to the content of Horace, his translational interventions are, like Roscommon's, rather pronounced, especially the way that he weaves in additional references to enslavement. Dunster's version is a facing-page translation—Latin on one side, English on the other—a structure that invites Latin-literate readers to monitor his translational choices at every turn. In addition, Dunster deliberately chooses to translate Horace's poetic works in prose, a form that ostensibly permits him to be more faithful to the source given the loosening of poetic restrictions. In Dunster's estimation, Horace's satires and epistles, unlike his odes, were meant "for the Instruction of Mankind" and "abound with many excellent Rules and Precepts, the Knowledge of which contributes very much to the Improvement of Life."[88] "This being the principle Design of our Poet," Dunster concludes that prose is more appropriate because he thinks it is clearer and more educational. "Another's Work may be easily made yours, if you carefully avoid too exact a Translation; if (like some servile Imitators) you follow not too closely your Author's method with which everyone one is acquainted; nor put your self under such Restraints, by representing every Circumstance of the Action, as you can't honourably extricate your self, without doing Violence to the Laws of Tragedy." Following Denham and Roscommon, Dunster's revealing translation also reads Horace's passage within the context of slavery. This is obvious in his rendering of "nec desilies imitator in artum" as "nor put your self under such Restraints"; Dunster uses "Restraints" to mean self-imposed fidelity to the source text that interrupts the free pursuit of aesthetic labor in the target language. In the anglophone context, this word also evokes the technologies of eighteenth-century slavery.

Of course, not all translators rendered these lines in the rhetorical language of slavery and freedom. Many did, and some did not, as two different versions from the same year show:

> A publick theme will then alone
> By lawful right become your own,
> If neither o'er a beaten ground
> You poorly tread the self-same round,
> Nor dully word for word translate,
> Nor, copying, run into a straight,
> Whence both the work's established law
> And shame forbids you to withdraw.[89]

> But publish'd matter is your own, with art,
> If duly you sustain the poet's part;
> Nor ramble, too circuitous your ring,
> Minutely to encompass every thing;
> And when your office is to imitate,
> In servile order word for word translate:

Nor imitate so closely as to lose
Against the rules, all freedom of your muse.[90]

The first is William Boscawen's version of Horace, and the second is from William Clubbe's, both dated 1797, at least two generations after the heyday of Denham's influence, and at a period when theories of translation were rapidly championing foreignizing technique over domesticating. And yet, in rhyming couplets, both translators adhere to a model of translation that is bound to sense but relatively free when it comes to style. Only Clubbe weaves into his translation a direct reference to translation as either "servility" or an exercise of "freedom," though Boscawen, for his part, slightly evokes the first in his original use of "dully" and "copying." One looks at these 1790s versions of Horace and they appear curious. After all, the 1790s was a period of revolutionary fervor. "Freedom" as a concept was ubiquitous. Likewise, the 1790s witnessed the dramatic rise of the anglophone abolition movement. The idea of "servility" or "slavishness" was equally widespread. Even though we do not see the vocabulary of slavery and freedom emphasized in both translations, it is safe to say that we see it woven into the "fabrick" of the most important translation theories of the late eighteenth century. The fifth chapter documents this claim further through readings of Alexander Fraser Tytler, Sir William Jones, William Julius Mickle, and George Campbell.

MULTILINGUAL LIVES

Joseph Emin

"Cacography" is a term that refers to bad or aberrant spelling or handwriting. It is often taken as the opposite of both "orthography" ("correct writing") and "calligraphy" ("beautiful writing"). Here, however, I want to use the term "cacography" in a different sense, to mean the written inscription of nonnormative forms of language—everything from unusual spellings, syntactical deviations, unfamiliar grammatical flourishes, and xenotropic stock expressions—when it originates from the pen of a multilingual subject. I arrive at this term by disambiguating cacography from the term dialect writing, which I have used sparingly so far to mean an intentional technology for simulating linguistic difference in print.[1] Whereas dialect writing is most often used to represent spoken language in the period, cacography has a different set of origins. Dialect writing is often highly deliberate, even if it seems extemporaneous, as when literate speakers and readers of Standard English juxtapose their normative language with nonnormative forms of living speech. In dialect writing, nonnormative forms of language are called into service for the political and aesthetic purpose of representing the limits of a linguistic community.[2] Cacography, on the other hand, is often incidental, the product of a multilingual anglophone writer's unique way of acting on and within anglophony. So whereas dialect writing emerges when a normative language user performs or exaggerates linguistic difference in print, cacography, by contrast, appears simply in a nonnormative subject's unsteady use of written language. In either case, to a normative reader, both dialect and cacography foreignize those subjects who are presumed to be the aberrant linguistic form's nontextual origins.

When we use language, we communicate our relationships to power and hierarchy as these are inscribed in and through language.[3] Spoken language is a learned behavior that communicates vectors of difference immediately—in mistakes and malapropisms but also much more subtly in the roundedness of a vowel, the palatalization of a consonant, or the epenthesis of a syllable. Our sounds, syntactical, and lexical choices tell others of our proximity to cultural power and our orientation to the linguistic communities of which we are a part. We divulge our personal histories, genders, affiliations, races, classes, and more. Writing is a learned technology that betrays relationships to literate communities in a way that is more obvious and more oblique. As when we speak, in writing we make choices (and, often enough, errors) that disclose our proximal or distal relationships to circulating standards of written propriety. So too when we read, and then later speak or write about what we have read, we risk divulging to others, as well as ourselves, literate misprisions that mark our subject position's relationship to linguistic normativity. Dialect writing and cacography, which are textual by nature, translate perceived interactional dynamics into print, in the first case by design and in the second by happenstance. These forms of writing place multilingual subjects beyond the boundaries of normative linguistic communities. In their difference from literate norms, dialect and cacography both represent cultural incompatibility. More specifically, they dramatize the tension surrounding a linguistic subject's ability to assert himself as a fully fledged subject of political life—and therefore aesthetic life and recognition.

Eighteenth-century writers were keenly aware of a particular language form's ability to situate subjects in speech or writing. This is among the most obvious stylistic conceits of popular outsider-looking-in texts. Oliver Goldsmith's *The Citizen of the World* (1760–61), for instance, features a narrator named Lien Chi Altangi, a persona whose writing voice is fluidly and recognizably Standard English in most instances. His voice is deliberately characterized as foreign mainly when it comes to grasping British customs. As far as mid-eighteenth-century anglophone writing practices are concerned, however, this persona is actually largely normative.[4] By this I mean that a reader finds fewer xenotropisms than might be expected. Lien is figured from the first of Goldsmith's columns as a "native of Honan in China," a simulation of a multilingual subject who, "by frequently conversing with the English" at Canton, has "learned the [English] language, though he is entirely a stranger to their manners and customs."[5] Goldsmith's editor's preface even reports to the reader that, "upon his first appearance here [Britain], many were angry not to find him as ignorant as a Tripoline ambassador, or an envoy from Mujac."[6] Instead, they were "surprised to find a man born so far from London . . . endued even with a moderate capacity."[7] And yet, despite this insistence on Lien Chi Altangi's anglophone fluency, Goldsmith still calls on xenotropisms in order to imitate and foreignize his invented narrator in certain contexts.[8] "But I submit to the stroke of heaven," Lien gushes in an early letter. "I hold the volume of Confucius in my hand, and, as I read, grow humble, patient, and wise."[9] Later, Goldsmith includes a note that reinforces this detail: "The Editor thinks proper to acquaint the reader, that the greatest part of the following letter seems to him to be little more than a rhapsody of sentences borrowed from Confucius, the Chinese philosopher."[10] The evocation of Lien's supposedly narrow philosophical universe ironizes and foreignizes his language of self-expression before a Standard English reader, no more so than when he addresses the invented Fum Hoam as "O holy disciple of Confucius."[11]

As the eighteenth century progressed, the aesthetic ideas anticipated by Goldsmith's depiction of Lien proliferated in different directions. A text that in recent decades has piqued numerous eighteenth-century and Romantic-era scholars, Elizabeth Hamilton's *Translation of the Letters of a Hindoo Rajah* (1796) is emblematic of these trends.[12] More so than Goldsmith, Hamilton's epistolary novel explicitly frames the voices of its three primary interlocutors with ethnographic flourishes that appear at the level of language as well as orthography.[13] Hamilton's "Zāārmilla" and "Māāndāāra" write in anglophone forms that are unambiguously marked by xenotropisms, including linguistic choices that are often heavy-handed. "Praise to Ganesa!" Zāārmilla writes to Māāndāāra, who begins his return letter, "Praise be to Veeshnû!" accompanying this invocation with the flattery that Zāārmilla's letter "hath kindled the fire of conflicting passions in the breast of Māāndāāra."[14] Beyond Māāndāāra's archaic third-person singular form of "to have" and his third-person references to the self, contemporary readers of this text would have noticed one terribly obvious visual feature of this text: macrons appear over some of the vowels in the names Zāārmilla and Māāndāāra. Drawing from the visual repertoire of both Latin textbooks and orientalist treatises that circulated in the period, these rigged spellings make the foreignness of the named characters more categorical than it would otherwise appear. Lien must continually cite his foreignness through references to Confucius, but for Hamilton's characters foreignness is continually made apparent at the level of print.

The potentially misleading fact is that not all early editions of Hamilton's book use these macrons, and those that do use them use them inconsistently. For example, the first London edition (1796) uses macrons uniformly over these names in chapter subtitles and but only haphazardly throughout the text. The first and second Dublin editions (1797, 1801) do not use these foreignizing macrons at all, and so readers are presented with names but no diacritics.[15] Nor does the fifth London edition (1811) use these macrons, although the first American edition (Boston, 1819), which appeared three years after Hamilton's death, uses them in the subtitles affixed to each of the letters but not at all in the letters themselves.[16] This discussion of the appearance or nonappearance of macrons is meant to allude to a larger linguistic context: writers and readers alike were intimately familiar with the strategies that print made possible for dressing language to appear unfamiliar.

In this printing context, anglophone writers who learned the language later in life were perhaps even more aware of language's ability to situate a subject in speech or in writing. This was the case of Joseph Emin ("Ameen son of Hovsep"), whose autobiographical *The Life and Adventures of Joseph Émïn, An Armenian. Written in English by Himself* (1792) repeatedly asks readers to overlook his writing almost as though he was certain they would find fault with it. Emin was a polyglot Armenian Christian, traveler, and mercenary who moved from his birthplace in the Persian Empire to Calcutta, where he stayed briefly before sailing for London and living there for four years. In London he gained friends and patrons like Edmund Burke and the Duke of Northumberland before studying at the Royal Military Academy, campaigning with the British military on the European continent, traveling the Ottoman Empire to inspire Armenian nationalism, and eventually returning to Calcutta.

The question of anglophone linguistic standards clearly consumes Emin's mind as a writer. He fears cacographies that will disclose him as an outsider. As a case in point, he describes how he has come to compose his life story in Standard English "with reluctance, not being very well versed in the English language."[17] The text begs his readers to "kindly pass over, any impropriety in his work" and to "consider the difficulty and labour by which he has attained the noble language of a foreign country, and that without either friend or money"—a far cry from Lien, whose English was apparently mastered by conversing with anglophone traders at Canton.[18] We can assume from Emin's apologia that he expected his writing would be read as an autoforeignizing text, marred by shibboleths, and communicative of its author's non-Englishness. Writing in the third person, Emin asks for sympathy: "If they could possibly dive into his [referring to himself] thoughts, to observe the hardship he undergoes in his task with an unpolished education, they would compare his mind to a blunt, rusty knife, cutting a thick bar of iron."[19] A blunt knife struggling to cut through iron is an apt metaphor for the "difficulty and labour" of learning another language so fluently that one blends unrecognizably into another linguistic community. The book ends just as it begins. "To conclude: The author humbly begs leave to remind the candid reader of his imperfect acquaintance with the native propriety of the English style."[20] Emin's comments confirm the point that communicative acts—even and especially written ones—can expose one to uncontrollable interpretations just as they confirm that language mastery is a costly, difficult, and often impossible barrier to community acceptance.

Upon arrival in Britain, the difficulties Emin faces as he tries to accede to the anglophone community are stark enough. He rents a room from an anglophone Swede who is married to an English woman. The Swede's candid advice to Emin for making his way in London, especially as it relates to language, is bleak. "Your best way I think will be, not to lose the opportunity of returning to Bengal, with the rest of the lascars. . . . Supposing that there were [someone to give you a reference], what would you do for want of the language, for you are hardly understood."[21] After describing Emin's many desultory pursuits in London after 1751—his time as a student, bricklayer, load carrier, law clerk, and potential Jamaican plantation worker, an indenture he later repudiated—Michael Fisher summarizes how Emin was read by Britons: "One potential employer cursed Emin for being a Frenchman. When Emin denied being French and began to explain what being an Armenian meant, the man identified him as a German."[22]

It is fitting then that both of his career-making encounters in Britain involve linguistic tests. After meeting Edmund Burke in the park, Emin describes their conversation and details the way he successfully proves his value to Burke through a literacy test. "When Mr. Burke understood that he [Emin] could read and write, he gave him the Tatler, and made him read a paragraph of it. He approved him; and said, 'Very well; lay it down. I am your friend as much as it lies in my power."[23] As for his second, more lucrative encounter, Emin is invited into the house of the Duke of Northumberland when he meets another Armenian who is serving as a groom to the duke. The man needs some words translated for his employer.[24] Emin shines in this role. Later, as he is writing to Northumberland, he includes a characteristic apology: "Forgive, my Lord, the language of a stranger. I have been in too low a condition to know how to write properly to your Lordship."[25]

The great irony surrounding Emin's anxiety about his anglophone self-presentation is that his life is a continual procession of multilingual encounters, most of which he deals with deftly. During his journeys through the Ottoman Empire, he understands many of the languages he encounters: Turkish, Armenian, "Curdish," and more.[26] His linguistic dexterity extends to eavesdropping: "They began to mutter to one another in the Tartarian language, saying, 'This man, while he is alone, has so great a liver, (The Asiatics commonly call a man of courage a man of liver)."[27] At other times, his linguistic skill comes across as an act of translation for the anglophone reader, as when he is traveling to meet the King of Georgia and must first "consult with Mahomed Khan the nutzal (which, in the Avar language, means a king)."[28] Later, Emin adds details to his translation of the Ottoman world in order to gesture toward a beauty in linguistic difference that anglophones might find enticing: "The word Karajagdy, in the Turkish language, signifies the first fall of snow."[29] With these robust linguistic faculties, it is almost preposterous that Emin should repeatedly anticipate and apologize for what might be perceived as anglophone impropriety. And yet he does apologize because the monolingual politics of language suggest that he should, especially given the literate world in which his text was to circulate.

A telling moment comes at the end of the narrative as Emin is making his final passage back to India. At Basra, he introduces himself to Henry Moore, a British East India Company agent: " 'My name is Emin: I am the son of Joseph Michael Emin of Calcutta, an Armenian by religion, and by birth a native of Hamadan in Persia.' Mr. Moore said, 'You seem to be an Irishman by your accent.' Emin, smiling, answered, 'You honour me much in thinking so; for the Irish are a brave nation, with a deserved renown.' "[30] Processing Emin's English, Moore identifies him as an anglophone Irishman, a thought that makes the former proud in spite of the fact that during his time in Britain Emin deliberately avoided all associations with Catholicism. To have attained the status of anglophone Irishman strikes Emin as a great coup, not least because he now understands the plight of the Irish to be analogous to that of Ottoman-occupied

Armenians. Emin's autobiography speaks to the many contours of late eighteenth-century anglophony. His cacographic self-assertions are one way that linguistic identity appears in eighteenth-century print culture. The next chapter turns directly to other ways in which print communicates identity.

CHAPTER 4

Literacy Fictions

Making Linguistic Difference Legible

Literacy and Legibility

Eighteenth-century dialect writing is implicitly entangled with the evolving meanings of literacy in the period. With this fact in mind, Peter Sloterdijk's 1999 essay "Rules for the Human Zoo" provides one way to approach larger questions surrounding literacy.

> We can trace the communitarian fantasy that lies at the root of all humanism back to the model of a literary society, in which participation through reading the canon reveals a common love of inspiring messages. At the heart of humanism so understood we discover a cult or club fantasy: the dream of the portentous solidarity of those who have been chosen to be allowed to read. In the ancient world—indeed, until the dawn of the modern nation-states—the power of reading actually did mean something like membership of a secret elite; linguistic knowledge once counted in many places as the provenance of sorcery. In Middle English the word "glamour" developed out of the word "grammar." The person who could read would be thought easily capable of other impossibilities.[1]

Sloterdijk's analysis of the "communitarian fantasy" or "dream" of shared literacy calls attention to the entwined histories of literacy and power that date from the beginning of large-scale vernacular reading and writing during the eighteenth century. Sloterdijk centers his comments around the "club fantasy" of "those who have been chosen to be allowed to read," by which he means a finite collection of arbiters who, by whatever vagaries or appropriations of force, have anointed themselves "chosen" to be included in the making of publicly operative definitions of how to read, what to read, what reading signifies, and what reading even is. To be "chosen," or among the literate elect, is to be authorized to participate in public discussions concerning aesthetic objects and/or political concerns as they relate to normative language. Not to be "chosen" is tantamount to exclusion based on ideals of linguistic normativity that are propagated by discourses like standardization and translation theory. "The power of reading"—and speaking and writing "properly," we might add—has been patrolled, regulated, imposed, and produced because, viewed from the angle of aesthetics, "it actually did," and still does, indicate "something like membership of a secret elite" to which not all have equal access and from which many are actively and continually banished.[2] Long before, and indeed long *after* the "dawn of . . . nation-states" (pace Sloterdijk), the notion that proper, sanctioned, or "elite" uses of language constitute the minimal conditions for a full engagement in public life and aesthetic practice remains embedded in the fabric of anglophone relationality even if the meaning of "sanctioned" or "elite" language has changed substantially.

The term "the power of reading" as I repurpose it here from Sloterdijk refers to the ability to participate in linguistic normativity. Consequently, it also refers to the ability to debate publicly the constitution of appropriate linguistic forms, a power that might also include the ability to have opinions on the appropriate means by which language is permitted to change. During the eighteenth century and today, this term "power of reading" differs from the more general term "literacy" in that the former's bivalence—power as ability and power as authority—evokes the superadded right to patrol or police language itself. Literacy alone refers to a variable range of technical skills, as well as their social significations. As I have already argued, specific powers underwriting and authorizing these "powers of reading" are brought into focus by two emergent and mutually reinforcing genres of eighteenth-century writing about language: the discourses of the standardization movement and translation theory. During this period, when Standard English defined the conditions of belonging for acceding to the dominant linguistic community, the discourse of standardization had considerable power. Translation, insofar as it was free and remunerative, defined the means by which the definition of proper Standard English could be allowed to change through the injection of admissible and compatible cultural material—cultural material for which a translator's labor can and should be compensated. Later in this chapter I will discuss "the power of reading" in terms of literary tropes that gesture toward the boundaries of the aesthetic, tropes that capture the liminality of language forms that cannot rise to the level of aesthetic contemplation because of their perceived linguistic nonnormativity, illegibility, incompatibility, or inhumanity. For now, however, I explore the meaning of literacy and the meaning of texts that deliberately pervert or fictionalize normative literacy's basic tenets through the deployment of dialect writing.[3]

I begin with Sloterdijk's essay because it helps open a new set of questions on the topic of literacy by defining this concept in terms of the normative exertion of power over the linguistically multiple and nonnormative. In total, however, "Rules for the Human Zoo" is a rather abstract rumination on what Sloterdijk calls "anthropotechnologies."[4] This term refers to technologies that produce the human in contradistinction to the animal that is the human's origin. These technologies produce the human by establishing horizons of linguistic mastery that one must cross in order to participate in different literary publics. Sloterdijk's close readings of Plato, Nietzsche, and Heidegger are only tangentially related to the present work's interest in the disciplinary and homogenizing operations of anglophone standardization and translation, but his figurations of language and literacy as they consolidate literate communities are transferable and generative. In particular, his analysis of standard language and literacy as technologies that "sharply divided our culture and created a yawning gulf between the literate and illiterate, a gulf that in its insuperability amounted almost to a species differentiation" offers one way of understanding the dynamics that I have been describing so far. Relative to the total population, the percentage of anglophones in the eighteenth century was very small, with a large spike toward the end. So any discussion of the definition of the "human" in this period should be wary. But there is a way to think eighteenth-century ideas of the human in relation to literacy, at least to the degree that written documents of the period encourage readers to imagine full humanity as newly contingent on literacy. This is another way of accounting for why the eighteenth-century anglophone archive's definition of the human generally comprises white, wealthy, and able anglophone bodies who, in addition, perform Standard English language and literacy appropriately. This much is a result of the politics of Standard English that takes shape over the period.

In spite of his theory's limitations, Sloterdijk's characterizations of the "portentous solidarity of those who have been chosen to be allowed to read" as well as his sense of the "power of reading" are ideal jumping-off points for thinking about the implications of literacy in the eighteenth-century anglophone world. For example, as I discuss later in this chapter, the "power of reading" is implicated in the way that nonnormative forms of writing are suddenly subject to standardizing translation toward the end of the century. As an added benefit, perhaps one more aesthetic than conceptual, the etymological relationship that Sloterdijk traces between "grammar" and "glamour" provides an aid for thinking about the social or "communitarian fantas[ies]" that subtend literacy. "Grammar," which in Sloterdijk means the learned rules of linguistic propriety, as well as the ability to read and decipher texts, and "glamour," which here might be taken to mean the aura, allure, or mystery that attends a learned individual's literate self-presentation, are mutually reinforcing semiotic concepts. By gesturing to the point of semantic overlap between these two words, Sloterdijk isolates the relationship between learning (grammar) and those mystifying powers and privileges that are derived from or contingent on learning (glamour). From this, we can say that grammar enables glamour just as glamour arrogates to itself the right to determine what counts as grammar. Adapting this circular operation to an eighteenth-century imperial context is revealing. The power to control grammar, by which I mean the power to control who uses what language and how, justifies itself by way of the cultural and commercial glamours assumed to accompany grammar. Likewise, the glamour sometimes adduced to imperial power is at least partially apparent in empire's tendency to continually interdict other human structures of making meaning in favor of those that are immediately autoaggrandizing to the linguistic systems put in place by imperial power itself.

To understand anglophony's notion of the "power of reading" as it is develops and endures as a feature of public identity into the present, one must first confront the eighteenth-century meaning of literacy, a concept with far finer gradations than illiteracy, its supposed opposite.[5] Whereas "illiteracy" names the total absence of a certain set of variable reading skills, literacy names a process of perpetual proof: proof of comprehension, proof of mastery, proof of participation in the reading of meaningful texts. Changes in the definition of the word "literacy" register Standard English's increasing importance. Inversely, they also register Latinity's dwindling currency during the eighteenth century. For example, many usages of the term "literacy" from this period continued to define the word strictly as written and reading fluency in the classical languages, Latin and Greek. According to the Oxford English Dictionary's 1748 quotation of Philip Dormer Stanhope, Fourth Earl of Stanhope's own gloss of the word, "The word illiterate, in its common acceptation, means a man who is ignorant of those two languages [Greek and Latin]." Interestingly, "illiteracy" likely also hearkened back to twelfth- and thirteenth-century ecclesiastical law stipulating that clergy, and later, laypeople, could stake a claim for *privilegium clericale* (benefit of clergy)—the right to be tried by a canon law court instead of secular court—based on the ability to read a biblical passage. Until 1706, when courts abolished the descendants of these literacy tests, an "illiterate" was defined as someone unable to claim that he or she understood Latin. By contrast, a person "literate" in Latin stood at the very boundary of the jurisdiction of secular law. This sense of the word persisted in that it provided a hierarchy of possible legal characters one could have with respect to the state. Similarly, it is during the mid- to late eighteenth century that "illiteracy" transitioned from meaning an inability to read in Greek and Latin to meaning an inability to read or write in any language, vernacular or otherwise.

Literacy's shifting technical definitions share a common semantic core: the ability to participate in publicly sanctioned acts of reading. Those who can participate in such acts experience literacy as a skill. Patrolling the boundary of acceptable uses of reading is the point of Hannah More's pamphlet *Village Politics* (1792), an antirevolutionary dialogue published repeatedly during the heady days of the early 1790s.[6] In this work, which is smattered with vernacularisms but does not necessarily rise to the level of full dialect writing, More invents two characters who fall under the text's address to "All the Mechanics Journeymen, and Day Labourers, in Great Britain." These two everymen are Tom Hod and Jack Anvil. More's dialogue engages Tom and Jack in a discussion of the politics of literacy and linguistic community. Though their discussion ranges widely among topics like freedom, constitutionalism, prices, revolutionary action, and sovereign rights, at heart it is an extended dialogue that interrogates the meanings of anglophone literacy for individuals whom More positions below political participation.[7]

From the moment the dialogue begins, when Jack asks Tom, "What book art reading? Why dost look so like a hang-dog?" and Tom gazes inquisitively at his book, responding, "Why I find here that I'm very unhappy, and very miserable; which I should never have known if I had not had the good luck to meet with this book," More creates a situation in which the literacy of the working class, especially the literacy of the working class as applied to political tracts like Paine's *The Rights of Man* (1791), tends toward being oppressive rather than liberatory.[8] Tom is put to the test immediately as Jack interrogates his reading comprehension. By virtue of this interrogation, Tom learns that reading is why he is unhappy. He has wasted his time reading illegitimate books filled with unsanitary political ideas. Through Jack, More recasts all of Tom's political dissatisfaction as a result of desultory reading practices that are extraneous rather than elemental to his laboring life. In Jack's view, unsanctioned forms of literacy taint one's otherwise positive experience of organic life in an orderly and hierarchical social system. As he puts it, it is a "good sign tho'; that you can't find out you're unhappy without looking into a book for it."[9] Jack consoles Tom, as though to say, at least in your actual laboring life you do not experience the same dissatisfaction as when you read about your laboring life.

Tom is figured as someone who is subliterate and who has a habit of reading the wrong texts in the wrong ways. The dialogue sets Jack up to become the instrument of Tom's reeducation. This reeducation is not organized around refining his reading practices but instead around erasing the conclusions he has arrived at independently through reading. It is not organized around increasing the copiousness or nuance of Tom's vocabulary, but instead around convincing him why the words that he has learned represent foreign cultural pollution. Beyond reeducation, Jack's tutoring at times amounts to deeducation:

> *Tom.* What is *Philosophy*, that Tim Standish talks so much about?
>
> *Jack.* To believe that there's neither God, nor devil, nor heaven, nor hell: to dig up a wicked old fellow's rotten bones, whose books, Sir John says, have been the ruin of thousands, and to set his figure up in a church and worship him.
>
> *Tom.* And what mean the other hard words that Tim talks about—*organization* and *function*, and *civisim*, and *incivisim*, and *equalization*, and *nviolability* [*sic*], and *imprescriptible*?
>
> *Jack.* Nonsense, gibberish, downright hocus-pocus. I know 'tis not English; Sir John says 'tis not Latin; and his valet de cham says 'tis not French neither.[10]

Just as quickly as words like "civism" and "equalization" enter into Tom's vocabulary, they are expelled by his conversation with Jack, who calls them "nonsense, gibberish, downright hocus-pocus," meaningless obfuscations that Tom should not waste his time trying to understand.[11] Jack's linguistic lesson consists of describing imported words as lacking origin or substance—" 'tis not English; Sir John says 'tis not Latin"—although his authority is subtly undercut by the expression "valet de cham" (*valet de chambre*), which More includes to show that even Jack renders borrowed French phrases in oral (rather than literate) terms.

More's lifelong investments in conservative, evangelical, but also abolitionist and poor-relief politics make the antiliterate content of *Village Politics* both unsurprising and counterintuitive according to certain narratives that link literacy and liberation.[12] She sutures these strains of thought together, however, around the idea of organic social hierarchy. In this instance, More's principle satiric enemy is French Revolutionary discourse. The specter of human enslavement is present but subdued, as in Tom's exclamation, "I don't see why we are to work like slaves, while others roll about in their coaches, feed on the fat of the land, and do nothing."[13] This is a false analogy with a reasonable explanation, Jack contends, one best captured in the "fable about the Belly and the Limbs" that he proceeds to tell. When the hands and limbs of the social body refuse to work, Jack argues, it is not the belly that suffers, but instead the hands and limbs themselves, who "for want of their old nourishment . . . fell sick, pined away, and would have died, if they had not come to their senses just in time to save their lives, as I hope you will do."[14] The rich are the belly in this fable, and they are formulated as the engine of social order. Rioting or rebelling against them hurts not them but everymen like Tom and Jack.

The principle gimmick of the dialogue as it concerns literacy, then, can be distilled as follows: an antirevolutionary Jack catechizes Tom, a faulty reader, on why he should leave off reading about foreign ideas like revolution and democracy that are spilling over from France in books, pamphlets, and other ephemeral forms. Jack convinces Tom that what he is spending his time reading is subversive and meaningless because foreign political ideas have no purchase in Britain. Jack rehearses Burkean arguments against radical change, and, after some weakly mounted attempts at debate, Tom gradually acquiesces that the time he has spent exercising his literacy and listening to local political organizer Tim Standish has been a waste.[15] Tom, who had initially trumpeted his reading of French Revolutionary thinking with the proclamation “I’m for a *Constitution*, and *Organization*, and *Equalization*,” finally abandons his interest in progressive politics in favor of the status quo—a distended belly with its dependent limbs. One way to interpret this is to say that Tom falls in line with Jack’s anodyne conclusion about the dubious value of literacy, a conclusion delivered at the end of the dialogue in a quotation from an unnamed pastor, who enjoins workers to “study to be quiet, work with your hands, and mind your own business.”[16]

Here I am most concerned with the fleeting parts of this well-known text that explicitly reference education and the value of literacy, some of which I have already indicated. The racist crudeness of several passages regarding education and cultural difference—“*Jack.* Why I’d sooner go to the Negers to get learning, or to the Turks to get religion, than to the French for freedom and happiness”—is juxtaposed to the clear and rigid separation that More creates between two forms of literate behavior, one dangerous and destabilizing (Tom’s), the other safe, sanitary, and, most appropriately, proper to an anglophone milieu as understood through the linguistic and literate assumptions of the time (Jack’s).[17] The moral lesson of the text is obvious: Tom wastes his time badly misreading and miscomprehending scandalous texts like *The Rights of Man*, whereas Jack, reporting on his own work ethic, provides a model of decorous literate behavior among the working class: “I have but little time for reading, and such as I should only read a bit of the best.”[18] Jack’s view of education and proper literate behavior is further captured in the following terms: “I read my bible, go to church, and think of a treasure in heaven,” and by this right he believes it is up to him to continually correct Tom, as in this contrapuntal exchange:

> *Tom.* What is the *new* Rights of Man?
> *Jack.* Battle, murder, and sudden death.
> *Tom.* What is it to be an *enlightened people*?
> *Jack.* To put out the light of the gospel, confound right and wrong, and grope about in pitch darkness.[19]

It is a simple but effective structure for a document of its kind. Everything that Tom has read relating to revolutionary politics is wrong. Every redefinition Jack provides on these subjects serves as an insightful linguistic lesson in appropriate forms of intercultural translation. The definition Tom has imbibed of the French Revolution from Paine, Tim Standish, and others is his most egregious act of literate misbehavior. Jack redefines the world-historical event in these terms for his misreading friend, " 'Tis all a lie, Tom. . . . 'Tis all murder, and nakedness, and hunger; many of the poor soldiers fight without victuals, and march without cloaths. These are your *Democrats!* Tom."[20]

Tom's complete capitulation to Jack's interventions into his literate understanding of the political world is expected. As the text progresses, Jack's speeches become longer and more elaborate; Tom's questions and interjections become shorter, simpler, and more sympathetic.[21] At one moment, Jack describes a potentially apocalyptic outcome of a revolution in Britain on French democratic ideals.

> *Jack.* . . . But, when this leveling comes about, there will be no firmaries, no hospitals, no charity-schools, no Sunday-schools, where so many hundred thousand poor should learn to read the word of God for nothing. For who is to pay for them? *equality* can't afford it; and those that may be willing won't be able.[22]

Jack turns the question of literacy back on Tom, who at this point in the dialogue is still asserting the idea that his reading of revolutionary literature has been meaningful to his understanding of himself as a political actor. Only the "belly" can subsidize the "charity-schools" and "Sunday-schools," in which "so many hundred thousand poor should learn to read the world of God for nothing," Jack seems to say. By protesting, leveling, and arguing for expanded rights, workers end up destroying the only route most of them have toward the acquisition of a meaningful and sanctioned form of literacy. Tom must choose: his freedom to read and interpret revolutionary literature or his class compatriots' privilege to read essential works like "the word of God." Choosing the former is exceedingly dangerous. Revolutionary France provides an instructive example of the social convulsions that are generated when people are unable to read and individually interpret the Bible. "Now that [a vernacular Bible] they had not in France: the bible was shut up in an unknown Heathenish tongue."[23] Unlike was the case in France, the King James Version of the Bible is here alluded to as a translation executed by highly educated members of the belly who were licensed to patrol literacy in the interest of those on whom this skill was bestowed.

Far from a fractious, exploitative, and "ruined" society, as Tom initially has it, Jack's lesson climaxes in a litany of blessings that, exterior to the free exercise of literacy, compensate for its absence.

> *Jack*. I'll tell thee how we are ruined.—We have a king so loving, that he would not hurt the people if he could; and so kept in, that he could not hurt the people if he would. We have as much liberty as can make us happy and more trade and riches than allows us to be good. We have the best laws in the world, if they were more strictly enforced; and the best religion in the world, if it was but better followed.[24]

The invocation of "trade and riches," "the best laws," and "the best religion" as the consolations of British life paints literacy as an ancillary need, a need that may be indulged only insofar as reading does not upset the ongoing stability of commercial, legal, and religious practice. It is both fitting and excessive that by this point Tom has been driven into an anti-Jacobin and antiliterate frenzy. He plots to reroute his revolutionary energy to a local pub where Tim Standish goes so that he can "put an end to that fellow's work."[25] He pauses before executing this plan in order to renounce nonbiblical reading altogether, frantically proclaiming, "No; first I'll stay to burn my book, and then I'll go and make a bonfire and—."[26] Here he is derailed by the last of Jack's lessons. Jack tells him there is no reason to drink, riot, or build a bonfire—these actions (like unregulated literacy) are antithetical to a stable society. While Jack chastises Tom for his plan to attack Tim Standish and build a bonfire, he says nothing about not burning Paine's book. More's dialogue between Tom and Jack concludes that Tom's capacity to freely exercise literacy is itself a fiction, as is his status as an effectual political actor.

Legibility and Translation

> We have often expressed a wish that our various dialects might be rescued from oblivion, while yet in existence. Even at this moment they are gradually vanishing: and, unless the last vestiges be speedily caught, it will be in vain to seek for them hereafter.[27]

I began this chapter with a close reading of More's *Village Politics* because the pamphlet represents a conservative turn against unsanctioned self-assertions of linguistic and literate practices that characterize the latter half of the eighteenth century. In this case, More anticipates (and recapitulates) the situations of Lyons and Ngũgĩ, as discussed in Chapter 1. More's pamphlet can be read as a signpost along the narrowing road through the aesthetic potentialities of nonnormative anglophone reading and writing, a road that leads to the formation of dialectology and ethnography as early as the late eighteenth century. In this respect, More's pamphlet brings together—but also to a certain extent closes the door on—a series of innovative writing practices within anglophony that assemble nonnormative language forms in order to act on and redraw the boundaries of aesthetic space. The texts I bring together in this second section of the chapter trouble the "power of reading" as it is policed in More's rendering of the conversation between the characters Jack and Tom. These texts deploy a daring repertoire of signifying practices in order to rescript possible meanings of literacy. Formally, they are interestingly complex.

Andrew Brice's *An Exmoor Scolding* (first published 1727; first extant edition 1746) and *An Exmoor Courtship* (1746) alongside the many versions of John Collier's *A View of the Lancashire Dialect by Way of Dialogue* (1746) represent a series of alluring paths not taken with regard to the aesthetic potential of anglophone dialect writing. These three "dialect dialogues," and others that I will mention here in passing, are conceptual ancestors to *Village Politics* in the way that they treat Standard English literacy as a fiction.[28] Archetypal rather than unique in the eighteenth-century archive, these texts contribute to contemporary understanding of how dialect writing is enfolded into Standard English literary practice, especially the domestic novel and regional poetry, during the nineteenth century and beyond. Moreover, as prose, these texts' ludic but loaded language games create a different picture of nonnormative language use than one gets through examination of poetry or the stage. One can chart the raucous archive of nonnormative eighteenth-century anglophone writing in a variety of complementary ways, but here I have chosen to focus my comments around two important features that these specific dialect dialogues have in common. First, they invoke the spectrum of anglophone linguistic and literate differences as generative literary tropes. Secondly, both Brice and Collier are translated into Standard English during the early nineteenth century, events that shed light on the limited range of ways in which readers received and categorized nonnormative writing by that time.

A retrospective accounting of the nineteenth-century publication records of London bookseller John Russell Smith and, later, the English

Dialect Society show the gradual winnowing of the reception criteria that were applied to nonnormative writing in a later era.[29] Born in 1810, Smith opened his shop on Old Compton Street in the early 1830s. From that point on, he became anglophone publishing's foremost bibliographer of dialect texts. Additionally, he reprinted and sold many such texts, especially those that captured or translated forms of anglophone identity that Smith believed were rapidly disappearing from British life. From his shop between London's Covent Garden and Soho, Smith dealt in books investigating the linguistic habits and particularities of the British archipelago's most remote corners. His hub's spokes extended widely, both in generic and geographical terms, and in this respect, his bibliographies (and later expansions of them) are an indispensable source for anyone interested in reactions to the imposition of Standard English as they erupted in the work of writers seeking visibility and aesthetic standing for nonnormative linguistic forms.[30]

Smith's *A Bibliographical List of the Works That Have Been Published Towards Illustrating the Provincial Dialects of England* (1839) offers an account of eighteenth- and early nineteenth-century forays into the written representation of oral anglophone lects.[31] The bibliography is organized geographically and contains more than one hundred listings under subheadings for English counties, cities, and regions. To take one short and representative listing, "Devonshire" provides a sampling of authors, titles, dates, and publication locations for texts that staged the particularities of the human voice in Devonshire. I have corrected authorship details, reordered the listings chronologically, shortened titles, excised notes, and condensed publication details in order to give a brief sampling of what a mid-nineteenth-century buyer of Smith's bibliography might expect to find:

(1) Andrew Brice, *An Exmoor Scolding, in the Propriety and Decency of the Exmoor Language, Between Two Sisters*, (*Gentleman's Magazine*, 1746); (A New Edition, London: 1839).

(2) John Walcot, "The Royal Visit to Exeter, by John Ploughshare, A Poetical Epistle by John Ploughshare," in *The Works of Peter Pindar*, Vol. 3 (1795).

(3) William Humphrey Marshall, *The Rural Economy of the West of England* (London, 1796);

(4) Mary Palmer, *A Dialogue in the Devonshire Dialect* (in three parts) (London, 1837);

(5) John Phillips, *A Devonshire Dialogue* (in four parts, to which is added a Glossary, for the most part by the Late Reverend John Phillips (London, 1839).[32]

The third title may seem like an ill-fitting outlier. Smith, ever thorough but not always accurate, includes this third title because, as his notes report, "Vol. 1, pp. 323–332, contains a Glossary of the Provincialisms of West Devonshire."[33] Indeed, all the Devonshire texts on Smith's list contain dialect glossaries. Important to my argument, four of the five texts grouped under "Devonshire" are fictive, inventive, and indeed literary rather than ethnographic or anthropological. However, later tradition treats them all as naturalistic representations of Devon's regional speech forms.

Smith's bibliography is an example of the evolving protocols of aesthetic reception relating to literacy that this chapter is interested in documenting.[34] His bibliography records two main types of works: works that make some effort to demonstrate or exemplify the diverse linguistic habits of British regional life, and works that seek to translate or make legible those linguistic habits for Standard English readers. At the level of organization, there is no attempt to mark those works that are the products of invention rather than ethnographic observation. Put plainly, Smith's ordering principles do not seem to include the idea that the texts he is compiling might carry aesthetic rather than narrowly documentary features. The bibliography amounts to a national linguistic census.[35] As in Francis Grose's *A Classical Dictionary of the Vulgar Tongue* (1785) and *A Provincial Glossary, with a Collection of Local Proverbs, and Popular Superstitions* (1787), Smith perhaps sees his project as a corrective or supplement to the normative lexicography of Samuel Johnson, whose dictionary disdained "cant" and regionalisms in favor of words with a standard linguistic currency. For these reasons, Smith's bibliographic work paints a much more saturated picture of British anglophony than Johnson does.[36]

Smith lists the first print appearance of *An Exmoor Scolding* as 1746. Book historian Ian Maxted, the keeper of a valuable digital repository relating to the British book trade, reports, "The early dialect work *An Exmoor Scolding* has also been attributed to him [Brice], the first part appearing in his newspaper [*Brice's Weekly Journal* (Exeter)] of 2 June 1727."[37] Smith's omission of this earliest version is understandable given that access to the archives of such a small publication would have been complicated. Nonetheless, 1746 is a convenient year to mark an important development in the history of regional British writing, and indeed, a crucial year for Andrew Brice.[38] I make this claim because it was during this one year—in fact over the course of a few summer months—that Brice's dialect writing came before a large anglophone public for the first time by way of the *Gentleman's Magazine*. Moreover, it was within the pages of this same publication and during this same year that John Collier's first dialect work, *A View of the Lancashire Dialect by Way of Dialogue*, reached its own nonregional audience.

D. M. Horgan summarizes the publication history of this single year as follows (I have added the relevant dates and article numbers in brackets): "The *Exmoor Courtship* was first printed in the *Gentleman's Magazine*, 16 (1746), 297–300 [June 1746, Article VII], followed by the first printing of *An Exmoor Scolding*, 353–5 [July 1746, Article VIII], which was only later published at Exeter. This in turn is followed by (pp. 405–8) *An Exmoor Vocabulary* [August 1746]. . . . The same issue of the *Gentleman's Magazine*, in sharp contrast, gives a very dismissive account (pp. 527–8) of Tim Bobbin's first published work, *A View of the Lancashire Dialect* [October 1746]."[39] Between June and October, in other words, four separate and quite different anglophone dialect texts—three separate dialect dialogues and one glossary by two different writers—were presented to an anglophone readership. Except for the glossary, each of these texts was also published in stand-alone form in 1746 and frequently thereafter.[40] In researching these titles, I have located and examined the 1746 editions, an individual edition of *An Exmoor Scolding* that was published at Exeter in 1750 (fourth edition), as well as combined editions of *An Exmoor Scolding* and *An Exmoor Courtship* that were published at Exeter in 1768 (sixth edition), 1771 (seventh edition), 1775 (eighth edition), 1782 (ninth edition) and 1788 (tenth edition).[41]

We can start to mark an important set of developments relating to translation during the latter half of the century. Beginning with the seventh edition in 1771, all later combined editions of *An Exmoor Scolding* and *An Exmoor Courtship* advertise on the title page that the volume includes "Such Marginal NOTES, and a VOCABULARY or GLOSSARY, at the End, as seem necessary for explaining uncouth Expressions, and interpreting barbarous Words and Phrases." More revealingly, starting with an unnumbered edition published in 1794, the title page also announces that "A Collateral Paraphrase in Plain English, For explaining barbarous Words and Phrases" is "adjoined" to the dialogues (Figure 4). Further editions published in 1795,

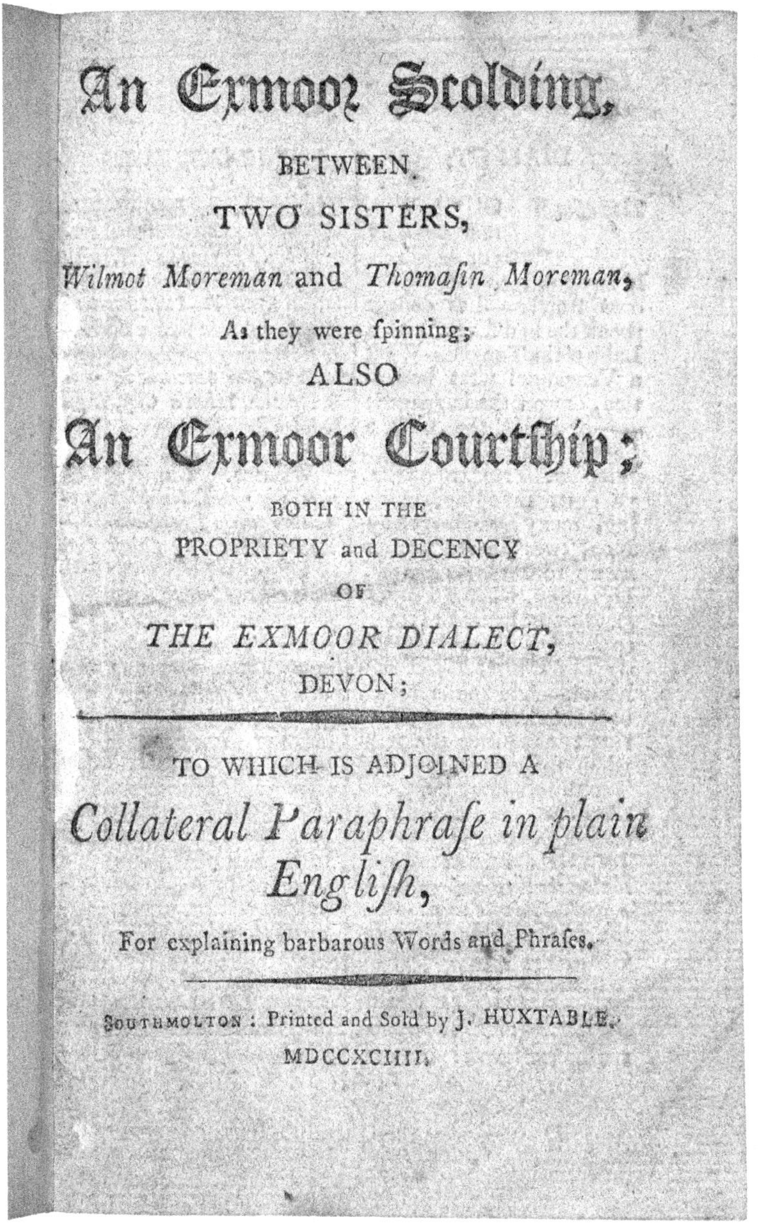

An Exmoor Scolding,

BETWEEN

TWO SISTERS,

Wilmot Moreman and *Thomaſin Moreman*,

As they were ſpinning;

ALSO

An Exmoor Courtſhip;

BOTH IN THE

PROPRIETY and DECENCY

OF

THE EXMOOR DIALECT,

DEVON;

TO WHICH IS ADJOINED A

Collateral Paraphraſe in plain Engliſh,

For explaining barbarous Words and Phraſes.

SOUTHMOLTON: Printed and Sold by J. HUXTABLE.

MDCCXCIIII.

FIGURE 4. The 1794 edition of *An Exmoor Scolding* is the first to be printed in two columns with the dialect text on the left and a "Collateral Paraphrase in plain English, for explaining barbarous Words and Phrases," on the right. Reproduced with permission courtesy of the British Library.

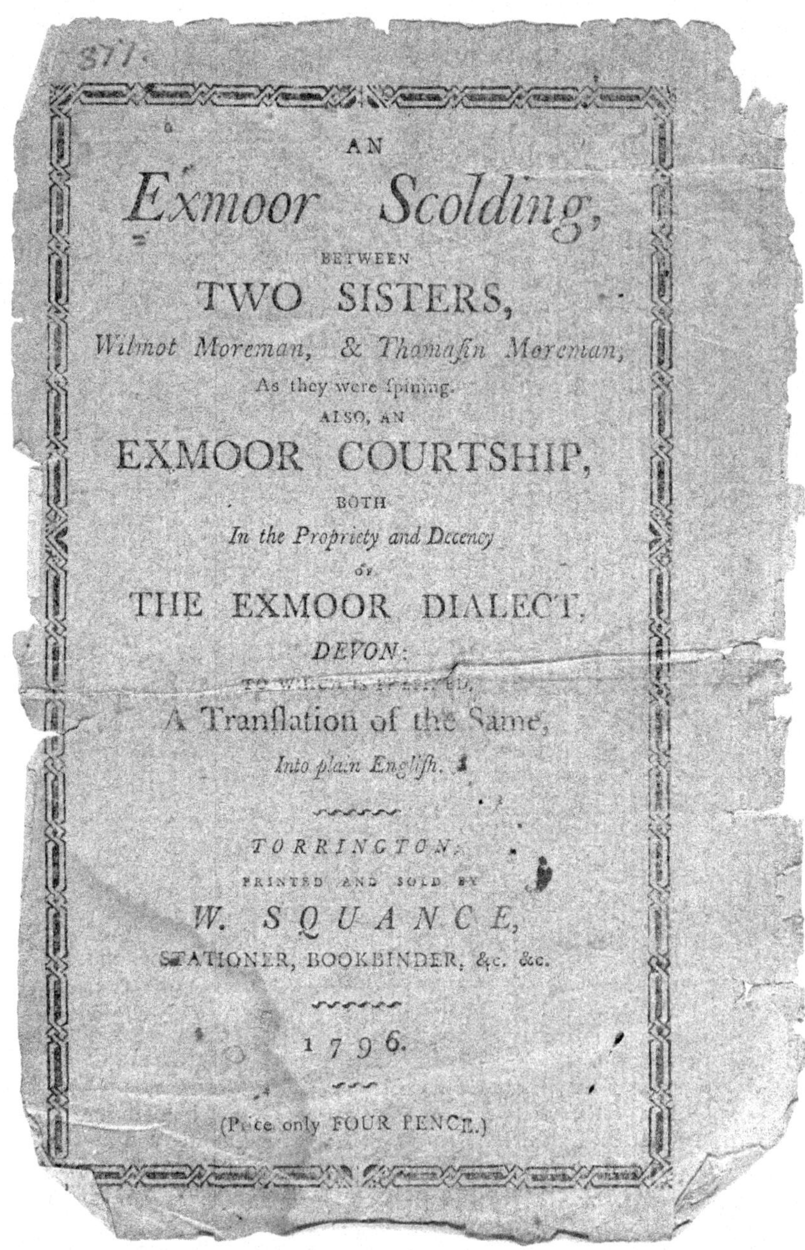

AN

Exmoor Scolding,

BETWEEN

TWO SISTERS,

Wilmot Moreman, & Thomaſin Moreman;

As they were ſpining.

ALSO, AN

EXMOOR COURTSHIP,

BOTH

In the Propriety and Decency

OF

THE EXMOOR DIALECT,

DEVON:

TO WHICH IS PREFIXED,

A Tranſlation of the Same,

Into plain Engliſh.

TORRINGTON:

PRINTED AND SOLD BY

W. SQUANCE,

STATIONER, BOOKBINDER, &c. &c.

1796.

(Price only FOUR PENCE.)

FIGURE 5. Following the exceedingly rare 1795 edition, several editions of *An Exmoor Scolding* refer to the Standard English accompaniment as a "translation." Pictured here is the 1796 edition. Reproduced with permission courtesy of Harvard University Library.

1796, and after modify alter this textual commodity dramatically.[42] Not only do they swap "paraphrase" for "translation" on the title page, they also announce that "A Translation of the Same, Into plain English," is "perfixed" to the dialogues, "perfix" here meaning "to fix firmly or definitively" (Figure 5).[43] For the rest of this chapter, all the quotations from Brice's Exmoor dialogues will be presented in "bilingual" facing-page format as it appears in these late eighteenth-century editions.[44]

The continuous, nearly one-hundred-year publishing afterlife of Brice's dialogues exemplifies the way that fictive dialect dialogues are gradually taken to be accurate and naturalistic representations of regional lectic speech and behavior over the course of the nineteenth century, which Brice could never have anticipated. According to Maxted's short biography, Brice published newspapers in Exeter for most of his life. He was a doting father, quondam poet, and theater buff. According to the *Universal Magazine*, "more women were trained as printers in his office than in almost any office in England, it being common to see three or four at work."[45] There is little one can conclude regarding this reference to Brice's seemingly forward-looking practices relating to gender and work. If true, it is complicated by the fact that *An Exmoor Scolding* is, in effect, a ribald, theatrical, and at times violent dialect dialogue—a long exchange of visceral insults—between two women, sisters Thomasin and Wilmot Moreman, women who, largely lacking interiority, seem all at once to detest and rely on one another. There are small moments of fellow feeling and mutual care between the sisters, but these are not the rule. In general Brice's fictionalization of Exmoor women emphasizes their mutual antagonism as it plays out in bawdy wordplay (Figure 6).

The structures of both *An Exmoor Scolding* and *An Exmoor Courtship* are relatively simple. Drawing on the principles of staged verbal performance in the theater, *An Exmoor Scolding* sees Thomasin and Wilmot trade insults, one for one. They accuse one another of things like promiscuity, ugliness, stupidity, irreverence, and laziness, accusations that make for a sometimes exhausting back and forth that culminates in a physical altercation in which one sister tries to strangle the other. Intensifying the combative flavor of this text, the 1794, 1795, and 1796 editions are divided into two parts: "Bout the First," and "Bout the Second," whereas the initial editions had no such division. The quotations below provide a sense of *An Exmoor Scolding*'s dialect writing as it appears next to its anonymous, Standard English intralingual translation in 1794 and beyond:

AN EXMOOR SCOLDING.

ORIGINAL LANGUAGE.

Thomaſin. LOCK! *Wilmot,* vor why vor ded'ſt roily zo upon ma up to *Challacomb* Rowl?—Ees dedent thenk tha had'ſt a be zich a Labbo' tha Tongue.—What a Vengance! wart betwatled, or wart tha baggaged;—or had'ſt tha took a Shord, or a paddled?

Wilmot. I roily upon tha, ya gurt, thonging, banging, muxy Drawbreech?—Noa, 'twas *thee* roil'ſt upon *me* up to *Doraty Vogwill's* Upzitting, whan tha *vungſt* (and to be hang'd to tha!) to *Rabbin.*—Should zem tha wart zeek arter Me-at and Me-al—And zo tha mearſt, by ort es know, wey guttering; as gutter tha wutt whan tha com'ſt to good Tackling.—But zome zed *Shoor and ſheer tha ded'ſt bet make wiſe, to ſee nif tha young* Joſy Heaff-field *wou'd come to zlack thy boddice, and whare a wou'd be O vore or no.*——Bet 'twas the old Diſyeaſe, Chun.

Thomaſin. Hey go! What Diſyeaſe deſt me-an, ya gurt duggedteal'd, ſwapping, rouſling Blowze? Ya gurt Roile, tell ma. Tell ma, a zey, what Diſyeaſe deſt me-an?—Ad! chell ream my Heart to tha avore Iſe let tha lipped.—Chell tack et ou wi' tha to tha true Ben fath! Tell ma, a zey, what Diſyeaſe deſt me-an, that tha zeſt cham a troubled wey?

Wilmot. Why; ya purting

TRANSLATED.

Thomaſin. ALACK! *Wilmot,* wherefore did'ſt thou rail ſo againſt me up to *Challacomb* Revel?—I did not think thou had'ſt been ſuch a Blab.—In the name of Vengeance! wer't befooled, or bewitched;—or had'ſt thou taken a Cup, or got fuddled?

Wilmot. I rail againſt thee, you great, longing, unwieldy, dirty Draggle-tail?—No, *thou* rail'ſt againſt *me,* at *Dorothy Fogwell's* Chriſtening-Feaſt, when thou ſtood'ſt Godmother (hang thee!) to *Robin.*—It ſeems thou wert ſick after Meals—and ſo thou migh'ſt, for aught I know, with guttling; as guttle thou wilt when thou comeſt to good Victuals——But ſome ſaid, *Truely thou did'ſt but counterfeit: to try whether the young* Joſeph Heathfield *would come to ſlacken thy Stays, and whether he would be anxious about thee or not.*—But 'twas thy old Diſeaſe, Quean.

Thomaſin. Heydey! What Diſeaſe doſt mean, you great draggletail'd, clumſy, ruſtling Slammerkin? you great Hoyden, tell me. Tell me, I ſay, what Diſceaſe doſt mean?—Egad! I'll ſplit my Lungs, before I let thee reſt.—I'll ſcold it out with thee to the purpoſe, faith! Tell me, I ſay, what Diſeaſe doſt mean, that thou ſay'ſt I'm troubled with

Wilmot. Why; you pou-

FIGURE 6. The dual columns of the 1796 edition of *An Exmoor Scolding* make for a reading experience in which Standard English is a framing device. Reproduced with permission courtesy of Harvard University Library.

Promiscuity in *An Exmoor Scolding*:

Thomasin: . . . How dedst thee stertlee upon the Zess last Harest wey the young *Dick Vrogwell*, whan *George Vuzz* putch'd? He told me the whole Fump o' the Besneze.

Thomasin: . . . How didst though wriggle upon the Mow last Harvest with the young *Dick Frogwell*, when *George Furze* stacked the Hay!—He told me every circumstance of the affair.

Wilmot: . . . Nif tha dest bet go down into the Paddick, to stroak the Kee, thee wut come oll a gerred, and oll horry zo vurs tha art a vorked; ya gerred teal'd panking, hewstring Mea-zel!

Wilmot: . . . If thou dost but go down into the Park, to Milk the Cows, thou will come home all bemired, and all dawbed, as high as thou art forked; you dirtytail'd, panting, wheezing Sow!

Ugliness in *An Exmoor Scolding*

Wilmot: . . . Pitha dest think enny Theng will e'er vittee or dooddee wey zich a whatnozed, haggle-tooth'd, stare-bason, timersome, rizy, wapper' ee'd Then as thee art?

Wilmot: . . . Prithee, dost think any thing will go well or prosper with such a red-nosed, haggle-tooth'd, bare-faced, headstrong, quarrelsome, goggle-eyed thing as Thou art?

Irreverence in *An Exmoor Scolding*:

Wilmot: . . . And whan tha dest zey mun [prayers], 'tis bet wilst tha art scrubbing, hewstring, and rittling abed. . . . 'Tes a Mail if e'er tha comst to Hewn only to zey men, zence tha ne'er zest men, chell warndy, but whan tha art half azlape, half-dozy, or scrubbing o' tha scabbed Yess.

Wilmot: . . . And when thou dost say them [prayers], it is only when thou art scratching, and coughing, and wheezing in bed. . . . 'Tis a Wonder if e'er thou goest to Heaven for saying they Prayers, since though never sayest them, I'll warrant, but when thou art half-asleep, half-drowsy, or scrubbing thy scabbed A—.[46]

The effect of the juxtaposition of dialect and its Standard English translation is to estrange the dialect and its speakers. At the same time, this estrangement is a familiar estrangement. Vocalized, phonetic reading of the text increases this feeling of anglophone familiarity and intelligibility. Read aloud, "He told me the whole Fump o' the Besneze" does not sound like "He told me every circumstance of the affair." However, it does resemble "He told me the whole fump of the business," a less domesticating rendering that quite clearly captures the sense of familiar estrangement I am describing. Whereas earlier, nontranslated versions of the text plunged readers into a difficult experiment with literacy's limits, the perfixed translations added in editions after 1795 encourage the reader to continually compare written norms with their oral foils.

At the level of plot, *An Exmoor Courtship* is straightforward. Andrew, a young farmer, proposes marriage to his cousin Margery—conceivably the same Margery from *An Exmoor Scolding*, though this is conjecture. Margery asks Wilmot for her advice. Later, when Andrew and Margery take a walk to her elderly grandmother's house, Margery learns that she stands to inherit some money. "Oh!" she tells Andrew, "Grammer's wor Vower Hundred Pounds, recken tha Goods indoor and out a door" ("Oh! Grandmother is worth Four Hundred Pounds, reckoning the Goods within Door and without").[47] Ultimately Andrew and Margery agree to marry.

As in *An Exmoor Scolding*, Brice's dialect writing queries the fictionality of Standard English literacy. I arrive at this interpretation in the following way. Brice's method is to transcribe lectic forms of speech in alphabetic writing. Alphabetic writing was known to most literate anglophones only through standardizing texts.[48] Orally, these forms of speech would have been comprehensible to a certain variety of anglophones. In writing, however, they take on a more pronounced air of difference and estrangement. To read Brice, readers must exercise their techniques of literacy differently, for truly, the meaning of literacy here is different. It is worth emphasizing that this is precisely the situation of literacy that I described in relation to Reverend Lyons. Lyons is troubled by the trend that those who are capable of reading Irish are *also and primarily* capable of reading Standard English. Similarly, and given the way literacy education works, those who are capable of reading dialect writing are *also and primarily* capable of reading Standard English. The copresentation of dialect and standard allows a reader to move between these two forms. Pleasure exists in their difference and comparability.

In at one moment of the courtship, Andrew and Margery discuss whether or not Andrew will be charged for defending Margery in a physical altercation:

> *Margery*: Well, es thenk ye, Cozen *Andra*, for taking wone's Peart zo.—Bet cham agest he'll go vor a Varrant vor ye, and take ye havore tha Cunsabel; and than ye may be bound over, and be vorst to g'in to Exter to Zizes; and than a mey zvear tha Peace of es, you know.—Es en et better to drenk Vriend and make et up?

> *Margery*: Well, I thank you, Cousin *Andrew*, for taking my part so.—But I am afraid he'll go for a Warrant for you, and take you before the Constable; & then you may be bound over & be forced to go to *Exeter* at the Assizes; and then he may swear the Peace of us, you know.—Is it not better to drink and be Friends, and make it up?[49]

These counterpoised forms of literacy make an interesting case for analysis. The dialect text is readable; it requires only that the normative reader make small and relatively regular syntax and sound substitutions. Reading both texts together troubles the coherence of linguistic normativity itself. After all, normative forms of print and literacy enable and condition one's reading experience of the nonnormative forms. Like most good reading, Brice's Exmoor dialogues invite one into these dimensions of linguistic multiplicity. Recourse to a glossary or editorial notes is not necessary, but it is educational. If a contemporary reader opts for reading only the translation, that reader overlooks the aesthetic dimensions of dialect texts like these, texts that are designed to put Standard English's political and aesthetic dimensions into question by engaging readers in new and heterodox modes of reading.

John Collier's *A View of the Lancashire Dialect by Way of Dialogue* is formally similar to Brice's Exmoor dialogues, though substantially different in plot and theme (Figure 7). Collier's language as filtered through the pseudonym Tim Bobbin is meant to be a creative rendering of lectic speech as it exists in Lancashire. In Collier, the stories of village life are a bit more episodic. They are also more upbeat, happy-go-lucky, but not uncritical in tone and atmosphere. In addition, Collier leaves a far larger imprint on the eighteenth-century archive than Brice's works. J. A. Hilton, writing in 1970, summarizes the complex story of this text's publication history in the following statistics: "There were seven reprints in the author's lifetime, the

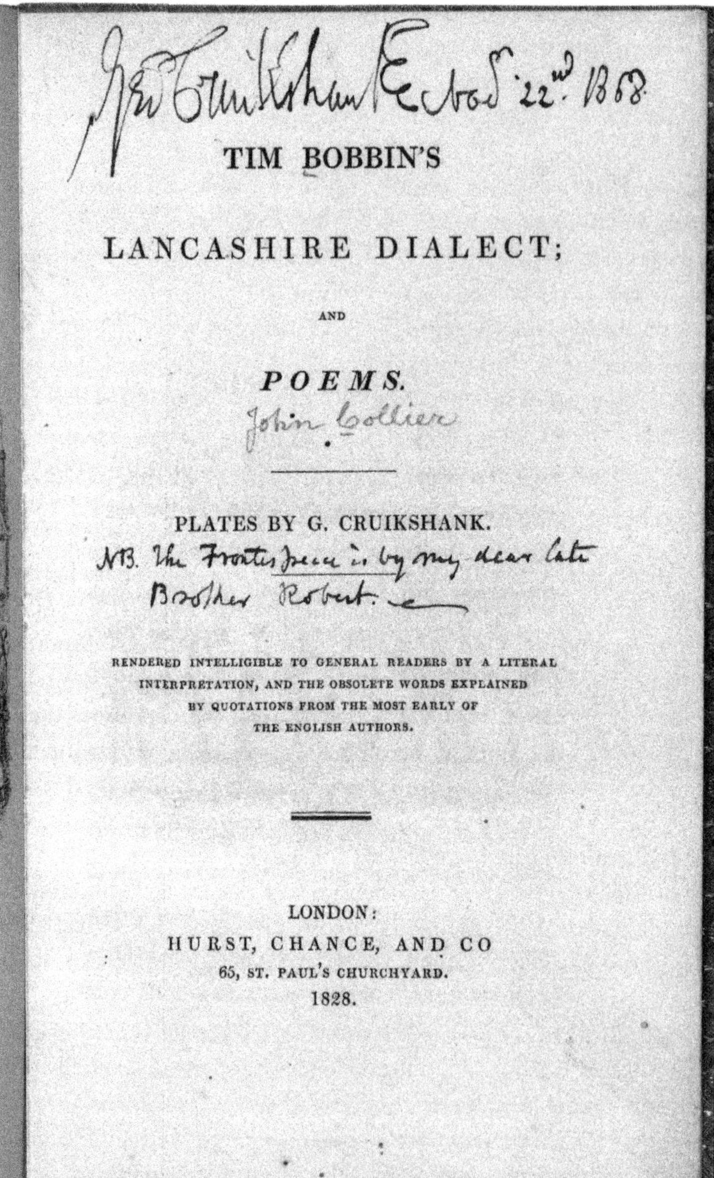

TIM BOBBIN'S

LANCASHIRE DIALECT;

AND

POEMS.

PLATES BY G. CRUIKSHANK.

RENDERED INTELLIGIBLE TO GENERAL READERS BY A LITERAL INTERPRETATION, AND THE OBSOLETE WORDS EXPLAINED BY QUOTATIONS FROM THE MOST EARLY OF THE ENGLISH AUTHORS.

LONDON:
HURST, CHANCE, AND CO
65, ST. PAUL'S CHURCHYARD.
1828.

FIGURE 7. The 1828 reprint of *The Lancashire Dialect* includes a translation into Standard English that renders the text "intelligible to general readers by a literal interpretation" because, as the introduction notes, "many have regretted they could not enter into the spirit of the work for want of such 'humble knowledge.'" Reproduced with permission courtesy of Harvard University Library.

edition of 1775, selling 6,000 copies, there were numerous pirated versions, a mark of success, and in one form or other it ran to a total of sixty-four editions by the end of the nineteenth century."[50] Collier was also a skilled caricaturist. He wrote multiple texts under the name Tim Bobbin. His dialect dialogues were published in combination with a substantial number of dialect poems over the course of the period Hilton mentions. As was true for the Exmoor dialogues during the 1790s, *A View of the Lancashire Dialect by Way of Dialogue* was "rendered intelligible to general readers by a literal interpretation, and the obsolete words explained by quotations from the most early of the English authors" in 1828.[51]

Structured as the conversational retelling of a picaresque series of unfortunate, degrading, and surprising episodes in one local man's life, Collier gets a lot of traction out of the bumbling miscomprehension of the main character Tummus and his bad luck.

Bad Luck in *A View of the Lancashire Dialect by Way of Dialogue*

Tummus: Mark whot e tell the Meary; for I think lunge rot fok liv'n an'th' moor mischoances they han.	*Thomas*: Mark what I tell thee, Mary; for I think the longer that folks live, the more mischances they have.
Tummus: Odds heart, howd teh tung, *Meary*; far I oather angurt some he witch, or the dule threw his club o'er meh that morning when eh geete up: far misfartins coom on me os thick os leet.	*Thomas*: Dear heart, hold thy tongue, Mary; for I had vexed either some he-witch, or the devil threw his club over me that morning when I got up, for misfortunes came on me as thick as lightning.[52]

An example of what today we might call slapstick comedy, but slapstick with a parodic edge, Tummus is a good-natured character who relates his mishaps to Meary, a romantic interest, in generally optimistic terms. For example, he tells her a farcical story about trying to catch an owl in a barn and falling off a ladder after having had some local bullies throw their urine all over him.

Slapstick in *A View of the Lancashire Dialect by Way of Dialogue*

Tummus: Eigh, faw eigh, for I thowt I'd brok'n th' crupper-booan o meh—boh it wur better in lickly; for I'd naw hurt boh th' tone theawm stunnisht, on th' skin bruzz'd off th' whirlbooan o meh knee, ot mede meh t'hawmpoo o bit.	*Thomas*: Ay! Fall! Ay! For I thought I'd broken the crupper-bone of my bottom; but it was better than I expected, for I'd no hurt but one thumb sprained and the skin bruised of the round bone of my knee, that made me limp a bit.[53]

Outrageous episodes like these accumulate as the text progresses.

Eventually these episodes add up to a political critique of class hierarchy and the asymmetrical power imbalance of London over the British regions. For example, Thomas worries throughout the text about his master beating or even killing him. These fears culminate toward the end of the text in an oblique moment of political intervention. Through Tummus, Collier points out that misfortune is rarely just misfortune but instead organized subjection. In another instance, Tummus asks, "Had not this a strong savour of fair cheating; nay downright biting of poor folk?" And Mary replies, "But great folks often do what they will, with little ones, right or wrong, what care they?"

Hierarchy/Intervention in *A View of the Lancashire Dialect by Way of Dialogue*

Tummus: . . . for th' last oandurth boh one me measter had lik't o killt meh: on just neaw, os shure os thee and me ar stonning here, I'm actilly running meh country. (1828; 4).	*Thomas*: . . . for the last evening but one, my master had like to have killed me; and just now, as thou art standing there, I'm actually running my country! (1828; 5).
Tummus: . . . I'r feeared o eawer fok seeching meh, on meh measter beasting me when he geet whooam . . . boh meh mind moot os weel o line on o pissmotehoyle, or in o rook o hollins or gorses, for it wur one o'clock ofore eh cou'd toyn me een (1828; 52).	*Thomas*: . . . I was afraid of our folk seeking me, and my master beating me when I got home . . . my mind might as well have lain in an ant's hole, or on a heap of holly or gorse, for it was one o'clock before I could close my eyes (1828; 53).

Tummus: . . . Had naw this o strung savor of fere cheeoting; ne deawn-reet nipping o poor fowk?	*Thomas*: . . . Had not this a strong savour of fair cheating; nay downright biting of poor folk?
Meary: . . . Boh great fok oft dun who te win wi littleons, reet or rank, whot kere'n they? (1828; 92).	*Mary*: . . . But great folks often do what they will, with little ones, right or wrong, what care they? (1828; 93).

The translation not only makes Collier's subtle social critiques more obvious and legible; it also dilutes them. For all his jokes and ribald gaffes, Tummus is a round, critically thinking character whose ideas ought to be read in the context of the way the text itself invests in them. The critique of Standard English literacy that is implicit in *A View of the Lancashire Dialect by Way of Dialogue*—as in Brice's Exmoor dialogues—is often most visible when juxtaposed to its translation.

Consider the way the preface to the seventh edition of Brice's *An Exmoor Scolding* appeals to the "Truth" of anecdotal observation in order to naturalize the text as a "genuine Specimen" of anglophony in that region, even at the level of syntax: "It having been alleg'd, that in the Exmoor *Scolding* particularly, the Substantives have frequently too many Adjectives annex'd to them . . . & and that the objurgatory Wenches in that Part of the country have not such a *Copia Verborum* as is here represented: But we may appear for the Truth of the contrary."[54] The editor here confirms the "Truth" that women of this region do indeed possess "a *Copia Verborum*" ("an abundance of words"). More interesting still, the seventh edition preface contains a Rousseauvian origin story that explains the regular attribution of this text to a man named Peter Lock even as it also tries to attest to the documentary "Truth" of the language used: "The following Collection was originally made, about the beginning of the present Century, by a blind itinerant Fidler. . . . His more common Converse with the lower Class of People gave him frequent Opportunities of hearing and observing their Phrases and diction; and as Persons deprived of Sight have generally a good Memory, he was thereby the better enabled to retain and repeat them."[55] The seventh edition preface even goes so far as to claim that *An Exmoor Scolding*—made up of a tissue of brutal insults—is so true-to-life that it "may be of some Use to such Lawyers as go on the Western Circuit, by whom the evidence of a Country-man is sometimes mistaken, for want of a proper Interpretation of his Language."[56]

A GLOSSARY

OF

LANCASHIRE WORDS AND PHRASES.[1]

IN WHICH MANY OF THE USELESS CORRUPTIONS ARE OMITTED, AND WHEREIN THE READER MAY OBSERVE,

That words marked	A. S.	*come from the*	Anglo-Saxon.
	Bel.		Belgic.
	Br.		British.
	Da.		Danish.
	Du.		Dutch.
	Fr.		French.
	Sw.		Swedish.
	Teu.		Teutonic.

[Many of the words in the Glossary are not found in *A View of the Lancashire Dialect*].

A

ACKERSPRIT, *a potatoe with roots at both ends.*

Actilly, *actually.* 41.

Addle, *to get; also unfruitful.* A. S.

Afterings, *the last of a cow's milk.*

Agate, *on the way.*

Agog, *set on, begun.*

Aighs, *an ax.* A. S.

An, { *if.* / *and.* } *(passim).*

Ancliff, *ancle.* A. S.

Anent, *opposite.* A. S. 57.

Appern, *apron.* 62.

Appo, *an apple.*

Ar, *are.* 41

Are, / Eawer, } *an hour, also our.*

Areawt, *out of doors.*

Ark, *a large chest.* A. S.

Arnt, *errand.* 43.

Arr (An), *a mark or scarr.*

Arren, *arrant, downright.* 45.

Arsewood, *backward, unwilling.* A. S.

Arsey-versey, *heels over head.* A. S. 49.

Ashelt, *likely, probable.* 49.

Ash, / Ax, / Axen, / Ash'n, } *ask.* A. S. *(passim).*

Ashes, / Axes, } *asks.*

Ashler, *large free stone, or moor stone.*

Asht, / Axt, } *asked.* 43.

Asker, *a nute.*

Astite, *as soon.* A. S.

At't, *at it.*

Awf, *an elf, an earthly demon.* Bel. 37.

Awkert, *untoward; also comical.* A. S. 73.

Awlung, *all owing to, because, &c.* 46.

Awlus, *always.* 41.

Awmeety, *Almighty.* 33.

Awnsert, *answered.*

[1] This Glossary is from the Sixth Edition, which contains 800 words more than were in any of the five former editions. The figures following a word indicate the page of the Dialogue where the word occurs.

FIGURE 8. The 1894 edition of John Collier's works reproduces the sixth edition of *The Lancashire Dialect*'s (1757) amplified glossary. Additionally, this late version notes the etymological origin of the words. Reproduced courtesy of the Library of Congress.

If we follow Collier's *A View of the Lancashire Dialect by Way of Dialogue* over the same period as Brice's Exmoor dialogues, we see similar but distinct patterns. Though Collier's first edition contains a small glossary, it is substantially enlarged in later editions, starting with the second edition of 1748, an edition dubbed as "very much Improv'd, with an Addition of above Five hundred *Lancashire* Words, not in the first Impression."[57] The sixth edition of 1757 goes further in that it contains "above 800 *Lancashire* Words, that never were in any of the Five first Impressions" as well as "a few Observations for the better Pronunciation of the Dialect" (Figure 8).[58] Editions in 1770, 1775, 1782, 1787, 1797, 1798, 1800, and 1819 contain these same paratexts—a glossary and pronunciation notes—but they also add poems, other episodes, engravings, and various occasional writings by Collier that flesh out his character of Tummus the "Lancashire Clown." Large collected editions of all Collier's work as Tummus come out in 1775, 1790, 1793, and 1818. Each of these stresses Collier's dedication to folkloristic philology: "Collier had been for many years," the 1818 edition records, "collecting, not only from the rustics in his own neighbourhood, but also wherever he made excursions, all the awkward, vulgar, obsolete words and *local* expressions which ever occurred to him in conversation amongst the lower class. A very retentive memory brought them safe back for insertion into his vocabulary or glossary."[59]

Charting the publication history of *An Exmoor Scolding* and *A View of the Lancashire Dialect by Way of Dialogue* is to chart the accumulation of explanatory paratexts that attempt to render dialect absolutely legible in Standard English terms. Understood another way, these texts sport with normative literacy. However, even as they reveal aesthetic qualities of the dialect writing, editorial and publishing additions eschew the dialect literacies that the texts ask readers to engage in. Standard English's delimiting clarity accretes around these texts, which gradually become examples of natural speech. Instead of being read as literary innovations or countermodels of anglophone writing's many possibilities, publishing apparatuses that were added over the course of these texts' commodity lives transform them into unmediated "true" representations of "real" speaking subjects. Echoing Daines Barrington's interest in preserving Dorothy Pentreath, the preface to the 1828 edition of *A View of the Lancashire Dialect by Way of Dialogue* claims, "The present work may prove an useful document to perpetuate the genuine English Provincial Dialect."[60] Hilton, writing a century and a half later, believes that Collier's fictive work "deserves acknowledgement as the first scientific attempt at a survey of the Lancashire dialect," a claim he backs up with reference to Collier's studies in Old and Middle English as well as his "good library."[61] Like Brice, the journalist, Collier the caricaturist certainly was a scholar and skilled observer of language. The etymologies presented in the glossary to his text make this clear. Nonetheless, ascribing scientificity to his dialect writing is to miss the significant and critical engagement with the spread of standard forms of literacy that Collier enacts through his unique linguistic choices.

An important function of the late eighteenth- and early nineteenth-century translations of these texts into Standard English is to obviate the reading process that had made these texts what they were in their dialect forms. A reader unfamiliar with the written dialect no longer needs to examine the paratexts to glean information and arrive at interpretive meanings. Instead, these translations set up a false equivalency between dialect and Standard English: two separate lects, two separate worlds, one hierarchical organization wherein Standard English is the explanatory key. These translations, in other words, register the emergence, sometime around the turn of the nineteenth century, of a Standard English reading community that now digests dialect only as naturalistic representation of regional reality rather than as the groundwork for a linguistic and literate counterpublic. In this context one finds the emergence of a new, hybrid type of dialect writing in which Standard English's explanatory and translational mechanisms are crucial to the work's aesthetic architecture.

Brogues and Bulls

> Whoever attends to the phraseology of the lower Irish may, at this day, hear many of the phrases and expressions used by Shakespeare.[62]

The domestication at work in the translations of Brice's and Collier's dialect writings is emblematic of larger late eighteenth-century trends. Works that address Standard English readers try to include anglophone linguistic difference as an aesthetic feature.[63] Whereas early, nontranslated editions of Brice and Collier posited readerships that would have been able to adapt to the form of literacy their texts demand, later dialect writing evinces more robust Standard English explanatory mechanisms and translations. Readers are encouraged to treat anglophone linguistic differences within any one text not as a metonym for alternative forms of being in language in the world but instead as evidence of dialect speakers' historical anachronism.

This is true of Charles Johnson's edited collection *Specimens of the Yorkshire Dialect* (1808), which contains, among other things, a simple verse poem that comes as close as any other dialect dialogue to succinctly capturing the power dimensions at the heart of how anglophone linguistic diversity was evolving during the period. The poem is called "The Old and New Pocket-Books, a Dialogue" and is attributed to one D. Lewis. As the poem's title suggests, the dialogue features two anthropomorphized pocketbooks having a conversation in iambic tetrameter. The old and tattered pocketbook speaks Yorkshire English whereas the shiny new one speaks in a posh register of Standard English. At one point, the new pocketbook haughtily asks himself what in the devil he is doing in such a poor, remote, and rustic house—and in the company of an old haggard pocketbook no less. In answer, the old pocketbook says that the new one has come as a replacement. The old pocketbook prophetically adds that extended use will wear the young pocketbook down too, degrading his new leather exterior until it is ragged and shabby. The young and relatively snooty pocketbook bristles at the summary of this dismal future,

Dost thou compare thyself with me?
If thou couldst but thy picture see,
Thy ragged coat, thy dirty look,
Scarce worthy of the name of book.
And must I to the fields retire,
Be prostituted to the lyre,
Companion of a rustic swain,
And ne'er return to town again?[64]

Understandably, the old pocketbook takes offense at the young upstart's pretensions,

True, thoo of higher kin may boast,
Of finer shap, an bigger cost;
Thoo's neeat an' smart, Ah mun alloo,
Bud, thoo will quit that bonny hue,
When thoo, like me, hes hardships born,
An' been by toil an' labor worn.[65]

In these two excerpts, dialect is old, beaten down, and on the verge of being discarded. The young pocketbook, a representation of the upstart invasiveness of Standard English in Yorkshire, appears haughty and cocksure, yet unaware of its own ephemerality and the contingency of its cultural appeal. As a representation of Standard English language and literacy, the new pocketbook has yet to bear hardships or be worn by labor, or so says the old pocketbook. The mode of address here is complicated. The reader is encouraged to identify with the old pocketbook—Yorkshire authenticity—but can do nothing to prevent the arrival of the new pocketbook, a harbinger of unavoidable linguistic and cultural change.

A well-known inversion of this dynamic, an inversion in which Standard English is figured as a happy rather than lamentable replacement for nonnormative linguistic practices, characterizes many of Maria Edgeworth's novels and essays. These works, especially *Castle Rackrent* (1800) and *Essay on Irish Bulls* (1802), articulate a literate pleasure that is the distinct privilege of Standard English speakers, those capable of reading a nonnormative text in conjunction with explanatory mechanisms that deform, alter, and radically recategorize the speech and thoughts of Irish anglophones. Edgeworth does this by letting language difference careen around within stately, carefully controlled Standard English prose frames. Unlike Brice and Collier, she is her own translator, in a sense. In order to understand both her approach to anglophone linguistic difference and her use of anglophone multilingualism in aesthetic practice, it is first necessary to take a short detour through Edgeworth's educationalist theories.

Edgeworth's comments regarding language learning in the second volume of *Practical Education* (1798) make clear that she has specific convictions about language and education that underwrite her fictive works. Her feelings, she says, derive from her own experiences observing her siblings' entry into language via badly formed grammars. Children waste time studying books of grammar that they are ill equipped to understand, Edgeworth declares. Children have no training in grammatical terminology, and hence, "absurd grammar, and exercise-books" lead them hopelessly astray.[66] Before students are exposed to grammars, grammatical education must begin with parents in a personal, conversational, and comfortable setting. Parents must guide their children's discovery of how linguistic forms arise from natural relationships among objects in the world. Edgeworth's pragmatic metaphor is "Much of the time that is spent in teaching boys to walk upon stilts might be more advantageously employed in teaching to walk without them."[67] Like Wordsworth, who sought the language of English peasants, and like Sir William Jones, who similarly obsessed over the "natural" expressive patterns of pastoralists from the East, Edgeworth thinks the best in language arises imminently from one's everyday confluence with family and household things.

Edgeworth's didactic writings stress that parents must discuss grammar with children because proper linguistic behavior is a habit built on close relationships, discipline, and guided study. The process should be deliberate but unhurried. When parents have figured grammar as a naturally occurring feature of the world instead of as an artificial code, children excel in literacy without trepidation. "When children have thus by degrees, and by short and clear conversations, been initiated in general grammar and familiarized to its technical terms, the first page of tremendous Lilly [William Lily, Latin grammarian] will lose much of its horror."[68] Students do not then have to flounder around the artificial structures of grammar texts; instead, the grammar of the classical languages becomes accessible, Lily's Latin grammar, as well as grammars of ancient Greek. Though Edgeworth believes that one can never actually know the "genius, pronunciation, melody, and idiom" of ancient Greek, she still concludes that classical languages like Greek are necessary in education because of the way they inform Standard English.[69] She asserts, "It is not the ambition of a gentleman to read Greek like an ancient Grecian, but to understand it as well as the generality of his contemporaries, to know whence the terms of most sciences are derived, and to be able, in some degree, to trace the progress of mankind in knowledge and refinement."[70] Ancient Greek's use value is a matter of contemporary practicality.

Given Edgeworth's argument that language is a set of personal, communicative acts that must be learned and regulated, it makes perfect sense that she should stress the necessity of learning English as quickly and thoroughly as possible. It also follows that she should be interested in accessing and broadcasting nonnormative language's quirks as both an aesthetic and educative act. If students understand and observe language the way she does, they become empowered to improve their own linguistic behavior. This is one of the things that the Edgeworths' *Essay on Irish Bulls* demonstrates thematically and textually. In this work, Standard English suggests polished fixity and resolve while the embedded examples of "Hiberno-English" dialect connote uncouth and excessive emotionality. Standard English translates and regulates dialect as it erupts. This is a work built around linguistic asymmetry.

Coauthored with her father, Richard Lovell Edgeworth, *Essay on Irish Bulls* combines theoretical and performative passages written in a hodgepodge of tones. The Edgeworths' text is playful, anecdotal, and personal. Like Brice's and Collier's works, it demands several forms of anglophone literacy but also undercuts the value of those multiple literacies at every turn. The work's structure is casual, lacking anything but the most schematic argumentative arc, sporadically alternating between imaginative ruminations on the nature of Irish anglophone speech patterns and elaborate tales of the fictive characters supposed to produce those speech patterns. Without fail, the text sternly defends Irish speech patterns, even while exaggeratedly mocking them along the way. Only in the conclusion does the father-daughter authorial team announce, "Unable any longer to support the tone of irony, we joyfully speak in our own characters, and explicitly declare our opinion, that the Irish are an ingenious, generous people."[71] As the Edgeworths acknowledge, the eighteenth-century Irish regularly fall victim to unjustified ethnic, religious, and political contempt. Consequently, it is imperative that self-flattering figures like the Edgeworths reclaim Irish "bulls" and "blunders" as literary feats. According to the authors, these "bulls" are a result of the laudable tendency of Irish anglophones to use "figurative and witty language."[72] This spirited defense of Irish anglophones runs counter to their subtler and more demeaning attacks on the dialect.

The Edgeworths do not identify any of the causes of differences in Hiberno-English and Standard English. We can suggest some of them here. The majority of Irish with whom the Edgeworths had contact were bilingual. Certainly, they experienced intrusions from their linguistic substrates when speaking as anglophones. Additionally, long-term colonization by the English meant that the Irish anglophone community had developed its own distinctive anglophone ethnolect. It necessarily diverged from British anglophone forms even though it was likely mutually intelligible with most. Finally, as one linguistic historian has written, "Native Irish chose to learn English because of the stigma attached to the Irish language as the language of poverty."[73] This configures the acquisition of Standard English as an aspirational act. These sociolinguistic explanations would have been unknown to the Edgeworths. The reader must settle for their quaint and paternalistic conclusion that the Irish are by nature figurative and witty people. On the one hand, they extol the Irish as "ingenious" and "generous." On the other hand, they cheapen Irish linguistic coinages by locating their origin in ethnic whimsy rather than a specific community's anglophone linguistic practices.

In "Chapter Eight: The Dublin Shoeblack," the Edgeworths exemplify the role of expert intralingual translators by glossing Irish verbs for untutored, Standard English readers. Ironically citing and then ventriloquizing Hugh Blair's *A Critical Dissertation on the Poems of Ossian, the Son of Fingal* (1763), the father-daughter team identifies Irish verbs, their origins, and their discursive contexts. What does it mean when an Irishman spouts with the phrase "To sky a copper," they ask. Their answer does nothing less than transform this metaphoric figure of speech into an inspired feat of mind, "To sky is a new verb, which none but a master hand could have coined. . . . The lofty idea of raising a metal to the skies is substituted for the mean thought of tossing up a halfpenny."[74] Similarly in their excursus on the expression "to flesh," which they gloss as, "to cheat your opponent," the Edgeworths applaud Irish creativity for its ability to euphemize cheating in elevated terms.[75] Following this logic, criminality is built into Irish language forms. The analysis takes on a sinister hue. Not only do the Irish cheat, they verbalize their cheating in opaque (but witty) terms. This subtext is offset by more explicit references to Irish charity and integrity, of course, but nonetheless, moments like the discussion of "to flesh" are obvious in the text.

As the *Essay on Irish Bulls* digs deeper into Irish anglophone speech patterns, complimenting the Irish for speaking figuratively becomes broader and more complex in reference. The Irish may express sordid actions with dignified phrases, but they also corroborate John Horne Tooke's claim that untutored speakers are masters of dispatch and efficiency.[76] The Edgeworths cite several specific examples of phrasal verbs formed only from English prepositions.[77] "He ups with" and "I outs with" are two such examples.[78] While praised for its verbal acuity, the semantic contraction of "I outs with my bread-earner" is immediately juxtaposed to the violence of "I gives it to him up to the Lamprey in the bread-basket." Teasing out these anglophone Irishisms—"bread-earner" means "knife," "Lamprey" means "hilt," and "bread-basket" means "stomach"—the Edgeworths narrate this brutal act as naturally within the ambit of Irish language and behavior.

Two literary comparisons accompany this intimation of Irish violence, however. The juxtaposition of these with anglophone Irish speech patterns results in a final picture that is highly intricate. First, the Edgeworths mention that Thomas Warton's commentary on Pope's "Rape of the Lock" celebrated the metonymy that allowed Pope to avoid continually repeating "scissors." In their view, anglophone Irish people exhibit the same poetic skills when using "bread-winner" for "knife." Second, jamming a knife up to the hilt in someone's stomach may turn some readers' stomachs, but the Edgeworths assure them that Vergil was in touch with the same poetic spirit as an ordinary Irish shoeblack. As comparison, they quote from *The Aeneid*: "Cervice orantis *capulo tenus* abdidit ensem (Up to the hilt his shining fauchion sheathed)."[79] The real heft of the argument comes in its equation of everyday Irish anglophone speech with illustrious exemplars from the European poetic canon. Vergil and Pope have received accolades immemorial for their linguistic stylings notwithstanding the carnage. The Edgeworths claim that the anglophone Irish should receive them too.

In a similar vein, the Edgeworths assert that the Irish speak no worse than Milton himself writes. They cite three blunders in Milton's language, the purpose being to point out that an anglophone Irishman, had he spoken them, would have been "laughed to scorn."[80] On the surface this is a radically leveling gesture in which a nonnormative anglophone form's "bulls" are placed on the same plane as mistakes made by a celebrated poet. The Edgeworths finally arrive at the idea that Irish anglophones are at once better than average Standard English speakers and fully equal to the best exemplars of all poetic traditions. In chapter 11, "The Brogue," they state plainly, "We are only going to candidly confess, that we think the Irish, in general, speak *better English* than is commonly spoken by the natives of England."[81]

These sorts of equations figure in many late eighteenth-century textual commodities and take spoken language as a starting point for writing about and aestheticizing difference. Nonnormative speakers are poets, and their poetry can be translated into something more palatable. Nonnormative speakers possess forms of language that can be made aesthetic when interwoven and regulated through Standard English frames. These are the main premises the Edgeworths work with. These are also the premises of the final book I mention in this chapter, Samuel Pegge's *Anecdotes of the English language* (1803), a book that is as casually organized, rollicking, and full of paradox as the Edgeworths' *Essay on Irish Bulls*. Pegge's rich metalinguistic descriptions of the dialect of London translate and praise Cockney speech. Detailed grammatical analysis doubles as aesthetic analysis, treating locutions like doubled negatives ("I didn't know nothing about it"), metathesis ("aks" or "ax" for "ask"), and nonnormative verb forms ("fit" for "fought") as an engine for the production of a distinctly copious form of literary prose.[82] Pegge combines urban linguistic reportage with satire, criticism, literary allusion, and the discourse of antiquarianism, among others genres and devices, thereby mimicking the linguistic fluidity of those he describes. Cockney speakers are praised for their unique ability to move appealingly between different anglophone registers: "Thus a Cockney will say to his companions, on a Sunday after dinner, when the *ennui* is coming on, 'Let us *fetch* a walk.' Again, in the past tense, he will tell them what 'a prodigious pretty walk he *faught* on the preceding Sunday.' "[83] While his details about London anglophones are tantalizing, at times it is difficult to discern whether Pegge is praising Londoners' linguistic dexterity or his own. This is not to say that Pegge invents these Cockney phrases and locutions, but instead that the complexity and syncretism he sees in them are also features of his own multilingual work.

Pegge's commentary projects the copious qualities of his own work onto the speakers that he remolds into his literary object. This is analogous to the way that the Edgeworths transform a known fact of vernacular Irish life into an occasion for aesthetic contemplation, and, indeed, into a commodity. When Pegge announces, "we must not expect a Hackney-coachman, who is an *Ubiquary*, and who picks up his Language (as well as his Fares) in the streets, to be quite so correct as an *Antiquary*," he is both aestheticizing Cockney anglophones and authorizing his own work as commodity through a satiric engagement with antiquarianism.[84] Pegge himself is the ubiquary in this etymological pun. His book contains an antiquarian-like study of the language of "everywhere," in Latin, "ubique." If the notion that "there is food for an Antiquary in the daily dialect of London" sounds a bit like a sales pitch, or at least an attempt to reach an established audience, it is because it is one.[85] The fifth and final chapter of this book turns to questions of translation, value, and commodification more intensively. The commodification of anglophone difference as it exists in the Edgeworths, Pegge, and a host of other texts is a fitting transition.

MULTILINGUAL LIVES

Antera Duke

January 21 the 1785
at 5 am in aqua Landing with fine morning so I go Captin Savage for tak goods for slav

January 21, 1785
At 5 a.m. at Aqua Landing, a fine morning. I went to Captain Savage to take goods [to be exchanged for slaves].

January 25 the 1785
about 4 am in Eyo Willy Honesty house so wee walk up to see Willy Honesty in yard so his killd 1 Big goat for wee soon after we walk up to see wee town & Did tak one great guns to putt for canow for two Egbo Young men Bring hom in aqua Landing so wee join to Henshaw Town and com Back and at 3 clock noon wee Everry Body go com to Deash Eyo Willy Honesty Daught . . . 1496 Rods besides cloth & powder & Iron so wee play all day befor night

January 25, 1785
About 4 a.m. we were in Eyo Willy Honesty's house and we walked up to see Willy Honesty in his yard. He killed 1 big goat for us. Soon after that we walked up to see our town and took one great gun [cannon] to put in a canoe for two of Egbo Young [Ofiong's] men to bring home to Aqua Landing. We went together to Henshaw Town and came back, and at 3 o'clock in the afternoon we and everybody went to "dash" Eyo Willy Honesty's daughter . . . 1496 rods besides cloth, gunpowder, and Iron. We "played" all day before night[fall].

January 28 the 1785
about 6 am in aqua Landing with fine morning so I hav work for my

January 28, 1785
About 6 a.m. at Aqua Landing, a fine morning. I worked in my small

small yard after 2 clock noon wee two go Bord Captin Smal with 3 slave so his tak two and wee com back	yard. After 2 o'clock in the afternoon we two went on board Captain Smale's ship with 3 slaves. He took two slaves and we came back.[1]

Antera Duke is the anglophone penname of Ntiero Edem Efiom, an Efik slave trader, patriarch, and diarist from Duke Town in the commercial region of the Calabar and Cross Rivers on the coast of what is today southeastern Nigeria.[2] Antera Duke, who lived from roughly the 1730s until between 1805 and 1809, kept an anglophone diary from January 18, 1785, until January 31, 1788.[3] Though he likely kept other diaries over the course of his career as a trader, the only surviving writings cover this small slice of the late 1780s. My interest in this text stems from the fact that, like the other multilingual lives I have described so far, it reveals new wrinkles in the complex texture of eighteenth-century anglophony. Unlike Daines Barrington's glossing of the life and death of Dorothy Pentreath, however, which stemmed from a curious encounter in public, Antera Duke's diary is a private account of a linguistic life in a rare anglophone form.

Scholars have held up Antera Duke's diary as an invaluable primary text for historians of African history, and in particular for historians of Ekpe practices, as well as for historians of the transatlantic slave trade.[4] In the intimate space of the private diary, Antera Duke records his day-to-day habits and relations with other people, all of which shed light on cultural practices in this region before and during the arrival of European slave traders. He records happenings in his family, his choice of clothes, alcohol consumption, celebrations, religious devotions, feuds, travel, and multilayered commercial networks. His descriptions of the kinship structures, social arrangements, religious practices, and trade linkages between Old Calabar, European slave traders, and other entrepôts along the African coast have been particularly generative for historians.[5]

As a case in point, Antera Duke's diary "records the anglicized names of 101 men and 5 women from Old Calabar and several surrounding Cross River settlements . . . the greatest number of names from any single source from the beginning of European trade at Old Calabar in the mid-1600s to 1805."[6] In addition to inscribing anglophone forms of these names into the historical record—names of powerful Ekpe dignitaries like Duke Ephraim as well as powerless local slaves like Andam Nothing—Antera Duke also records the names of European slave traders whose ships and journeys can be cross-referenced against extant ship records. The editors' elaborate discussion of slaving and trade networks reports that Antera Duke's diary corroborates many pieces of historical evidence, "In his [diary] entries from January 1785 to January 1788, Antera Duke references forty-two slaving voyages. . . . By comparing Antera's list with the slavers compiled in *Voyages*, the online slave trade database, we find that the diarist identifies thirty-eight of the forty-nine European vessels at Calabar in the three-year period."[7]

While the historical value of this document is immeasurable, for my purposes Antera Duke is discussed here as an example of a multilingual anglophone who chronicles his habits, relations, and interiority in the linguistic form of his own choosing. The linguistic form is worth examining at length from a historical perspective, just as it is worth, by way of experiment, examining it from a literary perspective that stresses rhetoric, metaphor, and expressive dexterity. Antera Duke wrote his diary in what his most recent editors call "trade English," an anglophone medium of communication borne out of the "daily contact between British mariners and African traders" that arose after the Royal African Company (established in 1672) began "encourag[ing] British commercial endeavors in the Lower Cross River."[8] As his editors describe the language of Antera Duke's diary, "It contains 10,510 words and reveals that Antera Duke had a working vocabulary of 400 English words."[9] This notwithstanding, the scholarly assessment is that his diary, by far the longest "trade English" text of its kind, contains a more elementary vocabulary than comparable writings.[10] The editors continue their appraisal of Antera Duke's language skills by noting, "His vocabulary and sentence structures, we contend, suggest that he learned English informally in the Cross River region by hearing spoken words and seeing them written in captains' accounts and letters."[11] This is a plausible explanation of Antera Duke's facility with the anglophone lect developing at that period of time in that particular location. A successful trader will advance by knowing the language in which the most profitable business in his area is transacted. The editors suggest that Antera Duke's almost osmotic education in "trade English" derived from seeing and overhearing European anglophones speaking. He thus uses the diary as a space within which to practice the language that would allow him to sell slaves and other commodities such as "textiles, iron bars, beads, powder kegs, guns, and copper rods" to European traders.[12] This explanation frames everything in terms of language's transactional component: Antera Duke is evidence of the fact that anglophony is a marketable skill in the period, a form of linguistic identity that was lucrative in certain spaces of economic exchange. This angle is not insignificant. It attests to the joint penetration of anglophony and capitalism into diverse linguistic communities around the globe during the period. However, it tells little about the man's ability to read and write, crucial biographical details lost to history.[13]

Before getting to the question of the market values of anglophone translation skills, which I take up at length in the next chapter, I would like here to examine Antera Duke's choice to write an anglophone diary at all, as well as the way in which this primary document is seen as one that must be translated in order to be read. Seeing this diary only as the imitation of European linguistic practice for commercial ends is to consign it to the realm of strict documentary reporting while reducing its author to a person with substandard or developmental linguistic skills that must be rerendered in a digestible form of Standard English.[14] These assumptions and the work of intralingual translation—which are necessary for the admirable work the editors set out to do—efface potential aesthetic features that appear at the moment of reading, effectively disqualifying them from notice. Literary scholars who are attuned to language's expressive capacities and interested in the heterogeneous scenes of eighteenth-century anglophone writing can do more with Antera Duke's diary. I believe that beyond the question of an anglophone language as remunerative instrument—"trade English"—one also finds in this diary a multilingual subject's deliberate experimentation with inhabiting and perhaps even reformulating a nonlocal language by using it as a medium for diary composition, which is an undeniably personal form of writing, one that is inseparable from the self-understanding of this particular literate multilingual.

The editors of Antera Duke's diary are most interested in explaining the historical conditions that the text charts, and they attend to these conditions with absolute ethnographic precision. I have no interest in questioning their meticulous work here. Their mode is the pursuit of transparent historical truth, and rightly so. This type of thinking and writing makes the past accessible in a way other disciplinary formations cannot. Their volume surrounds Antera Duke's writing with an impressive battery of prefatory, explanatory, and appendixed historical knowledge. Without question, it is useful for eighteenth-century scholars as a whole given the care with which the editors track and elucidate historical references that are made in the text. By prioritizing the ethnographic disclosure of historical data populating Antera Duke's life and times, they paint a vivid picture of late eighteenth-century life in a part of the world that was entwined with expanding global systems of commerce, especially the slave trade.

In the highly readable, facing-page Standard English translation that they have produced, editorial interventions fix meanings within discrete cultural and historical contexts while crowding out the aesthetic valences of Antera Duke's anglophone localism.[15]

February 23 the 1785	February 23, 1785
. . I go Bord Captin Loosdam for break book for 3 slave so I break for one at Captin Savage so I tak goods for slav at Captin Brown and com back.	. . . I went on board Captain Langdon's ship to "break book" [make an agreement] for 3 slaves. I "broke trade" for one slave with Captain Savage. Then I took goods for slaves from Captain Burrows and came back.[16]

Beyond altering the number of periods in the ellipsis that begins this entry, the translation corrects the exonyms "Loosdam" and "Brown" that Antera Duke uses to refer to the European slave traders "Langdon" and "Burrows." This correction in itself is relatively minor and can perhaps be accounted for by Antera Duke's confusion, miscomprehension, or inability to spell these names.[17] Another plausible explanation that preserves a certain aesthetic ambiguity is the idea that there were local anglophone terms for referring to the European slavers. The main detail of interest in this passage is the way that Antera Duke metaphorizes the idea of making an agreement with the evocative expression "break book." A footnote after the bracketed expression "[make an agreement]" in the Standard English column reads, " 'Break book' signifies the establishment of a trading agreement and derives from the European trader opening his account book to enter the transaction."[18] This is a worthy glossing of Antera Duke's metaphor, but it does not see the expression as a metaphor, but instead as a nonnormative gaffe born out of a misapprehension relating to the signification of the opening of a European trader's book as the conducting of business. Like so many other metaphors, this might also be creative linguistic substitution at work that is only reduced through translation.

The editors are straightforward and reasonable regarding their interventions. They are also linguistically rigorous, but still something critical seems lost in each translation, as though the need to translate itself is the problem, and not at all the translations they have produced.[19] Some interventions are dramatic, but seemingly required by the nature of Standard English, which demands, among other things, a close attention to temporal sequencing. "Our new 'translation' has changed 10 to 15 percent of the words from the 1956 Wilkie-Simmons translation," they write, "in many cases placing verbs in the past tense."[20] These excerpts from May 1787 are emblematic of the rigor with which the Standard English translation recodes Antera Duke's writings in precise sequential logic:

May 26 the 1787	May 26, 1787
. . . so I hear 18 men slave tak Boat and Run way from John Cooper Last night and 5 clock noon wee hear som them slave be to aqua town	. . . I heard that 18 men slaves took a boat and ran away from John Cooper last night, and at 5 o'clock in the afternoon we heard that some of those slaves are at Aqua Town.
May 27 the 1787	May 27, 1787
. . . we have see all Captin John family com to see about one the Daught marry Ego Young was fight with another the wife and Break Toothes out so the com to Break another wife Toothes out again so wee Did mak Jimimy antera for tak Toothes out for the wife his Ephrim Robin Henshaw Daught	. . . . All Captain John's family came to see us because one of their daughters who married Egbo Young [Antera] had fought with another wife and had had her teeth broken out. Then they came to break the other wife's teeth out. We made Jimmy Antera take the teeth of the wife, the daughter of Ephraim Robin Henshaw.[21]

I am of the opinion that, from the perspective of literary and cultural studies, the currency or readability of the left-hand column is the wrong question to ask of this text. For the purposes of historical research, it makes sense to treat Antera Duke's writing as aberrant and correctable. For the purposes of literary history and analysis, which try to stitch together narratives regarding how it is our anglophone signifying practices have arrived where they are, I believe that the translation detracts from and diminishes our knowledge of anglophone writing in all its plenitude. These two entries, one of which tells of a slave escape, and the other of which tells of a fight between two women, are legible, albeit in such a way that demands that reader reorient his grammatical, syntactical, and aesthetic perceptions.

Without a translation, Antera Duke's act of private, rhetorical sovereignty demands that the anglophone reader approach the diary with a flexible sense of what constitutes legibility. Reading his work takes time, study, and mental adaptation. It is in this spirit, then, that I present the following excerpt, which recounts news of a coronation and three family births, without its facing-page translation. The main details to know, which are spelled out in the footnotes (rendering the translation moot anyway) is that "coomy" refers to anchorage fees paid by Europeans and that "Efik regarded the birth of twins as a dire calamity," a detail that adds a different emotional tincture to the passage:[22]

> October 25 the 1787
>
> about 6 am in aqua Landing with small Rain morning so I walk up to see Esim and Egbo Young so I see Jimimy Henshaw come to see wee and wee tell him for go on bord Rogers for all Henshaw family coomy and wee have go on Rogers for mak Jimimy Henshaw name to King Egbo in Coomy Book . . . soon after 2 clock time wee com ashor and I hear one my Ephrim abashey Ebgo Sherry women have Brun two son one Day in plower andam Duke wife Brun young girl in aqua town[23]

CHAPTER 5

The "Alien Wealth" of "Lucky Contaminations"

Freedom, Labor, and Translation

The Values of Translation

When I describe eighteenth-century translations as commodities, I am alluding to more than the simple fact that translations were executed and sold in large numbers. Instead, to call an eighteenth-century translation a commodity is to name an assembly function that bundles a diverse array of metalinguistic forms into a salable book by calculating its potential market worth. Antera Duke's 1785 diary is not a commodity in this sense. The 2010 edition of his diary, however, is. Seen as commodities, translations are packaged with (1) prefaces and essays that have a tendency to read as rather free-form linguistic and cultural histories; (2) footnote and citational apparatuses that gesture to previous or competing commodities in related domains; (3) glossaries that provide intercultural equivalences; and (4) advertisements or book lists that point readers in new commodity directions. The intralingual translations of Brice's Exmoor dialogues and Collier's *A View of the Lancashire Dialect by Way of Dialogue* described the ways in which an accumulation of explanatory paratexts and advertising protocol naturalized these works in a Standard English literacy framework wherein aesthetic quality is subverted to ethnolinguistic documentation. The Edgeworths' *Essay on Irish Bulls*, while not a translation per se, still mimics the structural heterogeneity of the period's translation commodities by being—just like Thady Quirk's "An Hibernian Tale" in *Castle Rackrent*—a hodgepodge of fictive prose and translational notes, all preceded by a delimiting preface. Brice's Exmoor women, Collier's Tummus, the Edgeworths' Irish underclass, Pegge's Cockneys: the linguistic difference of all these figures is repackaged in translational commodities that address the demands of the market through their very multiplicity.

A rigorous survey of the *17th–18th Century Burney Collection Newspapers* database reveals patterns relating to the labor and circulation of translations during the eighteenth century, patterns that inform the process of commodification that anglophone translations of the period underwent. The database, which many scholars of the period know and use, "totals almost 1 million pages and contains approximately 1,270 titles."[1] It returns search results for periodicals published between 1604 and 1804 from 1,521,918 documents with the important caveat that the collection becomes denser as this period progresses.[2] Equipped with robust and advanced search functionality, the database permits a researcher to limit results based on place of publication (Barbados, England, France, Germany, India, Ireland, Italy, Jamaica, Netherlands, Scotland, United States) and publication language, although the options here are less diverse than the place of publication choices might initially suggest (Dutch, English, French, Italian, Latin—German is a notable absence given the developed state of periodicals in that language at the time, none of which Charles Burney collected).[3] A researcher can additionally limit by publication frequency and choose to execute a search that returns results drawn only from certain basic periodical sections (Advertising, Arts and Sports, Business News, and News). One can also execute a "fuzzy search," which, like other such database tools of its kind, looks for terms near to the search term while also returning things an OCR scanner might have misread.[4] However one searches, it is imperative to be cautious of results based on the varied and complex methodological questions this database poses.[5]

Nevertheless, this tool can be of tremendous use value if one is attentive to these questions. For example, a nonfuzzy search for the tokens "translation" or "translated" that appear only in "Advertising" sections of newspapers published between 1604 and 1804 returns 5,742 hits. Specifically, these results represent at least 5,742 individual pages from periodical advertising sections of anglophone newspapers in the Burney Collection in which either "translation" or "translated" or both is used on that page, although not necessarily in the same ad, as any given page contains a variable number of ads. While these 5,742 hits amount to less than half of 1 percent of the total number of pages contained within the database, this number is still substantial. Examining even this small subset of the eighteenth-century advertising archive is laborious and time consuming and resists strict quantitative conclusions. Nonetheless, it is edifying, especially regarding the qualitative development and rhetoric of translation advertising.

In terms of qualitative development, consider the textured understanding that one can glean from the numbers alone, even despite the limitations I have mentioned. Of the 5,742 pages in which either "translation" or "translated" or "translation" and "translated" occurs at least once, only one of these is published before 1700, and this is in an advertisement for a book said to contain, "*The Lives of Clement Alexandrinus, Gregory Nazianzen and Prudentius the Christian Poet* . . . written originally in French by Monsieur *le Clerk* and now translated into English."[6] The word "translation" does not appear in this ad at all. In fact the token "translated" hits far earlier in time than "translation" in this database. Whereas one can find advertising references to commodities on the market that are noted as being "translated from" such and such original language beginning in 1696, the first reference to a textual commodity labeled as a "translation" does not appear until 1728: "*In the Press, A* Translation *of* A Supplement to the *New Cyropedia*: Or, The Reflections of Cyrus upon his Travels," a volume to be sold at the low-to-moderate price of 7 shillings 6 pence.

If one examines those 5742 hits over course of the eighteenth century, a general though not unchecked pattern of increase is observable (Table 1). Clearly, the numerical trajectory is upward, and increasingly so, as the century advances. Even so, some of the numbers seem to defy the interpretation that there was unchecked or regular expansion. For example, a discursive lag between 1750 and 1780 is apparent. Additionally, the 1790s alone see more commodities advertised as "translated from" or as "translations" than all previous decades of the century combined. This explosion can be partially explained by the astonishing number of texts during this revolutionary decade that describe themselves as being translations of or translated from French (2,369, or about 81 percent of the total for that decade). If one extrapolates from the limited data available between January 1, 1800, and December 31, 1804, a time period that represents only 40 percent of the decade, a reasonable prediction—assuming that the latter 60 percent of the decade would see comparable numbers—is that, *caeteris paribus*, approximately 1,563 such references would occur. If this data were true, that would mean a decrease of almost 50 percent from the last decade of the eighteenth century as compared with the first decade of the nineteenth.

Table 1. Burney Collection Pages from Advertising Sections That Contain "Translation," "Translated," or Both

Decade (January 1 of first year to December 31 of last)	*Number of pages*
1700–1709	4
1710–19	13
1720–29	64
1730–39	217
1740–49	298
1750–59	239
1760–69	151
1770–79	276
1780–89	927
1790–99	2,927
1800–1804*	625*

*decadal data incomplete

Acknowledging that the Burney Collection is not comprehensive, I would like to still suggest here that the explosion of the 1790s primarily represents a series of competitive commodity publishing programs directed at circulating material relating to one primary xenotrope: Revolutionary France.

Even as larger, interlinguistic translation trends such as this one are visible, so too are rhetorical trends in translation advertising that increase our sense of what translation actually meant, politically and aesthetically, to literate consumers in the period. Advertisements in this century reach out to consumers by stressing the aesthetic values of the anglophone translation, as in an ad for a "Free Translation of that elegant and justly admired poem, written by the Abbé de Lille, entitled Les Jardins," a work in which, quoting from a review in the *English Review* (January 1790), "The language is flowing and poetical, the versification generally easy and melodious, and the pauses are regulated with an equal attention to smoothness and variety" (price 4s.).[7] Or, ads speak to the aesthetic beauty of the book itself as commodity. When William Beloe's *Miscellanies* was published in 1795, for example, an advertisement placed in the *Sun* described the volume, "consisting of Poems, Classical Extracts, and Oriental Tales, translated from the original Arabic," in appealing material terms: "Elegantly printed in Three small Volumes, Duodecimo, on a fine woven Paper" (price 10s. 6d.).[8] In terms of translations as relatively expensive and artful products, one can mention an advertisement for John Hoole's translation of Ariosto's *Orlando Furioso*, which sold as a bound octavo volume with colored plates for the price of 1l. 12s. 6d.[9]

Some advertisements solicit readers based on the claim that a translation has improved, updated, or positively altered an earlier translation and that these improvements will be rapidly before the reading public.[10] In 1732, "A New Translation of Homer's Iliad" appeared before the reading public, and the advertising campaign stressed both the attractiveness of the final object and the speed with which it was to be delivered to market. "Now in the Press, and will be Publish'd with all convenient Speed, beautifully Printed in Three Pocket Volumes, the Types being all new" (no named price).[11] A few years earlier, an ad for "A Translation of Mr. Limborch's Friendly Conference with a Learned Jew About the Christian Religion" containing "an Appendix on Miracles and Prophecy" promised readers that the improved retranslation is currently "in the press, and will speedily be delivered to the Subscribers" (no named price).[12] The sporadic absence of pricing details notwithstanding, across the long eighteenth century, these appeals to beauty, speed, and especially added value speak to consumer desire for accessible and attractive objects bearing xenotropic information from extra-anglophone contexts.

Given the state of elite education in the period, which was addressed in Chapter 3, it is unsurprising to find that many ads for translations, especially translations from classical languages, orient themselves not toward the luxury market but instead toward a pedagogical one. These ads announce new and innovative implements that teachers may use to instruct their pupils. An ad for a translation of Ovid's *Epistles*, for example, says that the translation is intended, "not as a help to scholars [students] in construing their lessons, but as a means of habituating their ideas to take a poetical turn, when requisite, by being read to them at the conclusion of each epistle or lesson, as their teachers shall think proper" (price 6s., sewed).[13] This translation is pitched less in terms of the meaning of the source text than it is in terms of encouraging students to allow Ovid to inspire their own attempts at anglophone poetry. As in poetics, translations served in moral instruction, although not in the limited ways one might expect. A fascinating advertisement from the *Oracle and Daily Advertiser* that was published in December 1800 informs readers that they may purchase "The Tales of the Genii; or Moral Lessons, faithfully translated from the Persian Manuscript by Sir CHARLES MORELL; abridged and adapted for the Instruction and Amusement of Youth by ELIZABETH SOMERVILLE, in 3. vols, each embellished with a Frontispiece, price 4s. 6d. bound."[14] Sir Charles Morrell is the penname of James Ridley, a writer whose two-volume pseudotranslation *The Tales of the Genii* (1764) purported to be a real translation of a Persian-language manuscript.[15] I have been unable to locate a copy of Somerville's rerendering of these tales here described, but there is no doubt that close attention to her strategies for reformulating the ten stories in Ridley's text as (amusing) moral exempla would prove fascinating.

The rhetoric of advertisements for translations in this period additionally registers a palpable interest in Britain's past and present in a rapidly changing and increasingly connected world system. In the late 1780s, during the Ossian controversy, the *World and Fashionable Advisor* carried a curious ad for three separate commodities: (1) a book called "The Originals of Ancient Poems of Ossian, Orran, Ullin, &c" (price 6s.); (2) a book called "Gaelic Antiquities . . . A Dissertation on the Authenticity of Ossian's Poems" (price 16s. 6d.); and (3) curiously, "The Psalms of David, and many passages from the New Testament; translated into Gaelic" (price 2s. 6d.).[16] These three composite commodities run the range of anglophone metalinguistic forms as they relate to Ossian. First, a reproduction of the "originals" from which MacPherson's poems are supposedly translated; second, an essay that sets out to demonstrate the veracity of MacPherson's work; and finally, a translation of the Psalms into Gaelic, presumably so that the author could prove the authenticity of Ossian by juxtaposing Ossian's work to the Psalms, a known form of poetry that was perceived to be ancient, artful, and edifying. The idea that there would be a readership for an inexpensive, Gaelic-language version of the Psalms in London in 1787 is a provocative detail.

In addition to the rhetorical developments described above, one of the most prominent features of eighteenth-century advertisements for translations as commodities is that they solicit anglophone readers through appeals to a newly formed sense of the "global." Britain's cultural and commercial position in an increasingly connected world is one of the primary sales pitches for many advertisements. And, as the examples below show, this market interest is regularly channeled through imperial institutions that anglophones would have known. Hence, one finds the legitimation of a translator's credentials by way of the East India Company in the description of a "handsomely printed," "One Volume Octavo" of "*Tales, Anecdotes, and Letters.* Translated from the Arabic and Persian by Jonathan Scott, Of the East India Company's Service, Persian Secretary to the late Governor General Warren Hastings, Esq." (price 6s.).[17] Conversely, one turns up regular appearances of ads that speak to unfulfilled British imperial fantasies. Such is the case of the repeatedly published ad for the translation of Christian Frederick Damberger's "Travels through the Interiour of Africa, from the Cape of Good Hope to Morocco," translated from German and offered to readers in octavo at the price of "half a guinea."[18] The repetition of advertisements for the translation of Damberger's *Travels* suggests either that the publisher was regularly trying to eliminate remaindered inventory or that there existed a strong market for xenotropic tales of travel from Africa's interior. Such tales, after all, might translate into economic opportunity while feeding curiosity about different cultural and linguistic spaces as seen through the eyes of a German. Unfortunately for those investors (and translation readers) with this in mind, Damberger's *Travels* were eventually understood to be a forgery "by some needy man of letters."[19]

A better way to sell translations was either to justify the translation by way of the translator's fame and experience or by way of an organization's recommendation that selected books were occupationally valuable to the maritime economy. These more reliable devices for advertising translations were deployed by a number of booksellers, including the prolific John Murray, whose advertisement below, in addition to many others, was published in several newspapers during the 1780s and 1790s, including the *World and Fashionable Advertiser*, the *World*, and the *Sun*:

For GENTLEMAN going to INDIA

Books printed for J. Murray, No. 32, Fleet-street, London, and recommended by the Honourable the Court of Directors and their Governors, Councils, and other Servants abroad.

This day is published,

Very handsomely printed at the Clarendon Press, Oxford, in Two large Volumes in Folio, price Ten Guineas bound,

A Dictionary; Persian, Arabic, and English, and English, Persian, and Arabic.

By John Richardson, ESQ. F.S.A.

Of the Middle Temple, and of Wadham College, Oxford.

Where may be had,

1. A Grammar of the Arabic Language, 4to. price 13s. bound. By the same.
2. A Grammar of the Persian Language; by Mr. Jones, 4to. price 13s. bound.
3. Letters chiefly from India, containing an Account of the Military Transactions on the Coast of Malabar, during the late War; together with a short Description of the Religion, Manners, and Customs of the Inhabitants of Indostan; by John Le Couteur, Esq. Captain in His Majesty's Hundredth Regiment of Foot. Translated from the French. The above book may be had in French, price 4s. sewed.
4. A Code of Gentoo Laws; or Ordinations of the Pundits, from a Persian Translation; made from the Original, written in the Shanscript Language, 8v. 7s. 6d. bound.
5. Institutes of Timour, improperly called Tamerlane, translated from the Persian by Major Davy and Mr. White, with Notes and Cuts, Persian and English, 4to. 1l. 11s. 6d. boards.
6. Girdlestone's Essays on the Hepatitis and Spasmodic Affections in India.
7. Bentius's Account of the Diseases which prevail in the East-Indies, 8vo. 5s. bound.
8. Dr. Lind's Essay on Diseases incident to Europeans in Hot Climates, 8vo. 6s. bound.
9. Dr. Blane's Observations on the Diseases incident to Seamen. Just published, large 8vo. 7s. bound.
10. Campbell's Lives of the British Admirals, with plates, brought down to 1779, four vols. large 8vo. Price 8s. bound.
11. The English Review for January 1790, and all the preceding Numbers, 2s. each.[20]

Beyond anything, this ad testifies to the canonization of anglophone orientalist thought in the form of Sir William Jones's *Persian Grammar* (1773), Nathaniel Brassey Halhed's *A Code of Gentoo Laws, or, Ordinations of the Pundits* (1776), and John Richardson's *A Dictionary, Persian, Arabic, English* (1777). Additionally, crucial to the sales pitch for these volumes is the fact that they are "recommended by the Honourable Court of Directors and their Governors, Councils, and other Servants abroad." In a competitive commodity environment, an advertisement must state those ways in which a product differs from competing commodities. The vectors of commodity differentiation go in many directions, but the explicit authorization of translations through East India Company recommendations is a powerful selling point.

In light of the evidence from the *17th–18th Century Burney Collection Newspapers*, it is clear that value inheres in commodities that are the products of translation to the degree that that translation differentiates itself from competing commodities, whether through authorial or institutional validation or economic, historical, pedagogical, or aesthetic self-justifications, among others. This is related to the question of "domesticating" versus "foreignizing" translation, but also quite different. While intralingual anglophone translations can be said to acquire value through editorial interventions that make the text legible to a Standard English audience, seen through the scrim of advertising, the eighteenth-century market valorizes interlingual translation in more varied ways. Interlingual translations, when they are real and not forged, are consumed with the expectation that linguistico-cultural information surrounds the translation, thereby authorizing it from an intellectual perspective and justifying its existence from a labor or commodity perspective.

"The Art of Translating"

Given this highly developed advertising context, one that speaks to the total embeddedness of the translation as a material commodity within an increasingly complex market and distribution system, it is unsurprising that four of the most notable late eighteenth-century translators should all envision—and also richly describe—translations and translating not just in terms of freedom and servility but also in terms of commodities and labor. The next section of this chapter turns to commodity life of translations in the work of Sir William Jones, William Julius Mickle, and George Campbell. For the time being, the present section investigates the work of Alexander Fraser Tytler, a man who, in a way, invented his own variety of translational commodity, the stand-alone anglophone treatise on translation (itself translated from French models, as Tytler makes clear). Unprecedented in anglophony in the period, Tytler's translation treatise seeks to define rules for the decorous importation of nonanglophone cultural material into Standard English. More to the point, the treatise reenvisions the binary of free and servile anglophone translation that was so prevalent during the eighteenth century. Tytler's vision clarifies the meaning of free translation as it relates to commodification in that he positively evaluates only translations in which the translator has added something to the original work that embellishes and improves Standard English. If a cultural injection is incompatible with his vision of Standard English, it is either unremarkable or bad.

Though it is unseemly to discuss the position of the translator relative to a source text as though it is somehow comparable to a slave's relation to a master, this is the comparison that Tytler's translation theory obliges one to make again and again. This is clear in *Essay on the Principles of Translation*, the most wide-ranging statement of anglophone thinking about translation that the late eighteenth century has to offer. In spite of this text's visibility during the Romantic period, Susan Bassnett, one of the pioneers and contemporary luminaries of the field of translation studies, laments that the work is "barely known today."[21] True, the text is relatively obscure and conceptually divorced from the standards and scientificity of more recent developments in linguistics as they relate to translation, but Tytler's essay remains an essential document for scholars who are eager to understand the complex linkages between standardization, translation, and aesthetics during the mid- to late eighteenth and early nineteenth centuries, which was a watershed moment for translation into (and out of) the English language. Jeffrey Huntsman, the essay's most recent modern editor, makes the case for Tytler this way: "Tytler stands in the history of translation much as Samuel Johnson does in lexicography; he summarized and in some sense epitomized the practice of translation for the preceding generations and endured as a model of that kind of translation for generations to follow."[22] Despite its contemporary obscurity, then, Tytler's essay merits an interpretation that positions his work (and translation studies in general) in relation to his analogue in the discourse of standardization, Samuel Johnson.

As a wide-ranging "amateur-expert," Tytler was a product and practitioner of the Scottish Enlightenment, both a theorist of translation and a translator; his biography informs his ideas and practice. Born in Edinburgh in 1747, Tytler was a precocious student who received his earliest schooling in that intellectually pulsating city. At the age of sixteen he was sent to England for two years of further education at the academy of James Elphinston, a fellow Scot, in Kensington. Given that Elphinston published *The Plan of Education at Mr. Elphinston's Academy, Kensington* in 1760, we have a sense of the exacting course of education that Tytler would have received during his two years there. Elphinston's pedagogical tract advances a theory of education based on "*Language* [as] Education's first object in the culture of the mind."[23] As in Edgeworth's *Practical Education*, the curriculum's rigorous study of Standard English grammar and elocution prepares students for equally rigorous study of Latin, Greek, Hebrew, French, and translation. In the educationalist's words, "When the theory of the native tongue is once exhibited by Grammar, and riveted both by reading and conversation, it cannot too soon or too constantly be applied to *writing*, whether in translation, or in composition. Translation improves the knowledge of both languages, but especially of that practiced by the pen. It is therefore important to translate, not only from foreign tongues, but into them; and this preparatory to composition, which may often be necessary in foreign living tongues, and sometimes be requisite in dead ones. If practice best rivets theory in prose, so must some, even foreign versification be proper, in order to have a taste of foreign poets ancient or modern."[24] By pointing out the linguistic pedagogy employed by the headmaster of a school that Tytler attended for only two years, I merely mean to suggest that, long before completing his studies at the University of Edinburgh, studying law, becoming a barrister, a historian, and later a translator and theorist of translation, Tytler was a multilingual anglophone subject who had dense early experience in multiple languages. He carried these practices on into his later life and interests.[25]

Though translators and readers of translations have always commented on their practice and experience of translation, in both specific and general terms, before Tytler's 1791 essay, few anglophone theorists had posed larger theoretical questions relating to translation outside of the domain of translation as practice. For this reason, Bassnett begins her chapter "The Origin and Development of Translation Studies" with Tytler's work precisely because "individual translators have, from time to time, commented on their practice, in prefaces, essays, notes, and letters, but the first extended critical account of translation in English is generally held to be Alexander Fraser Tytler's *Essay on the Principles of Translation*."[26] This assessment that Tytler's work exhibits a more general theoretical account of translation echoes the self-authorizing statements that Tytler himself puts forth in his essay's introduction, including that "it is much to be regretted, that they who were so eminently well qualified to furnish instruction in the art itself"—by which he means Quintilian, Cicero, and Pliny the Younger—"have contributed little more to its advancement than by some general recommendations of its importance."[27] Though the claim about the history of translation studies is inaccurate, Tytler still understands himself to be part of an illustrious but sparse, generative and yet "mutilated" intellectual lineage.[28] In his own self-appraisal, he aims at doing what, to his knowledge, others had only attempted to do in limited and bidirectional cases: Quintilian and Cicero on the translation of Greek into Latin, for example, or D'Alembert and Batteux on the translation of Latin into French. In opposition to attempts that he depicts as desultory, Tytler strives to deduce and catalogue evaluative criteria for translation from any language to any other. In so doing, he offers commentary on examples of translations of, in, and among a larger but still quite narrow range of European languages: English, French, Greek, Latin, and Spanish.[29]

Huntsman claims that because Tytler "lacks a precise terminology for either the linguistic or the literary aspects of his problem," he "attempts a precision by focusing his attention on particular problems in turn and by discussing, usually at some length, examples of both good and bad practice."[30] Filtering his assessment of Tytler through contemporary translation theory, Huntsman goes on to note, "The central terms in Tytler's aesthetic are *genius*, *wit*, and especially, *taste*. They are used almost as if they were technical terms—palpable, real, self-evident, virtually inescapable."[31] Huntsman is correct to point out that Tytler's method is empirical and that terms of eighteenth-century philosophy like "*genius*, *wit*, and especially, *taste*" permeate the text. These qualities certainly vitiate the degree to which the theory of translation that he proposes can be considered "technical." Huntsman is also right to historicize Tytler's practice between the common sense school of philosophy as it grew up around the work of Thomas Reid, George Campbell, Henry Home (Lord Kames), Alexander Girard, and James Beattie and the "the rustic but naturally honest views exemplified in the traditional balladry and the writings of Ramsay, Burns, and Scott."[32]

Far from "lacking a precise terminology," however, Tytler's essay repeats the specific and freighted evaluative vocabulary that I have charted through translations of *Ars Poetica*. The evaluative binaries that characterize his celebration of translational acts of freedom and liberty over servile and bound acts of imitation are especially instructive in that they are embedded in an era of translation whose precepts have shifted to become dramatically different from Denham's vision of fluent translation as it was imitated from the mid-seventeenth through the mid-to-late eighteenth century. As Burwick points out, Tytler's definition of good translation is unambiguously foreignizing, that "in which the merit of the original work is so completely transfused into another language, as to be distinctly apprehended, and as strongly felt, by a native of the country to which that language belongs, as it is by those who speak the language of the original work."[33] In addition to this, Tytler's rhetoric further poses a set of provocative questions about how scholars should understand the historical and cultural emplacement of a text like this one, a text that purports to offer lucid and transferrable rules for literary practice even as it is wholly inflected with the overdetermined language of the transatlantic slave system.

Echoing Horace as digested through Denham, Tytler speaks of translation as though translators can be divided into two camps: those who are bound, servile, and slavish to their source texts and those who are free or liberated from such constraints. Tytler's thesis, which comes out in his commentary on individual translators, is that a regulated form of nonlicentious but still "free" translation is far superior to servile translation. Tytler dismisses Ben Jonson as the quintessential example of an overly literal or "servile" translator, criticizing his efforts in the following way: "So in Jonson's translations from the Odes and Epodes of Horace, besides the most servile adherence to the words, even the measure of the original is imitated."[34] In short, Jonson's translations add no value to the original texts. For Tytler, Jonson falls into the pattern of "the English writers of the 16th, and the greater part of the 17th century, [who] seem to have had no other care than (in Denham's phrase) to translate language into language, and to have placed their whole merit in presenting a literal and servile transcript of their original."[35] Jonson's lack of invention fails Tytler's injunction that the best translations not be "servile." However, free translation also creates a certain amount of risk, he argues, because a free translation cannot be overly free lest it run the risk of wanton deviation from the source material. As he notes, "The difficulty indeed is, where so much freedom is allowed, to define what is to be accounted licentiousness."[36]

Better models of translation come into view when Tytler praises John Dryden.[37] Tytler describes Dryden's domesticating influence with overextended metaphors: "It was to Dryden that poetical translation owed a complete emancipation from her fetters." Because of Dryden's influence, "the danger now was, that she ['poetical translation'] should run into the extreme of licentiousness," the gendered implications of this form of "licentiousness" being particularly provocative.[38] So even though Tytler says that Dryden's translation of Vergil's *Aeneid* (1697) liberated poetic translation from a bonded relationship to the source text as exemplified by translators like Jonson, this "emancipation" of the text from its "fetters" occasioned its own problems. Invoking the "spirit of *English* liberty" that worked to regulate the standardization movement in the latter half of the eighteenth century, Tytler analogizes that in Dryden's wake "a judicious spirit of criticism was now wanting, to prescribe bounds to this increasing licence, and to determine to what precise degree a poetical translator might assume to himself the character of an original writer."[39] Early eighteenth-century translation practice in Dryden's wake was risky in Tytler's eyes. He accuses Dryden's overly "licentious" followers—but certainly not Dryden himself—of treating "fidelity" to semantic content as "but a secondary object."[40] Tytler's Dryden is thus an exciting but dangerous model of translation "exulting in her new liberty," a phrase that might be unpacked as an oblique reference to British anxiety surrounding the tumultuous early days of the French Revolution.[41]

Given that the first edition of Tytler's essay is published in 1791, it is difficult to read his text's repeated evocations of liberty and servility as though the text itself were divorced from a host of historical circumstances relating to the questions of power and sovereignty as they were circulating at the time. The French Revolution, the Haitian Revolution, slavery, and abolition: these events and the public debates and discussions surrounding them mediate Tytler's descriptions of translation. The idea that "emancipation" might be followed by excessive exultation in "new liberty" and the necessity of "prescribing bounds to this increasing licence" is one that resonates with the rhetoric both of Burkean conservatism and antiabolitionist texts of the period. Even the less metaphorical notion that criticism was needed "to determine what precise degree a poetical translator might assume to himself the character of an original writer" smacks of the questioning of traditional models of sovereignty and representation that the late eighteenth century's upheavals brought to the forefront of public consciousness. Who gets to represent whom, in translation, and in government? I do not mean to claim that Tytler's treatise is a coded investigation of these other topics of social and political import. Instead, my narrower assertion is that beyond just registering these ongoing conversations about the changing nature of sovereignty, Tytler's treatise also participates in them by invoking Standard English's permeability to new linguistic forms.

The easiest way to see this is to consider first the way that Tytler expresses his conviction that different language systems possess different expressive capacities that are proper to them, for "if the genius and character of all languages were the same, it would be an easy task to translate from one into another"; that is, all that would be required is "fidelity and attention."[42] This conception that linguistic (and perhaps cultural) difference is central to the problem of translation is also clear in statements like "The Latin language admits of a brevity, which cannot be successfully imitated in the English"; "The French language admits of a brevity of expression more corresponding to that of the Latin"; and "The Latin and Greek languages admit of inversions which are inconsistent with the genius of English."[43] Languages and language may "participate" with one another through translation, but within each linguistic system there are conventional practices that prevent direct and unproblematic transmission from one to the other.

Interlinguistic incompatibilities, while not rigorously generalized as cultural differences, are the variables that condition whether or not a translator will need to be "freer" or more "bound" with a source text. As Tytler puts it, "The different genius of the languages of the original and translation, will often make it necessary to depart from the manner of the original, in order to convey a faithful picture of the sense."[44] By this logic, languages that are more dissimilar from one another require that the translator assert more "freedom," a dangerous prospect in the imperial world of contact and asymmetric power. Yet there is a caveat: the exertion of that freedom must be organized around recreating "sense" rather than "manner," by which he means "national genius."[45] The act of transference from one linguistic system to another must render a work from the parameters of one "national genius" into the parameters of the other. As Tytler opines on the question of translating idiomatic expressions, when a translator "makes a Greek or a Roman speak French or English, he unwittingly puts into his mouth allusions to the manners of modern France or England."[46] Incompatibility between linguistic systems as they relate to cultural and political practices implicates the translator, whose job it is to calibrate his exertions of freedom in translation based on his own judgment about the degree of cultural incompatibility that obtains.

Tytler's overdetermined use of the vocabulary of freedom and bondage makes more sense in the context of the compatibility of linguistico-cultural systems. "An ordinary translator sinks under the energy of his original," Tytler writes, but "the man of genius frequently rises above it."[47] The translator must be "thoroughly master of the language" and kept in "restraints," but he also has at hand various freedoms, such as the "liberty of adding to or retrenching from the ideas of the original" and the freedom to "correct what appears to him a careless or inaccurate expression of the original."[48] A translator risks "presenting a literal and servile transcript of their original [language]," however, because, "to one who walks in trammels, it is not easy to exhibit an air of grace and freedom."[49] Rather than conforming to the binary of domesticating and foreignizing, Tytler's model of translation emphasizes the appropriate exertion of freedom, which can only be judged based on the transferability of different cultural practices into different linguistico-cultural settings. Thus, a "free" translation might be domesticating or foreignizing as it is read in the target culture just as a "servile" translation might be. The key difference is that a "free" translation injects appropriate cultural material into the target culture whereas a "servile" translation pollutes that target culture. The primary goal of the translator is that "he must adopt the very soul of his author, which must speak through his own organs."[50] The act of translation is the process whereby "the very soul" of another cultural context is transmuted through the written and spoken "organs" of the target. Its evaluation emerges from a consideration of how seamlessly the transcendental "soul" and corporeal "organs" fit together.

Tytler's discussion of "*the* [literary] *Art of Translating*" is meant to transcend time, place, and language. It tries to resolve an intercultural and aesthetic problem of importance to the late eighteenth-century marketplace.[51] Tytler says several times that translation is the motor of cultural exchange and improvement, and so what he views as its current state of undertheorization hampers the open exchange of information and creativity. To recapitulate the phrase from the lexicographer Nathan Bailey that appeared in Chapter 2, exchange and translation are the primary means by which historical periods, geographical locations, and disparate languages "participate" with one another. Echoing this, Tytler celebrates "the daily experience of the advantages of good translations in opening to us all the stores of ancient knowledge, and creating a free intercourse of science and of literature between all modern nations."[52] This laissez-faire rhetoric anticipates his survey of his own present, in which he does not hesitate to claim that "the utility of translations is universally felt, and therefore there is a continual demand for them."[53]

In essence, the free translator adds to source texts in such a way that the target culture benefits from the investment of translational labor. Tytler calls the end result of free translation "superaddition," by which he means the translator's active remaking of the text in such a way that "the idea shall have the most necessary connection with the original thought, and actually increase its force."[54] Whereas Denham and others arguing for adaptive translation worked with slavery as a metaphor for dogged subjection to a source text, one way to understand Tytler is that he uses the concept of slavery as it relates to the value of labor. The slavish or servile translator is the one whose labor results in inappropriate injections of irrelevant cultural ideas. This labor is valueless according to the terms of the system and cannot be remunerated. By contrast, the free translator is the one whose efforts toward making sure that a specific translated text is as "distinctly apprehended, and as strongly felt, by a native of the country to which that language belongs, as it is by those who speak the language of the original work" is the free exertion of individual labor that will be rewarded in the marketplace. The inversion here is remarkable. Whereas freedom results in cultural injections that are palatable, useful, or flattering—not unlike copious additions to English—servility is evidenced by an oddly obvious cultural or linguistic incompatibility, a supplementary and irreducible difference that does not fit within commonsense notions of propriety.

Free Extraction

> The peculiar, and without exaggeration we may say providential, felicity of the English language has been made its capital reproach—that, whilst yet ductile and capable of new impressions, it received a fresh and large infusion of alien wealth. It is, say the imbecile, a "bastard" language, a "hybrid" language and so forth. And thus, for a metaphor, for a name, for a sound, they overlook, as far as depends on their will, they sign away the main prerogative and dowry of their mother tongue. It is time to have done with all these follies. Let us open our eyes to our own advantages.[55]

To differing degrees and through varied metaphors, Sir William Jones, William Julius Mickle, and George Campbell all cast their acts of translation as free labor resulting in composite commodities that will serve the public good. In each case, the translator's sense of the interlingual benefits of his translation is different. However humbly, these three figures all present themselves as prospectors for what Thomas De Quincey would later call "alien wealth," that is, additional "fresh and large infusions" of "ductile" linguistic and cultural material that will accord with or embellish Standard English. Jones, Mickle, and Campbell each attempts to estimate the value of the "alien wealth" he is introducing into anglophony. That value is affixed to some aspect of the source context that the translator valorizes as culturally transmissible.

The pursuit of "alien wealth" from nonanglophone languages accords with discussions of anglophony's ambivalent "copiousness" as they unfold in grammars and other proto–linguistic texts of the period, books that describe the current state of the language as the outcome of intersecting peoples within Britain. Surveying the "proliferating variances" of anglophony in the culturally imbricated Caribbean, Glissant suggests that interlingual contact inevitably leads to "lucky contaminations" from each to each.[56] "Lucky contaminations" bears a different charge from "alien wealth." Whereas most commentators in the period—Defoe, Swift, Johnson, and others—can be said to think of anglophone linguistic patrimony as a history of "lucky contaminations," the future-oriented search for "alien wealth" that one sees in translation practice of the late eighteenth-century period tries to reformulate the potentialities of linguistic contact away from "contamination," however fortuitous, and instead toward resource extraction.[57]

Several scholars have observed a future-oriented interest in "alien wealth" in the work of Sir William Jones. His "Essay on the Poetry of Eastern Nations" argues for the value of interlingual translation from Asia—and also the value of his own volume of "Asiatick" poetry—by pointing out that his literary transcreations are inspired by imported models. Jones famously suggests, "If the languages of the Eastern nations were studied in our places of education . . . a new and ample field would be open for speculation. . . . We should be furnished with a new set of images and similitudes, and a number of excellent compositions would be brought to light, which further scholars might explain, and future poets might imitate."[58] Referencing this and other passages that code the process of translation in terms of mining, Mulholland picks up on the commodity aspects of Jones's conception of translation and discusses them as such: "Jones saw Indian knowledge as a valuable resource—like cotton or silk—that could provide Europe with something it lacked. As a resource, it was meant to be extracted."[59] In Mulholland's astute reading, Jones's poetry, and its effects on the anglophone conception of poetic voice are the end result of this extraction, a fact with which Jones himself would have likely been pleased. In his analysis of the cocreation of occident and orient, Makdisi, too, zeroes in on those aspects of Jones's thinking that the orientalist poet couches in commodity terms: "What Jones proposed, then, was to establish a cultural and literary parallel to the extraction of material wealth from the East and to transfer both sets of treasures back to Britain."[60]

Rangarajan, who gives one of the most illuminating readings of Jones to date, sees the orientalist as an importer of raw material that would later be repackaged according to scripts that made inherent difference compatible or "knowable." Rangarajan writes, "His India was not exotic in the conventional sense; he experimented with translating it into a somewhat 'knowable' entity whose foreignness was containable. . . . It was up to other readers to liberate the images he provided from his signifying constraints."[61] Jones's poetry finishes raw materials from India into knowable and salable commodities.[62] "Foreignness" was not only "containable," but marketable as well. As Rangarajan helps us understand, in Jones, xenotropisms should enter anglophony in a regularized way: translators should import compatible works from culturally relevant linguistic contexts and transform them into commodities.[63] At a later remove, students who study those translations synthesize them into pioneering poetry in their own vernaculars, which, too, then becomes a marketable commodity.[64] As Jones writes in the preface to his 1772 volume of syncretic poems, "I am persuaded that a writer, acquainted with the originals, might imitate them very happily in his native tongue, and that the publick would not be displeased to see the genuine compositions of *Arabia* and *Persia* in *English* dress."[65] As Chapter 4 sought to show, this process was not unique to orientalist attempts to translate the East. It is within the compass of eighteenth-century translation theory to view the process of translation not just as the transportation of semiotic content from one language to another, but also as the free assembly of diverse metalinguistic texts into legible commodities. Further, these commodities announce, almost as branding, the specific translational interventions that make them valuable anglophone commodities in the first place.

Whereas the value of Jones's 1772 volume of poetry is a function of its future dividends in anglophone poetic practice, William Julius Mickle, a contemporary of Jones's, sees the commodifiable value of his translational work differently. Mickle's 1776 translation of Luís Vaz de Camões's *Os Lusíadas* (1572), often considered to be the Portuguese national epic, refigures

Portuguese imperial failures as instructive examples for imperial Britain going forward. Quoting Horace's injunction "Nec Verbum Verbo, Curabis Reddere, Fidus Interpres," on its title page, *The Lusiad; Or, The Discovery of India. An Epic Poem* is prefaced by an intricate, value-adding document in which Mickle describes his translational work as imperially advantageous and good for Britain, not in terms of cultural injection and anglophone poetic invigoration, but in terms of clarifying and encouraging a new, globally expansive British imperial identity. "Ignorance of the true principles of commerce, that great cause of the fall of the Portuguese empire, does not at present threaten the British," Mickle opines near the end of his introduction. "Nor is the only natural reason of that fall [the Portuguese empire's fall] applicable to Great Britain."[66] To summarize his argument, by translating the Portuguese imperial epic and reinterpreting it as a story of failures in commerce and governance, Mickle's translation can help Britain solidify a sense of its own imperial values.

Mickle's preface to his translation is an example of an eighteenth-century translation preface that rises to the level of intricate work of composition in its own right. From justifying why he chooses to translate Camões's epic poem of maritime discovery to describing what the poem's translated use value represents for British imperial practice, Mickle's introduction does powerful ideological work. In quantitative terms, his dense prefatory writing runs to 155 pages—nearly one-third of the 484 pages of the entire volume, introduction and translation taken together. Of these 155 pages of introductory material, nearly 120 of them are devoted to topics that, by all intents and purposes, exceed the technical question of what translation is and how it is best to render one language's expressive architecture in another's. Mickle is most interested in imperial practice. The dynamics of translation are present but subdued in his preface.

In order to fully grasp Mickle's intervention, and to conceive of the commodity he is offering to the marketplace, first it is crucial to know the basic fact that Camões's poem dramatizes fifteenth- and sixteenth-century Portuguese maritime exploration.[67] Prince Henry the Navigator, Bartolomeu Dias, and Vasco da Gama are Camões's principal heroes—fifteenth-century sailors reprocessed through long-standing European tropes surrounding maritime icons like Odysseus and Aeneas.[68] At heart, Camões's poem is about contact and expansion, imperial self-adulation, and the future fantasy of permanent Portuguese maritime preeminence. As reread through Mickle's translation, the epic becomes a precise lesson in imperial failure, a lesson that emphasizes Portuguese lassitude and misrule in contradistinction to British sense and rectitude. "The transactions of the Portuguese in India are peculiarly the wars and negociations of commerce, and therefore offer instructions to every trading country, which are not to be found in the campaigns of a Caesar or a Marlborough."[69] The point is that British imperialists must learn from others' mistakes. Britain has the capacity to avoid imperial errors, Mickle suggests. Translating and propagating the missteps of Portugal will help by providing a guidebook of errors imperialists might make.

Mickle's preface begins by examining Camões's epic poetry as a literary form and then proceeds into a disquisition pertaining to the nature of commerce. The value of the "alien wealth" he has reaped in his translation, from Mickle's point of view, is that the Portuguese imperial project can inform and improve British expansionary goals, not at the level of language, but at the level of culture. Detailed stories of Portuguese maritime exploration along the African and Asian coasts, badly organized territorial skirmishes in India, and grotesque courtly decadence are woven into a cautionary tale for British imperial practice that stresses intelligent planning, commercial acumen, and moral integrity. Put another way, Mickle's introduction to his translation of *Os Lusíadas* is—quantitatively and qualitatively—less a treatise on the practice of translation than it is a manifesto for building the right and most moral kind of empire. The primary value of the translation, as Mickle puts it, is in its scrupulous attention to Portuguese mistakes in empire's execution: "But it was neither foreseen nor foretold, that the unexampled misconduct of the Portuguese would render the most lucrative commerce of the world an heavy, and at last insupportable expence on the treasury of Lisbon or Madrid; nor was it foretold, that the shameless villainy, the faithless piracies and rapine of their countrymen would bring down destruction upon their empire."[70] Another value Mickle expresses is that his translation represents instructive cultural fusion that will benefit imperial practice: "The birth of Learning and Commerce may be different, but their growth is mutual and dependent upon each other," he writes, and "the intercourse of mankind is the parent of both."[71]

Mickle's image of translation is refracted through a vision of history in which commerce improves all parties equally, especially when pursued on the classical Greek model. "Where the Grecian commerce, confined as it was, extended its influence, the deserts became cultivated fields, cities rose, and men were drawn from the woods and caverns to unite in society,"

Mickle writes.[72] In his praise of commerce, Mickle's prose becomes increasingly grandiose. He rejoices in the reputation of Don Henry, "Prince of Portugal" and patron of Portuguese imperial conquest, a man born, in Mickle's words, "to give to the whole world every advantage, every light that may possibly be diffused by the Intercourse of unlimited commerce."[73] Even the story of the dissemination of alphabetic script is, in essence, a story of commercial expansion to Mickle, and so he reads it through his knowledge of Phoenician trading networks, themselves an anticipation of transnational European trading networks to come: "It was that nation of merchants, the Phoenicians, which diffused the use of letters through the ancient, and Commerce will undoubtedly diffuse the same blessings through the modern world."[74] In a context where commerce is held up as the precondition for the formation and development of society, a context in which language's elements—its written form as well as its literate tropes and conventions—are envisioned as exchangeable commodities, translation itself becomes a commercial endeavor designed to spread cultivation.[75] Mickle's translation from the Portuguese will lead to the translation of British commerce to India, the preface assumes.

As a form of commerce, translations must appear in the marketplace as useful products, not extraneous or luxurious ones. "The superfluities of life, the baubles of the opulent, and even the luxuries which enervate the irresolute and administer disease, are introduced by commerce," but nonetheless, "the benefits which attend it are also to be considered."[76] Similarly, "Rapacity, avarice, and effeminacy are the vices ascribed to the increase of Commerce," but "infinitely more dreadful," are the vices that attend commerce's absence.[77] Jones was similarly careful that translations be pitched as a virtue of commerce rather than a negative result of commerce, as they appear in Johnson. Jones continually emphasized that translation from Asian languages needed to focus on "Asiatick writings" of value. Translational value could be deduced only through comparison with known writings of value: "It must not be supposed from my zeal for the literature of *Asia*, that I mean to place it in competition with the beautiful productions of the *Greeks* and *Romans*. . . . We always return to the writings of the ancients, as to the standard of true taste."[78] Similarly, the most basic premise of Mickle's preface is that the commodity he is offering to the anglophone public must communicate the lesson that "ignorance of the true principles of commerce" was "that great cause of the fall of the Portuguese empire."[79] This ignorance "does not at present threaten the British," though it might if Britons lose the foundations of their commercial strength.[80]

Roughly contemporaneous to the works of Jones and Mickle, George Campbell's influential work in the domain of scriptural translation has little obvious connection to British imperial aspirations. Instead, Campbell's two-volume work *The Four Gospels, Translated from the Greek. With Preliminary Dissertations and Notes Critical and Explanatory* (1789) encapsulates a different life for eighteenth-century translational commodities, commodities that rise or fall in the marketplace based on the "superadditions" that they offer reader-consumers, to recall Tytler's phrase. Across the 513 pages that make up Campbell's twelve dissertations on translating New Testament Greek into English—or, roughly one-third of the entire commodity—Campbell demonstrates an understanding that his work will contribute to ongoing conversations about Christianity only to the degree that it convinces readers of its value. Hence the dissertations' detailed argumentation and general volubility. "In an age like the present, wherein literary productions are so greatly multiplied . . . the press teems daily with the labors of the learned,"[81] Campbell writes. "Plenty in this, as in every other commodity, makes people harder to be pleased."[82] Contrary to the "ancient" period in which the Gospels were composed and canonized, in the eighteenth-century anglophone world, "learning is in more hands. Critics are multiplied. The press is open; and every cavil, as well as every argument, is quickly circulated."[83] Campbell knows well that, as was the case with Jerome's Vulgate, the success of his of his endeavors will depend on the widespread adoption of "perspicuous" translations, adoption that in this case is equivalent to purchase.[84]

Campbell's picture of a competitive literary marketplace would seem to confirm a fact that he vociferously denies. "As to the remarks to be found in the Dissertation and Notes, nothing was further from my purpose than, in any instance, to sacrifice truth to novelty."[85] The novelty or "superaddition" of the translation, Campbell tells the reader, is not its reinterpretation of known Christian doctrine. Instead, the novelty that this translation offers is a more informed understanding of the history of biblical Greek and the multilingualism of those who have used it as a medium of composition. As does Mickle, but less crudely, Campbell offers contemporary anglophone readers a set of transferable lessons or added values to a relatively saturated market of biblical retranslations. As I argue here, for Campbell, the language of the New Testament offers insights that are applicable to religious interpretations of scripture just as they are central to Campbell's own understanding of Standard English. Indeed, his translation practice, which moves a Hellenistic Greek source into a Standard English target, must attend to the multiplicities, compatibilities, and incompatibilities of both languages in order to be valuable. This is no easy feat. Given the complexities introduced by the fact that the Greek of the Gospels is "the barbarous idiom of a few obscure Galileans" and that most of the text's speakers are "men perfectly illiterate, and taken out of the lowest class of people," Campbell has set a high bar for himself.[86]

The lessons of Campbell's lengthy preface begin in the careful and approachable way that Campbell describes the Hellenistic Greek language to readers who might be unfamiliar with its internal complexities. Narrating the history of the Greek linguistic system such that it appears as a distant template for anglophony's diverse vectors of internal difference, Campbell points out, "In a language spoken, as Greek was then, in many distant countries there inevitably arise peculiarities in the acceptation of words in different regions."[87] He stresses that the authors of the Gospels were Hellenistic Jews and that they were thus always in the process of translating their internal experience of Aramaic and other languages into the more current Greek, thereby risking the way "one mingles in his speech the idioms of his native tongue," a feature of linguistic life that the Edgeworths exploited to great effect relative to Standard English.[88] Campbell goes on to point out that an attentive reader of the Gospels must understand that in certain places, as regards the language, "the phraseology is Hebrew and the words are Greek."[89] This is the milieu in which the skilled scriptural translator must work. The translator must attend to the linguistic multiplicities of the authors who are being translated. The translator must offer readers every opportunity to comprehend how those multiplicities can be analogized to their present so as to encourage proper interpretation.

Campbell's approach to translation is underwritten by contemporary theories of language that he helped codify through his *The Philosophy of Rhetoric* (1776), especially this tome's interest in proper forms of public elocution. The central claims of this earlier work anticipate his approach to language in *The Four Gospels*. When Campbell asks the question, "With regard to those rules which constitute purity in the language of any country, what are they, in effect, but the conventions which have happened to obtain among the natives, particularly those of the higher ranks," an attentive reader of *The Philosophy of Rhetoric* would answer as Campbell suggests in that text. Rules that constitute the language of any country are nothing but conventions. Conventional rules that can be studied and mastered through proper attention to rhetoric's varying techniques.[90] Campbell later asks why Jesus Christ chose the linguistically mixed and multiple as the delivery mechanism of his "truths." His conclusion is that the apostles and evangelists were chosen *because of* rather than *in spite of* their mixed linguistic identities. Their speech, "without artificial periods" or "a studied elocution," communicated authenticity at its most basic, and this was crucial "lest to human eloquence that success should be ascribed, which ought to be attributed to the divinity of the doctrine, and the agency of the Spirit, in the miracles it wrought in support of it."[91] As a translator, Campbell presents this form of authenticity in the anglophone voices of his apostles and evangelists.

Capturing this authenticity is difficult, however, because as he puts it, "translation . . . is a sort of leveler." When different books of a larger work have different authors, as in the case of the Gospels, "there will be more or less of an assimilating quality, by which the works translated are brought, in point of expression, to bear some resemblance to the ordinary style of the translator" instead of accurately representing the copious diversity of authors and voices within the original text. Only highly skilled translators "can adapt themselves to different styles more easily than others" and in such a way that lofty registers remain lofty and humble registers remain humble.[92] Added to this, the translator must at all moments keep in view the fact that the voice of "our Lord," unlike the apostles, "always spoke his mother tongue." Whereas the apostles might display linguistic difference in translation, the translator can take no such liberty with God. This injunction is homologous to the patterns this book has traced so far. The communication of linguistic difference must be regulated and controlled by protocol that conforms to the tenets of propriety within any linguistic system—in this case a system in which God, rather than a "barbarous Galilean," is a source of revelation.[93]

For Campbell, the difficulties of translation do not stop there, and nor do the potential values. By thinking through multiplicity as it resides in the linguistic identities of the Gospels' authors, a translator can arrive at a tolerable but not exceptional anglophone rendering. Implicitly, this produces a salable commodity, especially if the translator is in colloquy with the range of commodities that have already attempted, but fallen short, of achieving the best translation.[94] Referencing the dynamism of the scriptural translation marketplace, Campbell opines that that he has "never yet seen a translation of the Bible, or of any part of it, into any language I am acquainted with, which I did not think might be, in several places, altered for the better."[95] In addition to overlooking the idioletic voices of each of the Gospel's authors, the principle errors scriptural translators make have to do with the fusing of two different linguistic systems, between which untranslatables obtain. Vexing problems attend the translation of weights, measures, and monetary systems, for example, as invariably they do not conform to one another. Furthermore, some languages are "scant," like "the ancient oriental languages," which suffer from a "penury of words."[96] Others are "copious" like Standard English.[97] In their attempts to bridge the gap between these two extremes, bad translators "never fail to render obscure and enigmatical in the translation what is perspicuous and simple in the original."[98]

These considerations lead Campbell to promulgate three primary areas of concern for the work of translation. A translator must give a just representation of the sense of the original. A translator must be consistent with regard to the "genius" of the source language, and in particular, to the genius of any individual writer of the source language. Finally, a translator must "take care that the [translated] version have at least so far the quality of an original performance, as to appear natural and easy, such as shall give no handle to the critic to charge the translator with applying words improperly, or in a meaning not warranted by use, or combining them in a way which renders the sense obscure, and the construction ungrammatical, or even harsh."[99] This final form of concern is oriented explicitly toward the "critic," by which Campbell means an actual critic in the anglophone public sphere, a writer who might attack the improprieties of the translation's language as a way to devalue its status as commodity. In this way, the evaluative criteria of the target language (in this case Standard English) govern the translation's execution.

Concluding that a translation should be both "close" and "free," as context demands, but never "servilely literal," Campbell puts into circulation a theory of translation that bears much in common with Tytler, Jones, Mickle, and others of his period.[100] All four theories are contained within multipart commodities. All four theories of translation stress the benefits—aesthetic, political, and religions—that will accrue to anglophony as a result of the translator's free labor. All four theories of translation evince a sense that the transmission of linguistic content from one medium to another unfolds against the backdrop of linguistico-cultural compatibility as well as market demand; languages communicate differences that must be preserved only to the degree that their preservation in translation does not upset the target language's already-existing ways of making meaning.

MULTILINGUAL LIVES

Sequoyah

"In the winter of 1828, a delegation of the Cherokees visited the city of Washington, in order to make a treaty with the United States," writes Samuel Knapp near the end of the first lecture of his *Lectures on American Literature*, published in 1829.[1] "Among them was See-quah-yah, the inventor of the Cherokee alphabet," about whom Knapp continues, "His English name was George Guess; he was a half-blood; but had never, from his own account, spoken a single word of English up to the time of his invention, nor since" (Figure 9).[2] The story Knapp relates regarding Sequoyah's first-person account of the invention of the Cherokee syllabary—"from the lips of the inventor himself"—is offered up as an object lesson in linguistic manifest destiny on the North American continent. "As Empire travels westward with us [white Euro-American anglophones] . . . this language, whose origin and history, copiousness, strength, beauty, sweetness, and importance, have occupied our past hour, will carry with it the blessings of sound political and civil institutions, the blessing of letters and science, of virtue and religion."[3] Knapp summarizes Sequoyah's achievements as part of a celebration of the "copious, beautiful, sweet, majestic, [and] strong" English language because, for him, Sequoyah is a perfect example of the way that "blessings of letters and science, of virtue and religion" fertilize and modernize those nonanglophone cultures with which anglophony comes into contact. "The Indians themselves are becoming philologists and grammarians," Knapp delightedly concludes, "and [they are] exciting the wonder of the world, by the invention of letters."[4]

The man whose reputation is attached to his Cherokee name, Sequoyah, rather than the anglophone names George Guess and George Gist, by which he is identified in some early texts, was born in a Cherokee town called

FIGURE 9. Sequoyah, by Henry Inman, after Charles Bird King, c. 1830, oil on canvas, National Portrait Gallery, Smithsonian Institution.

Tuskegee in what is today eastern Tennessee sometime between 1760 and 1776. Knapp's conversation with Sequoyah, which occurred through the mediation of "two interpreters, one a half-blood, Capt. Rogers, and the other a full-blood chief, whose assumed English name was John Maw," happened just seven years after Sequoyah had revealed his graphic invention to the Cherokee tribal council in 1821. The moment when Knapp records his translated conversation with this "stoick" and "grave" man is thus the beginning of a great efflorescence in Cherokee literacy, anglophone as well as Sequoyan.[5] It was also a moment of cultural crisis in which the system that Sequoyah developed in order to "promote Cherokees' improvement and autonomy" was regularly being pressed into service as a helpmate to Christian evangelism.[6]

According to Knapp, Sequoyah's initial inspiration for the syllabary came from an experience with a U.S. prisoner of war captured during Major General Arthur St. Clair's defeat at the Battle of the Wabash River in 1791, an important native victory in the Northwest Indian War (1785–95). "In this campaign, or some one that followed it, a letter was found on the person of a prisoner. . . . The question arose among them, whether this mysterious power of *the talking leaf*, was the gift of the Great Spirit to the white man, or a discovery of the white man himself?"[7] The trope of "*the talking leaf*" as a tantalizing foretaste of literacy's power echoes and reframes "the trope of the talking book" in Ukasaw Gronniosaw, Olaudah Equiano, Frederick Douglass, and other authors of the black Atlantic tradition even as it foreshadows the intersection of indigenous and European intellectual traditions, an intersection that is memorably staged in Claude Lévi-Strauss's descriptions of the Nambikwara tribe in Brazil.[8] Lévi-Strauss, after observing the "chief's genius in instantly recognizing that writing could increase his authority," concludes, "My hypothesis, if correct, would oblige us to recognize the fact that the primary function of written communication is to facilitate slavery. . . . The fight against illiteracy is therefore connected with an increase in governmental authority over its citizens. Everyone must be able to read, so that the government can say: Ignorance of the law is no excuse."[9] The comparison between Lévi-Strauss's descriptions of the Nambikwara chief and Knapp's descriptions of Sequoyah is a distant but informative one.

While contemporary scholars might be comfortable seeing Sequoyah as someone who, like the Nambikwara chief, intuits foreign literacy's power and then invents native literacy (and numeracy) for his people, not as a way to gain power—as in Lévi-Strauss—but instead as an end-run around anglophone cultural incursions, Knapp interprets Sequoyah's invention as a backformation of anglophone linguistic practice—the uplifting result of the American empire's westward movement. As part of his case, Knapp uses disability as a narrative prosthesis, noting that Sequoyah does not have an opportunity to engage in his linguistic speculations until long after his first encounter with "*the talking leaf*," at a moment when the "swelling on his knee confined him to his cabin" and "made him a cripple for life, by shortening the diseased leg."[10] Only at this moment, when disability has forced Sequoyah to abandon his native predilections toward the mobile "excitements of war, and the pleasures of the chase," is he able, in Knapp's estimation, to direct his mind toward the "mystery of the power of *speaking by letters*."[11]

Evoking Rousseau's *Essai sur l'origine de langues* (1781), Knapp claims that Sequoyah observed the communication of animal passions in the natural world as a linguistic prototype. In a strangely infrahuman chain, Knapp then states that Sequoyah reasoned inductively "from the cries of wild beasts, from the talents of the mocking-bird, from the voices of his children and his companions" in order to come up with the idea of parsing the Cherokee language into discrete sounds that would each be represented by "pictorial signs, images of birds and beasts to convey these sounds to others, or to mark them in his own mind."[12] Knapp's narrative of the invention of the Cherokee syllabary climaxes as Sequoyah gradually abandons images of birds and beasts in favor of graphic abstraction, thereby distancing himself from the perceived organicism of indigenous lives. In Knapp's telling, Sequoyah alights on the idea of the conventional or arbitrary sign, and his insights quicken. Because of these insights, he becomes progressively alienated from his compatriots. "By this time he [Sequoyah] had become so abstracted from his tribe and their usual pursuits, that he was viewed with an eye of suspicion."[13]

Sequoyah at last creates a syllabary of "about two hundred characters," which number is later reduced to "eighty-six" with the help of his daughter's "acute ear."[14] By inventing this system for the rapid implementation of Cherokee literacy, he humanizes himself in Knapp's eyes. Knapp describes Sequoyah as seizing for himself and his people the power of literacy even if that power is to be exercised outside and as a challenge to anglophone systems of authority through literacy. Sequoyah's humanization, however, works (conversely) to demote those Cherokees who are suspicious of their tribesman's investigations into language. "There was some lurking suspicion of necromancy in the whole business," Knapp reports, forcing Sequoyah to strip his invention "of all supernatural influence."[15] Sequoyah must demonstrate for all onlookers his invention's scientificity, that is, its testability and reproducibility. This he does by having tribal elders pass information to him by using his daughter as Cherokee-language scribe. What follows this momentous performance is the tribe's celebratory epiphany, here heralded in Knapp as: "See-quah-yah became at once schoolmaster, professor, philosopher, and chief," a chain of attainments that equates titles drawn from the discourses of education with a revered position within some Native American tribal structures. "How nearly is man alike in every age!" Knapp exclaims before narrating how the Cherokees throw a feast in which Sequoyah is the guest of honor and held "in reverence as one favoured by the Great Spirit."[16]

Describing Sequoyah's successful proof that his syllabary could be used to communicate ideas across a distance and without speaking, Knapp concludes that the evidence worked "in such a manner as not only to destroy their [his kinsmen's] infidelity, but most firmly to fix their faith." In this way, Sequoyah is scripted into history as a figure who endows his tribe with what Knapp considers to be necessary conditions of modernity. For Knapp, Sequoyah becomes a sort of prophet in whom one has faith—that is, he elevates his people by virtue of his transcendent and transcultural linguistic intelligence. Knapp spares no praise in enumerating Sequoyah's uniquely impressive mind, which unfortunately reads as though his commendations are actively arguing against Sequoyah's indigeneity. Because of this, Sequoyah's ability to translate graphic technology back to his people cannot alter the fact that Sequoyah ceases to be a member of that people at all. "An Indian of the strictest veracity and sobriety," Sequoyah becomes a "man of diversified talents," a man who "passes from metaphysical and philosophical investigations to mechanical occupations with the greatest ease." He becomes an "American Cadmus" whose "habits are those of the most assiduous scholar" and whose "disposition is more lively than that of any Indian I ever saw."[17] Knapp finally defines the primary criterion of Sequoyah's exemplarity: "He understood and felt the advantages the white man had long enjoyed, of having the accumulations of every branch of knowledge, from generation to generation, by means of a written language, while the red man could only commit his thoughts to uncertain tradition."[18] Sequoyah is the supremely free translator of the late eighteenth century. He proves his translational skill to Knapp by adapting and circulating a technology that many anglophones deemed to be requisite for and coeval with "humanity" and "civilization."

Transcendent and transcultural, Sequoyah's perspective is believed to be transracial and translingual as well, or at least insofar as he takes from Europe and transmits to others. He proves to Knapp that, in "the western wilderness," "man has started up, and proved that he has not degenerated since the primitive days of Cecrops."[19] Sequoyah endorses the literate tradition with which Knapp associates himself. His story is recast as a narrative that flatters the uplifting potential of anglophone dispersal westward. After all, Sequoyah's initial idea came from "*the talking leaf*" of a U.S. soldier. "The western wilderness is not only to blossom like the rose," Knapp futurizes; it will also reveal more vectors for anglophone self-praise.

The five previous interludes on multilingual lives of the long eighteenth century that have been included in this book are fundamentally different from this final one, a brief semibiography in which I have described an interlingual contact with anglophony as experienced by a nonanglophone Cherokee and mediated through an American scholar of literature and history. The previous five narratives attempted to argue, by anecdote, for the narrative generativity of anglophone multilingualism. Peros, Jack, Neptune, and Cupid, who seep into the anglophone record as multilingual subversives with extra-anglophone ties that facilitate the disruption of plantation life's racist routines; Reverend Lyons, whose fantasies about the conditions of possibility for the emergence of a "*mere Irish scholar*" amount to an artful eulogy to a moribund tongue; Dorothy Pentreath and William Bodener, two elderly Cornish multilinguals whose apparent ephemerality echoes a broad anglophone interest in the superseded linguistic practices of bygone days; Joseph Emin, a writer who anxiously inscribes his own foreignness into an anglophone autobiography that abounds with extra-anglophone linguistic plenitude; and, last, Antera Duke, an anglophone multilingual who reformulates Standard English as a way to access its lucrative valences, a man who produces a dramatic piece of language-repurposing prose that cannot be reduced to a mere epiphenomenon of the unconscious processes of his linguistic substrata.

The story of Sequoyah, however, adds a new and important element. Sequoyah's story is about a relationship with anglophony that occasions a wholesale rejection of its premises. Sequoyah's story is about seizing linguistic sovereignty for a community that is encroached on. Taken together, then, the six multilingual lives I have included in this book chart several different itineraries. Together they speak (in many tongues) to the ungeneralizability of eighteenth-century anglophone experience. They speak to anglophony's many directions, its entanglements, and its many forms of relation—all of which occur as prefiguration to a present in which the dynamics I have described have intensified and changed. They also speak to forms of linguistic resistance. "Opacities must be preserved," Glissant writes. "An appetite for opportune obscurity in translation must be created; and falsely convenient vehicular sabirs must be relentlessly refuted."[20] Telling these six stories is about the preservation of such opacities just as it is about the embarrassment of monolithic and monolinguistic forms of thought that take a Standard English "sabir" as global destiny.

CONCLUSION

Anglophone Futures

Globalization and Divination, Language and the Humanities

The Life and Death of a Book

Samuel Ward Francis's *An Autobiography of a Latin Reader by Samuel Syntax, Esq.* (1859) is a novel of circulation, or "it-narrative," in true eighteenth-century style.[1] The novel's titular object begins its life as a rag. The rag is transformed into paper and, as paper, suffers the great pain of being cut into a book's pages. These newly cut pages find themselves at a printer's shop, fit to be inked, and, in a surprising feat of self-consciousness, they begin to muse, "I had a great desire to be a book of deep research, [a book] that would be consulted by the great men of the times, fill the young mind with useful information, arouse the weary, influence the old, and do honor to my country."[2] This disembodied voice of paper imagines different forms of "useful" book it might aspire to be—a book of arithmetic, a book of mythology, a "spelling-book," a history book, or perhaps a novel, which "would be purchased by rich and poor, young and old."[3]

These fantasies of utility and accessibility are rearranged after the printing process, when the book exclaims, "Reader, imagine my astonishment when, having received a stamp, my brain was instantly filled with Latin verbs, prepositions, adverbs and conjunctions."[4] Finding itself in the shape of a "Latin Reader," more specifically, a collection of didactic readings from figures like Horace, Cicero, and others, the book is delighted. "I now felt happy that I was printed for a higher class of persons than novel-readers," it exults.[5] This exultation is a sad mistake. As the Latin Reader soon learns. "I was not the kind of book [that was] in demand."[6]

In an upswing of fate, a curious boy purchases the Latin Reader. The book accompanies him to a boarding school, where, to its chagrin, it is shoved into a desk in favor of other instruments of learning. "I remained there, I should think, for nearly three months, seeing daylight only, when the desk was opened by my owner, to get a history, an arithmetic, or a spelling-book."[7] This is the first in a chain of misfortunes suffered by this book. Others include being spilled on, written on, scuffed up, and neglected as though valueless. The Latin Reader's worth in suspension, the book is hawked for a trifle to a bookseller who tosses it on a tall stack of other discarded texts. The book's commodity circulation—and therefore its story—appears to have come to an end.

The death of the Latin Reader is initiated in spectacular fashion. A fire consumes the bookseller's stall. The book fearfully reports, "In one corner of my berth I heard a deep groan emanating from a burning book in dying agonies. . . . I shut my eyes and shuddered."[8] Losing its bizarre form of consciousness, the book awakens to find itself scorched and waterlogged, unlovingly heaped on a pile of trash in the street. Believing itself to have escaped combustion, and thankful to remain alive, the remnants of the Latin Reader are scavenged by a child who wants to repurpose the book's paper for a kite. Its relief is short lived. A servant of the child's family finds the remnants of the half-burnt book and uses them as kindling, the hellish return of a destiny that the book believed it had escaped.

Before its death, this contemplative book philosophizes over the vagaries of fate that engender this or that embodiment or objectification. "How differently persons are placed in this life," the book thinks while fantasizing about the free movements of a gnat or fly.[9] We can read the Latin Reader's desire to be a common fly rather than a collection of didactic Latin writings as a reaction to feeling useless and seeing the self as useless in commodity terms. A fly exists outside the circulation of commodities, after all, and the Latin Reader sees this extraeconomic existence as desirable and liberatory. The book's fly fantasy encapsulates one implicit claim made in this novel: the Latin language, in addition to the historical, political, rhetorical, and aesthetic values that inhere therein, are anachronistic to the structures of education in mid- to late nineteenth-century America. The book's embodiment fantasies and double combustion point to its self-understanding as a finite commodity made of matter. Metaphorically, the demise of this material points to the politics of language as they shift educational priorities and reorder communities—often dramatically—over time.

In our contemporary moment, it is difficult not to read the book's "it-narrative" as an allegory pertaining to the value of knowledge as commodity. By this I mean that the "Latin" of the "Latin Reader" is not the most important thing to be lost in the book's destruction. Instead, the Latin Reader's misfortune is that its lessons are no longer viewed as instrumental or remunerative in the day-to-day lives of people in 1859. Of course Latin and other classical languages are still (thankfully) studied and researched, but that is not the main point of this heuristic. I have chosen to close with this strange conceit because the primary drama of the book's life is a crisis of pedagogical confidence, a feeling of valuelessness in the face of large-scale cultural and economic developments, a feeling that may be familiar to humanities scholars in the present.

Teleologies of English

We also know that change will have to be undertaken soon, or, things will change: task or event.[10]

Scholars of anglophone literature have been living through a fascinating conjunction, a conjunction relating to the commodity lives of the disciplines we teach and the institutional functions we perform. One sees this conjunction in the fact that two contrasting visions of the future of anglophone education clash in the marketplace. On the one hand, each day adds a new voice to the discordant choir of those who futurize the humanities—particularly fields like literature—as a crisis leading to death.[11] The illness in these fields is signified by shrinking major numbers, falling enrollments, hiring freezes, labor casualization, and, more generally, the perception that aesthetic education no longer has valuable skills to transmit or meaningful lessons to teach. Circulating alongside these gloomy futures, recent writing has also witnessed a tremendous efflorescence in popular works that herald the future of "Global English," "World English," "Globish," et cetera.[12] These latter works, which I discuss below by way of closing, paint the global reach of anglophony in sublime terms.[13] In various forms of future fantasy, they argue that we are living through "boom times" relating to the global influence of anglophone tongues.[14] They argue that there is a pressing cultural need to organize anglophony's expanding heft as proof of ongoing economic globalization, itself a portent of more globalization to come: so much so that narrating a global "it-narrative" of the "English" language has become a salable intellectual project with a sizeable readership. Unlike the curricula of many U.S. American humanities departments, the object of knowledge these books purport to explore is widely assumed, prima facie, to be urgent and therefore valuable.[15]

What, if anything, do narratives celebrating the anglophone dimensions of globalization have to do with the narrative of crisis surrounding the humanities? More importantly, what, if anything, does this conjunction tell us about ways forward in the humanities? These are the questions this conclusion tries to synthesize by looking critically at contemporary celebrations of anglophone expansionism against the eighteenth-century linguistic history that I have charted so far. Within this genre, the best books are well researched and ethically responsible attempts to locate anglophony's functioning in global capitalism as well as in global flows of cultural capital. Many of these works document the importance of anglophony to science and technology by citing language publication statistics.[16] They document the language system's importance in global communication by discussing anglophony in relation to the technical protocol and written content of the digital present and computer science more generally. They chart the importance of anglophony to global business, politics, and diplomacy by citing its official adoption by international organizations relating to the governmental, nonprofit, and for-profit sectors. To differing degrees, this genre discusses the pressures exerted on nonanglophone communities by the active exportation of diverse anglophone language practices in the form of commodities and popular culture. The more troubling representatives of this genre, however, have a tendency to drift into narrowly imagined cost-benefit analyses in which the economic benefit of anglophone incursions into other linguistic spaces outweigh any and all cultural costs. In some cases these "costs" are not seen as costs at all.

One of the most fascinating aspects of this genre is that these texts reproduce, and often in sanguine terms, certain strains of eighteenth-century anglophone ideologies relating to language, ideologies that were produced in and through empire. Even as recent anglophone futurologies try to root themselves in a dehierarchized, globalized, and networked present, a present in which transnational dialogue and exchange are desirable, they nevertheless parrot ideas about linguistic difference that can never be washed clean of their association with imperial mentality. These texts on "Global English" reconstitute the absorptive ideologies of the discourse of "copiousness," not as something to be glorified, but as an organic and causeless development that was always already predicted by anglophony's felicitous geographical and natural properties—the language's initial mixity, for example, its subsequent flexibility, and its absorptive capacity for taking in foreign words and expressions and rewrapping them in domestic dress. By actively disavowing the coercive historical forces that produced the naturalness of these "natural properties," and by overwriting the active but sometimes futile resistance that certain linguistic communities have attempted to marshal (and continue to marshal) as defense, these teleologies of English can omit more than they contain.

David Northrup, an important scholar of African transatlantic history, one of the three coeditors of the *Diary of Antera Duke*, cited extensively above, claims that his book *How English Became the Global Language* (2013) is "neither a celebration of global English and globalization nor a manifesto against their spread."[17] At times, however, this book reads like an excessive celebration of "Global English's" position in the world economy. This is particularly true in the book's final section, when Northrup sets out to counter the "prominent coterie of intellectuals who denounce globalization and global English on moral grounds."[18] The author digs in on this point regarding linguistic relativists and "moralists": "Even if they had their facts straight, such critics are tilting at windmills," he claims; "they neither understand the larger processes nor the personal choices made by individuals around the world."[19] Caricaturing sophisticated and worthy critics of neocolonialism and neoliberalism by challenging their control of the "facts," Northrup is partially right to note that deliberate individual and community choices have worked to perpetuate and extend the rapid spread of anglophony in the postcolonial period. He is also partially right in that individual choices, as he puts it, "have turned the spread of English from an imperialist plot to a more nuanced and more complex narrative."[20] But he is wrong in that anglophony's "more complex narrative" includes the axiom that, at the level of large-scale linguistic and economic systems, individual choices matter only in aggregate. When huge numbers of people "choose" anglophony, these are not the deliberate choices of free subjects, but instead, symptoms of larger economic and cultural events that are underway. At what point does a choice made out of economic necessity or cultural pressure cease to be a choice at all but instead an obligation?

The species of thought one sees in analyses like Northrup's values language to the degree that it is universal rather than culturally particular. This line of thought hearkens back to another era, one that believed in the project of universal, disinterested knowledge and abstract human subjects who, as in a fantasy, all have equal access to economic and political self-determination. When Northrup drifts into this mode, "however interesting the variations in English can be, the uniformity and mutual intelligibility of English across its major variations is the far more remarkable phenomenon"; or, when Scott Montgomery thinks through anglophone hegemony in science by writing, "Local tongues and possibly cultures are affected. . . . Casualties exist, in other words"; or, when Robert McCrum waxes into sublimity at the global extent of anglophone penetration, stating, "Estimates that about half the world's population . . . have knowledge of, or acquaintance with, some kind of English point to an aspiration driven by the deepest, most ancient impulse for a global community"; then crucial analytical dimensions are missing.[21] These critics are thinking linguistic culture and community in terms of efficiency, benefit, speed, profit, and globality, optics that align precisely with neoliberal discourse surrounding maximal economic benefit with minimal nonproductive drag. In other words, they are thinking within the same market-oriented logics that are institutionally marginalizing inquiry in the humanities.[22] This criticism is by no means intended to cast suspicion or aspersion on the importance of inquiry into the state of anglophone life in the global present. Writing a teleology of English is a form of humanistic work after all. Instead, I mean to suggest, as I have sought to do throughout *Multilingual Subjects*, that terms derived from a narrow vision of efficiency and profitability are insufficient when it comes to understanding the historical, political, and aesthetic complexities of the soft-power anglicization of the world to come.

James F. English's *The Global Future of English Studies* (2012) is a compactly executed, compelling, but still uneasy synthesis of our contemporary moment's twinned metalinguistic discourses—planetary anglophone futurology plus the narrative of crisis in humanities disciplines like "English" literature. English argues that "if we consider the global future of English studies," the picture is much less bleak than it is typically described, for English is becoming an ever more dominant language of a rapidly expanding global higher education system."[23] The picture of linguistic globalization this book presents comes from a pragmatic attempt to conceive of the future of "English studies" outside of the narrative of crisis and collapse that seems to have attended the field's entire existence, only recently having been severely exacerbated.[24] The density of statistical analysis surrounding

Standard English as global language of instruction confirms an intuition among many that "English studies" is being off-shored in a way that is analogous to what European and North American companies have been doing with manufacturing and other industries since at least the 1970s.[25] As James English makes clear to argue, however, this is not to say that the internationalization of "English studies" represents a diminishment, but instead that it represents a field-changing opportunity in which studied attention to the global confraternity of anglophone educators can preserve and cultivate spaces of free inquiry. In a way, this author is documenting necessary changes in the nature of the educational commodity that "English" or "literature" departments might have on offer if they enter "global" space under the rebrand "English studies." Scholars should think critically about these changes, for as Glissant points out, "Development thus has linguistic stakes, with consequences that can be neither codified nor predicted."[26]

The futurist manifesto that ends James English's volume on "English studies" is sensible, future-oriented, and careful. It attempts to sketch out the most fundamental ways in which a rechristened discipline like "English studies" must be cognizant of the global scope of anglophone life and institutional pedagogy as it plots its own institutional future. The manifesto's section on enrollments, after noting the global multiplication of disciplinary concentrations in recent years, concludes, "English studies is just one player on this vast and busy [disciplinary] field."[27] The author goes on to register the educational marketplace's competitiveness, noting, "But it is positioned as a natural winner."[28] In the section "Faculty," English attacks the casualization of academic labor and points to improvements in public relations as a way for faculty to justify themselves. "The story we need to be spreading is not about our unmet needs and desires but about the quality of student education."[29] The scandal of adjunct labor is what "students, parents, and university ranking services need to hear."[30] The final section on "Curriculum" asks scholars to attend to the reality of the global expanse of "English studies" as a discipline: "We are approaching a turning point at which, in strictly quantitative terms, the most consequential decisions about what and how we teach will be made on the seeming peripheries of the discipline."[31]

Scholars of the "Anglophone and European base," which he calls the "presumptive center," need to listen to and incorporate the work of scholars on the "periphery," because, in this unevenly globalizing moment, "The tail of foreign [anglophone] variants is becoming long enough to wag the dog of domestic English lit."[32] English's suggestions for how these evolutions in curriculum might play out are tantalizing. South Africa and Nigeria offer new models for a "less London-oriented syllabus in postcolonial African literature."[33] Similarly, and crucially, "departments in Brazil and Mexico can help to shape a new canon of American literatures and develop the new models we require for a bi- or trilingual American literary studies."[34] I would echo but also depart from these last two points only to say that African departments of literature might also offer bi- or trilingual models of literary studies just as literature departments in Brazil and Mexico already provide nonanglophone models of the deterritorialization of linguistic systems—the lusophone, the hispanophone—that scholars of anglophony might make central to their own teaching.

English's suggestions are illuminating but optimistic. As he points out, the future of anglophone education cannot be based around the reproduction of its primary institutional premises only elsewhere. Education must change; institutions must change too. To think about the future of anglophone education in these terms poses an interesting set of question. Does buying into a potential "global future of English studies" mean accepting anglophony's role as a continuing instrument of uneven forms of globalization? Does it mean stewarding the language into spaces where it might be economically advantageous but culturally destructive? "Local tongues and possibly cultures are affected. . . . Casualties exist, in other words"?[35] These questions are among those that Gayatri Spivak tarries with in her brilliant collection of essays *An Aesthetic Education in the Era of Globalization* (2012). Spivak answers both in the affirmative. Endorsing "global English studies" does indeed mean accepting anglophony's role as a continuing instrument of globalization. Endorsing "global English studies" does indeed mean stewarding the language into spaces where it might be economically advantageous and also culturally destructive.

In her discussion of forms of aesthetic education that can "supplement the necessary uniformization of globalization with linguistic diversity," Spivak figures anglophone scholarship as arriving at a decision point.[36] She writes, "We also know that change will have to be undertaken soon, or, things will change: task or event," challenge or inevitability.[37] Reading the question of global "English studies" through Spivak, we come face to face with the fact that, in spite of the ongoing crisis, we can conceptualize meaningful (but perhaps not valuable) forms of aesthetic education that work to challenge globalization's economic premises. "In our dwindling isolation cells," she writes, "we must plumb the forgotten and mandatorily ignored polarity of the social productivity and social destructiveness of capital and capitalism . . . by way of deep language learning, qualitative social sciences, philosophizing unconditional ethics."[38] To be worthy of the troubling term "global," any and all forms of education must perforce be multilingual.

The crisis in the humanities might be rescripted by coupling a global view of the field's expansion with attention to the multiplicities of any one language as well as to linguistic multiplicity itself, which I have been suggesting throughout *Multilingual Subjects*. Even so, this coupling does not necessarily arrest the ongoing diminution of the linguistic multiplicities that we are supposed to contemplate. As we try in the classroom to bring the multilingualism of our diverse students into conversation with the fields and periods we study, we are still facing a set of global economic developments that are antagonistic to both native and taught multilingualism. We face a future in which the world's remaining linguistic diversity stands in stark contrast to the way that anglophone institutions of primary, secondary, and higher education in North America are becoming increasingly monolingual at the level of curriculum, thereby failing at the pressing task of engaging students in extra-anglophone constellations of linguistic multiplicity. A close study of the dynamics of eighteenth-century anglophony suggests that crucial conditions that sustained an important variety of linguistic relationality are now absent, eliminated by the ideologies with which Standard English has tended to travel: colonialism, racism, sexism, classism, capitalism, and others.[39] Analyzing a crucial period in the history of eighteenth-century anglophony in terms of politics, aesthetics, and representation is my attempt to engage some historical forms of linguistic multiplicity that matter immensely as an inheritance of the present.

This primary conceptual balancing act, I think, is anticipated in the epigraphs that are prepended to this book. "If I know not the meaning of the voice, I shall be unto him that speaketh a barbarian," Paul writes in the First Epistle to the Corinthians, "and he that speaketh *shall* be a barbarian to me." Even as this passage makes an assertion regarding linguistic relationality, it also poses a set of questions. Interpreting the passage and its context loosely, it suggests that because there are "so many kinds of voices in the world" speaking in "unintelligible tongues" always demands an interpreter. An interpreter or translator allows an unintelligible tongue to be rendered in its relationship to the future of the community. Not only does this idea reverberate through the chain of centuries in Rangarajan's claim that "at the heart of every colonial encounter lies an act of translation," it gestures to the way in which the coming community depends on the "interpreter" or "translator."[40]

In Glissant's mandate that "opacities must be preserved" and that "an appetite for opportune obscurity in translation must be created," one finds a very different take on the human stakes of communication and exchange.[41] In 1 Corinthians, language difference must be overcome; in Glissant, it must be preserved. The future of "English studies" within an anglophone frame must synthesize these two ideas, insofar as it is possible, by grounding itself in the pedagogical value of linguistic multiplicity as a challenge to global economic uniformity. Many works of scholarship are doing this already, and *Multilingual Subjects* has sought to engage and further that scholarship by presenting an eighteenth-century picture of the enduring dialectic of linguistic universality and particularity.

Perhaps instead of a global future for "English studies" we should desire a future in which teleologies of English become progressively more parochial and provincialized, when "English" itself becomes parochial and provincialized.[42] Gikandi is right to say that this desire is a way of defending several segments of the public sphere—literature, aesthetics, and politics—against those who would disavow their value in contemporary conversations regarding the way of the world. Desiring anglophone provincialization is one way to argue in favor of our disciplinary future. Only under the make-believe conditions in which anglophony is somehow decoupled from globalization can an open and active attitude toward multilingualism and linguistic nonnormativity be cultivated across divergent and multilingual spaces as educational practice. Only when anglophony becomes but one example among many accessible linguistic counterexamples can critical study of anglophone literature be defensible and meaningful. Only then can critical translation flourish. In these circumstances, anglophony is seen not in the light of its imperial or global dimensions, but instead for its irreducible singularity—in the same way that all other forms of linguistic subjectivation are absolutely singular, and therefore wonderful. Only in these circumstances is anglophony seen as one way of being in the world among many. To echo Glissant, "Relation . . . is spoken multilingually," or, as Spivak theorizes, "Linguistic diversity can only curb the global."[43]

APPENDICES

Appendix A

Selected “Dialect” Prose

Appendix B

Selected “Dialect” Poetry

Appendix A. Selected "Dialect" Prose

Dialect	*Year*	*Author*	*Title*	*Publisher*	*Place*	*Type*	*Edition Noted*	*Preface*	*Glossary*
Cornish	1824	A Physician	*A Cornish Dialogue Between Grace Penvear and Mary Treviskey in A Guide to the Mount's Bay and the Land's End*	Printed and Published by W. Phillips	London and Edinburgh	Poetic Dialect Dialogue	Second	Many other Materials	No
Cornish	1846	Treenoodle	*Specimens of Cornish Provincial Dialect, Collected and Arranged by Uncle Jan Treenoodle, with some Introductory Remarks, and a Glossary, by an Antiquarian Friend, and A Selection of Songs and Other Pieces Connected with Cornwall.*	John Russell Smith	London	Prose Dialect		Yes	Yes
Craven (West Riding of Yorkshire)	1824	A Native of Craven	*Horae Momenta Cravenae, or, The Craven Dialect, Exemplified in Two Dialogues, Between Farmer Giles and his Neighbour Bridget. To which is Annexed a Copious Glossary*	Printed for Hurst, Robinson, and Co.	London and Leeds	Prose Dialect Dialogue	First	Yes	Yes
Craven (West Riding of Yorkshire)	1828	A Native of Craven (William Carr in hand)	*The Dialect of Craven, in the West-Riding of the County of York, With a Copious Glossary, Illustrated by Authorities from Ancient English and Scottish Writers, and Exemplified by Two Familiar Dialogues . . . In Two Volumes*	Printed for Wm. Crofts	London and Leeds	Prose Dialect Dialogue	Second, "Much Enlarged"	Many More Paratexts than First Edition	Yes

Appendix A (*continued*)

Dialect	*Year*	*Author*	*Title*	*Publisher*	*Place*	*Type*	*Edition Noted*	*Preface*	*Glossary*
Cumberland	1811		*Jollie's Sketch of Cumberland Manners and Customs: Partly in the Provincial Dialect, in Prose and Verse. With A Glossary*	Printed by F. Jollie and Sons	Carlisle and London	Dialect Poetry and Prose Letter by Isaac Ritson, "Manners and Customs of Cumberland"		Yes	Yes
Devonshire	1837	"A Lady" (Glossary by J. F. Palmer)	*A Dialogue in the Devonshire Dialect, (In Three Parts) By A Lady: To Which is Added a Glossary by J. F. Palmer*	Longman, Rees, Orme, Brown, Green and Longman; and P. Hannaford	London and Exeter	Prose Dialect Dialogue		Dedication and Advertisement	Yes
Devonshire	1839	Mary Palmer (edited by Mrs. Gwatkin)	*A Devonshire Dialogue, In Four Parts. To Which is Added A Glossary, For the most part by the late Rev. John Phillipps, of Membury, Devon.*	G. B. Whittaker and Co.	London and Plymouth	Prose Dialect Dialogue		Advertisement	Yes (glosses also in endnotes)
Exmoor	1746		*An Exmoor Scolding; In The Propriety and Decency of Exmoor Language, Between Two Sisters, Wilmot Moreman and Thomasin Moreman, As they were spinning.*	Printed and Sold by Andrew and Sarah Brice	Exon (Exeter?)	Prose Dialect Dialogue	Third	No	No
Exmoor	1750		*An Exmoor Scolding; In The Propriety and Decency of Exmoor Language, Between Two Sisters, Wilmot Moreman and Thomasin Moreman, As they were spinning.*	Printed and Sold by Andrew Brice	Exon (Exeter?)	Prose Dialect Dialogue	Fourth	No	No

Appendix A (*continued*)

Dialect	*Year*	*Author*	*Title*	*Publisher*	*Place*	*Type*	*Edition Noted*	*Preface*	*Glossary*
Exmoor	1768		*An Exmoor Scolding; In The Propriety and Decency of Exmoor Language, Between Two Sisters, Wilmot Moreman and Thomasin Moreman, As they were spinning. Also, an Exmoor Courtship*	Printed and Sold by A. Brice and B. Thorn	Exon (Exeter?)	Prose Dialect Dialogue	Sixth	No	No
Exmoor	1771		*An Exmoor Scolding; In the Propriety and Decency of Exmoor Language, Between Two Sisters, Wilmot Moreman and Thomasin Moreman, As they were Spinning. Also an Exmoor Courtship.*	Printed and Sold by A. Brice and B. Thorn	Exon (Exeter?)	Prose Dialect Dialogue	Seventh	Yes	Yes
Exmoor	1775		*An Exmoor Scolding, In the Propriety and Decency of Exmoor Language, Between Two Sisters, Wilmot Moreman and Thomasin Moreman, As they were spinning; Also, an Exmoor Courtship.*	Printed and Sold by B. Thorn	Exeter	Prose Dialect Dialogue	Eighth	Yes	Yes
Exmoor	1782		*An Exmoor Scolding, Between Two Sisters, Wilmot Moreman and Thomasin Moreman, As they were spinning, Also An Exmoor Courtship. Together with Notes, and a Vocabulary for explaining barbarous Words and Phrases*	Printed by B. Thorn and Son	Exeter	Prose Dialect Dialogues	Ninth ("Care-fully corrected and revised")	Yes	Yes
Exmoor	1788?		*An Exmoor Scolding; In the Propriety and Decency of Exmoor Language, Between Two Sisters, Wilmot Moreman and Thomasin Moreman, As they were Spinning. Also an Exmoor Courtship.*	Printed by E. Grigg; and sold by W. Grigg	Exeter	Prose Dialect Dialogue	Tenth	Yes	Yes

Appendix A (*continued*)

Dialect	*Year*	*Author*	*Title*	*Publisher*	*Place*	*Type*	*Edition Noted*	*Preface*	*Glossary*
Exmoor	1794		*An Exmoor Scolding, Between Two Sisters, Wilmot Moreman and Thomasin Moreman, As they were spinning, Also An Exmoor Courtship; Both in the Propriety and Decency of the Exmoor Dialect, Devon; To Which is Adjoined a Collateral Paraphrase in plain English, for explaining barbarous Words and Phrases*	Printed and Sold by J. Huxtable	South Molton	Prose Dialect Dialogue with Paraphrase		No	No
Exmoor	1795		*An Exmoor Scolding, Between Two Sisters, Wilmot Moreman and Thomasin Moreman, As they were spinning, Also An Exmoor Courtship; Both in the Propriety and Decency of the Exmoor Dialect, Devon: To Which is Prefixed, A Translation of the Same, Into plain English.*	Printed and Sold by J. McKenzie and Son	Exeter	Prose Dialect Dialogue with Translation		No	No
Exmoor	1796		*An Exmoor Scolding, Between Two Sisters, Wilmot Moreman and Thomasin Moreman, As they were spinning, Also An Exmoor Courtship; Both in the Propriety and Decency of the Exmoor Dialect, Devon: To Which is Prefixed, A Translation of the Same, Into plain English.*	Printed and Sold by W. Squance	Torrington	Prose Dialect Dialogue with Translation		No	No

Appendix A (*continued*)

Dialect	*Year*	*Author*	*Title*	*Publisher*	*Place*	*Type*	*Edition Noted*	*Preface*	*Glossary*
Exmoor	1818		*An Exmoor Scolding, In the Propriety and Decency of Exmoor Language, Between Two Sisters, Wilmot Moreman and Thomasin Moreman, As they were spinning; Also, an Exmoor Courtship.*	Reprinted from an Edition of 1771, by Penny and Son	Exeter	Prose Dialect Dialogue	"A New Edition"	Yes (Preface to the Seventh Edition, 1771)	Yes
Exmoor	1839		*An Exmoor Scolding; In the Propriety and Decency of Exmoor Language, Between Two Sisters, Wilmot Moreman and Thomasin Moreman, As they were spinning, Also, an Exmoor Courtship. A New Edition, With Notes and A Glossary Explaining Uncouth Expressions and Interpreting Barbarous Words and Phrases*	John Russell Smith	London	Prose Dialect Dialogue	"A New Edition"	Yes ("Preface to the Eighth Edition, 1771")	Yes
Kendal (Westmorland?)	1785	De Worfat	*A Bran New Wark, By William De Worfat Containing A True Calendar of his Thoughts Concerning Good Nebbe-rhood. Naw first printed fra his M.S. For the use of the hamlet of Woodland.*	Printed and Sold by all the Booksellers in Great-Britain	London	Prose Dialect	First	Yes ("The Prologue")	Yes
Lancashire	1746		*A View of the Lancashire Dialect; By way of Dialogue. Between Tummus o'William's, o'Margit o'Roaph's, and Meary o'Dicks, o'Tummy o'Peggy's.*	Printed and Sold by R. Whitworth . . .	Manchester	Prose Dialect Dialogue	First	No	Yes

Appendix A (*continued*)

Dialect	*Year*	*Author*	*Title*	*Publisher*	*Place*	*Type*	*Edition Noted*	*Preface*	*Glossary*
Lancashire	1746		*A View of the Lancashire Dialect; By way of Dialogue, Between Tummus o'Williams, o'Margit o'Roaf's, an Meary o'Dicks, o'Tummy o'Peggy's. Containing the Adventures and Misfortunes of a Lancashire Clown*	Printed for and Sold by the Booksellers in Town and Country	London	Prose Dialect Dialogues		No	Yes
Lancashire	1748	Bobbin—"Fellow of the Sisyphian Society of Dutch Loom Weavers, and an old Adept in the Dialect"	*A View of the Lancashire Dialect; By way of Dialogue. Between Tummus o'William's, o'Margit o'Roaph's, and Meary o'Dicks, o'Tummy o'Peggy's. Shewing in that Speech, the comical Adventures and Misfortunes of a Lancashire Clown. To which is prefix'd (by way of Preface,) a Dialogue between the Author and his Pamphlet.*	Printed and sold by James Lister	Leeds	Prose Dialect Dialogue	Second	Yes (Dialogue between Author and his Pamphlet)	Yes
Lancashire	1755	Bobbin—"Fellow of the Sisyphian Society of Dutch Loom Weavers, and an old Adept in the Dialect"	*A View of the Lancashire Dialect; By way of Dialogue. Between Tummus o'William's, o'Margit o'Roaph's, and Meary o'Dicks, o'Tummy o'Peggy's. Shewing in that Speech, the comical Adventures and Misfortunes of a Lancashire Clown. To which is prefix'd (by way of Preface,) a Dialogue between the Author and his Pamphlet.*	Printed for and sold by J. Robinson	London	Prose Dialect Dialogue	Fourth	Yes (Dialogue between Author and his Pamphlet)	Yes

Appendix A (*continued*)

Dialect	*Year*	*Author*	*Title*	*Publisher*	*Place*	*Type*	*Edition Noted*	*Preface*	*Glossary*
Lancashire	1757	Bobbin—"Fellow of the Sisyphian Society of Dutch Loom Weavers, and an old Adept in the Dialect"	*A View of the Lancashire Dialect; By way of Dialogue. Between Tummus o'William's, o'Margit o'Roaph's, and Meary o'Dicks, o'Tummy o'Peggy's. Shewing in that Speech, the comical Adventures and Misfortunes of a Lancashire Clown. To which is prefix'd (by way of Preface,) a Dialogue between the Author and his Pamphlet. With a few Observations for the better Pronunciation of the Dialect.*	Printed and Sold by Josehp [*sic*] Harrop	Manchester	Prose Dialect Dialogue	Sixth	Yes (Observations on Pronunciation + "Spon-new Cank between th' Eawther and his Buk")	Yes ("Above 800 words that never were in last five impressions")
Lancashire	1763		*Tim Bobbin's Toy-Shop open'd, Or, His Whimsical Amusements*	Printed and Sold by Joseph Harrop	Manchester	Prose Dialect Dialogues + Poem		Yes	Yes
Lancashire	1770	Tummus a Williams &c	*A View of the Lancashire Dialect: With a Large Glossary: Being the Adventures and Misfortunes of a Lancashire Clown.*	Printed and Sold in Pater-noster Row, and by the Booksellers in Lancashire	London	Prose Dialect Dialogue		No	Yes
Lancashire	1775		*The Miscellaneous Works of Tim Bobbin, Esq; Containing his View of the Lancashire Dialect; With large Additions and Improvements. Also his Poem of the Flying Dragon and the Man of Heaton Together with his Whimsical Amusements in Prose and Verse. Some of which never before Published.*	Printed for the Author, and Mr. Hastingden, Bookseller	Manchester	Prose Dialect Dialogues + Poem + Other		Yes	Yes

Appendix A (*continued*)

Dialect	*Year*	*Author*	*Title*	*Publisher*	*Place*	*Type*	*Edition Noted*	*Preface*	*Glossary*
Lancashire	1782	Tummus à Williams	*A View of the Lancashire Dialect: With a Large Glossary: Being the Adventures and Misfortunes of a Lancashire Clown.*		London	Dialect Prose		No	Yes
Lancashire	1787		*A View of the Lancashire Dialect; By way of Dialogue, Between Tummus o'Williams, o'f Margit o'Roaf's, an Meary o'Dicks, o'Tummy o'Peggy's. Containing the Adventures and Misfortunes of a Lancashire Clown.*	Printed for J. Binns	Leeds	Prose Dialect Dialogue		No	Yes
Lancashire	1790	Bobbin	*The Miscellaneous Works of Tim Bobbin, Esq; Containing his View of the Lancashire Dialect; With large Additions and Improvements. Also his Poem of the Flying Dragon and the Man of Heaton Together with his Whimsical Amusements in Prose and Verse.*	Printed for A. Millar, W. Law, and R. Cater	London and York	Prose Dialect Dialogues + Poem + Other		Yes (Observa-tions useful to Strangers to Lancashire Pronunciation + "Spon-new Cank between th' Eawther and his Buk")	Yes
Lancashire	1793	Bobbin	*The Miscellaneous Works of Tim Bobbin, Esq; Containing his View of the Lancashire Dialect; With large Additions and Improvements. Also his Poem of the Flying Dragon and the Man of Heaton Together with his Whimsical Amusements in Prose and Verse.*	Printed for J. Haslingden	Manchester	Prose Dialect Dialogues + Poem + Other		Yes (Observa-tions useful to Strangers to Lancashire Pronunciation + "Spon-new Cank between th' Eawther and his Buk")	Yes

Appendix A (*continued*)

Dialect	*Year*	*Author*	*Title*	*Publisher*	*Place*	*Type*	*Edition Noted*	*Preface*	*Glossary*
Lancashire	1797	Bobbin, Esq. An Old Adept in the Dialect	*A View of the Lancashire Dialect; By way of Dialogue, Between Tummus o'Williams, o'f Margit o'Roaf's, an Meary o'Dicks, o'Tummy o'Peggy's. Containing the Adventures and Misfortunes of a Lancashire Clown. To which are Added, The Flying Dragon and the Man of Heaton, The Blackbird—The Goose, The Gardener and the Ass—The Pluralist and Old Soldier, and a Glossary of the Lancashire Words and Phrases.*	Printed for the Booksellers		Prose Dialect Dialogues + Poem		No	No
Lancashire	1798		*Tim Bobbin's View of The Lancashire Dialect; With Large Additions and Improvements. Also a Glossary of Lancashire Words and Phrases*	Printed for A. Millar, W. Law, and R. Cater	London and York	Prose Dialect Dialogue		Yes (Observations useful to Strangers to Lancashire Pronunciation + "Spon-new Cank between th' Eawther and his Buk")	Yes
Lancashire	1800	a Williams &c	*A View of the Lancashire Dialect: With a Large Glossary: Being the Adventures and Misfortunes of a Lancashire Clown.*	P. Charles	London	Prose Dialect Dialogue		No	Yes

Appendix A (*continued*)

Dialect	*Year*	*Author*	*Title*	*Publisher*	*Place*	*Type*	*Edition Noted*	*Preface*	*Glossary*
Lancashire	1819	Bobbin	*A View of the Lancashire Dialect; By way of Dialogue, Between Tummus o'Williams, o'f Margit o'Roaph's, an Meary o'Dicks, o'Tummy o'Peggy's. Shewing in that Speech the Comical Adventures and Misfortunes of a Lancashire Clown. To which are Added (By way of Preface), A Dialogue between the Author and his Pamphlet. With a few Observations for the better Pronunciation of the Dialect. With a Glossary of all the Lancashire Words and Phrases therein used.*	Printed by J. Littlewood	Rochdale	Prose Dialect Dialgue		Yes (Observations useful to Strangers to Lancashire Pronunciation + "Spon-new Cank between th' Eawther and his Buk")	Yes
Lancashire	1828	Bobbin	*Tim Bobbin's Lancashire Dialect; and Poems. Rendered Intelligible to General Readers by a Literal Interpretation, and the Obsolete Words Explained by Quotations from the Most Early of The English Authors*	Hurst, Chance and Co.	London	Prose Dialect Dialogue + Translation		Numerous	Yes
Scottish	1788		*Poetical Dialogues on Religion, in the Scots Dialect, Between Two Gentleman and Two Ploughmen*	Printed for Peter Hill	Edinburgh	Poetic Dialect Dialogues	First?	No	No
Sheffield	1831	A Shevvild Chap	*The Sheffield Dialect, in Conversations "Uppa Are Hull Arston" Between a Gentleman's Guild and Jack Wheelswarf. Parts I. and II. With a Copious Glossary. And an Introductory Note on the Sound of the Letters A and O.*	Printed and Sold by J. Blackwell, and All Booksellers	Sheffield	Prose Dialect Dialogue + "Found Texts"?	Not First (see Introduction)	Introduction	Comparative Glossary

Appendix A (*continued*)

Dialect	*Year*	*Author*	*Title*	*Publisher*	*Place*	*Type*	*Edition Noted*	*Preface*	*Glossary*
Sheffield	1839	Bywater	*The Sheffield Dialect*	G. Chaloner	Sheffield and London	Prose Dialect Dialogues and Other Dialect Prose Writings	First?	Preface?	No
"Village"	1793	Chip, A Country Carpenter	*Village Politics: Addressed to All the Mechanics, Journeymen, and Day-Labourers, in Great Rritain [sic]*	Printed and Sold by G. Walker	York	Prose Dialogue	Fifth	No	No
"Children"	1800	Eves	*The Grammatical Play-Thing, Or, Winter Evening's Recreation for Young Ladies from Four to Twelve Years Old*	Printed at T. A. Pearson . . . and Sold by John Marshall	Birmingham and London	Grammar	First?	No (Dedication)	No
Westmorland	1790	W.	*The Westmorland Dialect, in three Familiar Dialogues: In Which an Attempt is Made To Illustrate the Provincial Idiom.*	Printed by James Ashburner	Kendal	Prose Dialect Dialogues	First	Yes	Yes
Westmorland	1802	Wheeler	*The Westmorland Dialect, in four Familiar Dialogues: In Which an Attempt is Made to Illustrate the Provincial Idiom.*	Printed for W. J. And J. Richardson; Wilson and Spence; B Walmsley; M. Branthwaite	London, York, Lancaster, Kendal	Prose Dialect Dialogues	Second	Yes	Yes
Westmorland	1821	Wheeler	*The Westmorland Dialect, with the Adjacency of Lancashire and Yorkshire, in Four Familiar Dialogues: In Which an Attempt is Made to Illustrate the Provincial Idiom.*	Printed by M. And B. Branthwaite	Kendal, London	Prose Dialect Dialogues + 2 Speeches + 2 Songs	Third	Yes	Yes

Appendix A (*continued*)

Dialect	*Year*	*Author*	*Title*	*Publisher*	*Place*	*Type*	*Edition Noted*	*Preface*	*Glossary*
Westmorland and Cumberland	1839	Various (Including Ann Wheeler)	*Westmoreland [sic] and Cumberland Dialects. Dialogues, Poems, Songs, and Ballads, by Various Writers, in the Westmoreland and Cumberland Dialects, Now First Collected: With a Copious Glossary of Words Peculiar to those Counties.*	John Russell Smith	London	Prose Dialect Dialogues + Poetic Dialect Dialogues	?	Yes	Yes
Westmorland	1840	Wheeler	*The Westmorland Dialect, in four Familiar Dialogues: In Which an Attempt is Made to Illustrate the Provincial Idiom. A New Edition. To which is Added a Copious Glossary of Westmoreland and Cumberland Words.*	John Russell Smith	London	Prose Dialect Dialogues	?	Yes	Yes
Yorkshire	1808		*Specimens of the Yorkshire Dialect. To which is added, A Glossary of Such of the Yorkshire Words as are Likely Not to be Understood By those unac-quainted with the Dialect*	Printed and Sold by Hargrove and Sons	Knaresbrough and "Book-sellers in the County of York"	Prose Dialect Dialogues + Poetic Dialect Dialogues	Second	No	Yes
Yorkshire	1833		*York Minster Screen, Being a Specimen of the Yorkshire Dialect, As Spoken in the North Riding.*	Printed by R. Smithson	Malton	Poetic Dialect Dialogues	First?	No	No, but glosses in endnotes
Yorkshire	1839		*The Yorkshire Dialect, Exemplified in Various Dialogues, Tales, and Songs, Applicable to the Country. To which is Added, A Glossary of Such Words as are likely not to be understood by those unacquainted with the dialect.*	John Russell Smith	London	Prose Dialect Dialogues + Poetic Dialect Dialogues	?	No	Yes

Appendix B. Selected "Dialect" Poetry

Dialect	*Year*	*Author*	*Title*	*Publisher*	*Place*	*Type*	*Edition Noted*	*Preface*	*Glossary*
Canting	1737		*Bacchus and Venus: Or, A Select Collection of near 200 of the most Witty and diverting Songs and Catches in Love and Gallantry . . . To which is Added, A Collection of Songs in the Canting Dialect with a Dictionary . . .*	R. Montague	London	Dialect Songs and Poetry		Yes, Several	Yes
Cumberland	1747	Josiah Relph	*A Miscellany of Poems*	Printed by Robert Foulis for Mr. Thom-linson in Wigton	Glasgow	Dialect Poems		Yes	Yes
Cumberland	1780	Robert Nelson	*A Choice Collection of Poems in Cumberland Dialect*	Printed by R. Wetherald	Sunderland	Dialect Poems		Yes	No
Cumberland	1790	John Stagg	*Miscellaneous Poems*	Printed by M. Dennison and Son	Carlisle	Dialect Poems, Classical Translations, etc.		Yes	No
Cumberland	1805	R. Anderson	*Ballads in the Cumberland Dialect . . . with Notes and a Glossary*	Printed by W. Hodgson	Carlisle	Dialect Poems (Ballads)		Yes	Yes
Cumberland	1805	John Stagg	*Miscellaneous Poems, Some of which are in the Cumberland Dialect*	Printed by W. Borrowdale	Workington	Dialect and Mixed Poems	Second	Yes	No
Cumberland	1807	John Stagg	*Miscellaneous Poems, Some of which are in the Cumberland and Scottish Dialects*	Printed by R. Hetherton	Wigton	Dialect and Mixed Poems		Yes	No

Appendix B (*continued*)

Dialect	*Year*	*Author*	*Title*	*Publisher*	*Place*	*Type*	*Edition Noted*	*Preface*	*Glossary*
Cumberland	1815	R. Anderson	*Ballads in the Cumberland Dialect, Chiefly by R. Anderson, with Notes and a Glossary: The Reminder by Various Authors, Several of which have been Never Before Published*	Printed by E. Rook	Wigton	Dialect Poems (Ballads)	Second	No (Dedication)	Yes
Cumberland	1821	John Stagg	*The Cumbrian Minstrel; Being a Poetical Miscellany of Legendary, Gothic and Romantic Tales, The Scenes and Subjects of which are principally laid in the Border Counties of England and Scotland; Together with Several Essays in the Northern Dialect; Also a Number of Original Pieces, Never before Published, And a Variety of Translations as well Modern as Classical*	Printed by T. Wilkinson	Manchester	Dialect Poems, Classical and Modern Translations, etc.		No (Poetical Address to Readers)	No
Cumberland	1842	Henry Lonsdale	*The Poetical Words of Susanna Blamire "The Muse of Cumberland"*	John Menzies	Edinburgh	Dialect Poetry		Yes	No
Essex	1839	Charles Clark	*John Noakes and Mary Styles; Or, "An Essex Calf's" Visit to Tiptree Races: A Poem, Exhibiting Some of the Most Striking Lingual Localisms Peculiar to Essex. With a Glossary.*	John Russell Smith	London	Dialect Poetry		No	Yes

Appendix B (*continued*)

Dialect	*Year*	*Author*	*Title*	*Publisher*	*Place*	*Type*	*Edition Noted*	*Preface*	*Glossary*
Dorsetshire	1844	William Barnes	*Poems of Rural Life, In the Dorset Dialect: With a Dissertation and Glossary*	John Russell Smith	London	Dialect Poetry	First	Yes (Dissertation on Dorset Dialect)	Yes
Newcastle	1827	Various (5 +)	*A Collection of Songs, Comic, Satirical, and Descriptive, Chiefly in the Newcastle Dialect, And Illustrative of the Language and Manners of the Common People on the Banks of the Tyne and Neighbourhood*	Printed by John Marshall	Newcastle upon Tyne	Dialect Poems		Yes (Editors Address)	No
Newcastle	1850	J. P. Robson	*Songs of the Bards of the Tyne; Or, A Choice Selection of Original Songs, Chiefly in the Newcastle Dialect. With a Glossary of 500 Words*	Published by P. France and Co.	Newcastle upon Tyne	Dialect Poems		Yes	Yes
Scottish	1720	Mr. Mitchell	*The Doleful Swan; A Pastoral Poem. Written Originally in the Scotch Dialect with an English Version*	T. Jauncy	London	Dialect Poetry		Yes	No
Scottish	1720	Allan Ramsay	*Patie and Roger: A Pastoral, by Mr. Allan Ramsay, in the Scots Dialect*	J. Pemberton and T. Jauncy	London	Dialect Poetry		Yes	No
Scottish	1748	Various	*Poems in the Scottish Dialect By Several Celebrated Poets*	Printed and Sold by Robert Foulis	Glasgow	Dialect Poetry		No	No
Scottish	1759		*Rural Love, A Tale In the Scottish Dialect To Which is Added a Glossary, or Alphabetical Explanation of the Scotish* [sic] *Words and Phrases*	Printed by Francis Douglas and sold by J. Coot	Aberdeen and London	Dialect Poetry		Yes (Advertisement)	Yes

Appendix B (*continued*)

Dialect	*Year*	*Author*	*Title*	*Publisher*	*Place*	*Type*	*Edition Noted*	*Preface*	*Glossary*
Scottish	1768	Alexander Ross	*The Fortunate Shepherdess, A Pastoral Tale in Three Cantos in the Scottish Dialect*	Printed by, and for Francis Douglas	Aberdeen	Dialect Poetry		Yes (Advertisement)	No
Scottish	1776	A Student at Marischal College	*Farmer's Ha': A Scots Poem*	Printed by J. Chalmers and Co.	Aberdeen	Dialect Poetry		No	No
Scottish	1777	David Fergusson	*A Select Collection of Scots Poems, Chiefly in the Broad Buchan Dialect*		Edinburgh	Dialect Poetry		No	Yes
Scottish	1778	Alexander Ross	*Helenore, Or the Fortunate Shepherdess, A Poem, in the Broad Scotch Dialect*	J. Chalmers and Co.	Aberdeen	Dialect Poetry	Second, "Carefully Corrected" (cf. 1768)	Yes (Dedication)	Yes
Scottish	1781	Forbes Stephen	*Rural Amusement; Or, A New Miscellany of Epistles, Poems, Songs, &c. Written in the Scotch Dialect*	J. Chalmers and Co.	Aberdeen	Dialect Poetry		No	No
Scottish	1785	David Fergusson	*A Select Collection of Scots Poems, Chiefly in the Broad Buchan Dialect. To which is added a Collection of Scots Proverbs*	T. Ruddiman	Edinburgh	Dialect Poetry	Second? (cf. 1777)	No	No
Scottish	1786	Robert Burns	*Poems, Chiefly in the Scottish Dialect by Robert Burns*	Printed by John Wilson	Kilmarnock	Dialect Poetry	First	Yes	Yes
Scottish	1787	Robert Burns	*Poems, Chiefly in the Scottish Dialect*	Printed for the Author, and Sold by William Creech	Edinburgh	Dialect Poetry	Second	No (Dedication ["Caledonian Hunt" + Subscribers])	Yes

Appendix B (*continued*)

Dialect	*Year*	*Author*	*Title*	*Publisher*	*Place*	*Type*	*Edition Noted*	*Preface*	*Glossary*
Scottish	1787	Robert Burns	*Poems, Chiefly in the Scottish Dialect*	Printed and Sold by James Magee	Belfast	Dialect Poetry		No (Dedication ["Caledonian Hunt" + Excerpt from Lounger Review])	Yes
Scottish	1787	Robert Burns	*Poems, Chiefly in the Scottish Dialect*	Printed for A. Strahan; T. Cadell; and W. Creech	London and Edinburgh	Dialect Poetry	Third	No (Dedication ["Caledonian Hunt" + Subscribers])	Yes
Scottish	1788	Ebenezer Picken	*Poems and Epistles, Mostly in the Scottish Dialect. With a Glossary*	Printed by John Neilson	Paisley	Dialect Poetry	First	Yes (Dedication + Preface)	Yes
Scottish	1788	Robert Galloway	*Poems, Epistles and Songs, Chiefly in the Scottish Dialect. To which are Added A Brief Account of the Revolution in 1688, and a Narrative of the Rebellion in 1745–46, continued to the Death of Prince Charles in 1788*	Printed by W. Bell	Glasgow	Dialect Poetry		Yes	No
Scottish	1789	Alexander Ross	*Helenore, Or the Fortunate Shepherdess, A Poem, in the Broad Scotch Dialect*	Printed and Sold by J. Boyle	Aberdeen	Dialect Poetry	Third ("Corrected Edition")	No (Dedication)	Yes
Scottish	1789	David Davidson	*Thoughts on the Seasons, &c. Partly in the Scottish Dialect*	Printed for the Author and Sold by J. Murray and W. Creech	London and Edinburgh	Dialect Poetry		Yes	Yes

Appendix B (*continued*)

Dialect	*Year*	*Author*	*Title*	*Publisher*	*Place*	*Type*	*Edition Noted*	*Preface*	*Glossary*
Scottish	1790	David Morison	*Poems, Chiefly in the Scottish Dialect*	Printed by David Buchanan	Montrose	Dialect Poetry		No (Dedication + Subscribers)	Yes
Scottish	1790	Andrew Shirrefs	*Poems, Chiefly in the Scottish Dialect*	Printed for the Author by D. Willison: And Sold by W. Creech and B. Hill	Edinburgh and London	Dialect Poetry		No (Dedica-tions + Subscribers)	No
Scottish	1791	Robert Cumming	*Essay, Delivered in the Pantheon on Thursday, April 14. 1971. On the Question "Whether have the Exertions of Allan Ramsay or Robert Ferguson done most Honour to Scottish Poetry." To which is Added Willie and Jamie, an Eclogue, in the Scottish Dialect.*	Printed for T. Brown	Edinburgh	Poetic Essay + Dialect Poetry		No	No
Scottish	1791	John Burness	*Poems, Chiefly in the Scottish Dialect*	Printed by T. Colvill for the Author	Dundee	Dialect Poetry		No	No
Scottish	1792		*Airdrie Fair, A Poem in the Scottish Dialect*		Glasgow	Dialect Poetry		No	No
Scottish	1792	The Author of The Shepherd's Wedding	*New Year's Morning, In Edinburgh; And Auld Handsel Monday, In the Country: Two Poems in the Scottish Dialect*		Edinburgh	Dialect Poetry		Yes	No

Appendix B (*continued*)

Dialect	*Year*	*Author*	*Title*	*Publisher*	*Place*	*Type*	*Edition Noted*	*Preface*	*Glossary*
Scottish	1792	Robert Galloway	*Poems, Epistles and Songs, Chiefly in the Scottish Dialect. To which are Added A Brief Account of the Revolution in 1688, and a Narrative of the Rebellion in 1745–46, continued to the Death of Prince Charles in 1788*	Printed by E. Miller for the Author	Glasgow	Dialect Poetry	Second ("With Additions")	Yes	No
Scottish	1793	Robert Gray	*Poems in the Scots and English Dialect*	Printed for the Author	Glasgow	Dialect and Mixed Poetry		No (Dedicatory Poems)	No
Scottish	1793	Samuel Thomson	*Poems, on Different Subjects, Partly in the Scottish Dialect*	Printed for the Author	Belfast	Dialect and Mixed Poetry		Yes (Dedications, one to Robert Burns)	No
Scottish	1796	John Lauderdale	*A Collection of Poems, Chiefly in the Scottish Dialect*	Printed for the Author, by J. Robertson	Edinburgh	Dialect Poetry		Yes (Dedication)	No
Scottish	1796	Unclear	*The Twa Cuckolds; and the Tint Cow, or Thrawart Maggy. Two Tales in the Scottish Dialect*	Printed for and sold by the booksellers	Edinburgh	Dialect Poetry		No	No
Scottish	1798	David Crawford	*Poems, Chiefly in the Scottish Dialect, on Various Subjects*	Printed for the Author, by J. Pillans and Sons	Edinburgh	Dialect Poetry		No	No
Scottish	1799	An Obscure Edinburgher	*A Butter'd Slice, To the Obscure Auld Magistrate Wha Answered Bailie Smith's Address. And A Waefu' Tale; Or An Address to the Lord Provost, on Account O' The Present Dearth O' The Meal and Bread. Two Poems in the Scottish Dialect*	Printed by J. Pillans and Sons, for the Author	Edinburgh	Dialect Poetry		Yes (Prefatory Poem)	No

Appendix B (*continued*)

Dialect	*Year*	*Author*	*Title*	*Publisher*	*Place*	*Type*	*Edition Noted*	*Preface*	*Glossary*
Scottish	1801	James Thomson, Weaver in Kenleith	*Poems, in the Scottish Dialect*	Printed by J. Pillans and Sons	Edinburgh	Dialect Poetry		Yes (Life of the Author)	No
Scottish	1801	James Hogg	*Scottish Pastorals, Poems, Songs, &c. Mostly Written in the Dialect of the South*	Printed by John Taylor	Edinburgh	Dialect and Mixed Poetry		No	No
Scottish	1801	Berwickshire Sandie	*Poems, Mostly in the Scottish Dialect*	Printed for the Author, By Mundell and Son	Edinburgh	Dialect Poetry		Yes	No
Scottish	1803		*Songs, Chiefly in the Scottish Dialect*	Printed for Manners and Miller	Edinburgh	Dialect Poetry		No	No
Scottish	1806	Alexander Douglas	*Poems, Chiefly in the Scottish Dialect*	Printed by R. Tullis, for the Author	Cupar, Fife	Dialect Poetry		Yes (Life of the Author + Subscribers)	Yes
Scottish	1809	John Skinner	*Amusements of Leisure Hours: Or Poetical Pieces, Chiefly in the Scottish Dialect*	Printed by John Moir	Edinburgh and Aberdeen	Dialect Poetry		Yes (Life of the Author)	Yes
Scottish	1809	Thomas Donaldson	*Poems, Chiefly in the Scottish Dialect; Both Humorous and Entertaining*	Printed at the Apollo Press by and for Wm. Davison	Alnwick	Dialect Poetry		Yes (Dedication + Preface)	Yes
Scottish	1811	George Bruce	*Poems and Songs, on Various Occasions*	Printed by the Author for Oliver and Boyd	Edinburgh	Dialect Poetry		Yes (Dedication + Preface)	No

Appendix B (*continued*)

Dialect	*Year*	*Author*	*Title*	*Publisher*	*Place*	*Type*	*Edition Noted*	*Preface*	*Glossary*
Scottish	1811	Andrew Scott	*Poems, Chiefly in the Scottish Dialect*	Printed by Alexander Leadbetter for the Author	Kelso	Dialect Poetry		Yes	No
Scottish	1812	Peter Forbes	*Poems, Chiefly in the Scottish Dialect*	Printed by R. Menzies, Lawnmarket, for the Author	Edinburgh and Dalkeith	Dialect Poetry		Yes	No
Scottish	1813	Ebenezer Picken	*Miscellaneous Poems, Songs, &c. Partly in the Scottish Dialect with a Copious Glossary*	Printed by James Clarke	Edinburgh, Glasgow, Paisley, and London	Dialect Poetry		Yes	Yes
Scottish	1815	Robert Tannahill	*Poems and Songs, Chiefly in the Scottish Dialect*	Printed by Longman . . .	London, Edinburgh, Glasgow, Paisley	Dialect Poetry	Third	Yes (Life of the Author)	No
Scottish	1815	James Alexander Linen	*Poems, In the Scots and English Dialect, on Various Occasions*	Printed for the Editor	Edinburgh	Dialect Poetry		Yes (Life of the Author)	No
Scottish	1816	James Aikman	*Poems, Chiefly Lyrical, Partly in the Scottish Dialect*	Printed for Macredie, Skelly and Muckersy	Edinburgh, Glasgow, and London	Dialect and Lyric Poetry		Yes	No
Scottish	1817	Robert Tannahill	*Poems and Songs, Chiefly in the Scotish [sic] Dialect.*	Published by Longman . . .	London, Edinburgh, and Glasgow	Dialect Poetry	Fourth	Yes (Life of the Author)	No
Scottish	1822	Robert Wilson	*Poems, Chiefly in the Scottish Dialect*	Printed for the Author	Edinburgh	Dialect Poetry		No (Dedicatory Poems)	No

Appendix B (*continued*)

Dialect	*Year*	*Author*	*Title*	*Publisher*	*Place*	*Type*	*Edition Noted*	*Preface*	*Glossary*
Scottish	1826	David Anderson	*Poems, Chiefly in the Scottish Dialect*	Printed at the Star Office, For the Author	Aberdeen	Dialect Poetry	Second	Yes	No
Scottish	1827	John Imlah	*May Flowers. Poems and Songs: Some in the Scottish Dialect*	Baldwin, Cradock, and Joy	London	Dialect Poetry		Yes (Dedication + Preface + Subscribers)	No
Scottish	1827	John Watt	*Poems, Chiefly in the Scottish Dialect*	Printed for the Author	EdinburghDi-alect Poetry		No (Dedicatory Poems)	No	
Scottish (Galloway)	1828	William McDowall	*Poems, Chiefly in the Galloway Dialect*	Printed for the Author, By J. McNairn	Newton-Stewart	Dialect Poetry		Yes (Description of Galloway)	No
Scottish	1831	Robert Shennan	*Tales, Songs, and Miscellaneous Poems, Descriptive of Rural Scenes and Manners; Chiefly in the Scottish Dialect*	Printed by John McDi-armid and Co.	Dumfries	Dialect Poetry		Yes (Dedication + Preface)	No
Scottish	1837	Thomas Daniel	*Poems, Chiefly in the Scottish Dialect*	Printed for the Author by R. King	Peterhead	Dialect Poetry	Second	Yes (Dedicatory Poem)	No
Scottish	1845	Peter Still	*The Cottar's Sunday, And Other Poems, Chiefly in the Scottish Dialect*	Henry Longstreth	Philadelphia	Dialect Poetry		Yes	No
Scottish	1853	Walter Watson	*Poems and Songs, Chiefly in the Scottish Dialect*	David Robertson	Glasgow	Dialect Poetry		Yes (Life of the Author)	No

Appendix B (*continued*)

Dialect	*Year*	*Author*	*Title*	*Publisher*	*Place*	*Type*	*Edition Noted*	*Preface*	*Glossary*
Shropshire	1844	James Orchard Halliwell	*The Poems of John Audelay. A Specimen of the Shropshire Dialect in the Fifteenth Century*	Printed for the Percy Society	London	Historic Dialect Poetry	First	Yes	No
Somersetshire	1776	"By the Author of the New Bath Guide"	*An Election Ball in Poetical Letters, in the Zomerzetshire Dialect, From Mr. Inkle, a Freeman of Bath, to His Wife at Glocester: With a Poetical Address to John Miller, Esq. At Batheaston Villa*	Printed for the Author by S. Hazard	Bath	Dialect Poetry	First	No	No
Somersetshire	1843	James Orchard Halliwell	*A Collection of Pieces in the Dialect of Zummerzet.*	John Russell Smith	London	Dialect Poetry and Prose		No	No
Yorkshire	1850	John Castillo	*The Bard of the Dales, Or Poems and Miscellaneous Pieces. Partly in the Yorkshire Dialect*	John Hughes	London	Dialect Poetry		No	No

NOTES

Introduction

1. Samuel Johnson, *Journey to the Western Islands of Scotland* (London: W. Strahan and T. Cadell, 1775), 75.

2. In Mikhail Bakhtin's work, "heteroglossia" is the foil of a stable and unitary language. One moment in Bakhtin stands out for its relevance here: "The processes of centralization and decentralization, of unification and disunification, intersect in the utterance; the utterance not only answers the requirements of its own language as an individualized embodiment of a speech act, but it answers the requirements of heteroglossia as well; it is in fact an active participant in such speech diversity. And this active participation of every utterance in living heteroglossia determines the linguistic profile and style of the utterance to no less a degree than its inclusion in any normative-centralizing system of a unitary language." By contrast, the translators of this volume point out in their glossary that "polyglossia" refers to "the simultaneous presence of two or more national languages interacting with a single cultural system (Bakhtin's two historical models are ancient Rome and the Renaissance)." See Bakhtin, *The Dialogic Imagination: Four Essays by M. M. Bakhtin*, Michael Holquist, ed., Caryl Emerson and Michael Holquist, trans. (Austin: University of Texas Press, 1981), 272, 431.

3. I mount a rigorous argument for using the term "anglophone" in the coming sections of this introduction. For the time being, and in anticipation of that argument, I dwell here on the distinctions Johnson tries to make in this passage.

4. James Mulholland makes this point convincingly in *Sounding Imperial: Poetic Voice and the Politics of Empire, 1730–1820* (Baltimore: Johns Hopkins University Press, 2013). As Mulholland summarizes this aesthetic inheritance, "While the British expanded their dominion in North America, the Caribbean, and Asia, and while they explored the Pacific Islands and Africa, they were also idealizing the oral traditions they found there and impersonating overseas speakers," 2.

5. See Lynda Mugglestone, *"Talking Proper": The Rise of Accent as Social Symbol* (Oxford: Oxford University Press, 2003).

6. My invocation of Standard English here owes a great debt to recent scholarship on this topic. Andrew Elfenbein suggests, "Before English's standardization, linguistic common ground for educated men meant Latin and Greek, along with the entire apparatus of learning that accompanied knowledge of those languages; for members of particular language communities, the spoken vernacular, in the form of local languages ranging from Scots to Manx, was part of common ground. What was missing was a language that could, at least at the level of social myth, be common ground for all Britons." See Andrew Elfenbein, *Romanticism and the Rise of English* (Stanford, Calif.: Stanford University Press, 2009), 21–22. See also theoretical work on the politics of standardization as they have been pioneered by Olivia Smith, *The Politics of Language 1791–1819*

(Oxford: Oxford University Press 1984); Tony Crowley, *Standard English and the Politics of Language*, 2nd ed. (New York: Palgrave Macmillan, 2003); Richard Maggaraf Turley, *The Politics of Language in Romantic Literature* (New York: Palgrave Macmillan, 2002); William Keach, *Arbitrary Power: Romanticism, Language, and Politics* (Princeton, N.J.: Princeton University Press, 2004); and Marcus Tomalin, *Romanticism and Linguistic Theory* (New York: Palgrave Macmillan, 2009).

7. The best recent assemblage of essays on Samuel Johnson and his contexts can be found in Jack Lynch, ed., *Samuel Johnson in Context* (Cambridge: Cambridge University Press, 2012).

8. Sir Walter Scott, *Waverley; or, 'Tis Sixty Years Since*, vol. 2 of 3 (Edinburgh: James Ballantyne, 1814), 209.

9. Scott, *Waverley*, 209.

10. Scott, *Waverley*, 10.

11. Lest the representation of multilingualism in Scott be understood only as a way to screen characters and readers alike from what the plot will bring, it should be said that a more common use of multilingualism in narration is to invoke the practice of translation, and with it ideas of transformation, dynamism, communication, and change. For example, Flora Mac-Ivor's Scottish Gaelic song leads naive Waverley into an exoticizing fixation. Flora's subsequent translation and performance of the song is a moment in which translation is the engine of seductive intrigue. See Scott, *Waverley*, 171–80.

12. I take the term xenotropism, which refers to the written inscription of foreignness, from Srinivas Aravamudan's *Enlightenment Orientalism: Resisting the Rise of the Novel* (Chicago: University of Chicago Press, 2012), 37, 39.

13. Among others see Katie Trumpener, *Bardic Nationalism: The Romantic Novel and the British Empire* (Princeton, N.J.: Princeton University Press, 1997); Janet Sorensen, *The Grammar of Empire in Eighteenth-Century British Writing* (Cambridge: Cambridge University Press, 2000); Felicity Nussbaum, *The Limits of the Human* (Cambridge: Cambridge University Press, 2003); Kathleen Wilson, ed., *A New Imperial History: Culture, Identity, and Modernity in Britain and the Empire, 1660–1840* (Cambridge: Cambridge University Press, 2004); Srinivas Aravamudan, *Tropicopolitans: Colonialism and Agency, 1688–1804* (Durham, N.C.: Duke University Press, 2006); Simon Gikandi, *Slavery and the Culture of Taste* (Princeton, N.J.: Princeton University Press, 2011); Srinivas Aravamudan, *Enlightenment Orientalism*; David Simpson, *Romanticism and the Question of the Stranger* (Chicago: University of Chicago Press, 2013); Evan Gottlieb, *Romantic Globalism: British Literature and the Modern World Order, 1750–1830* (Columbus: Ohio State University Press, 2014); Saree Makdisi, *Making England Western: Occidentalism, Race, and Imperial Culture* (Chicago: University of Chicago Press, 2014).

14. James Adams, *The Pronunciation of the English Language Vindicated from Imputed Anomaly and Caprice* (Edinburgh: J. Moir, 1799), 3.

15. Murray Cohen compares the latter half of the eighteenth century with the first half and provides the numbers in *Sensible Words: Linguistic Practice in England, 1640–1785* (Baltimore: Johns Hopkins University Press, 1977); William St. Clair's *The Reading Nation in the Romantic Period* (Cambridge: Cambridge University Press, 2004) provides relative and absolute publishing statistics on some linguistic teaching texts.

16. Sir William Jones, "The Third Anniversary Discourse, on the Hindoos," delivered 2 February, 1786, in *Works of Sir William Jones*, Lord Teignmouth, ed., vol. 1 of 13 (London: John Stockdale, 1807), 34.

17. It bears noting that other scholars who have studied linguistic multiplicity and difference have opted for different terminologies. Jonathan Hsy's *Trading Tongues: Merchants, Multilingualism, and Medieval Literature* (Columbus: Ohio State University Press, 2013), for example, opts for

the term "translingual" as a way to describe the imbrications of Middle English, Latin, French, Flemish, and other languages in medieval London. Hsy writes, "If 'multilingual' denotes the fact that languages coexist and occupy the same di- or tri-glossic space, then 'translingual' emphasizes the capacity for languages within such spaces to interact: to influence and transform each other through networks of exchange," 6–7. This is a tremendously useful piece of terminology. Throughout this book, however, I will use the term "multilingual" far more frequently because, as I hope to show, "multilingualism" is the explicit foil of Standard English as the long eighteenth century progresses. Put another way, discussing similar phenomena as Hsy in the language of "multilingualism" allows me to bring into focus hierarchical power relations obtaining within anglophony in the period. To the degree that translingualism in Hsy as well as Lydia Liu's *Translingual Practice: Literature, National Culture, and Translated Modernity, China 1900–1937* (Stanford, Calif.: Stanford University Press, 1995) is a way of generating new forms of linguistic identity through circulation, one of the interests of the present book is that the eighteenth century witnesses the delimitation and restriction of certain forms of linguistic identity and exchange.

18. See Ingrid Tieken-Boon van Ostade, *Grammars, Grammarians, and Grammar-Writing in Eighteenth-Century England* (Berlin: Mouton de Gruyter, 2008), and Ingrid Tieken-Boon van Ostade, *The Bishop's Grammar: Robert Lowth and the Rise of Prescriptivism in English* (Oxford: Oxford University Press, 2011).

19. See Kathleen Wilson, *New Imperial History*, and Michael Fisher, *Counterflows to Colonialism: Indian Travellers and Settlers in Britain, 1600–1857* (Delhi: Permanent Black, 2004).

20. On the question of ethnicity in the period, especially as it relates to language and nationalism, see Colin Kidd, *British Identities Before Nationalism: Ethnicity and Nationhood in the Atlantic World, 1600–1800* (Cambridge: Cambridge University Press, 1999).

21. This quotation was not chosen casually. The links between the English language and the expansion of the global marketplace are well known. The full context of Marx's quotation is, "The need of a constantly expanding market for its products chases the bourgeoisie over the entire surface of the globe must nestle everywhere, settle everywhere, establish connexions everywhere." From a certain point of view, these two sentences describe English's role in the imperial world over the past two and a half centuries as well as Marx's concept of the bourgeoisie. Karl Marx and Friedrich Engels, *The Communist Manifesto* (London: Verso, 1998), 39.

22. Gayatri Chakravorty Spivak's *An Aesthetic Education in the Era of Globalization*, which I discuss in detail in the conclusion, gestures toward the lack of multilingualism in contemporary U.S. American education, noting, "Already it is the relatively glamorous think tanks and monolingual 'interdisciplinarity' (read shrinking diversity and Americanized monoculture) that are gaining funding. U.S. 'core curricula'—minimally 'politically correct' by including 'multicultural' classics—again in English translation—are traveling internationally." In *An Aesthetic Education in the Era of Globalization* (Cambridge, Mass.: Harvard University Press, 2012), 26.

23. Susan Buck-Morss, *Hegel, Haiti, and Universal History* (Pittsburgh: University of Pittsburgh Press, 2009), 134.

24. Susan Buck-Morss, *Hegel, Haiti, and Universal History*, 111.

25. See in particular Simon Gikandi's *PMLA* essays "From Penn Station to Trenton: The Language Train," in vol. 128, no. 4 (October 2013), 865–71; "Provincializing English," in vol. 129, no. 1 (January 2014), 7–11; and "The Fragility of Languages," in vol. 130, no. 1 (January 2015), 9–14.

26. Gikandi, "Provincializing English," 7, 8. In "From Penn Station to Trenton," the author also cites U.S. English-only movements; he writes, "I often ask myself why Spanish creates terror

in some parts of the United States, triggering the rise of English-only movements. Why are these movements driven by anxiety about Spanish (in Texas, for example) and not Portuguese (in New Bedford, Massachusetts) or Swedish (in Minnesota)? Is it about numbers, country of origin, or the fear that Spanish might one day acquire the power of monolingualism?" Gikandi, "From Penn Station to Trenton," 867. See also Dipesh Chakrabarty, *Provincializing Europe*, 2000, (Princeton, N.J.: Princeton University Press, 2008).

27. "Who are those people," Gikandi asks in another passage of people whose languages are moribund. "What is their sense of being in the world? What happens to the last speakers of a language when they talk and all they hear is the echo of their own voices? What is the status of an address without an addressee? What does it mean for a language to die?" Gikandi, "Fragility of Languages," 11.

28. Gikandi, "Provincializing English," 7.

29. Gikandi, "Provincializing English," 12.

30. The collective noun "anglophony" is first attested in the *Oxford English Dictionary* in 1969. It appears as a backformation from *francophonie*. The first instance of its usage is a quotation from the *Journal of Contemporary History* that reads, "This does not mean France would adhere to *francophonie*, any more than the USA adheres to *anglophonie*." As a proper noun, "Anglophone" has longer history dating back to 1900: "In Canada two-thirds of the white population are Anglophones, and the rest Francophones." Throughout this book I will opt for a lowercase spelling of the noun form of the word. As an adjective, "anglophone" is of a similar vintage as "anglophony," showing up first in the dictionary in 1965 and in a postcolonial context: "His intimate knowledge of affairs in Africa (Francophone as well as Anglophone) . . . equips him outstandingly to point out not only what has gone wrong in West Africa . . . but what should be done to put it right." See "Anglophony, n." and "anglophone, n. and adj." in *OED Online*, March 2014, Oxford University Press, http://www.oed.com/view/Entry/7603 (accessed May 4, 2014).

31. See Julie Coleman, *A History of Cant and Slang Dictionaries*, vol. 1, *1567–1784* (Oxford: Oxford University Press, 2004.

32. Watts and Trudgill point directly to this fact when they observe, "These are varieties [of English] which have been marginalised by historical linguistics because they have been regarded as non-standard, and/or which have been ignored because they have been considered to be socially or geographically peripheral in some way. We would point out, as justification for this, that there are very many more non-standard than standard varieties of English in the world; that they are spoken by many more people than Standard English; and that to ignore them does our understanding of the history of the English language no service at all." Richard Watts and Peter Trudgill, "The History of Non-Standard Varieties of English," in *Alternative Histories of English*, Watts and Trudgill, eds. (London: Routledge, 2002), 27.

33. On Scots, education, and anglophony, see Robert Crawford, *Devolving English Literature* (Oxford: Oxford University Press, 1992).

34. I describe other limitations to this term below, but one of the most important is that the very idea of anglophony might be misconstrued as a universalizing gesture.

35. David Hume, *Essays on Suicide, And The Immortality of the Soul* (London: M. Smith, 1783), 11.

36. John Collier, *A View of the Lancashire Dialect by Way of Dialogue* (Manchester: R. Whitworth, 1746), 3. The Standard English translation of Collier's anglophone line is taken from an 1828 reproduction of the work, one of many, as described in the fourth chapter. John Collier, *Tim Bobbin's Lancashire Dialect; and Poems* (London: Hurst, Chance, 1828), 2–3.

37. Stephen Behrendt, A. J. H. Latham, and David Northrup, eds., *The Diary of Antera Duke, an Eighteenth-Century African Slave Trader* (Oxford: Oxford University Press, 2010), 140–41. I discuss Antera Duke in the chapter interlude entitled "Multilingual Lives: Antera Duke."

38. Gilles Deleuze and Félix Guattari, *Milles Plateaux* (Paris: Éditions de Minuit, 1980), 13–14.

39. Deleuze and Guattari, *Milles Plateaux*, 13–14.

40. In *The Order of Things*, Michel Foucault makes a similar set of points relating to language's disorganized contingency. He writes in the chapter "Speaking" that "the history of the various languages is no longer anything more than a question of erosion or accident, introduction, meetings, and the mingling of various elements; it has no law, no progress, no necessity proper to it. . . . This is because languages evolve in accordance with the effects of migrations, victories and defeats, fashions, commerce; but not under the impulsion of any historicity possessed by the languages themselves." In *The Order of Things*, 1966 (New York: Random House, 1994), 100.

41. Peter Trudgill's chapter "The History of Lesser-Known Varieties of English" provides helpful histories of the arrival of anglophony in a variety of places. In *Alternative Histories of English*, Watts and Trudgill, eds., 29–44.

42. Compare the shifting uses of these terms in works like Crawford, *Devolving English Literature*; John Kerrigan, *Archipelagic English: Literature, History, and Politics, 1603–1707* (Oxford: Oxford University Press, 2008); and Alok Yadav, *Before the Empire of English: Literature, Provinciality, and Nationalism in Eighteenth-Century Britain* (New York: Palgrave Macmillan, 2004).

43. Édouard Glissant, *Poetics of Relation*, 1990, Betsy Wing, trans. (Ann Arbor: University of Michigan Press, 1997), 95.

44. Benedict Anderson, *Imagined Communities*, 1983 (London: Verso, 1991), 38.

45. It must be said that Anderson was himself profoundly multilingual, which his perhaps why he invests so much in arguing against multilingualism as a facile accomplishment. His final work, *A Life Beyond Boundaries: A Memoir* (London: Verso, 2016), details the energy and delight that Anderson invested in language learning.

46. Anderson, *Imagined Communities*, 152.

47. Glissant, *Poetics of Relation*, 19.

48. Glissant, *Poetics of Relation*, 118. Bakhtin similarly dissects "unicity": "Language—like the living concrete environment in which the consciousness of the artist lives—is never unitary. It is unitary only as an abstract grammatical system of normative forms taken in isolation from the concrete, ideological conceptualizations that fill it, and in isolation from the uninterrupted process of historical becoming that is a characteristic of all living language," in *Dialogic Imagination*, 288.

49. Ngũgĩ wa Thiong'o, *Decolonising the Mind: The Politics of Language in African Literature* (London: J. Currey, 1986), 11.

Multilingual Lives: Peros, Jack, Neptune, and Cupid

1. For broad approaches to these types of advertisements, see—among others cited throughout this section and the following chapter—Lathan Windley's *Runaway Slave Advertisements: A Documentary History from the 1730s Until 1790* (Westport, Conn.: Greenwood, 1983), and Marcus Wood, *Blind Memory: Visual Representations of Slavery in England and America, 1780–1865* (New York: Routledge, 2000).

2. Considering the "commonness" of eighteenth-century fugitive advertising, David Waldstreicher argues, "Runaway advertisements, in effect, were the first slave narratives—the first published stories about slaves and their seizure of freedom." Waldstreicher, "Reading the Runaways: Self-Fashioning, Print Culture, and Confidence in Slavery in the Eighteenth-Century Mid-Atlantic," *William and Mary Quarterly*, 56, no. 2 (April 1999): 243–72.

3. Correspondence with Mary Thompson, a research historian at the Fred W. Smith National Library for the Study of George Washington, suggests that it is highly likely that Washington wrote this advertisement himself, especially because his name is included in full. Other instances of runaway slaves from the Mount Vernon complex or from the Washington family generated advertisements that are signed by a farm manager or household steward rather than Washington himself. Mary Thompson, e-mail message to author, March 3, 2016.

4. "Advertisement for Runaway Slaves, 11 August 1761," Founders Online, National Archives, http://founders.archives.gov/documents/Washington/02-07-02-0038 (last update: June 29, 2015), from *The Papers of George Washington*, Colonial Series, vol. 7, *1 January 1761?–?15 June 1767*, W. W. Abbot and Dorothy Twohig, eds. (Charlottesville: University Press of Virginia, 1990), 65–68. In 2010, the Papers of George Washington began offering their work on the Founders Online Website, http://founders.archives.gov/, a resource that was established in 2010 by the U.S. National Archives in order to gather the complete papers of John Adams, Benjamin Franklin, Alexander Hamilton, Thomas Jefferson, and James Madison in addition to those of George Washington.

5. See Chapter 1.

6. In a dense passage that places Deidre Lynch's *The Economy of Character: Novels, Market Culture, and the Business of Inner Meaning* (Chicago: University of Chicago Press, 1998) in conversation with J. G. A. Pocock, Nancy Gallagher, and Slavoj Žižek, Ian Baucom provides the complex and economically motivated meaning of "type" that I am working with here: "To this general fictional type (*the* type of the aggregate subject of finance capital), the novel . . . added a second sort of type: not only the generalizable, average, new social person, but also the typical representative of a specified rank of person active in commercial society—the typical banker, shopkeeper, suitor, trading partner, or other 'sort' of person whose character and credibility readers were increasingly called on to interpret if they were to transact social life successfully." Here and in the next chapter, I show ways in which other forms of fictive writing like fugitive advertising circulate such types. Ian Baucom, *Specters of the Atlantic: Finance Capital, Slavery, and the Philosophy of History* (Durham, N.C.: Duke University Press, 2005), 70.

7. Spivak frames this gap in characteristically stark terms: "Top-down police breaches of Enlightenment principles are more rule than exception." In *Aesthetic Education in the Era of Globalization*, 4. On the mutual implication of enlightenment humanism and slavery, see Simon Gikandi, *Slavery and the Culture of Taste* (Princeton, N.J.: Princeton University Press, 2011).

8. Donald Sweig provides a detailed account of the commercial and fiscal mechanisms by which Washington acquired slaves. Sweig writes, "Washington, for example, bought slaves in Maryland [to avoid a 10 percent duty in Virginia]. From the mid-1750s until about 1770, he was increasing his slave force by frequent purchases." See Sweig, "The Importation of African Slaves to the Potomac River, 1732–1772," *William and Mary Quarterly*, 42, no. 4 (October 1985), 515–16.

9. "At about the same time that he was drawing up his will, Washington made a list of the adult and child slaves on each of the Mount Vernon farms, usually giving ages, occupations, and other pertinent information. His list of 317 slaves includes the names of 124 who belonged to him outright and were to be freed when Martha Washington died, 153 who were Martha Washington's

dower slaves [see notes 10 and 11 below] and at her death would go to the Custis heir-at-law, her grandson George Washington Parke Custis, and 40 others leased by GW from his neighbor Penelope Manley French." See note 2 to "George Washington's Last Will and Testament, 9 July 1799," Founders Online, National Archives, http://founders.archives.gov/documents/Washington/06-04-02-0404-0001 (last update: September 29, 2015), *The Papers of George Washington*, Retirement Series, vol. 4, *20 April 1799–13 December 1799*, W. W. Abbot, ed. (Charlottesville: University Press of Virginia, 1999), 479–511.

10. Upon his death, Washington's estate passed to Martha Washington, who outlived her husband by two and a half years. Respecting the three categories of slaves who worked Washington's lands—those owned outright by Washington, those owned by Martha Washington, and those leased from others—Washington's will reads as follows: "Upon the decease [of] my wife, it is my Will & desire th[at] all the Slaves which I hold in [my] own right, shall receive their free[dom]. To emancipate them during [her] life, would, tho' earnestly wish[ed by] me, be attended with such insu[pera]ble difficulties on account of thei[r interm]ixture by Marriages with the [dow]er Negroes, as to excite the most pa[in]ful sensations, if not disagreeabl[e c]onsequences from the latter, while [both] descriptions are in the occupancy [of] the same Proprietor; it not being [in] my power, under the tenure by which [th]e Dower Negroes are held, to man[umi]t them." Washington could not, in other words, manumit slaves originally belonging to his wife's first husband, and nor could he manumit leased slaves.

11. "Dower slaves" belonged to Martha Washington for the duration of her natural life, at which point they reverted to the heir of the estate of her first husband, Daniel Parke Custis.

12. Sweig also discusses the advertisement under examination here as it relates to the four slaves' provenance, writing, "An advertisement by Washington for four runaway slaves in the *Maryland Gazette* of August 1761 provides additional evidence of clandestine importations to Virginia. Washington identified two of the four, Neptune and Cupid, as having been 'brought from an African Ship in August 1759.' As no ship carrying slaves entered at South Potomac between 1754 and 1760, where had Washington purchased these Africans? . . . The accounts do indicate that, in 1759, in addition to buying some Virginia-born blacks, whose names he recorded, he also purchased nine blacks from a 'Col° Churchill' for £406.28. Col. Henry Churchill, a wealthy Fauquier County planter, might well have bought slaves in Maryland for Washington and perhaps other Virginians as well. That Washington did not list these blacks by name [Neptune and Cupid], as he did others, supports the contention that they were newly imported Africans." These facts also support the conclusion that Washington was profiting from a loophole in the law regarding intercolonial transportation of slaves to avoid taxation in Virginia. Sweig, "Importation of African Slaves to the Potomac River, 1732–1772," 518–19.

13. See note 1 of the annotations to "Advertisement for Runaway Slaves, 11 August 1761," Founders Online, National Archives, http://founders.archives.gov/documents/Washington/02-07-02-0038 (last update: June 29, 2015). Source: *The Papers of George Washington*, Colonial Series, vol. 7, *1 January 1761–15 June 1767*, ed. W. W. Abbot and Dorothy Twohig, 65–68.

14. See note 4 of the annotations to "Advertisement for Runaway Slaves, 11 August 1761," 65–68.

15. Jacques Derrida, *The Monolingualism of the Other; or, The Prosthesis of Origin*, 1996, Patrick Mensah, trans. (Stanford, Calif.: Stanford University Press, 1998), 48.

16. Elizabeth Alexander, "Praise Song for the Day: A Poem for Barack Obama's Presidential Inauguration," recited in Washington, D.C., January 20, 2009. The first two stanzas of the poem

are equally appropriate for this context. They read as follows: "Each day we go about our business, / walking past each other, catching each other's / eyes or not, about to speak or speaking. / / All about us is noise. All about us is / noise and bramble, thorn and din, each / one of our ancestors on our tongues."

17. Citing S. W. Koelle's *Polyglotta Africana; or, A Comparative Vocabulary of Nearly 300 Words and Phrases in More Than 100 Distinct African Tongues* (London: Church Missionary House, 1854), David Northrup writes, "An indication of the linguistic diversity that could exist among enslaved Africans comes from the small British colony of Sierra Leone, where 160 distinct African languages were counted among those liberated from slave ships and resettled there, mostly between 1815 and 1835, by the British Anti-slave Trade Patrol." In Northrup, *How English Became the Global Language* (New York: Palgrave Macmillan, 2013), 11.

18. Sweig, "Importation of African Slaves to the Potomac River, 1732–1772," 515–16.

19. By contrast, Washington's letters display an insecure reverence for certain European languages, Latin, Greek, and French in particular. Writing to the Comte de Grasse in 1784, for example, Washington states, "I thank you for the memorials you have had the goodness to send me; it is unhappy for me however that I am not sufficiently Master of the French language to read them without assistance; this, when fully obtained will, I have no doubt, enable my judgment to coincide with my wishes; which are as favorable as those of your warmest friend, and greatest admirer can be." George Washington to the Comte de Grasse, May 15, 1784, *The Writings of George Washington from the Original Manuscript Sources, 1745–1799*, John C. Fitzpatrick, ed., vol. 27 (Washington, D.C.: U.S. Government Printing Office, 1931–43), 401. I am indebted to research historian Mary Thompson for sharing with me her meticulous research and citations relating to Washington's views of nonanglophone languages.

20. It is seems all at once necessary and superfluous to quote here Thomas Jefferson's well-known dismissal of these two anglophone multilinguals on racial grounds: "Religion indeed has produced a Phyllis Whately [*sic*]; but it could not produce a poet. The compositions published under her name are below the dignity of criticism. The heroes of the *Dunciad* are to her, as Hercules to the author of that poem. Ignatius Sancho has approached nearer to merit in composition; yet his letters do more honour to the heart than the head. They breathe the purest effusions of friendship and general philanthropy, and shew how great a degree of the latter may be compounded with strong religious zeal. He is often happy in the turn of his compliments, and his stile is easy and familiar, except when he affects a Shandean fabrication of words." I address the linguistic dimensions of Wheatley's poetic oeuvre in the fourth section of the next chapter. See Thomas Jefferson, *Notes on the State of Virginia*, 1785, (London: John Stockdale, 1787), 234.

Chapter 1. The Multilingualism of the Other

1. Rev. Lyons, "Education in Ireland: Irish Society" (London: Andrews, 1827), 3.

2. Ngũgĩ, *Decolonising the Mind*, 11.

3. "It was after the declaration of a state of emergency over Kenya in 1952 that all the schools run by patriotic nationalists were taken over by the colonial regime and were replaced under District Education Boards chaired by Englishmen. In Kenya, English became more than a language: it was *the* language, and all the others had to bow before it in deference." Ngũgĩ, *Decolonising the Mind*, 11.

4. Viswanathan departs from a premise that remains valid, timely, and extensible: "This book sets out to demonstrate in part that the discipline of English came into its own in an age of colonialism, as well as to argue that no serious account of its growth and development can afford to ignore the imperial mission of educating and civilizing colonial subjects in the literature and thought of England, a mission that in the long run served to strengthen Western cultural hegemony in enormously complex ways." Gauri Viswanathan, *Masks of Conquest: Literary Study and British Rule in India* (New York: Columbia University Press, 1989), 2.

5. I use the term "dialectic" in the sense of the term that Andrew Cole provides through his long history of dialectical thinking. Keeping with this, in this book I will describe the linguistically normative and linguistically nonnormative as two immediacies that are gradually sharpened into fixed ideas over the course of the long eighteenth century. See Andrew Cole, *The Birth of Theory* (Chicago: University of Chicago Press, 2014).

6. Rev. Lyons, "Education in Ireland. Irish Society," 1.

7. Ngũgĩ, *Decolonising the Mind*, 17, 9.

8. Ngũgĩ, *Decolonising the Mind*, 9.

9. Ngũgĩ, *Decolonising the Mind*, 16.

10. I take the term "transtemporal" from Rita Felski's critique of historicism in "Context Stinks," in *New Literary History*, 42 (2011), 573–91.

11. See Suzanne Romaine, *Bilingualism* (Oxford: Basil Blackwell, 1989), 217–18; Robert Phillipson, *Linguistic Imperialism* (Oxford: Oxford University Press, 1992); David Crystal, *English as a Global Language* (Cambridge University Press, 1997); and updates to the latter text in David Crystal, *English as a Global Language*, 2nd ed. (Cambridge: Cambridge University Press, 2003). By way of comparison with French imperial linguistic practice, Frantz Fanon, writing in 1952, notes, "Aux Antilles . . . la langue officiellement parlée est le français; les instituteurs surveillent étroitement les enfants pour que le créole ne soit pas utilisé. [In the Antilles . . . the language that is officially spoken is French; teachers closely monitor students to ensure that Creole is not used.]" *Peau noire masques blancs* (Paris: Seuil, 1952), 22.

12. Rajend Mesthrie, "Building a New English Dialect," in *Alternative Histories of English*, Watts and Trudgill, eds. (London: Routledge, 2002), 112.

13. Mesthrie captures enabling and disabling elements (what he calls the lighter and "darker sides") of anglophone linguistic imposition when he notes, "The adoption of English in the long run mirrored the advantages and weaknesses of colonisation. English brought Western education and access to some of the cultural and scientific elements of the West. In countries such as India and South Africa it enabled developing local leaderships to communicate with each other beyond the confines of traditional ties to region, and linguistic and ethnic group and ultimately led to new ideas of nationhood. The darker side of the spread was the devaluation of local languages and the destruction of local cultures." Rajend Mesthrie, "Building a New English Dialect," 112.

14. Mesthrie, "Building a New English Dialect," 112.

15. See in particular Janet Sorensen's discussion of the relationship between England and Scotland as mediated by language politics in *Grammar of Empire in Eighteenth-Century British Writing*.

16. The political and aesthetic agency of those resisting or attempting to dismantle anglophone linguistic impositions is displayed in recent studies of imperial educational practices in North America. See E. Jennifer Monaghan, *Learning to Read and Write in Colonial America* (Amherst: University of Massachusetts Press, 2005), and Sean Harvey, *Native Tongues: Colonialism and Race from Encounter to the Reservation* (Cambridge, Mass.: Harvard University Press,

2015). To cite another example, Hilary Wyss's *English Letters and Indian Literacies* describes technologies of alphabetic literacy pedagogy as they were visited on Native Americans "educated" in the missionary schools of late eighteenth- and early nineteenth-century North America. Noting that the scene of native learning was implicitly transatlantic and anglophone, Wyss points to ways that indigenous literacies both informed and outlasted native use of alphabetic literacy in spite of efforts on the part of educators to prevent those very facts. See Hilary Wyss, *English Letters and Indian Literacies: Reading, Writing, and New England Missionary Schools, 1750–1830* (Philadelphia: University of Pennsylvania Press, 2012).

17. The longevity of these political and aesthetic traditions is further demonstrated by first-hand accounts of those who survived the unashamedly linguicidal American Indian Residential School system. See David Wallace Adams, *Education for Extinction: American Indians and the Boarding School Experience, 1875–1928* (Lawrence: University of Kansas Press, 1995), and Allan Reyhner and Jeanne Oyawin Eder, *American Indian Education: A History* (Norman: University of Oklahoma Press, 2006).

18. It would be disingenuous but also false to describe the scene of language learning and literacy as though it were only a scene of unchecked violence and imposition. In a recent *PMLA* editor's column, Gikandi describes the Kenyan society in which he grew up as "a society where English was considered both pure and dangerous." Before going on to rehearse the main intellectual responses to English as a postcolonial language that positioned itself as a precondition to modernity, Gikandi frames the scene on the ground for those who lived through decolonization: "Desire for English had nothing to do with what has come to be known as colonial mimicry, for my parents, like other members of their generation, were proud of their mother tongue and their native culture, but they assumed that the future belonged to a new set of experiences and behaviors that was only available to them through English." Gikandi, "Provincializing English," 8.

19. In the final section of this chapter I discuss Robert Burns and Phillis Wheatley as paradigmatic examples of creative productivity in the face of linguistic impositions, but suffice it to say, there are many other figures who fit this model, a fact the rest of the book tries to demonstrate.

20. My use of the first term derives from Olivia Smith's investigation of the politics of language during the 1790s in Britain. Smith's close reading of the distinction produced between polite and vulgar language forms, not to mention her critical analysis of how each was represented in texts of the period, have been essential to the formulation of my argument. See Olivia Smith, *Politics of Language, 1789–1819*.

21. Derrida, *Monolingualism of the Other*, 40.

22. "Monolanguage" is Derrida's term for an imperial language that insists on its unity and regularity even though, strictly speaking, languages can have no such unity. He writes, "What I mean to say is that it is impossible to count languages. There is no calculability, since the One of a language, which escapes all arithmetic (ac)countability, is never determined. The One of the monolanguage of which I speak, and the one I speak, will hence not be an arithmetical identity or, in short, any identity at all. Monolanguage remains incalculable, at least in that characteristic. But the fact that languages appear strictly incalculable does not prevent them from all disappearing. In this century they are sinking each day by the hundreds, and this perdition opens the question of another rescue, or another salvation." Derrida, *Monolingualism of the Other*, 40, 30.

23. Yildiz notes, "The 'mother tongue' is the affective knot at the center of the monolingual paradigm and therefore a knot worth unraveling. . . . The 'mother' in 'mother tongue' stands in

for the allegedly organic nature of this structure by supplying it with notions of maternal origin, affective and corporeal intimacy, and natural kinship. Yet the emotional and ideological connotations of 'mother tongue' . . . are historical artifacts and not transhistorical constants." Yasemin Yildiz, *Beyond the Mother Tongue: The Postmonolingual Condition* (New York: Fordham University Press, 2013), 10.

24. Thomas Paul Bonfiglio, *Mother Tongues and Nations: The Invention of the Native Speaker* (Berlin: De Gruyter Mouton, 2010), 122–23. Bonfiglio's investigation into the history of the concepts of "the mother tongue" and "the native speaker" is less interested in aesthetic practice than Yildiz's. Suffice it to say, both scholars begin from a similar sense that the eighteenth-century codevelopment of imperial and nationalistic practice forms the heart of the matter.

25. Following Yildiz and Bonfiglio, we can and should date the maturation of this particular politics of monolingualism to the eighteenth century even if relevant precursors are identifiable before. Filling in the prehistory of Yildiz's analyses of mostly twentieth-century mixed language writing in, German, German Jewish, German Japanese, and German Turkish literary traditions it is also part of my argument that we can understand contemporary aesthetic implications of the political distinction between monolingualism and multilingualism that Yildiz posits through an examination of the eighteenth-century cultural agon between Standard English and emergent or residual anglophone Englishes, a dialectic I pursue in Chapter 4 by tracing the interactions of normative Standard English and nonnormative eighteenth-century anglophony in texts like Brice's *Exmoor Scolding* and John Collier's *View of the Lancashire Dialect.*

26. Frantz Fanon writes vividly of his own linguistic autosurveillance, spawned as it was by the politics of the French language's imperial status, "Oui, il faut que je me surveille dans mon élocution, car c'est un peu à travers elle qu'on me jugera. [Yes, I have to monitor myself in my elocution, because it's basically through that that I will be judged.]" *Peau noire masques blancs*, 15.

27. Bakhtin, *Dialogic Imagination*, 295.

28. Katie Wales, *Northern English: A Cultural and Social History* (Cambridge: Cambridge University Press, 2006), 2.

29. This fictive newspaper description of the mysterious and linguistically deft biloquist named Carwin appears in Charles Brockden Brown, *Wieland; or, The Transformation: An American Tale* (New York: Penguin Classics, 1991; 1798), 147.

30. The global anglophone archive of eighteenth-century fugitive and slave advertising is vast. For example, editor Lathan Windley's *Runaway Slave Advertisements* runs to four volumes, each of which concentrates on a specific colony/state: Virginia, Maryland, South Carolina, and Georgia. More detailed studies have mostly been undertaken using cross-sectional methodologies that, like Windley's, concentrate on a single geographical location or specific newspaper. One notable example of this kind is Richard Wojtowicz and Billy Smith's work, which points out that between its founding in 1728 and the end of the century, the *Pennsylvania Gazette* alone contained "thousands of notices of notices for runaways, most of whom fled masters who lived within the region." Wojtowicz and Smith, "Advertisements for Runaway Slaves, Indentured Servants, and Apprentices in the *Pennsylvania Gazette*," *Pennsylvania History*, 54, no. 1 (January 1987), 35. Other studies take on fugitive advertising from diverse perspectives. Thomas Agostini's study of advertisements for North American war deserters locates nearly two thousand such ads published between Georgia and Nova Scotia in the limited period from 1755 to 1762. See Thomas Agostini, "'Deserted His Majesty's Service': Military Runaways, the British-American Press, and the Problem of Desertion During the Seven Years' War," *Journal of Social History*, 40, no. 4 (Summer

2007), 957. Because gender is a key component of many fugitive ads, Jan Kurth focuses on female servants and female slaves as they appeared in the *Poughkeepsie Journal*. Kurth, "Wayward Wenches and Wives: Runaway Women in the Hudson Valley, NY, 1785–1830," *NWSA Journal*, 1, no. 2 (Winter 1988–89), 199–220. This is just a small sample. Other key works will be present in the notes throughout the rest of this chapter.

31. On the development of British periodical advertising practices, see Nicholas Mason, *Literary Advertising and the Shaping of British Romanticism* (Baltimore: Johns Hopkins University Press, 2013). This fine book's first chapter, "Advertising in the Romantic Century" (11–22), is particularly apropos.

32. On the question of the relationship between British and American advertising, Marcus Wood writes, "Representations of the fugitive slave, and the formulae for prose descriptions of escapees, had been developed out of the conventions of advertisements for runaway white indentured servants advertised commonly in colonial papers from the mid-eighteenth century." See Wood, *Blind Memory*, 80. On the question of the financial importance of slavery to newspapers, see David Waldstreicher's instructive tabulation of advertising revenue in Franklin's *Pennsylvania Gazette*. Waldstreicher, "Reading the Runaways," 250.

33. In this latter location, for example, where fledgling anglophone papers got off the ground in Calcutta only during the 1780s, the assumption that fugitive notices would constitute a part of a paper's revenue stream is clear. Indeed, early incarnations of many anglophone newspapers in South Asia—*Hicky's Bengal Gazette; or, Calcutta General Advertiser* (1780–82); *India Gazette, or, Calcutta Public Advertiser* (1781–88); *Calcutta Gazette; or, Oriental Advertiser* (1784–1816); and *Calcutta Chronicle; and General Advertiser* (1787–94)—carried fugitive ads from their beginnings. Additionally, Michael Craton's analysis of the Jamaican sugar estate Worthy Park gestures toward fugitive slaves and advertising in the Caribbean. Craton, *Searching for the Invisible Man: Slaves and Plantation Life in Jamaica* (Cambridge, Mass.: Harvard University Press, 1978).

34. Gwenda Morgan and Peter Rushton's reading of fugitive advertising is interested in the question of how social interaction was coded in text, but they omit the reciprocal constitution of language and body. As they write, "The obvious features to comment on were those most visible to observers and most likely to lead to confident identification by the reading public." Gwenda Morgan and Peter Rushton, "Visible Bodies: Subordination and Identity in the Eighteenth-Century Atlantic World," *Journal of Social History*, 39, no. 1 (Autumn 2005), 42. Waldstreicher does justice to the presence of linguistic details in fugitive slave advertising by structuring his argument around the interpenetration of four attributes present in many ads for escaped slaves. He writes, "Four of these attributes stand out in the advertisements: clothing, trades or skills, linguistic ability or usage, and ethnic or racial identity." Whereas Waldstreicher is more concerned with what references to language can tell us about slave resistance and agency, in this chapter I focus more on the intersection between fugitive advertising and textual representation of voices and bodies. Waldstreicher, "Reading the Runaways," 248.

35. The archive of anglophone fugitive advertising is massive. Unfortunately, I cannot offer here a comprehensive statistical accounting of the relative frequency of linguistic qualifications in such ads. Instead, I want to discuss how linguistic determinations function when they do appear, and then claim that this has something to say about language politics in the period and today.

36. It is interesting in this respect to consider fugitive advertising in conjunction with the performances, staged lessons, and pedagogical texts of the British elocution movement, which

was spearheaded in the mid-eighteenth century by Thomas Sheridan and later by John Walker. In the discourses of elocution, a student is taught to combine linguistic propriety with bodily grace. See in particular the bodily and linguistic cues in Thomas Sheridan's, *A Course of Lectures on Elocution* (London: W. Strahan, 1762), and John Walker, *The Elements of Elocution* (London: T. Cadell, 1781).

37. *Oracle*, April 8, 1791, no. 581.

38. Somersetshire sounds, as protoethnographer James Jennings recorded in 1825, "consist in their terminating, in the present tense of the indicative mood, all the third persons singular of the verbs in *th* or *eth* . . . *he lov'th, he read'th, he zee'th*." Jennings, *Observations on Some of the Dialect in the West of England* (London: Baldwin, Cradock, and Joy, 1825), 3.

39. As the *Oxford English Dictionary* attests, during the period "spinster" was widely used as both an occupational term and a disparaging term for an unmarried woman. "spinster, n." *OED Online*, March 2016, Oxford University Press, http://www.oed.com.proxygw.wrlc.org/view/Entry/186771?redirectedFrom = spinster (accessed April 30, 2016).

40. *Gazetteer and New Daily Advertiser*, Tuesday, February 5, 1771, no. 13084.

41. *Evening Post*, March 6–8, 1755, no. 4263.

42. For a recent and entertaining take on the history of canting crews, see Daniel Heller-Roazen *Dark Tongues: The Art of Rogues and Riddlers* (New York: Zone Books, 2013).

43. *Westminster Journal or New Weekly Miscellany*, May 9, 1747, no. 284.

44. *General Evening Post*, December 27–30, 1794, no. 9555.

45. William Wordsworth is of course the author of the central document addressing the relationship between linguistic difference and poesis in the late eighteenth and early nineteenth centuries. *Lyrical Ballads* (1798 and later editions) makes productive aesthetic use of the concept of "rustic life" and, in so doing, influences generations of readers, poets, and novelists to come.

46. *Gazetteer and New Daily Advertiser*, Tuesday, December 1, 1778, no. 15538.

47. *Caledonian Mercury*, January 12, 1789, no. 10508.

48. *Public Advertiser*, June 24, 1790, no. 17461.

49. *Public Advertiser*, June 24, 1790, no. 17461.

50. *St. James Chronicle or the British Evening Post*, December 2–14, 1793, no. 5612.

51. Indeed, efflorescent eighteenth-century elocution treatises take it as axiomatic that an individual's language practices are alterable and improvable, where improvement is defined as the imitation of artificially defined standards of propriety.

52. *North Carolina Minerva and Raleigh Advertiser*, December 27, 1816.

53. Waldstreicher's eye-opening reading of language in the transatlantic world points out that "multilingual slaves were the glue of maritime commerce, of a diverse America growing because of its trade with the world." The majority of the ads he cites, however, do not indicate that owners acknowledged this truth about slave multilingualism, and the majority of the ads he cites approach multilingual skills with trepidation. Waldstreicher, "Reading the Runaways," 259–61.

54. See also Mary Gallant, "Slave Runaways in Colonial Virginia: Accounts and Status Passage as Collective Process," *Symbolic Interaction*, 15, no. 4 (Winter 1992), 389–412; James Giganto, "Trading in Jersey Souls: New Jersey and the Interstate Slave Trade," *Pennsylvania History*, 77, no. 3 (Summer 2010), 281–302; Lorenzo Greene, "The New England Negro as Seen in Advertisements for Runaway Slaves," *Journal of Negro History*, 29, no. 2 (April 1944), 126–46; Daniel E. Meaders, *Advertisements for Escaped Slaves in Virginia, 1801–1820* (New York: Garland, 1997);

Daniel E. Meaders, *Dead or Alive: Fugitive Slaves and White Indentured Servants Before 1830* (New York: Garland, 1993); Daniel E. Meaders, "South Carolina Fugitives as Viewed Through Local Colonial Newspapers with Emphasis on Runaway Notices 1732–1801," *Journal of Negro History*, 60, no. 2 (April 1975), 288–319; Richard Wojtowicz and Billy Smith, *Blacks Who Stole Themselves*; and Jonathan Prude, "To Look upon the 'Lower Sort': Runaway Ads and the Appearance of Unfree Laborers in America, 1750–1800," *Journal of American History*, 78, no. 1 (June 1991), 124–59.

55. *Calcutta Gazette; or, Oriental Advertiser*, vol. 14, 1790–91, nos. 355, 356.

56. *Hicky's Bengal Gazette; or, Calcutta General Advertiser*, 1780, nos. 11, 12.

57. *Hicky's Bengal Gazette; or, Calcutta General Advertiser*, 1780–82, nos. 2–6.

58. Here I am transporting into linguistic terms Wojtowicz and Smith's concept of the escape from slavery as a theft of labor power. This appears in Richard Wojtowicz and Billy Smith, *Blacks Who Stole Themselves*.

59. *Calcutta Gazette; or, Oriental Advertiser*, vol. 11, 1789, nos. 271, 272.

60. "khidmutgar, n." *OED Online*, March 2016, Oxford University Press, http://www.oed.com/view/Entry/103208?redirectedFrom=khitmatgar (accessed May 8, 2016).

61. Robert Burns is a good example of a figure who remained within the realm of the aesthetic even though his writing is linguistically heterodox. As I point out in Chapter 4, many writers who deal in different anglophone forms have been confined to the realms of philology and historical linguistics.

62. Though I mean "stage" in a wider and metaphoric sense, the theater is an important place to look for nonnormative forms of English as spectacle. Michael Ragussis has recently and productively catalogued the unquestioned ubiquity of performed dialect on the stage in *Theatrical Nation: Jews and Other Outlandish Englishmen in Georgian Britain* (Philadelphia: University of Pennsylvania Press, 2010).

63. Henry MacKenzie, "The Surprising Effects of Original Genius, exemplified in the Poetical Productions of Robert Burns, an Ayrshire Ploughman," first published in the *Lounger* (December 1786), reprinted in the *European Magazine and London Review*, December 1786, and subsequently reprinted in the annual edition of *European Magazine and London Review* (London: J. Cornhill, 1786), 461.

64. Tobias Smollett, "Monthly Catalogue of Poetry. *Poems, Chiefly in the Scottish Dialect. By Robert Burns.* Printed at Kilmarnock," in *Critical Review*, 63 (London: A. Hamilton, 1787), 388.

65. See in this volume "Multilingual Lives: Peros, Jack, Neptune, and Cupid," n. 20.

66. Burns's revised dedication to the 1787 Edinburgh edition expressly addresses Scottish patrons—"To the Noblemen and Gentlemen of the Caledonian Hunt"—thereby inserting his project into a uniquely national mythos. The Kilmarnock preface (1786), on the other hand, speaks more abstractly about poetic authorship, citing Scottish luminaries Ramsay and Ferguson as influences alongside an apostrophe to Englishman William Shenstone as "that celebrated Poet, whose divine Elegies do honour to our language, our nation, and our species" (Kilmarnock, iv). The inclusive first-person pronouns in this apostrophe may surprise modern readers. Is Burns grouping himself with the English? Britishness? Anglophony? A universalist vision of humanity? The Edinburgh edition's dedication clears up any ambiguities on this front. First, Burns affirms that he is not so "hackneyed" as to have "prostituted Learning" (presumably to the anglicized Scottish elite) and then proceeds to "claim the common Scottish name with you, my illustrious Countrymen" (Edinburgh, vi). Nationalist rhetoric permeates the second edition's dedication in

a way that is absent from the first, thereby rebranding the poet as one whose concerns suffused Scotland but had little truck with the British tradition.

67. As an example, consider the multilingual toggling at work in the first three stanzas of Burns's celebrated poem "To a Mouse": "Wee, sleeket, cowran, tim'rous beastie, / O, what a panic's in thy breastie! / Thou need na start awa sae hasty, / Wi' bickerin brattle! / I wad be laith to rin an' chase thee / Wi' murd'ring pattle! / / I'm truly sorry Man's dominion / Has broken Nature's social union, / An' justifies that ill opinion, / Which makes thee startle, / At me, thy poor, earth-born companion, / An' fellow-mortal! / / I doubt na, whyles, but thou may thieve; / What then? poor beastie, thou maun live! / A daimen-icker in a thrave / 'S a sma' request: / I'll get a blessin wi' the lave, / An' never miss 't!" Whereas Burns's first and third stanzas invite anglophone readers into the texture of the Scots tongue, the second stanza's apology is far more legible to a primarily anglophone reader unfamiliar with Scots. By sandwiching this stanza between the others, Burns both ironizes Standard English and elevates Scots.

68. John C. Shields, "Wheatley, Phillis (*c.* 1753–1784)," *Oxford Dictionary of National Biography*, Oxford University Press, 2004, May 2008, http://www.oxforddnb.com/view/article/53405 (accessed September 12, 2014).

69. Vincent Carretta notes, "The Middle Passage that brought the future Phillis Wheatley to Boston on 11 July 1761 was in many ways exceptional. She arrived during an interruption of a more comprehensive decline of the transatlantic slave trade to Boston since the 1740s. Due to the Seven Years' War, her Middle Passage may have been the only shipment of enslaved Africans to arrive in Boson in 1761, and one of only three slave-trading voyages from Africa to any of Britain's North American or Caribbean colonies that year." Carretta, *Phillis Wheatley: Biography of a Genius in Bondage* (Athens: University of Georgia Press, 2011), 6.

70. John C. Shields, "Wheatley, Phillis (*c.* 1753–1784)," *Oxford Dictionary of National Biography*, Oxford University Press, 2004, May 2008, http://www.oxforddnb.com/view/article/53405 (accessed September 12, 2014).

71. John Wheatley, "Letter Sent by the Author's Master to the Publisher," in Phillis Wheatley, *Poems on Various Subjects, Religious and Moral* (London: Archibald Bell, 1773).

72. Archibald Bell, "Attestation," in *Poems on Various Subjects, Religious and Moral.*

73. Archibald Bell, "Attestation."

74. Carretta, *Phillis Wheatley: Biography of a Genius in Bondage*, 40.

75. Carretta, *Phillis Wheatley: Biography of a Genius in Bondage*, 37.

76. Phillis Wheatley, "On Being Brought from Africa to America," in *Poems on Various Subjects, Religious and Moral*, 10.

77. "On the Death of the Rev. Dr. Sewell," "On the Death of the Rev. George Whitefield," "On the Death of a Young Lady of Five Years of Age," "On the Death of a Young Gentleman," "To a Lady on the Death of Her Husband," "To a Lady on the Death of Three Relations," "To a Clergyman on the Death of His Lady," "A Funeral Poem on the Death of C.R., An Infant of Twelve Months," "To a Lady and Her Children, On the Death of Her Son and Their Brother," "To a Gentleman and Lady, On the Death of the Lady's Brother and Sister, and a Child of the Name Avis, Aged One Year," "On the Death of Dr. Samuel Marshall," "On the Death of J.C., An Infant," "To the Honorable T.H., Esq. On the Death of his Daughter," and "To His Honor, the Lieutenant-Governor, On the Death of His Lady, March 24, 1773."

78. "Niobe in Distress for her Children slain by Apollo" and "Farewell to America" are obvious examples, the latter especially so in that it implicitly redoubles an earlier departure from Africa.

79. For the classical context of elegy, which in the period of its formation has wide-ranging functions that are irreducible to requiem or mourning, see Antonio Aloni, "Elegy: Forms, Functions, and Communication," in *The Cambridge Companion to Greek Lyric*, Felix Budelmann, ed. (Cambridge: Cambridge University Press, 2009), 168–88.

80. Eric Ashley Harrison, "The Trojan Horse: Classics, Memory, Transformation, and Afric Ambition in *Poems on Various Subjects, Religions and Moral*," in *New Essays on Phillis Wheatley*, John C. Shields and Eric D. Lamore, eds. (Knoxville: University of Tennessee Press, 2011), 87.

81. This passage continues, "Her tone verges on outright admonishment at times, as she charges the subject of the elegy—the living relative(s) left behind—not to wish for the deceased's return, while she simultaneously celebrates the now bodiless state of the departed." Mary McAleer Balkun, "To 'Pursue Th' Unbodied Mind:' Phillis Wheatley and the Raced Body in Early America," in *New Essays on Phillis Wheatley*, 380.

82. Devona Mallory, "I Remember Mama: Honoring the Goddess-Mother While Denouncing the Slaveowner-God in Phillis Wheatley's Poetry," in *New Essays on Phillis Wheatley*, 32.

83. Phillis Wheatley, "On the Death of a Young Lady of Five Years of Age," 13–14.

84. Compare this to Wheatley's "A Funeral Poem on the Death of C.R., An Infant of Twelve Months," in which the infant takes "flight / To purer regions of celestial light" and there learns to speak in the "joyful" and "exulting" language of prayer even though "heaving" and "pensive bosoms" remain behind to "groan."

85. Tobias Smollett, "Monthly Catalogue of Poetry. *Poems, Chiefly in the Scottish Dialect. By Robert Burns.* Printed at Kilmarnock," 387–88.

86. In addition to Yasemin Yildiz's *Beyond the Mother Tongue*, Hsy's *Trading Tongues*, and Evelyn Nien-Ming Ch'ien's *Weird English* (Cambridge, Mass.: Harvard University Press, 2004), which I discuss below, one can also count as good and recent models Brian Lennon's *In Babel's Shadow: Multilingual Literatures, Monolingual States* (Minneapolis: University of Minnesota Press, 2010) and the edited collection by Axel Englund and Anders Olsson entitled *Languages of Exile: Migration and Multilingualism in Twentieth-Century Literature* (Bern: Peter Lang, 2013).

87. One exception to this claim is the attention scholars have paid to the story of the translation and authorization of the King James Version of the Bible. A forty-seven-person team produced the translation that came to be known as the Authorized Version in three centers of translation: Oxford, Cambridge, and Westminster. One of the stated operational principles of this team was to rely heavily on earlier versions such as the Geneva, Coverdale, Tyndale, and Bishops' Bibles, especially when it came to translating the so-called Old Testament. All these earlier Bibles and the King James Bible required textual and personal consultation and "multilingual exchanges" with the Jewish tradition and Jewish scholars. There was also an explicit attempt to maintain, as much as it was possible through translation, some of the grammatical and syntactical features of the Hebrew original. For more scholarly analyses, see in particular the introduction to the Oxford World Classics edition of the King James Bible (2008) and David Daiches's *The King James Version of the English Bible: An Account of the Development and Sources of the English Bible of 1611 with Special Reference to the Hebrew Tradition* (Chicago: University of Chicago Press, 1941).

Multilingual Lives: Reverend Lyons

1. As Ngũgĩ has argued, "Language carries culture, and culture carries, particularly through orature and literature, the entire body of values by which we come to perceive ourselves and our

place in the world. . . . Language is thus inseparable from ourselves as a community of human beings with a specific form and character, a specific history, a specific relationship to the world." The imposition of one language over another represents an event in the destruction of culture and community. Ngũgĩ, *Decolonising the Mind*, 16.

2. In the pamphlet containing Lyons's speech, the introductory paragraph glosses the Benevolent Society of St. Patrick as "an institution in Liverpool for educating the poor on the most liberal principles." Rev. Lyons, "Education in Ireland. Irish Society," 1. Many other Benevolent Societies of St. Patrick were established in Britain and North America during the late eighteenth and early nineteenth centuries. The London chapter, for example, was founded in 1783.

3. For a historical account of the British and Foreign Bible Society, see Leslie Howsam, *Cheap Bibles: Nineteenth-Century Publishing and the British and Foreign Bible Society* (New York: Cambridge University Press, 1991). For a much earlier examination that includes reference to the Hibernian Bible Society, see John Owen, *The History of the Origin and the First Ten Years of the British and Foreign Bible Society* (New York: James Eastburn, 1817).

4. Lyons closes his speech in terms that praise the group that has asked him to address them: "The Hibernian and Irish Societies are an incubus on the moral energies of the people. They never did, never will succeed, except in tearing up the very foundations of social intercourse between Protestants and Catholics. . . . If the English wish really to aid in educating the Irish poor, let them make the Benevolent Society of St. Patrick the depository of their funds, and they shall soon see Ireland another country." Lyons, "Education in Ireland. Irish Society," 5, 2.

5. Lyons, "Education in Ireland. Irish Society," 3.

6. Lyons, "Education in Ireland. Irish Society," 2.

7. Lyons, "Education in Ireland. Irish Society," 2.

8. Samuel Johnson, "Preface" to *A Dictionary of the English Language* (London: W. Strahan et al., 1755), paragraph 91. Hereafter I am following the paragraph numbering added to the text in Jack Lynch's contemporary online edition of the preface. Jack Lynch, ed. "Preface to the *Dictionary*. From Samuel Johnson, *A Dictionary of the English Language* (London, 1755)," https://andromeda.rutgers.edu/~jlynch/Texts/preface.html.

9. Here I am referring to the lines from Lyons that were quoted at the beginning of Chapter 1: "All of you recollect . . . when the square bit of timber, called *the score*, suspended from the neck of each new scholar, gave intimation to the master, by a notch on its angles, when the stammering urchin relapsed into his mother tongue at home," "Education in Ireland. Irish Society," 3.

10. Ngũgĩ too tackles the question of anglophone literacy, especially in his discussion of "cultural alienation." He notes that "English was the official vehicle and the magic formula to colonial elitedom" and that attaining this elite status came at a terrific cost irrespective of the benefits it engendered. "The language of an African child's formal education was foreign. The language of his conceptualisation was foreign. Thought, in him, took the visible form of a foreign language. So the written language of a child's upbringing in the school (even his spoken language within the school compound) became divorced from his spoken language at home. There was often not the slightest relationship between the child's written world, which was also the language of his schooling, and the world of his immediate environment in the family and in the community." Ngũgĩ, *Decolonising the Mind*, 12, 15.

11. Lyons, "Education in Ireland. Irish Society," 3.

12. Lyons, "Education in Ireland. Irish Society," 3.

13. Lyons, "Education in Ireland. Irish Society," 3.

14. "Pentateuch" is a typically Christian theological term derived from Greek that refers to Genesis, Exodus, Leviticus, Numbers, and Deuteronomy, the first five scrolls or books of the Hebrew Bible, or Torah. Lyons, "Education in Ireland. Irish Society," 3.

15. The idea that translation can be a tool of linguistic and political control rather than unmediated communication of ideas is one I take up in the third chapter of this book. Lyons, "Education in Ireland. Irish Society," 4.

16. The useful term "linguistic imperialism" is Robert Phillipson's. He defines this term in the following way: "A working definition of English linguistic imperialism is that the dominance of English is asserted and maintained by the establishment and continuous reconstitution of structural and cultural inequalities between English and other languages." See Robert Phillipson, *Linguistic Imperialism* (Oxford: Oxford University Press, 1992), 47; more generally, 38–78.

17. Lyons, "Education in Ireland. Irish Society," 3.

18. Lyons, "Education in Ireland. Irish Society," 3.

19. Lyons, "Education in Ireland. Irish Society," 3.

20. Ngũgĩ depicts the idea of monolingual lack in related terms: "I remember one boy in my class of 1954 who had distinctions in all subjects except English, which he had failed. He was made to fail the entire exam. He went on to become a burn boy in a busy company. I who had only passes but got a credit in English got a place at the Alliance High School, one of the most elitist institutions for Africans in colonial Kenya." Ngũgĩ, *Decolonising the Mind*, 12.

21. Lyons, "Education in Ireland. Irish Society," 3.

22. Derrida, *Monolingualism of the Other*, 53.

23. Lyons, "Education in Ireland. Irish Society," 4.

24. Lyons, "Education in Ireland. Irish Society," 4.

25. Lyons, "Education in Ireland. Irish Society," 5.

Chapter 2. De Copia

1. Marlon James, *A Brief History of Seven Killings* (New York: Riverhead Books, 2014), 631.

2. As one reviewer puts it, "The two outsiders, the journalist and the CIA man, think in 1970s-flavoured American English. Everyone else's inner voice slides around on a continuum between Jamaican English and patois, a predominately spoken language which James renders using standard American English spelling in order to make things easier for non-Jamaican readers. 'Deh' and 'yuh' and the like are reserved for scraps of dialogue, and their use is socially graded: Nina, a child—like her creator—of a respectable uptown household, starts 'chatting bad' only when she's angry or upset, and doesn't sound very different from the Americans most of the time. Papa-Lo's thoughts are rich with mixed registers ('Still I have to wonder 'bout the level of bangarang a man going to perpetrate when he won't even tell me about it'), while Bam-Bam, at the bottom of the heap, doesn't have many words to rub together." Christopher Tayler, "Goings-On in the Tivoli Gardens," review of *A Brief History of Seven Killings*, by Marlon James, in *London Review of Books*, November 5, 2015, http://www.lrb.co.uk/v37/n21/christopher-tayler/goings-on-in-the-tivoli-gardens.

3. See James F. English's reading of both "prestige" and the Booker Prize in *The Economy of Prestige: Prizes, Awards, and the Circulation of Cultural Value* (Cambridge, Mass.: Harvard University Press, 2008).

4. As I suggested in the Introduction, it is useful to differentiate between the term "lect" and the term "dialect." In this book's interventionist vocabulary, "lect" refers to actually existing speech whereas "dialect" refers to written representations of them. In other words, "dialect" refers to historically contingent techniques for rendering lectic forms of anglophony in text. In many cases the technique of dialect writing is so divorced from reality of lectic speech that what it really renders is merely the idea of linguistic difference rather than actual phonological or grammatical differences. "Dialect" can and should be understood as a technology of writing rather than the unmediated communication of spoken lectic forms onto the page. For example, the preface to the seventh edition of *An Exmoor Scolding* (1771), a fictive text I discuss at length in the fourth chapter, reads: "The following is a genuine specimen thereof [the Devonshire dialect] as spoken in parts of the country where the scene is laid." I stress the distinction between lect and dialect—which is also about a distinction between world and text—in order to work against prefatory statements like this one, a statement that attributes to the author's semi-invented language an almost documentary realism.

5. It is interesting to compare the reviews of Burns by MacKenzie and Smollett cited in the previous chapter to later opinions on the aesthetics of anglophone linguistic difference. In Ralph Waldo Emerson's estimation, for example, Burns provides "the only example in history of a language made classic by the genius of a single man." Similarly, in an 1886 essay celebrating the centennial of *Poems, Chiefly in the Scottish Dialect,* Walt Whitman celebrates Burns's use of linguistic localism as aesthetic object. For Whitman, Burns's ability to publicize "the Scotch idiom was undoubtedly his happiest hit." Ralph Waldo Emerson, "Robert Burns, Speech at the Celebration of the Burns Centenary, Boston, January 25, 1869," in *The Complete Works of Ralph Waldo Emerson*, vol. 11, *Miscellanies*, (Boston: Houghton Mifflin: 1904), 442; Walt Whitman, "Robert Burns as Poet and Person," *North American Review*, 143, no. 360 (November 1886), 428.

6. Aesthetics and politics are social behaviors that are closely related and formally analogous in Rancière's work. Consider Rancière's analysis of the limits of political space as they are drawn by language: "If there is someone you do not wish to recognize as a political being, you begin by not seeing him as the bearer of the signs of politicity, by not understanding what he says, by not hearing what issues from his mouth as discourse. . . . Traditionally, in order to deny the political quality of a category—workers, women, and so on—all that was required was to assert that they belonged to a 'domestic' space that was separated from public life, one from which only groans or cries expressing suffering, hunger or anger could emerge, but not actual speech demonstrating a shared *aisthesis*." Jacques Rancière, *Dissensus: On Politics and Aesthetics*, Steven Corcoran, ed. and trans. (London: Continuum Books, 2010), 38.

7. Jacques Rancière, *Aisthesis: Scenes from the Aesthetic Regime of Art*, Zakir Paul, trans. (London: Verso, 2013), x.

8. Rancière, *Aisthesis*, ix.

9. These discrete moments account for the way that representations like "the vulgar figures of genre painting," "the exaltation of the most prosaic activities in verse free from meter," and "industrial buildings and machine rhythms," among other things, have become discernible as artistic objects over the last two centuries. Rancière, *Aisthesis*, x.

10. "The essence of politics resides in the modes of dissensual subjectivation that reveal a society in its difference to itself." Rancière, *Dissensus*, 42.

11. "Political argumentation is at one and the same time the demonstration of a possible world in which the argument could count as an argument, one that is addressed by a subject

qualified to argue, over an identified object, to an addressee who is required to see the object and to hear the argument that he 'normally' has no reason either to see or to hear." Rancière, *Dissensus*, 39.

12. Implicitly stressing postcolonial and critical race theory's role in bringing about these aesthetic and political changes, Ahmad takes her title from the subtitle of Ken Saro-Wiwa's *Sozaboy: A Novel in Rotten English* (1985). It is by redeploying this title that Ahmad's anthology ties itself to an aesthetically, politically, and linguistically established oppositional tradition.

13. Ahmad summarizes the filiations between these and others, writing, "What we term Standard English, their work reminds us, is after all only one dialect among many—the one that happened to be spoken by the groups of people responsible for compiling dictionaries and assembling grammar manuals." In Dohra Ahmad, *Rotten English: A Literary Anthology* (New York: W. W. Norton, 2007), 17.

14. Ahmad, *Rotten English*, 26.

15. Rancière, *Aisthesis*, xii.

16. It also argues in favor of linking Burns to nonnormative anglophone writers of the Standard English eighteenth century—traditionally unheralded and anaesthetic writers who might reveal different aspects of these developments than Burns. As Susan Buck-Morss argues, the critical writing of history is "a continuous struggle to liberate the past from the unconscious of a collective that forgets the conditions of its own existence." Buck-Morss, *Hegel, Haiti, and Universal History*, 85.

17. Derrida, *Monolingualism of the Other*, 57.

18. Evelyn Nien-Ming Ch'ien, *Weird English* (Cambridge, Mass.: Harvard University Press, 2004), 26.

19. Nathan Bailey, *Universal Etymological Dictionary* (London: E. Bell et al., 1721), 1–2.

20. Nathan Bailey, *Universal Etymological Dictionary*, 2.

21. Like Nathan Bailey's, most dictionaries of the period included prefaces that justified their intervention into public language habits in similar ways, almost always by grounding themselves in nonanglophone textual traditions, especially those of the classical world.

22. Nathan Bailey, *Universal Etymological Dictionary*, 11.

23. See Tieken-Boon van Ostade, *Grammars, Grammarians and Grammar-Writing in Eighteenth-Century England* and *The Bishop's Grammar: Robert Lowth and the Rise of Prescriptivism in English*. These works are crucial to any understanding of eighteenth-century metalinguistic discourse, in particular, the question of grammar writing.

24. Anselm Bayly, *A Plain and Complete Grammar of the English Language* (London: G. Bigg, 1772), ix. See also Anselm Bayly, *An Introduction to Languages Literary and Philosophical; Especially to the English, Latin, Greek and Hebrew* (London: James Rivington et al., 1758).

25. Anselm Bayly, *Introduction to Languages Literary and Philosophical*, 11.

26. A recent study by Kenneth Haynes has convincingly described some of the grammatical and thematic ways that eighteenth-century Greek and Latin multilingualism altered formal and tropological textures in English literature. The intricacies of Haynes's readings are remarkable, but it is the general thrust of his argument that proves most constructive here. For him, Greek and Latin literacy had undeniable social implications. Training in the "learned languages" bisected society: one either had Greek and Latin along with the status they conveyed, or one did not. If we take the best-selling grammarians and lexicographers of the eighteenth century—"best-selling" being here a weak but correlative placeholder for "influential," which has few measures—

the patterns are self-evident. Greek and Latin training were almost a precondition for authorizing commentary on English, a notion that should surprise contemporary language and literature experts. See Kenneth Haynes, *English Literature and Ancient Languages* (Oxford: Oxford University Press, 2003).

27. Johnson, "Preface," paragraph 3.

28. Robert Lowth, *A Short Introduction to English Grammar* (London: J. Hughs, 1762), vi.

29. Thomas Sheridan, *A Course of Lectures on Elocution* (London: W. Strahan, 1762), 3.

30. Thomas Sheridan, *Course of Lectures on Elocution*, 217.

31. Jim Milroy, "The Legitimate Language," in *Alternative Histories of English*, Watts and Trudgill, eds., 13.

32. Robert Lass, ed. *The Cambridge History of the English Language*, vol. 3, *1476–1776* (Cambridge: Cambridge University Press, 1999), 8.

33. Thomas Sheridan, *Course of Lectures on Elocution*, 206.

34. Tieken-Boon van Ostade argues that grammars of the eighteenth century, especially Lowth's, are more descriptive and empirical than prescriptive, as has commonly been assumed. See *Bishop's Grammar*, 10–15.

35. Wolfram Schmidgen, *Exquisite Mixture: The Virtues of Impurity in Early Modern England* (Philadelphia: University of Pennsylvania Press, 2013), 1.

36. Schmidgen, *Exquisite Mixture*, 19, 18.

37. See Tony Crowley, *Standard English and the Politics of Language*. See also John Barrell, "The Language Properly So-Called: The Authority of Common Usage," in *English Literature in History 1730–80: An Equal, Wide, Survey* (London: Hutchinson, 1983), 110–75.

38. Desiderius Erasmus, *Copia: Foundations of the Abundant Style*, trans. Betty Knott, vol. 24 of *Collected Works of Erasmus* (Toronto: University of Toronto Press, 1978), 301.

39. Erasmus, *Copia*, 301.

40. Erasmus, *Copia*, 300.

41. An analysis of the self-conscious effort to formulate English into an imperial language with a worthy imperial literature can be found in Alok Yadav's *Before the Empire of English*.

42. Hugh Blair, *Lectures on Rhetoric and Belles Lettres*, vol. 1 (Dublin: Whitestone et al., 1783), 204.

43. Richard Carew, "The Excellencie of the English Tongue by R.C. of Anthony Esquire to W.C.," 1596, reprinted in William Camden, *Remaines, concerning Britaine: but especially England, and the Inhabitants thereof*, 1605, (London: John Legatt, 1614), 36–44.

44. Carew, "Excellencie of the English Tongue," 41.

45. William Camden, *Remaines*, 27.

46. William Camden, *Remaines*, 27–28.

47. Peter Heylyn, *Cosmographie* (London: Henry Seile, 1652), 265.

48. See Schmidgen, *Exquisite Mixture*, 101–45. See also Book III of Locke's *An Essay Concerning Human Understanding*, Pauline Phemister, ed. (Oxford: Oxford University Press, 2008).

49. There were other factors in the standardization movement's growth, of course, including expanded literacy and the new accessibility of books and leisure time. On the relationship between Locke and language theory, see Hans Aarsleff, *From Locke to Saussure: Essays on the Study of Language and Intellectual History* (Minneapolis: University of Minnesota Press, 1982).

50. Jonathan Swift, *A Proposal for Correcting, Improving, and Ascertaining the English Tongue*, 2nd ed. (London: Benjamin Tooke, 1712). An important reading of "ongoing debates about

empire in the period" can be found in David Armitage, *The Ideological Origins of the British Empire* (Cambridge: Cambridge University Press, 2000). Recently, eighteenth-century scholars have addressed Steven Pincus's challenge to rethink the way partisan politics rather than consensus "served to structure the reception and deployment of new economic information and policy recommendations" relative to empire. See Steven Pincus, "Rethinking Mercantilism: Political Economy, the British Empire, and the Atlantic World in the Seventeenth and Eighteenth Centuries" and "Reconfiguring the British Empire," *William and Mary Quarterly*, 69, no. 1 (January 2012), 3–34, 63–70.

51. James Harris, *Hermes: A Philosophical Inquiry Concerning Language and Universal Grammar* (London: H. Woodfall, 1751), 422.

52. For his part, Swift thought of Greek as a good model for English's imperial promise. Greeks, like Britons, were a seafaring—or as Defoe put it "amphibious"—people. Swift writes, "The *Grecians* spread their Colonies round all the Coasts of *Asia Minor*, even to the *Northern* Parts . . . in every Island of the *Ægean Sea*, and several others in the *Mediterranean*, where the Language was preserved entire for many Ages." Jonathan Swift, *Proposal for Correcting, Improving, and Ascertaining the English Tongue*, 16.

53. For a pan-European overview of the *Respublica literaria* and *République des belles lettres*, see Peter Burke, *Languages and Communities in Early Modern Europe* (Cambridge: Cambridge University Press, 2004), 43–88.

54. Peter Burke, *Languages and Communities*, 17.

55. James Greenwood, *An Essay Towards a Practical Grammar*, 5th ed. (London: J. Nourse, 1753; 1722), 10.

56. George Campbell, *Philosophy of Rhetoric* (London: W. Strahan and T. Cadell, 1776), 404.

57. Harris, *Hermes*, 409.

58. Harris, *Hermes*, 408.

59. Here I am again evoking the central problematics of Smith's *Politics of Language*. See also Marcus Tomalin's *Romanticism and Linguistic Theory*.

60. Daniel Defoe, "An Essay Upon Projects," in *The Works of Daniel Defoe*, vol. 3, William Hazlitt, ed. (London: John Clements, 1843), 36.

61. Defoe, "Essay Upon Projects," 36.

62. Many eighteenth-century usages of the term "literacy" defined the word as the ability to read classical languages. Until the mid- to late eighteenth century, "illiteracy" referred to a lack of education in Greek and Latin. See discussion in Chapter 4.

63. Defoe, "Essay Upon Projects," 36.

64. Defoe excludes female voices in spite of the fact that the same essay argues in favor of a women's academy by saying that sexual discrimination in education is "one of the most barbarous customs in the world." Defoe, "Essay Upon Projects," 42. Swift too repeats this limitation in his language committee even though he views women as a conservative linguistic force. As he writes, "Now, I would by no means give Ladies the Trouble of advising us in the Reformation of our Language; yet I cannot help thinking, that since they have been left out of all Meeting, except Parties at Play, or where worse Designs are carried on, our Conversation hath very much degenerated." Jonathan Swift, *Proposal for Correcting, Improving, and Ascertaining the English Tongue*, 29.

65. To Defoe, coinages based on fashion, whimsy, or artifice are unlawful. In a play on the word "coinage," Defoe asserts that under the regulation of his society " 'twould be as criminal

then to coin words as money." Inventing words without public sanction is a crime against the public because neologisms break the social compact of agreed-on values in the same manner as counterfeit money. Both acts circulate signifiers that lack customary real-world referents. Defoe, "Essay Upon Projects," 36.

66. Daniel Defoe, *The True-Born Englishman: A Satyr* (London, 1700), 17.

67. Spenser describes Chaucer with the phrase "well of English undefyled" in the *Faërie Queene*, IV. Samuel Johnson deploys the phrase in his "Preface": "So far have I been from any care to grace my pages with modern decorations, that I have studiously endeavoured to collect examples and authorities from the writers before the restoration, whose works I regard as *the wells of English undefiled*, as the pure sources of genuine diction." Johnson, "Preface," paragraph 61. Hereafter, all paragraph numbers are taken from Jack Lynch's edition of the "Preface," http://andromeda.rutgers.edu/~jlynch/Texts/preface.html (accessed March 2, 2014).

68. Schmidgen draws similar conclusions about this poem in *Exquisite Mixture*, 6–8.

69. Carried into the English language via translations of the Hebrew Bible, the word "shibboleth" connotes an irrepressible quality of language that betrays cultural, ethnic, or class extraction, and thus, supposed allegiances and affiliations. See Judges 12.

70. Daniel Defoe, *True-Born Englishman*, 25.

71. Daniel Defoe, *A Tour Through the Whole Island of Great Britain*, vol. 3 of 4, 4th edition (London: S. Birt, et al., 1748), 232.

72. Johnson, "Preface," paragraph 4.

73. Johnson, "Preface," paragraph 30.

74. Johnson, "Preface," paragraph 31.

75. Johnson, "Preface," paragraph 86.

76. Johnson, "Preface," paragraph 87.

77. Johnson, "Preface," paragraph 90.

78. Johnson, "Preface," paragraph 90.

79. Johnson, "Preface," paragraph 11.

80. Johnson, "Preface," paragraph 84.

81. Johnson, "Preface," paragraph 85.

82. Johnson, "Preface," paragraph 86.

83. Johnson, "Preface," paragraph 45.

84. Johnson, "Preface," paragraph 91.

85. Johnson, "Preface," paragraph 89.

86. Johnson, "Preface," paragraph 88.

87. Carew, "Excellencie of the English Tongue," 42.

88. Francis Grose's *Classical Dictionary of the Vulgar Tongue* (London: S. Hooper, 1788; 1785) is an interesting counterpoint to both Johnson and Spence.

89. Thomas Spence, "Preface" to *The Grand Repository of the English Language* (Newcastle: T. Saint, 1775), unpaginated.

90. Spence promises readers, "To read what is printed in this alphabet, nothing is required but to apply the same sound immutably to each character (in whatever position) that the alphabet directs." Spence, *A Supplement to the History of Robinson Crusoe* (Newcastle: T. Saint, 1782), i.

91. James Elphinston, *Propriety Ascertained in her Picture, Or, Inglish Speech and Spelling Rendered Mutual Guides* (London: W. Richardson, 1786), 1:xiii.

92. E. P. Thompson, *The Making of the English Working Class* (London: V. Gollancz, 1963); Christina Bewley and David Bewley, *Gentleman Radical: A Life of John Horne Tooke: 1736–1812*

(London: Tauris Academic Studies, 1998); Alan Wharam, *The Treason Trials, 1794* (Leicester: Leicester University Press, 1992).

93. John Horne Tooke, *Επεα Πτεροεντα*, or The Diversions of Purley (London: Richard Taylor, 1786; 1829), 6.

94. "Dispatch" was the force that drove linguistic condensation according to Tooke. Hence his title, *Epea Pteroenta*, meaning winged words.

95. Tooke, *The Diversions of Purley*, 304.

96. In the introductions to their works, Smith's *Politics of Language*, Tomalin's *Romanticism and Linguistic Theory*, Turley's *The Politics of Language*, and Keach's *Arbitrary Power* all cite Aarsleff as a powerful influence.

97. Hans Aarsleff, *The Study of Language in England, 1780–1860* (Princeton, N.J.: Princeton University Press, 1967).

98. Blair, *Lectures on Rhetoric and Belles Lettres*, 203–4.

99. Adam Smith, "Considerations Concerning the First Formation of Languages," appendix to *The Theory of Moral Sentiments* (London: A. Millar, 1767), 437–78.

100. Blair, *Lectures on Rhetoric and Belles Lettres*, 204.

101. Blair, *Lectures on Rhetoric and Belles Lettres*, 204.

102. Blair, *Lectures on Rhetoric and Belles Lettres*, 206.

Multilingual Lives: Dorothy Pentreath and William Bodener

1. Scholar P. A. S. Pool writes of Dorothy Pentreath, "She enjoyed a rather spurious posthumous reputation as the 'last speaker of the Cornish language'; this we know to be incorrect, but she may well have been the last native-speaker, brought up to speak nothing but Cornish." See P. A. S. Pool, *The Death of Cornish* (Penzance: Pool, 1975), 26. For the basic details of Pentreath's life, see Matthew Spriggs, "Pentreath, Dorothy (*bap.* 1692, *d.* 1777)," *Oxford Dictionary of National Biography*, Oxford University Press, 2004, http://www.oxforddnb.com/view/article/14692 (accessed May 19, 2015).

2. William Bottrell claims that Pentreath could "speak English pretty well when she was cool," meaning when she was not angry. William Bottrell, *Traditions and Hearthside Stories of West Cornwall* (Penzance: W. Cornish, 1870), 184.

3. Bottrell recounts a squabble between Pentreath and an anglophone man who knocked her "cowal full of fish" into a muddy ditch: "Dolly then forgot her English, and began to abuse in her native Cornish, which came more glibly to her tongue; at the same time casting mud, fish, and stones at Mr. Price as hard and fast as she could pelt them, the refrain of each sentence of abuse being an oath ending with '*Cronnack an hagar dhu.*' As Dolly was reputed to be a kind of half witch, as mentioned before, Mr. Price became terribly frightened at hearing what he dreaded might be some horrible incantation for laying a spell on him and his." This passage from Bottrell is analyzed in P. A. S. Pool's *The Death of Cornish*. Pool describes this curse as "one fragment" of Pentreath's speech that has survived "by the purest chance," an insult that Bottrell claims to have obtained from an "old lady of Sennen, who knew Dolly well." See Bottrell, *Traditions and Hearthside Stories of West Cornwall*, 184–85. See also P. A. S. Pool, *Death of Cornish*, 27.

4. As Rancière notes, change in the political and aesthetic space "consists in making what was unseen visible; in making what was audible as mere noise heard as speech and in demonstrating that what appeared as a mere expression of pleasure and pain is a shared feeling of a good or an evil." Rancière, *Dissensus*, 38.

5. Marilyn Butler gestures toward ways in which cultural and linguistic supersession can be grouped among the master or motivating tropes for the development of Romanticism when she writes, "Popular antiquarianism was part of a broader historical revival occurring in the third quarter of the eighteenth-century within France's largest neighbors, in the German princely states as well as in Britain. Pre-modern nativist cultural forms threatened the modern cultural dominance of France and of francophile governing élites. The ground was laid for a major shift not just in literary fashion but in social attitudes and group identities. Three basic narrative forms emerged in this revival and remained dominant through the Romantic period. First to become fashionable was the (medieval) popular ballad. . . . Second came the long verse romance. . . . Coinciding with both, the 'prose romance' or historical novel began to deploy supernatural incidents and characters, or to introduce ballads, scholarly materials, and elaborate framing narratives, all hinting at a process of transmission over time or across cultures. The actual ascendency of the historical manner in the half-century 1780–1830 sits oddly with some later critical suppositions—that the personal lyric is the dominant Romantic form, or that the period belongs to the writer of genius, supremely individualistic and self-generating." Marilyn Butler, "Antiquarianism (Popular)," in *An Oxford Companion to the Romantic Age: British Culture 1776–1832*, Ian McCalman, ed. (Oxford: Oxford University Press, 1999), 335.

6. By invoking Pentreath in this way, I am deliberately following one of the lines of inquiry in Katie Trumpener's *Bardic Nationalism*, a book that assesses the political and aesthetic outcomes of the subjection of the Celtic peripheries to England. Trumpener describes these diverse cultural spaces (Cornwall included) as places were "disparate cultures find themselves connected not only by their parallel modes of subordination within the empire but also by a constant flow of people—administrators, soldiers, merchants, colonists, and travelers—back and forth between different imperial holdings. . . . The most far-flung provinces of the empire (beginning with Scotland and Ireland) simultaneously develop a strange cosmopolitanism, which parallels that of the imperial center itself. Such self-awareness marks much early colonial writing. Yet most accounts of Britain's literary empire, seeing as their object of study a literature forged by the influence of English models on English colonists, have either emphasized the cultural subordination of periphery to center or traced the discrete national development of separate colonial literatures. The international address and transcolonial character of today's postcolonial fiction makes clear the need for a synchronous history of empire instead" (xiii–xiv).

7. Spriggs, "Pentreath, Dorothy," *Oxford Dictionary of National Biography*.

8. Spriggs, "Pentreath, Dorothy," *Oxford Dictionary of National Biography*.

9. One notable early text on Cornwall is Richard Carew's *Survey of Cornwall* (London: T. Bensley, 1811; 1602), which includes a note on the language habits of the people of Cornwall, claiming that "most of the Inhabitants can [speak] no word of *Cornish*, but very few are ignorant of the English; and yet some so affect their owne, as to a stranger they will note speake it; for if meeting them by chance, you inquire the way or any such matter, your answere shal be, *Meea navidna cowza sawzneck*, I can speake no Saxonage." Folklore associates the Cornish-language statement of refusal to speak English to an anglophone with Pentreath, but in fact it comes from this earlier passage in Carew. Citing the work of Nicholas Boson, a seventeenth-century Cornish scholar who wrote in both English and Cornish, Pool quotes a note in Boson's manuscript *Nebbaz Gerriau Dro Tho Carnoack* (*A Few Words about Cornish*) in which Boson laments, "Our Cornish tongue hath been so long on the wane that we can hardly hope to see it increase again, for as the English confined it into this narrow country first, so it presseth on still, leaving it no

place but about the cliff and sea. . . . The old men dying away, we find young men to speak it less and less, and worse and worse, and so it is like to decay from time to time." Pool, *Death of Cornish*, 12.

o. David Philip Miller, "Barrington, Daines (1727/8–1800)," *Oxford Dictionary of National Biography*, Oxford University Press, 2004, January 2008, http://www.oxforddnb.com/view/article/1529 (accessed June, 9 2015).

11. "My brother Captain Barrington brought a French East India ship into Mount's Bay, in the year 1746 (to the best of my recollection), who told me, that when he sailed from thence on a cruise toward the French coast, he took with him from that part of Cornwall a seaman who spoke the Cornish language, and who was understood by some French seamen of the coast of Bretagne, with whom he afterwards happened to have occasion to converse." Daines Barrington, "*On the Expiration of the Cornish Language. In a Letter from the Hon.* Daines Barrington, *Vice Pres. S.A. to* John Lloyd, *Esquire, F.S.A.* Read at the Society of Antiquaries, May 6, 1773," in *Archaeologia: Or Miscellaneous Tracts Relating to Antiquity*, vol. 3 (London, J. Nichols: 1776), 281.

12. With this phrasing I am again invoking Baucom's useful synthesis of much scholarship surrounding the eighteenth-century "type." He writes of Fielding and Hogarth's versions of Bridget Allworthy that she is "less entirely a person than she is a theory of a mode of personhood, an abstract emblem of a *real* human type, a composite drawn not from nature but from an aggregated variety of sources." So too Dorothy Pentreath, who in Barrington's mind is a specific type of known antiquarian object, a stunning example of a vanishing provincial multilingual. Baucom, *Specters of the Atlantic*, 277–78.

13. Barrington's journey and subsequent dispatches are directly in conversation with the earlier work of Dr. William Borlase, whom Pool calls, "the greatest Cornish scholar of the 18th century." Borlase authored *The Antiquities of Cornwall* (1754) and *The Natural History of Cornwall* (1758), the former of which contains a sizeable vocabulary of Cornish and the latter of which contains the conclusion, "That we may attend it to the grave; this language is now altogether ceased, so as not to be spoken any where in conversation." As Pool puts it, "this was for the adequate though astonishing reason that he knew nothing of them [surviving Cornish speakers]!" Barrington mentions Borlase's erroneous conclusions about Cornish's death several times in his first dispatch. William Borlase, *The Natural History of Cornwall* (Oxford: W. Jackson, 1758), 316; Pool, *Death of Cornish*, 24.

14. Barrington, "*On the Expiration of the Cornish Language*," 281.

15. Barrington, "*On the Expiration of the Cornish Language*," 281.

16. Barrington, "*On the Expiration of the Cornish Language*," 279, 284.

17. Barrington, "*On the Expiration of the Cornish Language*," 281. Compare the analogous "wager" used as framing device in Ann Wheeler, *The Westmorland Dialect in Four Familiar Dialogues* (London: W. J. and J. Richardson, 1802), ix.

18. Barrington, "*On the Expiration of the Cornish Language*," 281, 282.

19. By pointing out the importance of Pentreath's "two or three minute" speech, I am following the argumentative logic of Christopher Taylor's essay "'Most Holy Virgin Assist Me': Subaltern Transnationalism and Positively Possible Worlds." In this essay, Taylor describes the torture in British Trinidad of a "young free mulatta named Louisa Calderon," a woman who was accused of theft and whose testimony before her anglophone torturers included a variety of discursive registers. Taylor's point is that the legal interpretation of Calderon's speech glosses over her religious invocations (which are never translated in the transcript) and instead focuses

on gleaning positive content that might be called a "confession," as though such a "confession" could be winnowed out and isolated from her other modes of speech. Taylor asks the question, "But what if we were to refuse to read Calderon's invocations in the manner of her British judges, and instead read Calderon's invocations as an attempt to call upon another world, one illegible to her case's Anglo-centric interpreters?" In Pentreath's case, I would suggest a related reading. If Pentreath's untranslated Cornish is thought of only as abuse, insult, or screed, then one forecloses any possibility that the speech actually contains the coherent assertion of antianglophone political content. In Chapter 4, I read the tendency to see merely comedy in dialect writing in a similar fashion. Christopher Taylor, " 'Most Holy Virgin Assist Me': Subaltern Transnationalism and Positively Possible Worlds," *History of the Present*, 4, no. 1 (Spring 2014), 76.

20. Barrington mentions Edward Lhuyd's work at the beginning of "*On the Expiration of the Cornish Language*," 279. Lhyud's important work *Archaeologia Britannica*, vol. 1, *Glossography* (Oxford: Printed for the Author, 1707) contains grammars and vocabularies of several Celtic languages as well as lists of manuscripts in those languages and directions for reading and accessing them.

21. Barrington, "*On the Expiration of the Cornish Language*," 284.

22. Barrington, "*On the Expiration of the Cornish Language*," 282.

23. Barrington, "*On the Expiration of the Cornish Language*," 284.

24. The preface to Padma Rangarajan's *Imperial Babel: Translation, Exoticism, and the Long Nineteenth Century* (New York: Fordham University Press, 2014) opens with a brilliant reading of the "Malay" in Thomas De Quincey's *Confessions of an English Opium Eater*. Rangarajan uses the joke in this scene—that De Quincey believes Greek to be a language the "Malay" might understand because of Greece's nearness to the East—to begin making the case that "at the heart of every colonial encounter lies an act of translation" (vii). Barrington's linking of Cornish and Welsh is of course grounded in linguistic history, whereas De Quincey's linkage of Greek and "Malay" is a muddled conclusion. Nonetheless, both share a sense of the instrumentality of language and translation ways of managing cultural alterity, which is always irreducible to linguistic relationships.

25. Barrington, "*On the Expiration of the Cornish Language*," 284.

26. Daines Barrington, "*Mr.* Barrington *on some additional Information relative to the Continuance of the* Cornish *Language. In a Letter to* John Lloyd, *Esq. F.A.S.*" in *Archaeologia: Or Miscellaneous Tracts Relating to Antiquity*, vol. 5 (London, J. Nichols: 1779), 81.

27. Pool writes, "The Cornish text [of Bodener's letter] is of great interest as being the last passage of authentic Cornish writing to survive, and is an excellent piece of Late Cornish." He goes on to note that "Bodinar survived Dolly Pentreath by 12 years, dying in 1789, but it is noteworthy that he was not a native speaker like her; he had first learnt Cornish when going to sea with old fishermen, whereas she had learnt it in earliest childhood." Pool, *Death of Cornish*, 28.

28. Daines Barrington, "*Mr.* Barrington *on some additional Information relative to the Continuance of the* Cornish *Language*," 83.

29. Daines Barrington, "*Mr.* Barrington *on some additional Information relative to the Continuance of the* Cornish *Language*," 83.

30. See Gloria Anzaldúa, *Borderlands* / La Frontera*: The New Mestiza* (San Francisco: Spinsters/Aunt Lute, 1987); Mary Louise Pratt, "Arts of the Contact Zone," in *Profession* (1991), 33–40; and Mary Louise Pratt, *Imperial Eyes: Travel Writing and Transculturation* (Abingdon: Routledge, 2008; 1992).

Chapter 3. De Libertate

1. Johnson, "Preface," paragraph 90.

2. Anglophone interlingual translation practice—by which I mean the transportation of linguistico-cultural material from non-anglophone linguistic mediums into anglophony, whether through imitation, paraphrase, metaphrase, or other translational protocol—is becoming increasingly central to eighteenth-century literary studies.

3. "Calque" is a linguistics term that refers to a word-for-word or morpheme-for-morpheme loan translation from one language to another. An example of interlinguistic calques can be found in varied but morphemically analogous words for "translation," such as the French *traduction* and the German *Übersetzung*. More theoretically, because it introduces a new and perhaps "foreign" linguistic form into a given system, a calque has much in common with Rancière's model of dissensual aesthetics and politics. As he writes, "A dissensus is not a conflict of interests, opinions or values; it is a division inserted in 'common sense': a dispute over what is given and about the frame within which we see something as given." Similarly, a calque asks language users to think differently about the perceptual infinity that language parses into discrete signs. Rancière, *Dissensus*, 69.

4. This excerpt from Johnson also gestures to a crucial context within which both standardization and translation unfold during the second half of the eighteenth century. In the final sentence above, Johnson's idea that translators will "reduce" Standard English into "a dialect of *France*" indexes the cultural competition that was perceived to exist between anglophone and francophone linguistic systems. Anglophone fear surrounding francophone linguistic practices comes to a head during the French revolutionaries' deliberate attempts to engineer a new French language for a democratic republic.

5. Lowth and Campbell are emblematic of the crossover between writers who addressed the topic of standardization and those who executed important translations. Lowth's notes on method and interpretation are collected in *De Sacra Poesi Hebraeorum Praelectiones Academicae Oxonii Habitae* (Oxford: Clarendon Press, 1753). The English version, *Lectures on the Sacred Poetry of the Hebrews*, was translated by George Gregory (London: J. Nichols, 1787). The enactment of Lowth's translational method appears in *Isaiah: A New Translation; With a Preliminary Dissertation, and Notes Critical, Philological, and Explanatory* (London: J. Nichols, 1778). These were vital reference points for a generation of translators and poets irrespective of their relationship to Hebrew just as his *A Short Introduction to English Grammar* was popular and influential in Britain and North America. I discuss Campbell at length in the fifth chapter.

6. See Stuart Gillespie and Penelope Wilson, "Publishing and Readership of Translation," and David Hopkins and Pat Rogers, "The Translator's Trade," in *The Oxford History of Literary Translation in English*, vol. 3, *1660–1790*, Stuart Gillespie and David Hopkins, eds. (Oxford: Oxford University Press, 2005), 38–51, 81–95.

7. Other writers of the period share this linguistico-political anxiety about French encroachment. Joseph Priestley claims in the preface to third edition of his *The Rudiments of English Grammar*, "If I have done any essential service to my native tongue, I think it will arise from my detecting in time a very great number of *gallicisms*, which have insinuated themselves into the style of many of our most justly admired writers; and which, in my opinion, tend greatly to injure the true idiom of the English language, being contrary to most established analogies." In *The Rudiments of English Grammar*, 1761, 3rd ed. (London: J. F. Rivington, 1772), x.

8. Mary Helen McMurran describes the English and French "language acquisition texts" (what I have been calling standardization texts) and their theories in the following insightful terms: "Eighteenth-century grammar books promoted the ease of translation between vernaculars without interlinear reading and rendering in the belief that visualizing equivalence and replacing vocabulary was sufficient. This unimpeded rendering process enforced in pedagogical texts was not merely the promotional rhetoric of their authors, but was based on the theoretical pretense that unlike ancient languages, modern vernaculars are guided by rational principles. According to the *Encyclopédie*, French and English, which they call 'analog' languages, follow a rational word order. . . . Analog languages facilitate reading and translating because of their natural analytical word order, while the artificial order of what they call 'transpositive' languages such as Latin and Greek required that they be first reduced to analog order, then translated." Mary Helen McMurran, *The Spread of Novels: Translation and Prose Fiction in the Eighteenth Century* (Princeton, N.J.: Princeton University Press, 2010), 12.

9. Tytler's *Essay on the Principles of Translation* was first published in 1791; it was reviewed at least six times in major publications; it was translated into German in 1793; and it was subsequently expanded and republished in 1797 and again in 1813. For the 1793 translation, see Renatus Gotthelf Löbel, trans., *Grundsätze der Kunst zu Übersetzen, ein Versuch aus Dem Englischen* (Leipzig: Mengandsche Buchhandlung, 1793). Jeffrey Huntsman remarks that the German translation "seems to have had some European popularity in this form," Alexander Fraser Tytler, *Essay on the Principles of Translation*, Jeffrey Huntsman, ed. (Amsterdam: John Benjamins B. V., 1978), xxxii–xxxiii.

10. Tytler, *Essay on the Principles of Translation*, 220.

11. Tytler, *Essay on the Principles of Translation*, 47.

12. Frederick Burwick writes, "In the Romantic period, too, the theory and practice of translation underwent radical change. The prevailing aim of translations in the first half of the 18th century was not simply to adapt the original to the target language, but also to meet the cultural expectations of stylistic form and aesthetic appeal." He continues by noting that late eighteenth- and early nineteenth-century translation practice was a "tug-of-war . . . between the principle of fidelity to the original and the principle of cultural adaptation. Maintaining the integrity of the foreign text vs. altering precisely the marks of its foreignness so that it could be fully appreciated in terms of familiar tastes and values." For her part, Padma Rangarajan extends this observation in her examination of the dialogic relationship between nineteenth-century translation practices and colonial thought. Locating an early origin for shifts in translational priorities in Herder's "recognition of language" as "a fundamental human diversity, or 'radical difference,'" Rangarajan charts an intellectual lineage through which "'foreignizing' translations, or translations that bend, or alter, the target language to allow room for the source language" gained favor. See Frederick Burwick, "Romantic Theories of Translation," *Wordsworth Circle*, 39, no. 3 (Summer 2008), 68, and Padma Rangarajan, *Imperial Babel*, 3–4.

13. Louis Kelly, "The Eighteenth Century to Tytler," in *The Oxford History of Literary Translation in English*, vol. 3, *1660–1790*, Stuart Gillespie and David Hopkins, eds. (Oxford: Oxford University Press, 2005), 67.

14. Domesticating translation in anglophony is often organized around explanation. For example, an advertisement for a text by "Edward Wells, D.D. late Rector of Colesbatch in Leicestershire" promises the following about the commodity on offer: "An Help to the more easy and clear Understanding of the HOLY SCRIPTURE: Being a compleat Paraphrase, with Annotations

on all Books of the OLD TESTAMENT, explained after the following Method, (viz) 1. The common English Translation render'd more agreeable to the Original. 2. A Paraphrase, wherein the Text is explained, and divided into proper Sections, and other lesser Divisions." In this instance, "The common English Translation render'd more agreeable to the Original" refers to a modernizing update of the KJV. The added features of a " Paraphrase" and more precise "Divisions" speaks to the way that domesticating translation—which often understood itself as being as close to texts as possible insofar as transcendental meaning was concerned—was also eminently interested in exact and universal semiosis. *Country Journal, or, The Craftsman*, October 26, 1728, no. 121.

15. Lawrence Venuti, *The Translator's Invisibility: A History of Translation*, 1995, 2nd ed. (Abingdon: Routledge, 2008).

16. An advertisement for Nathaniel Scarlett's 1798 *Translation of the New Testament* attempts to sell the product based on the premise that the translator has "taken care to avoid the two extremes of being too servile and literal on one hand, and too periphrastic in the other." This polarity between a "too servile" foreignizing translation and a "too periphrastic" domesticating translation generated by the seemingly natural periphrasis of anglophone multiplicity speaks to a enduring concern in the late eighteenth century with the nature of what Johnson would have called the "spirit of *English* liberty." In *Sun*, April 10, 1798, no. 1730. The quotation from Johnson can be found in "Preface," paragraph 90.

17. Glissant emphasizes the Caribbean plantation's multilingual, multiethnic, and multiracial character, writing, "It is there that multilingualism, that threatened dimension of our universe, can be observed for one of the first times, organically forming and disintegrating." Glissant, *Poetics of Relation*, 74.

18. In this instance, I am using "transcreate" and "transcreation" in the sense of Srinivas Aravamudan's discussion of Antoine Galland's *Mille et une nuits*. See Aravamudan, *Enlightenment Orientalism*, 52–54.

19. Lawrence Venuti's definition of translation is also useful here: "Translation is a process by which the chain of signifiers that constitutes the foreign text is replaced by a chain of signifiers in the translating language which the translator provides on the strength of an interpretation." In *Translator's Invisibility*, 13.

20. Rangarajan accounts for the initial assumption of difference underlying translation practice by beginning with Herder's dismissal of Enlightenment universality in favor the notion that "language arose organically from particular geographical and historical conditions, and, accordingly, varied widely across time and space." Rangarajan, *Imperial Babel*, 3.

21. Roman Jakobson defines intralingual and interlingual translation in the following way: "(1) Intralingual translation or *rewording* is an interpretation of verbal signs by means of others signs of the same language. (2) Interlingual translation or *translation proper* is an interpretation of verbal signs by means of some other language." See Maria Tymoczko, *Enlarging Translation, Empowering Translators* (New York: Routledge, 2007), 56.

22. In the fourth chapter, I discuss early nineteenth-century Standard English translations of anglophone dialect texts that were first printed in the 1740s. In terms of Classical Arabic, it is important to note that the first direct Arabic-English translation of the Koran was done by George Sale in 1734.

23. I consider the problems attending intralingual translation during the period in Chapter 4.

24. Similarly, I take up interlingual translation in Chapter 5.

25. My interest in sketching the capaciousness of this term is part of a larger intellectual commitment. Translation studies is intersecting more dramatically with traditional literary disciplines, and this is in large part because of intellectual imperatives brought about by theorists of colonialism, postcolonialism, and globalization, all of whom are to be credited with the welcome wane of nationally oriented, hermetically sealed literary traditions. Given the increasingly acknowledged insights of globally oriented scholarly trends like world systems theory, for example, continued examination of the premises and practices of global exchange is needed, and translation studies provides just such an opportunity. The field's insights are especially germane to eighteenth-century studies. Given the rapid development of British imperial systems during this period, and the deterritorialization of anglophony that these systems accomplished, the eighteenth century is one of the key eras during which one can undertake the larger project of situating anglophone literary practices then and now in their proper local and global contexts.

26. Lawrence Venuti, "Translation, Simulacra, Resistance" in *Translation Changes Everything: Theory and Practice* (Abingdon: Routledge, 2013), 141.

27. Priestley, *Rudiments of English Grammar*, xxi–xxii.

28. Emphasizing a similar imbrication, McMurran describes eighteenth-century translation practice in the following terms: "My approach to translation emphasizes that the translative fictional field reflects the historical situation in which translating was endemic to literary culture, and translating between English and French in particular was little more than an ordinary complement to the expected acquisition of languages and literacy." McMurran, *Spread of Novels*, 14.

29. The King James Version of the Bible (KJV) offers an important early case study in (what might be called foreignizing) translation and aesthetics. This Authorized Version was translated by a team of translators and completed in 1604. One of the translation's specific goals was to retain the linguistic differences latent in the text's biblical Hebrew portions. In keeping with this goal, the KJV's translation team had purposefully set out to mimic as closely as possible biblical Hebrew's cadences, vocabulary, and expressive patterns.

Examining the translation's details, it is clear that famous formulations like "Thus saith the LORD of hosts, Hearken not unto the words of the prophets that prophesy unto you" (Jeremiah 23:16) turn out to be word-for-word, and even morpheme-for-morpheme translations from biblical Hebrew. The KJV's wording appears as a string of syntactic calques, ultimately the result of a translation strategy highly invested in formal rather than functional equivalence. As an example of some of the linguistic details Jeremiah 23:16 retains, it is important to point out that in biblical Hebrew the verb-subject-object pattern is regular and unremarkable, often even obligatory; in Jacobean and Georgian English, however, its very irregularity makes it a distinctive pattern of reverent, providential language. In biblical Hebrew, the proximal repetition of "prophets" and "prophesy" is a poetic feature that plays sonically on regular word derivation patterns unique to the Semitic language family's systems of root consonants. In the KJV's English, there is a similar effect, a product of translational intention, but the word formation game is obviously lost. As many other examples from the KJV show, foreignizing translation occasions the constant incorporation of foreign-language patterns and structures into the target language.

Culture digests those new patterns and structures in diverse ways. Addison praised this translation's revolutionary achievements by explicitly invoking the way the KJV's improved the English language. In the *Spectator*, no. 405, June 14, 1712, Addison writes, "There is a certain coldness and indifference in the phrases of our European languages when they are compared with the oriental forms of speech: and it happens very luckily that the Hebrew idioms run into the English tongue with a particular grace and beauty. Our language has received innumerable elegancies and improvements, from that infusion of Hebraisms, which are derived to it out of the poetical passages in holy writ." Whether people were conscious of this translational history, like Addison, or utterly oblivious to it, as many parishioners must have been, the King James Bible domesticated Hebrew patterns into English, and the community of users invested them with poetic and theological significance. Eventually, Hebrew syntactic and lexical patterns were folded into anglophony as a distinct register.

30. The phrase is taken from the following quotation: "So, *exceeding* for *exceedingly*, however improper, occurs frequently in the vulgar translation of the Bible, and has obtained in common discourse." In Lowth, *Short Introduction to English Grammar*, 155–56, note.

31. Lowth, *Short Introduction to English Grammar*, 45.

32. Priestley, *Rudiments of English Grammar*, 78.

33. Tytler, *Essay on the Principles of Translation*, 124.

34. Tytler, *Essay on the Principles of Translation*, 137.

35. Tytler, *Essay on the Principles of Translation*, 210.

36. An ambivalence surrounding the achievements of the French language relative to anglophony animate much of the discourses of standardization and translation as they take shape during the eighteenth century. One the one hand, French was a model. The dedication to Brightland's *Grammar* uses French linguistic achievements in an admiring way: "A *Grammar* of the *French Language* was the First Labour of that Learned Body the *French Academy* . . . as YOUR MAJESTY's Arms have been Superior to those of *France*, so we hope that, by *Your Royal Influence*, You will give the same Superiority to *Our Arts* and *Sciences*, which are All built on *This* that is no Presented to YOUR SACRED MAJESTY." French linguistic achievements were also interpreted as threatening, as in the poem that is also prefaced to Brightland's grammar: "If only Martial Conquests we advance, / And yield the Muse's Bow'rs to vanquish'd *France*; / If here we fix our Pillars of Renown / Will not resenting *Britain's* Genius frown, / And, while our Troops politer Realm's o'er-run, / Cry, *So the* Vandals *and the* Goths *have done?* / When Honour calls my Sons to new Alarms, / And Grow in *Arts* victorious, as in *Arms*, / Our Language to advance, and prove our *Words* / No less design'd for Conquest than our *Swords*. / Till *Learning's* Banners thro' our Realms are spread, / And Captive *Sciences* from Bondage led; / Tho *Gallic* Trophies shall our Island fill, / Our Conqu'ring Wings are clipt, and Lewis triumphs still." See John Brightland, *A Grammar of the English Tongue*, 8th ed. (London: James Rivington and James Fletcher, 1759).

37. John Wallis, *Grammatica Linguae Anglicanae* (Oxford: Leon Litchfield, 1652).

38. Greenwood's grammar and other works show this same interest in balancing anglophone particularity with classical inheritance. *The London Vocabulary*, for instance, bills itself dually as a "new Method proper to acquaint the Learner with Things as well as Pure Latin Words." Essentially, the book is a categorized list of anglophone words and their Latin translations, the coincidence of which is meant to prepare specifically English students for understanding Latin without being "led thro' a Crowd of Modern Barbarisms, and loaded with a Multitude of Words which the Romans never heard of." In James Greenwood, *The London Vocabulary*, 3rd ed. (London: A. Bettesworth, 1713; 1711), 1–2.

39. Joseph Aickin, *The English Grammar; Or, the English Tongue Reduced to Grammatical Rules* (London: MB, 1693), title page.

40. Priestley, *Rudiments of English Grammar*, vi–vii.

41. Priestley, *Rudiments of English Grammar*, ix.

42. For example, Don Chapman notes that Joseph Priestley "attended Batley grammar school and a small school kept by John Kirkby, where he learned Latin, Greek and the rudiments of Hebrew, Chaldee, Syriac, and Arabic." Don Chapman, "The Eighteenth Century Grammarians as Language Experts," in Tieken-Boon van Ostade, *Grammars, Grammarians and Grammar-Writing in Eighteenth-Century England*, 24.

43. Women like Aphra Behn, Elizabeth Carter, Elizabeth Griffith, Eliza Haywood, Charlotte Lennox, Katherine Phillips, and Helen Maria Williams were some of the most important French-English translators of the seventeenth and eighteenth centuries.

44. Beyond French-English translation, several of these women also worked with texts originally in German, Greek, Italian, Latin, and Spanish. See Sarah Annes Brown, "Women Translators," in *The Oxford History of Literary Translation in English*, vol. 3, *1660–1790*, Stuart Gillespie and David Hopkins, eds., 111–20. Elizabeth Smith, whom I have written about elsewhere, was a notable translator of biblical Hebrew in the early nineteenth century. See Daniel DeWispelare, "An Amateur's Professional Devotion: Elizabeth Smith's Translation of the Book of Job," *Literature and Theology*, 25, no. 2 (May 2011).

45. Don Chapman, "Eighteenth Century Grammarians as Language Experts," 21.

46. Don Chapman, "Eighteenth Century Grammarians as Language Experts," 22.

47. Put another way, perhaps our contemporary model of a language expert—especially in national literature departments—is more narrowly monolingual than the amateur-expert model that characterizes eighteenth-century anglophony, thus preventing us from seeing certain aspects of literary and aesthetic history.

48. Don Chapman, "Eighteenth Century Grammarians as Language Experts," 23.

49. Don Chapman, "Eighteenth Century Grammarians as Language Experts," 24.

50. I take up these points in more detail in the Conclusion of this book.

51. See Stuart Gillespie and Penelope Wilson, "Publishing and Readership of Translation," and David Hopkins and Pat Rogers, "The Translator's Trade," in *The Oxford History of Literary Translation in English*, vol. 3, *1660–1790*, Stuart Gillespie and David Hopkins, eds. (Oxford: Oxford University Press, 2005), 38–51; 81–95.

52. Lawrence Venuti, "Retranslations: The Creation of Value," in *Translation Changes Everything: Theory and Practice* (Abingdon: Routledge, 2013), 96–108.

53. Brightland criticizes imitators and competitors doing similar grammatical work in the preface to *Grammar of the English Tongue*, iii–iv.

54. Anselm Bayly, *Plain and Complete Grammar of the English Language*, vi–vii.

55. Anselm Bayly, *Plain and Complete Grammar of the English Language*, x.

56. The sixteenth- and seventeenth-century search for a perfect or "universal grammar" is admirably described in Umberto Eco's *The Search for the Perfect Language* (Oxford: Blackwell, 1995), especially his chapter on John Wilkins's *Essay Towards a Real Character, and Philosophical Language*. Tracking a similar shift, but from the point of view of translation, Burwick writes, "A century later [ca. 1800], the translator served new audiences, each with a different set of expectations. The new audiences were shaped by the rising middle-class and the rapidly expanding literacy. Translations from the Greek and Latin were [still] familiar exercises in the schools, but the translator no longer served an audience trained in those exercises. The translation may once have been for many readers a supplement to their reading in the original. Now it was relied upon by a broader reading public as their sole access to an unknown language and culture." Burwick, "Romantic Theories of Translation," 69.

57. Alexander Adam, *The Rudiments of Latin and English Grammar*, 3rd ed. (Edinburgh: W. Gordon et al., 1786), iv.

58. Robert Lowth, *Short Introduction to English Grammar*, iii.

59. Robert Lowth, *Short Introduction to English Grammar*, 28.

60. See, for example, Hans Aarsleff, *The Study of Language in England, 1780–1860* (Princeton, N.J.: Princeton University Press, 1967), and Manfred Görlach, *Eighteenth-Century English* (Heidelberg: Universitätsverlag Winter Heidelberg, 2001).

61. John Denham, "To Mr. Richard Fanshaw, Esq; upon his Ingeneous Translation of *Pastor-Fido* into English," in *Coopers Hill A Poeme. The Second Edition with Additions* (London: Humphrey Moseley, 1650), 21–22.

62. Like Fanshawe, Denham was also a practicing translator. He translated several things, including part of the *Aeneid*. See Denham's *The Destruction of Troy: An Essay upon the Second Book of Virgil's Aeneid* (1636; 1656).

63. In addition to *Il Pastor Fido*, Fanshawe translated a variety of texts from Italian, Lain, and Portuguese during the 1640s and 1650s. One work, Fanshawe's translation of Camões's *Lusiads* (1655), would prove particularly important to a late eighteenth-century rendering of the text by Julius Mickle. Mickle's version is discussed in Chapter 5.

64. Lawrence Venuti, *Translator's Invisibility*, 50.

65. Lawrence Venuti, *Translator's Invisibility*, 35.

66. An advertisement in the *World and Fashionable Advisor* for "J.E.'s" translation of *Ovid's Epistles* done in 1787 walks a careful line between endorsing the premises of domesticating or foreignizing translation: "This Translation, keeping as close to the original as the difference of idiom, and the nature of poetry will allow, is recommended for the use of Schools; not as a help to scholars in construing their lessons, but as a means of habituating their ideas to take a poetical turn, when requisite." In *World and Fashionable Advertiser*, August, 8, 1787, no. 187.

67. Lawrence Venuti, *Translator's Invisibility*, 51.

68. Lawrence Venuti, *Translator's Invisibility*, 53, 69.

69. McMurran, *Spread of Novels*, 6.

70. McMurran, *Spread of Novels*, 6.

71. Gayatri Chakravorty Spivak, *Outside in the Teaching Machine* (New York: Routledge, 2009; 1993), 205.

72. In addition to the passage from the *Ars Poetica* that I will discuss below, translators frequently quoted from this line in Horace's *Epistles* (1.19.19–20): "o imitatores, servum pecus, ut mihi saepe bilem, saepe iocum vestri movere tumultus." Less frequently, translators invoked Cicero's phrase, "indisperti interpres" as it is used in *De Finibus* (3.15).

73. The history of the anglophone Bible demonstrates this transition. The brief background is that over the course of the eighteenth century, Protestants, Catholics, Dissenters, and Jews all circulated new anglophone translations of biblical material. Jonathan Sheehan's *Enlightenment Bible: Translation, Scholarship, and Culture* (Princeton, N.J.: Princeton University Press, 2005) outlines this process, claiming that eighteenth-century approaches to retranslating the Bible can be seen as efforts to rehabilitate the force of prophecy at a time when scripture appeared distant and antiquated rather than applicable and contemporary. Additionally, the new, sectarian retranslations of scripture occurred simultaneous to a sequence of religious and political controversies, the most obvious of which was the Jewish Naturalization Act of 1753. This suite of controversies is analyzed in great depth as it relates to translation practices in historian David

Ruderman's *Jewish Enlightenment in an English Key: Anglo-Jewry's Construction of Modern Jewish Thought* (Princeton, N.J.: Princeton University Press, 2000) and *Connecting the Covenants* (Philadelphia: University of Pennsylvania Press, 2007).

To see the implications for translation history, consider a brief set of statistics pertaining to translations of the Song of Songs. Between 1660 and 1750, two versifications, one paraphrasis, and ten works whose front matters nebulously identified them as verse paraphrases or verse translations were published. In almost all cases, the translators were reworking the King James Version of Song of Songs and generating fluently readable neoclassical anglophone poetry from it (intralingual translation). It is revealing to survey the ninety-year period between 1750 and 1840, during which there appeared in print fourteen separate Hebrew-to-English translations of Song of Songs alone and only a handful of paraphrases or versifications (interlingual translation). These new, direct translations pursue, to differing degrees, ways of foreignizing the biblical text in order to advance the interpretive logics of a particular religious ideology. Similar statistics exist for a number of books in the biblical Hebrew corpus, even to the point that one can claim, as Sheehan does, that biblical Hebrew retranslation was an important aspect of late eighteenth-century anglophone culture.

The historic development is fascinating. Whereas from the Restoration until roughly the mid-eighteenth century the King James Version serves as an engine for generating poetic practice via translations undertaken from one anglophone variety to another, from the mid-eighteenth into the early nineteenth century the goal of translation shifts, and scholars return to biblical Hebrew materials in order to produce exacting translations that all at once reinforce theological doctrine and lead into new theories of poetry and aesthetics. Biblical Hebrew is one context in which scholars can see in unequivocal terms the reciprocal development of translation and culture. As biblical Hebrew translation moves from paraphrastic reworking toward metaphrastic accuracy, theories of authority and authorship also alter. Translation, especially in its foreignizing varieties, became a way to stake claims about community and theology, as well as aesthetics.

74. Buck-Morss, *Hegel, Haiti, and Universal History*, 21.

75. Simon Gikandi's important book on the relationship between slavery and European culture reads "slavery as one of the informing conditions of modern identity." Gikandi, *Slavery and the Culture of Taste*, 29.

76. In the Loeb Classical Library, H. Rushton Fairclough translates this passage into prose in the following way: "In ground open to all you will win private rights, if you do not linger along the easy and open pathway, if you do not seek to render word for word as a slavish translator, and if in your copying you do not leap into the narrow well, out of which either shame or the laws of your task will keep you from stirring a step." *Horace: Satires. Epistles. The Art of Poetry* (Cambridge, Mass.: Harvard University Library, 1926), 461–63.

77. *Horace Of the Art of Poetry, In English Numbers* (London: J. Roberts, 1735), v–vi.

78. *Horace Of the Art of Poetry, In English Numbers*, v.

79. David Ferry's popular 2002 version reads as follows: "For if you don't just lazily saunter about / On easy paths of the public domain you'll earn / Your rightful ownership of part of it, / So long as you're not a pedissequous slave / Following foot for foot one foot at a time / Into the trap of timorous hyper-correctness." The expression "pedissequous slave" is a particularly extreme rendering. In Ferry, *The Epistles of Horace: Bilingual Edition* (New York: Farrar, Straus and Giroux, 2002), 160.

80. In this case, *pedem proferre* contrasts with *pedem referre*, meaning "to retreat."

81. This is visible in Drant's preface, wherein he mentions that one printer rejected his work in the following terms: "Sir your boke be wyse, and ful of learnyng, yet peraduenture it wyl not be so saileable" because "flim flames and gue gawes" are "soner rapte vp thenne are those which be lettered and Clarkly makings." Drant goes on to reference the "amarouse Pamphlets" that preoccupy readers instead of "bookes of learnynge." He finally settles on a marketing strategy that stresses its truth to the "learning, and sayinges of the author." Thomas Drant, *Horace his arte of Poetrie, pistles, and Satyrs, Englished and to the Earle of Ormounte by Tho. Drant, addressed, 1567* (London: Thomas Marshe, 1567), preface.

82. Drant's version is as follows: "A publique matter may be thought to cume from pryuate store, / If that one do not treade out right, the trodden, vsed waye. / Thou shalt haue no regarde at all word for word to oute lay. / If thou wouldest turne things faythfullye and do not imitate / So iumpingly, so precyselie and step, for step so strayte, / That what for shame to wade on still or ells to ende the thinge / As it began, thou canst not moue ne yet they foote out bringe." In *Horace his arte of Poetrie, pistles, and Satyrs*, 10.

83. Tytler writes, "So in B. Jonson's translations from the Odes and Epodes of Horace, besides the most servile adherence to the words, even the measure of the original is imitated," in *Essay on the Principles of Translation*, 66.

84. Ben Jonson, *Q. Horatius Flaccus: his Art of poetry. Englished by Ben: Jonson. With other workes of the author, never printed before* (London: I. Okes, 1640), lines 187–94.

85. Regarding Jonson's translation, Stuart Gillespie points out, "Horace thus sanctions the use of the common stock of cultural material, *publica materies*, and warns against the type of *fidus interpres* who will allow himself to be constrained by *pudor* or *lex operis*—by a sense of modesty or by the laws of the genre. Jonson seems to appreciate the creative freedom this formulation allows: his version is at this point itself an expansion, and handled more freely than he permits himself elsewhere." In *English Translation and Classical Reception* (Oxford: Wiley-Blackwell, 2011), 45.

86. Roscommon's importance in popular conceptions of translation theory is confirmed by a number of factors. For one, quotations from his version of the *Ars Poetica* show up in translation advertising, as in the case of an advertisement for a book called *The Life of Mahomet*, "translated from the French Original by the Count of Boulainvilliers." Below the description of the text, one finds Roscommon's couplet, "'*Tis true*, Composing *is the Nobler Part, / But good* Translation *is no easy Art*" as advertising copy. In *Grub Street Journal*, December, 10, 1730, no. 49. Other evidence attests to Roscommon's influence. Henry Ames, who translated the *Ars Poetica*, in 1727, writes " 'Tis certain my *Lord* Roscommon has not only excel'd in Justness of Version, and Elegance of Style, but has given his Poet all the Natural Beauties and Genteel Plainness of the English Dress; and makes him shine (even now) as distinguishingly Bright in our own Language, as he did near Two Thousand years ago in Ancient Roman." In *A New Translation of Horace's Art of Poetry, Attempted in Rhyme* (London: W. Pepper, 1727). Likewise, in the anonymously published translation from 1735 mentioned above, the translator's preface notes, "Should any Person not sufficient Master of the Tongue to read this Piece in the Original ask me 'What Books I thought would best assist him for Understanding of It,' if I thought on any other, I most certainly should recommend my Lord *Roscommon's* Version." In *Horace Of the Art of Poetry, In English Numbers*, iii.

87. Wentworth Dillon, Earl of Roscommon, *Horace's Art of poetry made English by the Right Honourable the Earl of Roscommon* (London: Henry Herringman, 1680).

88. Samuel Dunster, *Horace's Satires, Epistles, and Art of Poetry, Done into English, with Notes* (London: T.W. for W. Mears, F. Clay, and D. Browne, 1729), unpaginated.

89. William Boscawen, *The Satires, Epistles, and Art of Poetry of Horace, Translated into English Verse* (London: John Stockdale, 1797), 499–500.

90. William Clubbe, *The epistle of Horace to the Pisos, on the art of poetry. Translated into English verse. By William Clubbe, L.L.B. Vicar of Brandeston, Suffolk* (Ipswich: George Jermyn, 1797), 16.

Multilingual Lives: Joseph Emin

1. The ways dialect brings linguistic and other differences onto the page are informative. In the "Little Dominick" chapter of Maria and Richard Lovell Edgeworth's *Essay on Irish Bulls*, for example, little Irish Dominic suffers under the linguistic foibles of a Welsh schoolmaster exaggeratedly named Mr. Owen ap Davies ap Jenkins ap Jones. The repeated iterations of "ap"—a Welsh patronymic etymologically akin to the English genitive particle "of"—seems to assert and distort Welsh concern with genealogy. Mr. Owen's speech patterns exhibit the Celtic language tendency to devoice initial consonants in certain phonological positions, as in his exclamation, "Cot pless me, / you plockit, and shall I never *learn* you Enclish crammar?" Hard "g" sounds (/g/) lose their voicing to become "c" (/k/), just as the initial /b/ in "bless" and "blockhead" is translated into to "p" (/p/). Additionally, Mr. Owen also swaps the verbs "teach" and "learn." The Edgeworths keep this dialect game every time Mr. Owen speaks. "Day" becomes "tay," "danger," "tanger," and the phrase "by the advice of your guardian" is spelled, "py the atvice of your cardian." The Edgeworths' dialect writing is a simple cipher where certain graphemes are regularly swapped. See Maria Edgeworth and Richard Lovell Edgeworth, *Essay on Irish Bulls*, 1802, 2nd ed. (London: J. Johnson, 1803), 70.

2. Another interesting case study in deliberate eighteenth-century dialect writing can be found in visual depictions of eighteenth-century Anglo-Jewish types. In these, printers relied on their captions' idiosyncratic orthographies to supplement the inscription of cultural and physical difference. Two key orthographic alterations are emphasized in these surprisingly stable Anglo-Jewish dialects: the replacement of "s" with "sh'" and the replacement of "th" with "d." In an unattributed 1792 print sold by Carington Bowles, No. 69 St. Paul's Church Yard, a man with distorted features and a smarmy expression accompanies the brutally simplistic caption, "I've got the monish." The implication here is crude: the portrait's subject represents an imagined Jewish broker with distinctive linguistic features. Related, but different, George Woodward's "A Jew Pedlar, An English Politician" features an impoverished Jewish peddler whose strong accent can be heard in his sales pitch, "Dere ish de pictures of de King and de Queen—ash fine ash—de life itself—who buys? who buys? no more den twopence for de two—and de gold be worth all the monish without all de pictures." Linguistically, this sentence makes an interesting distinction to which few readers would have been consciously attuned. There are two phonemes in English represented by the grapheme "th:" a voiceless dental fricative /θ/ as in the word "think," and a voided dental fricative /ð/ as in the word "though." The best way to see these two phonemes in action is to view them as they function in minimal pairs, for they mark the phonetic and grammatical difference between near homophones like "breath" and "breathe," "bath" and "bathe," and "sheath" and "sheathe." The author of the caption changes only the voiced variety of "th" to "d." Hence, "the" becomes "de" and "there" becomes "dere," but he does not alter "worth" to

"word" nor "without" to "widout." In this way, the author of the caption actually obeys phonemic pairings common to most anglophone varieties. For these images and other images, see Frank Felsenstein and Sharon Liberman Mintz, curators, *The Jew as Other: A Century of English Caricature 1730–1830: An Exhibition, April 6–July 31, 1995* (New York: Library of the Jewish Theological Seminary of America, 1995), 15, 24.

3. This sentence synthesizes Erving Goffman's work on linguistic self-presentation in *The Presentation of Self in Everyday Life* (New York: Anchor Books, 1959) with the general insights of sociolinguistics as it was inaugurated—and subsequently expansively elaborated—by William Labov's work as well as that of those scholars in his intellectual lineage. The imprint of reading Labov's *The Social Stratification of English in New York City*, 1966, (Cambridge: Cambridge University Press, 2006) is intentionally visible here as throughout.

4. Citing Hamilton Jewett Smith's *Oliver Goldsmith's The Citizen of the World: A Study* (New Haven, Conn.: Yale University Press, 1926) and Arthur Lytton Sells's *Les Sources françaises de Goldsmith* (Paris: E. Champion, 1924), McMurran adds complexity to the question of anglophone writing, noting, "Oliver Goldsmith translated and inserted passages from Marquis d'Argens' *Lettres Chinoises* in his *Citizen of the World*, and some of the passages Goldsmith used were translated from d'Argens' own unacknowledged use of Du Halde's description of China." McMurran, *Spread of Novels*, 5.

5. Oliver Goldsmith, *The Works of Oliver Goldsmith*, vol. 3, J. W. M. Gibbs, ed. (London: George Bell, 1885), 13.

6. Oliver Goldsmith, *Works of Oliver Goldsmith*, 9.

7. Oliver Goldsmith, *Works of Oliver Goldsmith*, 9.

8. In one of his audiences with a "Lady of Distinction," Lien is shown into the room and the woman exclaims, "What an unusual share of *somethingness* in his whole appearance! . . . I would give the world to see him in his own country dress. . . . Pray, speak a little Chinese: I have learned something of the language myself." Oliver Goldsmith, *Works of Oliver Goldsmith*, 53–54.

9. Oliver Goldsmith, *Works of Oliver Goldsmith*, 31.

10. Oliver Goldsmith, *Works of Oliver Goldsmith*, 178.

11. Oliver Goldsmith, *Works of Oliver Goldsmith*, 154.

12. Srinivas Aravamudan reads Hamilton's novel as a "satirical and pseudoethographic text" that is emblematic of his key critical term "Enlightenment Orientalism," which he defines as "an investigative tool that offers an alternative to the uniform directionality of other fictional genres, including especially the nation-centered novel after the middle of the eighteenth century." In *Enlightenment Orientalism*, 102, 111. Padma Rangarajan's close reading of this text within the context of imperial translation techniques and pseudoethnographies characterizes Hamilton's novel as a "layered evocation of Hindu, colonial, and British customs" that "offered her readers a truly global vision of empire as the catalyst for useful transcultural praxis." In *Imperial Babel*, 142.

13. In this instance, "ethnographic" refers to the process by which the very surface of writing attempts to communicate the difference of the speaker. In other words, I am using this word in the specific sense of a graphic representation of ethnos.

14. Elizabeth Hamilton, *Translation of the Letter of a Hindoo Rajah*, Pamela Perkins and Shannon Russell, eds. (Peterborough, Ontario: Broadview, 1999; 1796).

15. It is interesting to note too that the first Irish edition of this text, which I have consulted, also does not contain the preliminary dissertation even though it is bombastically announced on the title page.

16. The use of macrons in the spelling of these names is unstable within any one of the editions that uses them.

17. Joseph Emin, *The Life and Adventures of Joseph Émïn, An Armenian. Written in English by Himself* (London, 1792), 3.

18. Joseph Emin, *Life and Adventures of Joseph Émïn*, 4.

19. Joseph Emin, *Life and Adventures of Joseph Émïn*, 4.

20. Joseph Emin, *Life and Adventures of Joseph Émïn*, 639.

21. Joseph Emin, *Life and Adventures of Joseph Émïn*, 54.

22. Michael Fisher sees these confusions in a positive light, arguing, "Thus, within Britain, Emin had some scope to negotiate his particular identity among the range of aliens whom Britons ranked hierarchically." Michael Fisher, *Counterflows to Colonialism*, 75. In a different essay, Fisher fleshes out the extralingual "scope" Emin would have had to negotiate his identity: "He made his Armenian Christianity a special marker of self-identification with Britons, and explicitly distanced himself from the Catholic French as well as Muslims and Jews. The relatively high social standing of such Asian men reflected signs of cultural status valued by most Britons: respectable social class, non-Catholic Christian associations, male gender, and English literacy and deportment." Michael Fisher, "Asians in Britain: Negotiations of Identity Through Self-Representation," in *New Imperial History*, ed. Kathleen Wilson, 97.

23. Joseph Emin, *Life and Adventures of Joseph Émïn*, 91.

24. "In the month of November, when one morning the author was going along Cheapside, he met a young man in a Turkish habit, and had the curiosity to speak to him in that language, as he found him to be an Armenian; both parties were glad to see each other. . . . The man had been sent over with an Arabian horse, as a groom, by the English merchants at Aleppo, for his Grace the late Duke (at that time Earl) of Northumberland. The Armenian groom desired him to call on him at Northumberland-house, as he was an entire stranger to the English, in order to explain some words to the people of the house; to which he agreed very gladly, not foreseeing the happy consequences of it." Joseph Emin, *Life and Adventures of Joseph Émïn*, 93.

25. Joseph Emin, *Life and Adventures of Joseph Émïn*, 99.

26. Joseph Emin, *Life and Adventures of Joseph Émïn*, 464.

27. Joseph Emin, *Life and Adventures of Joseph Émïn*, 216.

28. Joseph Emin, *Life and Adventures of Joseph Émïn*, 339.

29. Joseph Emin, *Life and Adventures of Joseph Émïn*, 416.

30. Joseph Emin, *Life and Adventures of Joseph Émïn*, 558.

Chapter 4. Literacy Fictions

1. Peter Sloterdijk, "Rules for the Human Zoo," 1999, Mary Varney Rorty, trans., *Environment and Planning D: Society and Space*, 29 (2009), 13.

2. See Lynda Mugglestone, *"Talking Proper": The Rise of Accent as Social Symbol.*

3. Earlier I defined "dialect" in a nontraditional sense. I treat "dialect" as a writing technique that reprocesses living forms of lectic speech into a written context, not in the interest of accurate or true representation of multilingual human subjects, but instead in the interests of characterology and narrative momentum.

4. Peter Sloterdijk, "Rules for the Human Zoo," 23.

5. By the late eighteenth century, though, "illiteracy" frequently applied to the condition of being unable to read or write in any language. The OED quotes an essay in William Martin's *Geographical Magazine* from 1782: "The illiteracy of Mahomet made it necessary for him to find some more learned associate." The novelty of this last sense of "illiteracy" indicates a milestone in the development of the Standard English definition. Once the condition of "illiteracy" includes all vernacular languages, it indicates the collapse of the previously accepted linguistic hierarchy. Put another way, enough material had by that point been written in the vernacular that an inability to read and write it was a social liability. An OED reference to Thomas Warton from the same era provides an interestingly ambiguous usage of "illiteracy" to mean ignorance in general. The passage in question is a 1774 extract from *The History of English Poetry* where Warton describes Scottish poet Gawen Douglass's trip to Paris around 1500. He relates that according to a decree of James I, it was necessary "to reform the illiteracy of the clergy. . . . No ecclesiastic of Scotland should be preferred to a prebend of any value without a competent skill in that science." Warton's comment clearly implies that the clergy needed to better their knowledge of canon law and thus their Greek and Latin. Yet, given that Warton was a professor of poetry and deeply attracted to the ongoing antiquarian ballad revival, we might put pressure on the literal reading so as to suggest that Warton was also interested in the clergy's lack of vernacular language skills, those nonnormative language forms spoken by parishioners. This deconstructive reading is more provocative, as it suggests the clergy's ineffectiveness derived from their deafness to the vernacular's importance and not because of their deficiencies in Greek or Latin. The evidence in this passage stinks of ambiguity but still does indicate that meanings of "literacy" and "illiteracy" were undergoing substantial transformations during this period. Without Latinity, education was becoming less exclusive. Latin and Greek were increasingly viewed as meaningful accomplishments only when affixed to gentlemen who possessed—in addition to land and status—the power to put classical knowledge into the maintaining an orderly status quo.

6. More's engagement with the double-edged sword of mass literacy in *Village Politics* is generally understood to be a formal and conceptual precursor to the "Cheap Repository" tracts that More produced after 1795. Jane Nardin fills in these details: "Many Evangelicals lamented their inability to teach the poor how to read the scriptures without enabling them to read immoral books as well. Confronting this problem in 1794, after her success with *Village Politics*, More devised a plan to provide literature for the poor that would be both uplifting and entertaining. This plan resulted in the publication of the "Cheap Repository" series of tracts, over a hundred of which appeared between 1795 and 1798. They were sold by street hawkers and distributed free by gentled fold to their dependents. So subsidized, the tracts were dramatically successful. By 1796 over two million copies had been disposed of." Jane Nardin, "Hannah More and the Problem of Poverty," *Texas Studies in Literature and Language*, 43, no. 3, (Fall 2001), 280. Susan Pederson provides crucial primary and secondary background to *Village Politics* as it relates to the "Cheap Repository" tracts in "Hannah More Meets Simple Simon: Tracts, Chapbooks, and Popular Culture in Late Eighteenth-Century England," *Journal of British Studies*, 25, no. 1 (January 1986), 84–113.

7. Mona Scheuermann's contextualized close reading of *Village Politics* assesses the simplistic anglophone register in which the dialogue is composed: "*Village Politics* is written in language so simple that a child would understand it; clearly, More's idea of the intelligence of her lower-class audience, notwithstanding her experience with Ann Yearsley, is that to be lower class is to be of low mental ability. Neither she nor her friends seem to hear the contemptuous quality of

an argument that is couched in diction and supported by logic that might be appropriate for a five year old." Mona Scheuermann, *In Praise of Poverty: Hannah More Counters Thomas Paine and the Radical Threat* (Lexington: University of Kentucky Press, 2002), 108.

8. Hannah More, *Village Politics. Addressed to All the Mechanics, Journeymen, and Day Labourers in Great Britain* (London: C. Rivington, 1792), 3.

9. Hannah More, *Village Politics*, 3.

10. Hannah More, *Village Politics*, 20.

11. Scheuermann notes, "But he [Tom] does not even know what he is asking for. It is clear that the big words he uses—'I'm for a *Constitution*, and *Organization*, and *Equalization*'—are not concepts he comprehends. Jack loses his patience a bit, as More intends her reader to do, with Tom's silliness." Scheuermann, *In Praise of Poverty*, 111.

12. Arguing that the pamphlet also demonstrates a certain sympathy for those who would identify "the failings of the rich," Nardin reads the subtle linking of these several forms of More's politics in the following terms: "Though Jack concludes his harangue by advising Tom to 'be quiet, work with your own hands, and mind your own business," the tract is not purely quietest in its implications. In a mild Tory way, it is reformist as well. In *Village Politics*, More managed to produce a pamphlet that delighted [Bishop Beilby] Porteus and other members of the ruling classes, yet was not completely innocent of social criticism." Jane Nardin, "Hannah More and the Problem of Poverty," 279.

13. Hannah More, *Village Politics*, 8.

14. Hannah More, *Village Politics*, 8.

15. Several critics see the explicit influence of Burke in Jack's anecdote regarding his boss, Sir John's castle: "When Sir John married, my Lady, who is a little fantastical, and likes to do everything like the French, begged him to pull down yonder fine old castle, and build it up in her frippery way. No, says Sir John; what shall I pull down this noble building, raised by the wisdom of my brave ancestors; which outstood the civil wars, and only underwent a little needful repair at the Revolution." Hannah More, *Village Politics*, 7.

16. Hannah More, *Village Politics*, 7, 24.

17. Hannah More, *Village Politics*, 13.

18. In response to Tom's question about whether or not he has read *The Rights of Man*, Jack replies that he would rather read *The Whole Duty of Man*, a reference to a devotional work by royalist churchman Richard Allestree first published in 1658. This work takes its title from Ecclesiastes 12. Lines 12–13 of this chapter are instructive, especially as they relate to More's sense that literacy could be immensely misleading: "12. And further, by these, my son, be admonished: of making many books there is no end; and much study is a weariness of the flesh. 13. Let us hear the conclusion of the whole matter: Fear God, and keep his commandments: for this is the whole duty of man" (KJV); Hannah More, *Village Politics*, 5–6.

19. Hannah More, *Village Politics*, 13.

20. Hannah More, *Village Politics*, 14.

21. Here I am echoing Scheuermann's observation, "From this point, however, until near the end of the story, Tom's comments for the most part are one-liners, essentially prompts for talks and vignettes designed to teach specific lessons of common sense, morality, and, of course, good citizenship." Scheuermann, *In Praise of Poverty*, 112.

22. Hannah More, *Village Politics*, 13.

23. Hannah More, *Village Politics*, 14.

24. Hannah More, *Village Politics*, 17–18.

25. Hannah More, *Village Politics*, 18.

26. Hannah More, *Village Politics*, 18.

27. Review of *Anecdotes of the English Language: Chiefly Regarding the Local Dialect of London and Its Environs* by Samuel Pegge, *Critical Review*, 2 (London: S. Hamilton, 1804), 214.

28. "Dialect dialogue" is a term I use here to refer to a specific literary form wherein conversations between characters stage linguistic and other particularities of regional life, thereby naturalizing linguistic and cultural difference along rural and urban lines. "Dialect dialogues" often transpire in a named region of Britain, as in Brice, in Collier, and in Ann Wheeler's *The Westmorland Dialect in Four Familiar Dialogues* (1800). By writing language as it was supposedly spoken, these texts relativize and trouble Standard English literacy by inviting readers to engage in different and more challenging forms of literacy. For more on "dialect dialogues" and Wheeler, see Daniel DeWispelare, "Dissidence in Dialect: Ann Wheeler's Westmorland Dialogues," *Studies in Romanticism*, no. 1 (Spring 2015). See also Appendix A.

29. For biographical details on John Russell Smith, see R. J. Goulden, "Smith, John Russell (1810–1894)," *Oxford Dictionary of National Biography*, Oxford University Press, 2004, http://www.oxforddnb.com/view/article/25864 (accessed January 25, 2013).

30. Other important bibliographic works by Smith that pertain to anglophone language practices include: *Bibliotheca Cantiana, a Bibliographic Account of What Has Been Published on the History, Topography, Antiquities, Customs, and Family Genealogy of the County of Kent* (London: John Russell Smith, 1837) and *A Catalogue of an Unique Collection of Ancient English Broadside Ballads, Printed Entirely in Black Letter* (London: John Russell Smith, 1856), which promises to gather together "the really vernacular fugitive ballads of the common people," v. In addition to these, Smith republished a wide array of earlier anglophone texts, including Francis Grose's *A Glossary of Provincial and Local Words Used in England* (London: John Russell Smith, 1839). This last volume is particularly interesting in that it includes at the end a fifty-six-page catalogue of "Books Published or Sold by John Russell Smith." One of these books, William Holloway's *A General Dictionary of Provincialisms, Written with a View to Rescue from Oblivion the Fast Fading Relics of By-gone Days* (Sussex: Baxter and Son, 1839), includes an eight-page prefatory listing of language books and glossaries published or sold by Smith.

31. In 1877, Walter Skeat and J. H. Nodal, members of the English Dialect Society, compiled *A Bibliographic List of the Works That Have Been Published, or are Known to Exist in MS., Illustrative of the Various Dialects of English* (London: Trübner, 1877), a work that would supersede Smith's curatorial work on anglophone particularities. Skeat and Nodal's listing is far more compendious, and yet still in debt to Smith. Their listing for "Devonshire," which was compiled and updated by John Shelley, runs to four pages with twenty-two separate entries.

32. The fifth text on the list is "another edition" of the forth, "but with so many material alterations, that they might be called a new set of [dialect] Dialogues." John Russell Smith, *A Bibliographical List of the Works that Have Been Published Towards Illustrating the Provincial Dialects of England* (London: John Russell Smith, 1839), 9.

33. John Russell Smith, *Bibliographical List*, 9.

34. Smith's listing on Devonshire includes an important set of details under the listing for Andrew Brice. He claims that Brice's *An Exmoor Scolding* was first published in 1746; he registers that this unique anglophone text had already run to ten printed editions in 1788, when a glossary was added; and he notes that he, John Russell Smith, published the newest edition in 1839.

Though Smith does not mention Brice's *An Exmoor Courtship*, which is a formally similar work that was frequently published as a companion piece to *An Exmoor Scolding*, and though he does not tabulate the many other editions of these singular writings, his reference to his most recent 1839 republication of the work speaks to his intuition that the text remained a salable commodity.

35. Smith is also uninterested in tabulating or compiling representations of anglophone difference outside of Britain.

36. Eighteenth-century tabulations of past literary traditions, however, do not necessarily appear in Smith's bibliography. Works like Percy's *Reliques of English Poetry* (1765), Warton's *History of English Literature, 1100–1603* (3 vols., 1774–81), and Grose's antiquarian catalogues are absent. In place of these, Smith includes texts invested in recording contemporary or near-contemporary anglophone diversity. Confirmation can be found by looking closely at those works by Grose that do appear. Whereas *Antiquities of England and Wales* (6 vols., 1773–87) and *Antiquities of Scotland* (2 vols., 1789–91) are not listed, Grose's *Provincial Glossary* (1787) appears on Smith's bibliography's first page. Even though the two former works contain a wealth of historical linguistic information, Smith omits them in favor of a regional glossary of living or recently living languages, "local proverbs and popular superstitions."

37. Ian Maxted, "Brice, Andrew (1692–1773)," *Oxford Dictionary of National Biography*, Oxford University Press, 2004, http://www.oxforddnb.com/view/article/3379 (accessed June 13, 2015); See also Ian Maxted, "Exeter Working Papers in Book History," 2015, http://book history.blogspot.co.uk/ (accessed September 10, 2015).

38. The first extant edition of *An Exmoor Scolding* is the third, dated 1746. Brice, who is listed as the printer, is assumed to be the author.

39. D. M. Horgan, "Popular Protest in the Eighteenth Century: John Collier (Tim Bobbin), 1708–1786," *Review of English Studies*, 48, no. 191 (1997), 314. As regards *An Exmoor Vocabulary*, this is in effect an approximately three-hundred-word reader-submitted glossary of "all such Words in the *Exmoor Scolding* and *Courtship*, the Meaning of which does not appear by the Sense, with the Addition of some others; all accented on their proper Syllables, to Shew the Method of their Pronunciation."

40. The title page of the first extant print edition of *An Exmoor Scolding* (1746) lists it as the third edition.

41. In this case, the edition numbers in parentheses correspond to what is announced on the title pages.

42. Besides John Russell Smith's 1839 edition, a reprint of the seventh edition—the first with a glossary and notes—appears at Exeter in 1818.

43. The editors of the OED note that "perfix" is an anglophone derivative of the etymon "prefix." "°perfix, v." *OED Online*, March 2016, Oxford University Press, http://www.oed.com .proxygw.wrlc.org/view/Entry/140753?redirectedFrom = perfix (accessed May 24, 2016).

44. Because the text is readable on its own without a translation, I include the translation here in order to stage the effect of intralingual translation on this text and to gauge some of the ideological implications.

45. Ian Maxted, "Brice, Andrew (1692–1773)."

46. Andrew Brice, *An Exmoor Scolding, Between Two Sisters, Wilmot and Thomasin Moreman, As they were Spinning; Also An Exmoor Courtship; Both in the Propriety and Decency of the Exmoor Dialect, To which is Adjoined a Collateral Paraphrase in Plain English, For explaining barbarous Words and Phrases* (South Molton: J. Huxtable, 1794), 3, 3, 4, 12.

47. Andrew Brice, .*Exmoor Scolding . . . Also An Exmoor Courtship*, 32.

48. This is the precise situation that Reverend Lyons describes. Those who are capable of reading Irish are also and primarily capable of reading English. Those who are capable of reading nonstandard writing are also and primarily capable of reading standard writing.

49. Andrew Brice, *Exmoor Scolding . . . Also An Exmoor Courtship*, 15.

50. J. A. Hilton, "'Tim Bobbin' and the Origins of Provincial Consciousness in Lancashire," *Journal of the Lancashire Dialect Society*, no. 19 (January 1970), 2.

51. John Collier, *Tim Bobbin's Lancashire Dialect; and Poems* (London: Hurst, Chance, 1828), title page.

52. John Collier, *Tim Bobbin's Lancashire Dialect; and Poems*, 4, 22.

53. John Collier, *Tim Bobbin's Lancashire Dialect; and Poems*, 20.

54. Andrew Brice, *An Exmoor Scolding; In the Propriety and Decency of Exmoor Language, Between Two Sisters, Wilmot Moreman and Thomasin Moreman, As they were Spinning. Also, An Exmoor Courtship* (Exon: A. Brice and B. Thorn, 1771), ii.

55. Andrew Brice, *Exmoor Scolding . . . Also, An Exmoor Courtship*, i.

56. Andrew Brice, *Exmoor Scolding . . . Also, An Exmoor Courtship*, i.

57. John Collier, *A View of the Lancashire Dialect; By way of Dialogue* (Leeds: James Lister, 1748), title page.

58. John Collier, *A View of the Lancashire Dialect; By way of Dialogue* (Manchester: Joseph Harrop), title page.

59. John Collier, *The Miscellaneous Works of Tim Bobbin, Esq. Containing his View of the Lancashire Dialect, With large Additions and Improvements; and a Glossary* (London: T. and J. Allman, 1818), xiii.

60. John Collier, *Tim Bobbin's Lancashire Dialect; and Poems*, v.

61. J. A. Hilton, "'Tim Bobbin' and the Origins of Provincial Consciousness in Lancashire," 3.

62. Maria and Richard Lovell Edgeworth, *Essay on Irish Bulls*, 198.

63. See the use of the word "dialect" in titles listed in Appendix A and Appendix B.

64. D. Lewis, "The Old and New Pocket-Books, a Dialogue," in *Specimens of the Yorkshire Dialect*, Charles Johnson, ed. (Knaresborough: Hargrove and Sons, 1808), 27.

65. D. Lewis, "Old and New Pocket-Books, a Dialogue," 27.

66. Maria Edgeworth and Richard Lovell Edgeworth, *Practical Education*, vol. 2 (London: J. Johnson, 1798), 388.

67. Maria Edgeworth and Richard Lovell Edgeworth, *Practical Education*, 408.

68. Maria Edgeworth and Richard Lovell Edgeworth, *Practical Education*, 403.

69. Maria Edgeworth and Richard Lovell Edgeworth, *Practical Education*, 387.

70. Maria Edgeworth and Richard Lovell Edgeworth, *Practical Education*, 387.

71. Maria Edgeworth and Richard Lovell Edgeworth, *Essay on Irish Bulls*, 300.

72. Maria Edgeworth and Richard Lovell Edgeworth, *Essay on Irish Bulls*, 300.

73. Elizabeth Gilmartin, "The Anglo-Irish Dialect: Mediating Linguistic Conflict," *Victorian Literature and Culture*, 32, no. 1 (2004), 3.

74. Maria Edgeworth and Richard Lovell Edgeworth, *Essay on Irish Bulls*, 131.

75. Maria Edgeworth and Richard Lovell Edgeworth, *Essay on Irish Bulls*, 133.

76. Maria Edgeworth was somewhat taken with Tooke's theories. Not only does she apostrophize him throughout *Essay on Irish Bulls*, but she also cites him in the footnotes to *Castle*

Rackrent, An Hibernian Tale (London: J. Crowder, 1800) and several times in the body of *Practical Education.*

77. In Tooke's linguistic schema, prepositions, among the most widely used particles in language, derive only from Anglo-Saxon words. Thus, the Hiberno-English speakers are in tune with the Anglo-Saxon heritage of the English tongue even though their speech may strike the Standard English ear as foreign.

78. Maria Edgeworth and Richard Lovell Edgeworth, *Essay on Irish Bulls*, 134.

79. Maria Edgeworth and Richard Lovell Edgeworth, *Essay on Irish Bulls*, 137.

80. Maria Edgeworth and Richard Lovell Edgeworth, *Essay on Irish Bulls*, 217.

81. Maria Edgeworth and Richard Lovell Edgeworth, *Essay on Irish Bulls*, 197.

82. Samuel Pegge, *Anecdotes of the English Language: Chiefly Regarding the Local Dialect of London and Its Environs* (London: J. Nichols, 1814; 1803), 80, 93, 156.

83. Pegge, *Anecdotes of the English Language*, 110.

84. Pegge, *Anecdotes of the English Language*, 110.

85. Pegge, *Anecdotes of the English Language*, 110.

Multilingual Lives: Antera Duke

1. Behrendt, Latham, and Northrup, *Diary of Antera Duke*, 136–37.

2. I will refer to Ntiero Edem Efiom with the two-name appellation "Antera Duke," as the majority of modern scholars and editors of his works have done. Behrendt, Latham, and Northrup write, "Efik naming patters help chart generations and ward development [ward refers to an extended family unit]. In Efik a father's name becomes the son's second name, for example, Nsa Efiom and Edem Efiom were the sons of Efiom Ekpo. . . . This naming sequence transferred to Anglicized trading names, and thus Duke Antera is Antera Duke's son, probably his eldest son with one of his principal wives." In Behrendt, Latham, and Northrup, *Diary of Antera Duke*, 16.

3. Citing Daryll Forde's 1968 study, *Efik Traders of Old Calabar* (London: Oxford University Press), Joan Fayer notes, "Antera Duke wrote the diary for his own personal use 'in a large folio volume—such as might have been used as a ship's log-book—which had apparently been given to him by one of the officers of a slave ship." Behrendt, Latham, and Northrup continue the interesting transmission history of Antera Duke's diary, the only version of which comes from a transcription made by chance in 1907 by Arthur W. Wilkie. Wilkie was a missionary in Old Calabar during the early part of the twentieth century. The only folio copy of the diary was shown to him on one of his trips back to Edinburgh by William Valentine, a clerk at the Foreign Mission Office of the Free Church of Scotland, where the manuscript had been deposited and forgotten during the nineteenth century. The original folio was likely destroyed during World War II, and as the editors point out, "it is not possible to double-check the accuracy of the transcription." Joan Fayer, "Pidgins as Written Languages: Evidence from 18th Century Old Calabar," *Anthropological Linguistics*, 28, no. 3 (Fall 1986), 314; Behrendt, Latham, and Northrup, *Diary of Antera Duke*, 120.

4. "Ekpe was an invisible forest spirit, which had to be propitiated for the well-being of Calabar. Similar beliefs in forest spirits exist in other communities in southeaster Nigeria and western Cameroon, and in many the spirit manifested itself as a leopard and traveled from the bush to interact with humans. Ekpe means 'leopard' in Ibibio and Efik. . . . Since humans captured the spirit, it tries devious ways to escape, and indeed it was revered as a trickster.

Leopard societies developed to worship the forest spirit and unite villagers around a supernatural entity." As a form of community consolidation, Ekpe practices led to the formation of an organizational social structure with different levels or grades as well as the circulation of a series of Ekpe laws and tributary systems that functioned as a kind of de facto governmental structure: "Ekpe, then, in these days, was an exclusively male society that enacted and enforced laws for the greater Efik community, helped reduce tensions between individuals and families, and stabilized the business environment for both local and overseas traders. A wealthy merchant, Antera Duke was a member of Nyampke, the highest of four Ekpe grades functioning during the last twenty years of his life." See Behrendt, Latham, and Northrup, *Diary of Antera Duke*, 27–36.

5. Stressing the diary's historical value, the editors note, "As a diary, Antera Duke's diary gives historians information otherwise not found in documents written by Africans in the precolonial era." Later they reiterate this point in more detail: "The diary, the most extensive Efik-authored writing, anchors local political, legal, and religious traditions in time." In Behrendt, Latham, and Northrup, *Diary of Antera Duke*, 3, 44.

6. Behrendt, Latham, and Northrup, *Diary of Antera Duke*, 221.

7. Behrendt, Latham, and Northrup elaborate the dynamics of the slave trade in the region where Antera Duke lived in the following terms: "African merchants based in the Cross River region sold slaves to European ship captains from the mid-seventeenth century, when Caribbean cash-crop plantations began developing, to the late 1830s and the final British-led diplomatic and naval push to abolish the transatlantic slave trade. Though Portuguese captains were the first to visit the Rio da Cruz (Cross River) . . . British captains dominated each decade of the Old Calabar slave trade until Parliament banned the trade in 1807–1808. Captains sailing from London, Bristol, or Liverpool purchased three-quarters of all enslaved Africans sold at Old Calabar, and from 1662 to 1807 at least one British captain traded with Efik merchants each year." Behrent, Latham, and Northrup, *Diary of Antera Duke*, 73, 48.

8. Behrendt, Latham, and Northrup, *Diary of Antera Duke*, 49. In a different piece of scholarship that focuses on an earlier period in Calabar history, Stephen Behrendt and Eric Graham write, "Creation of London-based monopoly companies helped secure the dominance of English-flagged vessels in the Cross River form the 1660s to 1713 [when the Royal Africa Company lost its slave-trading monopoly in Old Calabar], prompting local African merchants to learn broken English and adopt English-style names to facilitate trade." In Stephen Behrendt and Eric Graham, "African Merchants, Notables and the Slave Trade at Old Calabar, 1720: Evidence from the National Archives of Scotland," *History in Africa*, 30 (2003), 42.

9. Behrendt, Latham, and Northrup, *Diary of Antera Duke*, 3.

10. The editors inform readers, "We assume that Antera also penned letteres, notes, or cursory debt tallies in trade English, as there are seventeen such Efik-authored documents from the period 1767–1804. In two letters to Liverpool merchants in 1773, Grandy King George (Ephraim Robin John) wrote 1,608 words, and the next longest surviving Efik document [in "trade English"] contains 333 words. Of these sixteen documents, only six still exist in manuscript." On the question of the relative complexity of vocabularies of Efik writers in "trade English," Antera Duke's editors point out in a footnote, "the English vocabulary learned by Efik merchants may differ—Ephraim Robin John, for example, used more sophisticated verbs and nouns, correctly spelling 'acquaint' and 'acquaintances,' and attempting the difficult words, 'encouragement' (spelled 'In Curigement') and 'civility' ('sivellety'). He also employed sophisticated verbs such as to vex, hoist, cast, prevent, write, ought, consult, and insist. Antera had learned a more simplified vocabulary." Behrendt, Latham, and Northrup, *Diary of Antera Duke*, 3, 273–74 n 30.

11. Behrendt, Latham, and Northrup, *Diary of Antera Duke*, 120.

12. Behrendt, Latham, and Northrup, *Diary of Antera Duke*, 2.

13. One must speculate that he was trained or somehow observed the rudiments of anglophone writing, although the editors of his diary seem to distrust that possibility, insisting instead on the oral transmission of these skills. They write, "The best example of how Antera learned English—by hearing a sailor reading business correspondence—in his use of 'occasion.' Twice Antera writes the term: as 'Cosoin" in one passage and then as "cason" eighteen months later—in both instances translated by Simmons [an earlier translator] as 'cousin.'" Fayer provides a different possibility: "Antera Duke wrote his diary in Calabar Pidgin although there was another writing system that was known in Old Calabar. This was nsibidi, a pictographic writing system that was used by members of a secret male society [Ekpe]. As a prominent Efik trader and a member of this society, Antera Duke probably knew how to use this writing system." Fayer goes on to note its radical difference form anglophone alphabetic script, but it is possible this analogous technology influenced his understanding of anglophone writing. Behrendt, Latham, and Northrup, *Diary of Antera Duke*, 128; Fayer, "Pidgins as Written Languages: Evidence from 18th Century Old Calabar," 315.

14. This might account for the fact that versions of this text have regularly been published as internal translations into Standard English. Donald C. Simmons was the first to translate the text into Standard English, in 1956. Behrendt, Latham, and Northrup's newest version reproduces the fiat that one translate the text, but it also presents the reader with facing-page versions of Antera Duke's entries and translations of those entries into legible forms. The editors, like any good translators should, confirm that their version is an informed reading, not the transparent transmission of the source text in Standard English: "Readers should note that our standard-English rendition is the best attempt of three historians to elucidate fully the Efik writer's sentences; other scholars may decide upon alternate interpretations." Behrendt, Latham, and Northrup, *Diary of Antera Duke*, 129.

15. For example, in terms of historical accuracy, the editors are able to repair errors in chronology made either by Antera Duke at the moment of writing or by Arthur Wilkie at the moment of transcription. See Behrendt, Latham, and Northrup, *Diary of Antera Duke*, 125–26.

16. Behrendt, Latham, and Northrup, *Diary of Antera Duke*, 140–41.

17. See discussion of the name "Brown/Burrows" in Behrendt, Latham, and Northrup, *Diary of Antera Duke*, 138n30, 141n40, 146n58, and 160n112.

18. Behrendt, Latham, and Northrup, *Diary of Antera Duke*, 141n43.

19. "Linguistic analysis of Antera Duke's diary provided guidelines for revising the 'modern English' version written by Wilkie and Simmons. . . . The diarist begins sentences with temporal markers and conjunctions. Antera employs the subordinating conjunction 'so' either as an adverbial clause to indicate a sequential relationship or to indicate a causal relationship. We kept in mind how Antera might have heard words, or the types of words he would have seen written by captains, merchants, or other Efik. . . . There is a clear correspondence between vowel sounds and the letters he writes, as when Antera pens 'at' when he hears the number 'eight.'" Behrendt, Latham, and Northrup, *Diary of Antera Duke*, 127–28.

20. Behrendt, Latham, and Northrup, *Diary of Antera Duke*, 127.

21. Behrendt, Latham, and Northrup, *Diary of Antera Duke*, 202–3.

22. Behrendt, Latham, and Northrup, *Diary of Antera Duke*, 202n246.

23. Behrendt, Latham, and Northrup, *Diary of Antera Duke*, 202.

Chapter 5. The "Alien Wealth" of "Lucky Contaminations"

1. The "About" page of this database reads: "The newspapers, pamphlets, and books gathered by the Reverend Charles Burney (1757–1817) represent the largest and most comprehensive collection of early English news media. The present digital collection, that helps chart the development of the concept of 'news' and 'newspapers' and the 'free press', totals almost 1 million pages and contains approximately 1,270 titles. Many of the Burney newspapers are well known, but many pamphlets and broadsides also included have remained largely hidden." *17th–18th Century Burney Collection Newspapers*, Gale Cengage, 2014.

2. This is intuitive for this primary reason: the expansion of the periodical press over this period. However, the increase in hits as the eighteenth century draws toward an end also represents the rising importance and market penetration of translated texts during the period.

3. Actually the only document originally published in Germany (Hamburg) that is represented in the database is a broadside entitled *Price Current of the Principal Articles Imported from America in Our Currency & British Sterling Money*).

4. As Gale Cengage defines the use of this functionality, "Fuzzy search settings can enhance your search by retrieving near matches on a term or terms. This is a particularly valuable feature within a digital archive database in that it allows you to locate a word or words within works despite imperfect matches in spelling between the searched term and document content. This is a common occurrence due to the variant/approximate spellings often found in historical documents, and possibly due to Optical Character Recognition (OCR) scanning errors made during the data digitization process. Fuzzy search functionality greatly minimizes the impact that variant/approximate spellings and any OCR errors may have on your search results." *17th–18th Century Burney Collection Newspapers*, Gale Cengage, 2014.

5. The main methodological points I would like to make are two, the first more obvious than the second: (1) this database represents a curated selection of British newspapers, pamphlets, and books—it should not be confused with the entirety of all British newspapers, pamphlets, and books; (2) one should be careful in making developmental claims from this data because the density, and thus representativeness, of the archive fluctuates over the period.

6. *Post Man and Historical Account* (London), October 17–20, 1696, no. 226. If one does not limit oneself to "Advertising sections," other occurrences of this phrase occur as early as 1648. Obviously too, this is by no means the first occurrence of this phrase in advertising.

7. *St. James's Chronicle or the British Evening Post*, March 9–11, 1790, no. 4507.

8. *Sun* (London), October 17, 1795, no. 954.

9. *Sun* (London), December 27, 1800, no. 2580. This same advertisement, which was printed in several papers during December 1800, also advertises an edition of Helen Maria Williams's translation of *Paul and Virginia* (5s.) as well as an advertisement for a four-volume collection "Asiatic Researches; or, Transactions of the Society established at Bengal, by Sir William Jones and others" that was being sold for 3l. 4s.

10. Venuti notes, "In the case of retranslations, the translator's agency is distinguished by a significant increase in self-consciousness that seeks to take into account the manifold conditions and consequences of the translating." An attention to the commercial value of the retranslation is one of these manifold conditions. Venuti, *Translation Changes Everything*, 100.

11. This advertisement is also interesting in that, as a retranslation that does not name the translator, the advertiser still takes pains to stress the superadded value the volume represents: "As this Translation was undertaken by Gentlemen who UNDERSTAND GREEK, the Reader

may be sure he has the SENSE of the AUTHOR. . . . To this EDITION will be added some Remarks both on the Beauties and Imperfections of the Author, after the Manner of Mr. ADDISON'S Remarks upon Milton." *Daily London Journal*, July 26, 1732, no. 3607.

12. *London Evening Post*, May 21, 1730, no. 382.

13. *World and Fashionable Advisor*, August, 8, 1787, no. 187.

14. *Oracle and Daily Advertiser*, December 26, 1800, no. 22429.

15. Ros Ballaster, ed. *Fables of the East: Selected Tales, 1662–1785* (Oxford: Oxford University Press, 2005), 71–100.

16. *World and Fashionable Advisor*, August, 3, 1787, no. 183.

17. *Oracle and Daily Advertiser*, February 19, 1800, no. 22225.

18. This advertisement appears first in the London magazine *Porcupine*, December 23, 1800, no. 47, and is republished in the *Courier and Evening Gazette*, the *Morning Post and Gazetteer*, the *Sun*, the *Albion and Evening Advertiser*, and the *Oracle and Daily Advertiser* several times throughout the ensuing months.

19. Tobias Smollett, ed. *The Critical Review; or, Annals of Literature*, vol. 32 (London: S. Hamilton, 1801), 18.

20. This version is taken from *World*, February 23, 1790, no. 982. Many other versions exist.

21. Susan Bassnett, *Translation* (Routledge: London, 2014), 16.

22. In Tytler, *Essay on the Principles of Translation*, Jeffrey Huntsman, ed., xliii.

23. James Elphinston, *The Plan of Education at Mr. Elphinston's Academy, Kensington* (London: W. Owen, 1760), 2.

24. James Elphinston, *Plan of Education at Mr. Elphinston's Academy, Kensington*, 10.

25. Further biographical information can be found in Alexander Du Toit, "Tytler, Alexander Fraser, Lord Woodhouselee (1747–1813)," in *Oxford Dictionary of National Biography*, Oxford University Press, 2004, http://www.oxforddnb.com/view/article/27965 (accessed November 22, 2014).

26. Bassnett, *Translation*, 16.

27. Tytler, *Essay on the Principles of Translation*, 2. Huntsman makes a valid criticism of Tytler that is worth remembering: "Of works containing statements of importance for translation theory, Tytler remarks on only a few—for example, d'Alembert's comments in *Mélanges de literature*, Batteux's in the *Principles de la literature* (although he does not mention the English translation of the section on translation published in Edinburgh in 1760), Huet's *De Interpretatione* (1683), and, in the second and third editions, Campbell's "Dissertations" from the *Four Gospels* (1789). . . . But of the French theorists like Du Bellay and Dolet, and of English writers like Cowley, Creech, Golding, Humphrey, Mickle and Vicars, there is little or no mention." In Tytler, *Essay on the Principles of Translation*, Jeffrey Huntsman, ed., xxxiv.

28. Tytler, *Essay on the Principles of Translation*, 3.

29. I will not focus rigorously on Tytler's specific commentary on particular translations, though these might be of interest to scholars researching the eighteenth-century reception of particular texts. The translators Tytler discusses include: d'Alembert, Anguillara, Batteux, Bourne, Brown, Campbell, Castalio, Congreve, Cotton, Cowley, Cumberland, Delille, Dryden, Echard, Fanshawe, Hobbes, Huet, Hughes, Jarvis, Jortin, Lowth, Markham, May, Melmoth, Motteux, the Duke de Nivernois, Pitcairne, Pope, Rowe, Sandys, Smollett, Sterne, and Webb.

30. In Tytler, *Essay on the Principles of Translation*, Jeffrey Huntsman, ed., xxxvi.

31. In Tytler, *Essay on the Principles of Translation*, Jeffrey Huntsman, ed., xliii.

32. In Tytler, *Essay on the Principles of Translation*, Jeffrey Huntsman, ed., xii–xxx, xxii.

33. See Burwick, "Romantic Theories of Translation," 68; Tytler, *Essay on the Principles of Translation*, 14.

34. Tytler, *Essay on the Principles of Translation*, 66.

35. Tytler, *Essay on the Principles of Translation*, 54.

36. Tytler, *Essay on the Principles of Translation*, 201.

37. For recent readings of Dryden as a translator, see Judith Sloman, *Dryden: The Poetics of Translation* (Toronto: University of Toronto Press, 1985); David Hopkins, *John Dryden* (Cambridge: Cambridge University Press, 1986); and Paul Hammon, *John Dryden and the Traces of Classical Rome* (Oxford: Oxford University Press, 2000).

38. Tytler, *Essay on the Principles of Translation*, 79.

39. Tytler, *Essay on the Principles of Translation*, 80.

40. Tytler, *Essay on the Principles of Translation*, 80.

41. Tytler, *Essay on the Principles of Translation*, 79.

42. Tytler, *Essay on the Principles of Translation*, 12.

43. Tytler, *Essay on the Principles of Translation*, 169, 182, 184.

44. At times, Tytler does indeed seem to invoke fixed notion of national rather than linguistic character. At one point, for example, he criticizes Voltaire's translation of Shakespeare's *Hamlet*, lamenting how "wonderfully has he metamorphosed" and yet "how miserably disfigured him." For Tytler, this ambivalent translation was engendered by "the original difference of his genius and that of Shakespeare, increased by the general opposition of the national character of the French and English." Tytler, *Essay on the Principles of Translation*, 375.

45. "[It] would be highly preposterous to depart, in any case, from the sense, for the sake of imitating the manner." Tytler, *Essay on the Principles of Translation*, 215.

46. Tytler, *Essay on the Principles of Translation*, 248.

47. Tytler, *Essay on the Principles of Translation*, 47.

48. Tytler, *Essay on the Principles of Translation*, 203, 24, 59.

49. Tytler, *Essay on the Principles of Translation*, 64, 200.

50. Tytler, *Essay on the Principles of Translation*, 248.

51. Tytler, *Essay on the Principles of Translation*, 1.

52. Tytler, *Essay on the Principles of Translation*, 4–5.

53. Tytler *Essay on the Principles of Translation*, 8.

54. Tytler, *Essay on the Principles of Translation*, 39.

55. Thomas De Quincey, "The English Language," *Blackwood's Edinburgh Magazine*, 45 (April 1839), 455–62.

56. Glissant, *Poetics of Relation*, 99.

57. It is worth pausing here to recall the primary discourse of anglophone linguistic history as it is exemplified in the work of Nathan Bailey, who writes, "The English Tongue, the present Speech of *Great Britain*, and the Subject Matter of this Dictionary, is a compound of ancient Languages, as *British*, (*Welch) Saxon*, *Danish*, *Norman* and *modern French*, *Latin*, and *Greek*. . . . By this Coalition of Languages, and by the daily Custom of Writers to introduce any emphatical and significant Words, that by Travels or Acquaintance with foreign Languages they find, has so enrich'd the *English* Tongue, that it is become the most copious in *Europe*; and I may (I believe) venture to say in the whole World: So that we scarce want a proper Word to express any Thing or Idea, without a Periphrasis, as the *French* &c. are frequently obliged to do, by Reason of the Scantiness of their *Copia verborum*." Nathan Bailey, *Universal Etymological English Dictionary*, ii.

58. Sir William Jones, "Essay on the Poetry of Eastern Nations," in *Poems, Consisting Chiefly of Translations from the Asiatick Languages* (Oxford: Clarendon, 1772), 199.

59. James Mulholland, *Sounding Imperial*, 126.

60. Saree Makdisi, *Making England Western*, 12.

61. Rangarajan, *Imperial Babel*, 109.

62. Jones's view of interlingual translation as the purposeful extraction of value is paradigmatic for the period. In his preface to *A Grammar of the Persian Language* (London: J. Richardson, 1775), Jones claims that scholars, "most of whom have confined their study to the minute researchers of verbal criticism" are "like men who discover a precious mine, but instead of searching for the rich ore, or for gems, amuse themselves with collecting smooth pebbles and pieces of crystal," iii.

63. The process I am describing here is clear in Jones's rhetoric. It is one of the reasons, for example, why he frets over the dearth of Asian books: "Another obvious reason for the neglect of the Persian language, is the great scarcity of books. . . . The greater part of them are preserved in the different museums and libraries of Europe, where they are shown more as objects of curiosity than as sources of information; and are admired, like the characters on a Chinese screen, more for their gay colours than for their meaning." In Jones, "Preface" to *Grammar of the Persian Language*, ii.

64. Even in this earlier period (1770s), a decade before he went to India to take up his role as a jurist, Jones is well aware that, outside of linguistic wealth, there are other important commodities that attend study of and translation from the Persian language. "By one of those revolutions, which no human prudence could have foreseen, the Persian language found its way into India; that rich and celebrated empire, which, by the flourishing state of our commerce, has been the source of incredible wealth to the merchants of Europe." In Jones, "Preface" to *Grammar of the Persian Language*, ix.

65. Jones, "Preface" to *Poems, Consisting Chiefly of Translations from the Asiatick Tongues*, vii.

66. William Julius Mickle, "Preface" to *The Lusiad; Or, The Discovery of India. An Epic Poem. Translated from the Original Portuguese of Luis de Camoëns* (Oxford: Jackson and Lister, 1776), cii.

67. Balachandra Rajan's globally contextualized reading of both Camões's poem and Mickle's translation from the perspective of "the Asian Reader" declares, "Mickle resoundingly associates commerce with possession, and that association persisted even though nineteenth-century free traders questioned the empire not on moral grounds but on the grounds of its viability as a business concern." In a brilliant passage, Rajan debates the merits of potential readings of the poem given the history of the European epic, the imperial aspirations of eighteenth-century Britain, and the position of the postcolonial reader: "For such a reader, the heavy commercial freight that the poem carries and the characterizing of every Asian country exclusively in terms of its wealth and vulnerability are too dominantly foregrounded for *The Lusiads* to be approached as a heroic poem that swerves in to the commercial. The reverse reading of Camões's poem as a commercial poem that swerves into the heroic remains possible, but the magnitude of the swerve cannot be made significant to those aware of the exploitative realities, the destructive cooperation of commerce with possession, that history wrote as a postscript to the poem's final cantos." In Balachandra Rajan, *Under Western Eyes: India from Milton to Macauley* (Durham, N.C.: Duke University Press, 1999), 48, 48–49. Here I read this poem for its commercial-possessive qualities without considering any swerve into the heroic.

68. Mickle writes regarding the form of the classical epic as it pertains to Camões's, "In contradistinction to the *Iliad* and the *Aeneid*, the *Paradise Lost* has been called the Epic Poem of Religion. In the same manner may the *Lusiad* be named the Epic Poem of Commerce." In Mickle,."Preface" to *The Lusiad*, i.

69. Mickle, "Preface" to *The Lusiad*, cv.

70. In a later passage, Mickle declares, "But if the fall of the Portuguese empire be an example peculiarly held up to the British, still more particularly does the history of Portuguese Asia demand the attention of that stupendous Common Wealth, the United East India Company." Mickle, "Preface" to *The Lusiad*, cv, ci.

71. Mickle, "Preface" to *The Lusiad*, xii–xiii.

72. Mickle, "Preface" to *The Lusiad*, xxv.

73. Commerce is the link between classical models of maritime colonialism and eighteenth-century models. This is why Mickle sees the Greek city-states of the Mediterranean in such influential terms. In the case of Don Henry, Mickle claims that "the wealth and power of ancient Tyre and Carthage shewed him what a maritime nation might hope; and the flourishing colonies of the Greeks were the frequent topic of his conversation." Mickle, "Preface" to *The Lusiad*, xiii.

74. Mickle, "Preface" to *The Lusiad*, x–xi.

75. Mickle's description of commerce in Britain suggests this reading: "He who passes from the trading towns and cultured fields of England, to those remote villages of Scotland or Ireland, which claim this description, is astonished at the comparative wretchedness of their destitute inhabitants; but few consider, that these villages only exhibit a view of what Europe was, ere the spirit of Commerce diffused the blessings which naturally flow from her improvements," in "Preface" to *The Lusiad*, xiv.

76. Mickle, "Preface" to *The Lusiad*, i–ii.

77. Mickle, "Preface" to *The Lusiad*, xv.

78. Jones, "Preface" to *Poems*, vi.

79. Mickle, "Preface" to *The Lusiad*, cii.

80. Mickle, "Preface" to *The Lusiad*, cii.

81. George Campbell, *The Four Gospels, Translated from the Greek. With Preliminary Dissertations and Notes Critical and Explanatory*, vol. 1 of 2 (London: A. Strahan and T. Cadell, 1789), 19.

82. Campbell, *Four Gospels*, 19.

83. Campbell, *Four Gospels*, 35.

84. Campbell tells the textual history of the Vulgate like this: "The people very soon and very generally discovered, that, along with all the simplicity they could desire, it was in every respect more intelligible, and, consequently, both more instructive and more agreeable than the old. The immediate effect of this general conviction was greatly to multiply the copies, which proved, in a very few centuries, the total extinction of the Italic, formerly called the Vulgate version, and the establishment of the present Vulgate, or Jerome's translation, in its room." In *Four Gospels*, 24.

85. Campbell, *Four Gospels*, 19.

86. Campbell's use of the term "barbarous" in a more confined and textual sense is idiosyncratic for the period: "Nay, if such a one had even denominated the idiom of the New Testament *barbarous*, I should not have thought it an unpardonable offence. The word sounds harshly; but we know that, form the mouth of native Greeks, it could only mean that the idiom of that book is not conformable to the rules of their grammarians and rhetoricians, and to the practice of their writers of reputation." In Campbell, *Four Gospels*, 54, 50.

87. Campbell, *Four Gospels*, 48.

88. Regarding the constancy of translation, Campbell writes, "His apostles and evangelists, on the contrary, who wrote in Greek, were, in writing, obliged to translate the instructions received from him into a foreign language of a very different structure, and for the use of people accustomed to a peculiar idiom." Campbell, *Four Gospels*, 57, 48.

89. Campbell, *Four Gospels*, 48.

90. Campbell, *Four Gospels*, 50.

91. Campbell, *Four Gospels*, 50.

92. Campbell, *Four Gospels*, 58.

93. The conclusion I have drawn here that Campbell's translation is controlled by a certain set of anglophone cultural practices is contrary to what Campbell himself says. His claim, advanced in commercial rhetoric, is that "the translator's business is to convey them [the author's thoughts] unadulterated, in the words of another language. To blend them with his own sentiments, or with any sentiments which are not the author's is to discharge the humble office of translator unfaithfully." My sense of this statement, however, in light of the rest of the dissertations, translation, and notes, is that Campbell simply sees himself in agreement with the religious and political sentiments of the original author (in this case the "Holy Spirit"), and so he carries out his business effectively—indeed, in a translational situation like Campbell's, he can carry out his business *only* effectively because to introduce "originality" into the text would amount to religious heterodoxy. Though he expends great effort pointing out that scriptural translation can be hampered by the fact that one learns the lessons of religion before examining or translating the texts themselves, he does not (and perhaps cannot) adequately address how his own religious axioms inform his translation practice. Campbell, *Four Gospels*, 19.

94. Campbell gestures to these other commodities in many ways. At one point, he reports, "For the readings here adopted, I have been chiefly indebted to the valuable folio edition of the Greek New Testament published by Mill, and that published by Wetstein, but without blindly following the opinion of either. In the judgments formed by these editors with respect to the true reading, they appear to be in extremes: the former often acquiesces in too little evidence, the latter requires too much." A bit later, he cites more commodities: "For the ancient versions, where it appeared proper, I have had recourse to Walton's Polyglot; of some, as the Syriac, the Gothic, or as it is now with greater probability accounted, the Frankish, the Anglo-Saxon, the modern Greek, and the Vulgate, I have copies, as well as of all the modern translations quoted in this work." In *Four Gospels*, 21.

95. Campbell, *Four Gospels*, 22.

96. Campbell, *Four Gospels*, 77.

97. Campbell, *Four Gospels*, 92.

98. Campbell, *Four Gospels*, 255.

99. Campbell, *Four Gospels*, 340.

100. Campbell, *Four Gospels*, 141–42.

Multilingual Lives: Sequoyah

1. Samuel Knapp, *Lectures on American Literature, with Remarks on Some Passages of American History* (New York: Elam Bliss, 1829), 25.

2. Knapp, *Lectures on American Literature*, 25.

3. Knapp, *Lectures on American Literature*, 25, 22.

4. Knapp, *Lectures on American Literature*, 26.

5. Knapp, *Lectures on American Literature*, 26.

6. Sean Harvey captures this dynamic brilliantly in *Native Tongues.* The lines I have borrowed above are part of a much richer account of language difference in early America that dovetails with my own in its conclusion that, across this period, cultural and racial difference in society was something that, most immediately, was heard. Harvey writes, "While Sequoyah had intended the syllabary to promote Cherokee's improvement and autonomy, the syllabary offered an alternative to missionaries struggling to write down native languages, one that would aid the work of conversion immediately and could provide an intermediate step toward eventual English literacy and social assimilation. At the same time, amid increasing calls in Georgia and other states to remove the large southern nations, white-educated Cherokees held up the extraordinary invention as proof of Cherokee civilization, in the hopes of swaying public opinion against removal, while downplaying its obvious rejection of English literacy and its implications for preserving Native sovereignty. Different parties used the syllabary for competing ends, and different scholars and officials found the syllabary to represent divergent things: proof of independent 'civilization' or its impossibility without white influence. While many recoiled from the syllabary's demonstration that assimilation would not necessarily follow 'civilization,' missionaries to other Native people considered non-alphabetic writing systems perhaps more suited to Native languages and speakers. U.S. expansion, moreover, introduced Americans to languages seemingly unlike those they had previously encountered. Futile efforts to pronounce sounds and contain them within English alphabetical values fueled speculation about the difference of Native characters and bodies, deepening an expansive view of race as something that could be heard as well as seen." Harvey, *Native Tongues*, 115.

7. Knapp, *Lectures on American Literature*, 26. Harvey helps contextualize the question of whether writing was an invention or a divine gift, writing, "Nativist traditions circulating among northern, southern, and western nations around this time articulated the belief that writing marked eternal cultural difference between Indians and whites. Literacy was unsuited to Indians, in this view, because the Great Spirit had not given it to them. In marked contrast, contemporary Cherokee legends . . . illustrate both the propriety of Native literacy and white perfidy. The creator had originally given Indians the book, but the white man stole it. Sequoyah, who had invented the syllabary so his people could benefit from writing without submitting to the danger of missionaries' indoctrination or manipulation, could have been seen to reclaim writing for Cherokees." Harvey, *Native Tongues*, 115.

8. See Henry Louis Gates, *The Signifying Monkey: A Theory of African-American Literary Criticism*, 25th anniversary ed. (Oxford: Oxford University Press, 2014; 1988).

9. Claude Lévi-Strauss, *Tristes Tropiques* (New York: Atheneum, 1984), 299.

10. Knapp, *Lectures on American Literature*, 26.

11. In keeping with his general sense that it is the copiousness of a language that occasions the expansion of ideas, Knapp flatters Sequoyah's work while also flattering anglophony far further, noting that Sequoyah's invention of writing is made all the more spectacular given that "the very name of which [*speaking by letters*], of course, was not to be found in his language. Knapp, *Lectures on American Literature*, 26.

12. Knapp, *Lectures on American Literature*, 26.

13. Knapp, *Lectures on American Literature*, 27.

14. Knapp, *Lectures on American Literature*, 26.

15. Knapp, *Lectures on American Literature*, 27.

16. Knapp, *Lectures on American Literature*, 27.

17. Cadmus, the founder of Thebes, is a Phoenician prince traditionally credited with introducing Phoenician letters to the Greeks, who then adapted them in order to transform their language into a literate one. Knapp, *Lectures on American Literature*, 28–29.

18. Knapp, *Lectures on American Literature*, 29.

19. Cecrops is a legendary, prehistorical king of Athens who is credited with transmitting reading and writing to the Athenians. Knapp, *Lectures on American Literature*, 29.

20. Glissant, *Poetics of Relation*, 120.

Conclusion

1. For more on the variety, vitality, and cultural significance of eighteenth-century "it-narratives," especially insofar as they relate to the force of commerce in the period, see Mark Blackwell's excellent edited collection, *The Secret Life of Things: Animals, Objects, and It-Narratives in Eighteenth-Century England* (Lewisburg, Pa.: Bucknell University Press, 2007).

2. Samuel Ward Francis, *An Autobiography of a Latin Reader by Samuel Syntax, Esq.* (New York: Anson D. F. Randolph, 1859), 8.

3. Samuel Ward Francis, *Autobiography of a Latin Reader*, 8.

4. Samuel Ward Francis, *Autobiography of a Latin Reader*, 10.

5. Samuel Ward Francis, *Autobiography of a Latin Reader*, 11.

6. Samuel Ward Francis, *Autobiography of a Latin Reader*, 17.

7. Samuel Ward Francis, *Autobiography of a Latin Reader*, 33.

8. Samuel Ward Francis, *Autobiography of a Latin Reader*, 48.

9. Samuel Ward Francis, *Autobiography of a Latin Reader*, 46.

10. Spivak, *Aesthetic Education in the Era of Globalization*, 11.

11. As Ashley Cohen etymologizes, "A 'crisis' is a narratological event. From the Geek *krisis*, or decision, the earliest English use of the term refers to a specific moment of decision: the point when an illness turns, decisively, toward either recovery or death. This definition's implicit connection to diagnosis is drawn out further in the Greek *krinein*, from which *krisis* is derived. To decide, to judge, to separate, to sieve, to distinguish, and to sort, *krinein* and its proto-Indo-European root *krei* are also the source of "critique," as Heidegger, Nietzsche, and Derrida have all reminded us. This etymology imbues 'crisis' with a meaning very different from its seeming cognates 'disaster,' 'catastrophe,' 'calamity,' and so on. A crisis is not a fitting appellation for just any period of political or economic tumult; rather, it refers to an event or series of events whose effect is to sift out insight from the blindness of chaos. A crisis produces new clarity of vision." Ashley Cohen, "Imperial Crisis and Geographics of Corruption in Samuel Foote's *The Cozeners*," lecture, American Society for Eighteenth-Century Studies Annual Conference, Pittsburgh, March 31, 2016.

12. The texts I have consulted while writing this conclusion include, but are not limited to: Alastair Pennycook, *The Cultural Politics of English as an International Language* (New York: Longman, 1994); David Crystal, *English as a Global Language* (Cambridge: Cambridge University Press, 1997); David Graddol, *The Future of English* (London: British Council, 1997); David Crystal, *English as a Global Language*, 2nd ed. (Cambridge: Cambridge University Press, 2003); David

Crystal, *The Language Revolution* (Cambridge: Polity, 2004); Alastair Pennycook, *Global Englishes and Transcultural Flows* (London: Routledge, 2007); Barbara Birch, *The English Language Teacher in Global Civil Society* (London: Routledge, 2009); Robert McCrum, *Globish: How the English Language Became the World's Language* (New York: W. W. Norton, 2010); Philip Seargeant, *Exploring World Englishes: Language in a Global Context* (London: Routledge, 2012); Scott Montgomery, *Does Science Need a Global Language: English and the Future of Research* (Chicago: University of Chicago Press, 2013); and David Northrup, *How English Became the Global Language* (New York: Palgrave Macmillan, 2013).

13. Philip Seargeant's nuanced description of the problems of linguistic globalization still begins with the sublime axiom "Today, English is in an unprecedented linguistic position in that it is more widely used, and in more domains, than any other language across the globe. And this pervasiveness—and the diversity that accompanies it—is forcing a recalibration of basic notions of the relationship of language to everyday lived experience." In *Exploring World Englishes*, 2–3.

14. I borrow this phrase and the itinerant theories regarding futurology from Daniel Rosenberg and Susan Harding's *Histories of the Future* (Durham, N.C.: Duke University Press, 2005), a remarkable collection that interrogates the contemporary proliferation of "representations of the future" as well as the rapid supersession of these representations.

15. This is not to say that "English" departments are not dealing with urgent issues. As a teacher of these subjects, I believe that we are. However, I mean to suggest only that the public does not necessarily see the project of anglophone literary and cultural history, analysis, and critique with the same urgency as the project of documenting and interrogating anglophony's centrality to globalization.

16. Scott Montgomery describes the importance of Standard English to scientific exchange in sublime terms: "By the late 2000s, nearly all forms of written output, whether in print or online, whether in person or in video, whether in professional or informal settings, had already come to depend on this one tongue when the intended audience is the larger world community of researchers in any field." In *Does Science Need a Global Language*, 3.

17. David Northrup, *How English Became the Global Language*, 6.

18. David Northrup, *How English Became the Global Language*, 7.

19. David Northrup, *How English Became the Global Language*, 7.

20. David Northrup, *How English Became the Global Language*, 158.

21. David Northrup, *How English Became the Global Language*, 4; Scott Montgomery, *Does Science Need a Global Language*, 8; Robert McCrum, *Globish: How the English Language Became the World's Language*, 276.

22. Spivak theorizes that an aesthetic education in the global present should focus on deep language learning, qualitative social sciences, and unconditional ethics. However, as she notes, "Deep language learning and unconditional ethics are so out of joint with this immensely powerful brave new world-machine that people of our sort make this plea because we cannot do otherwise, because our shared obsession declares that some hope of bringing about the epistemological revolution needed to turn capital around to gendered social justice must still be kept alive against all hope." In *Aesthetic Education in the Era of Globalization*, 26.

23. James F. English, *The Global Future of English Studies* (Malden, Mass.: Wiley-Blackwell, 2012), 8.

24. James F. English, *Global Future of English Studies*, 6–7.

25. Articulating a binary that is closely related to "humanities crisis" and "global anglophone expansion," Spivak reads the "global" in contemporary education in a highly critical but perhaps

accurate light: "The increasingly corporatized and ambitious globalist university in the United States supervised the minimalization of the humanities and the social sciences—in order to achieve the maximum of some version of globalization." In *Aesthetic Education in the Era of Globalization*, 2.

26. Glissant, *Poetics of Relation*, 104.

27. James F. English, *Global Future of English Studies*, 190.

28. James F. English, *Global Future of English Studies*, 190.

29. James F. English, *Global Future of English Studies*, 190.

30. James F. English, *Global Future of English Studies*, 190.

31. James F. English, *Global Future of English Studies*, 191.

32. James F. English, *Global Future of English Studies*, 191.

33. James F. English, *Global Future of English Studies*, 191.

34. James F. English, *Global Future of English Studies*, 191.

35. Stephen Montgomery, *Does Science Need a Global Language*, 8.

36. Spivak, *Aesthetic Education in the Era of Globalization*, 28.

37. Spivak, *Aesthetic Education in the Era of Globalization*, 11.

38. Spivak, *Aesthetic Education in the Era of Globalization*, 27.

39. As Spivak notes, "We must also find something relating to 'our own history' to counteract the fact that the Enlightenment came, to colonizer and colonized alike, through colonialism, to support a destructive 'free trade,' and that top-down police breaches of Enlightenment principles are more rule than exception." In *Aesthetic Education in the Era of Globalization*, 4.

40. Rangarajan, *Imperial Babel*, viii.

41. Glissant, *Poetics of Relation*, 120.

42. Here I am again invoking Dipesh Chakrabarty's *Provincializing Europe* and Simon Gikandi's essay "Provincializing English."

43. Glissant, *Poetics of Relation*, 19; Spivak, *Aesthetic Education in the Era of Globalization*, 26.

WORKS CITED

Aarsleff, Hans. *From Locke to Saussure: Essays on the Study of Language and Intellectual History.* Minneapolis: University of Minnesota Press, 1982.

———. *The Study of Language in England, 1780–1860.* Princeton, N.J.: Princeton University Press, 1967. Abbot, W. W., ed. *The Papers of George Washington.* Retirement Series. Vol. 4, *20 April 1799–13 December 1799.* Charlottesville: University Press of Virginia, 1999.

Abbot, W. W., and Dorothy Twohig, eds. *The Papers of George Washington.* Colonial Series. Vol. 7, *1 January 1761–15 June 1767.* Charlottesville: University Press of Virginia, 1990. Adam, Alexander. *The Rudiments of Latin and English Grammar.* 3rd ed. Edinburgh: W. Gordon et al., 1786.

Adam, Alexander. *The Rudiments of Latin and English Grammar.* 3rd ed. Edinburgh: W. Gordon, 1786.

Adams, David Wallace. *Education for Extinction: American Indians and the Boaarding School Experience, 1875–1928.* Lawrence: University of Kansas Press, 1995.

Adams, James. *The Pronunciation of the English Language Vindicated from Imputed Anomaly and Caprice.* Edinburgh: J. Moir, 1799.

Addison, Joseph. *Spectator*, no. 405 (Saturday, June 14, 1712).

Agostini, Thomas. "'Deserted His Majesty's Service': Military Runaways, the British-American Press, and the Problem of Desertion During the Seven Years' War." *Journal of Social History*, 40, no. 4 (Summer 2007): 957–85.

Ahmad, Dohra. *Rotten English: A Literary Anthology.* New York: W. W. Norton, 2007.

Aickin, Joseph. *The English Grammar; Or, the English Tongue Reduced to Grammatical Rules.* London: MB, 1693.

Alexander, Elizabeth. "Praise Song for the Day: A Poem for Barack Obama's Presidential Inauguration." Recited in Washington, D.C., January 20, 2013.

Aloni, Antonio. "Elegy: Forms, Functions, and Communication." In *The Cambridge Companion to Greek Lyric.* Felix Budelmann, ed., 168–88. Cambridge: Cambridge University Press, 2009.

Ames, Henry. *A New Translation of Horace's Art of Poetry, Attempted in Rhyme.* London: W. Pepper, 1727.

Anderson, Benedict. *A Life Beyond Boundaries: A Memoir.* London: Verso, 2016.

———. *Imagined Communities.* 1983. London: Verso, 1991.

Anzaldúa, Gloria. *Borderlands* / La Frontera: *The New Mestiza.* San Francisco: Spinsters/Aunt Lute, 1987.

Aravamudan, Srinivas. *Enlightenment Orientalism: Resisting the Rise of the Novel.* Chicago: University of Chicago Press, 2012.

———. *Tropicopolitans: Colonialism and Agency, 1688–1804.* Durham, N.C.: Duke University Press, 2006.

Armitage, David. *The Ideological Origins of the British Empire.* Cambridge: Cambridge University Press, 2000.

Bailey, Nathan. *Universal Etymological Dictionary.* London: E. Bell et al., 1721.

Bakhtin, Mikhael. *The Dialogic Imagination: Four Essays by M.M. Bakhtin.* Michael Holquist, ed. Caryl Emerson and Michael Holquist, trans. Austin: University of Texas Press, 1981.

Ballaster, Ros, ed. *Fables of the East: Selected Tales, 1662–1785.* Oxford: Oxford University Press, 2005.

Barrell, John. *English Literature in History 1730–80: An Equal, Wide, Survey.* London: Hutchinson, 1983.

Barrington, Daines. "*Mr.* Barrington *on some additional Information relative to the Continuance of the* Cornish *Language. In a Letter to* John Lloyd, *Esq. F.A.S.*" In *Archaeologia: Or Miscellaneous Tracts Relating to Antiquity.* Vol. 5. London: J. Nichols, 1779.

———. "*On the Expiration of the Cornish Language. In a Letter from the Hon.* Daines Barrington, *Vice Pres. S.A. to* John Lloyd, *Esquire, F.S.A.* Read at the Society of Antiquaries, May 6, 1773." In *Archaeologia: Or Miscellaneous Tracts Relating to Antiquity* In *Archaeologia: Or Miscellaneous Tracts Relating to Antiquity.* Vol. 3. London: J. Nichols, 1776.

Bassnett, Susan. *Translation.* New York: Routledge, 2014.

Baucom, Ian. *Specters of the Atlantic: Finance Capital, Slavery, and the Philosophy of History.* Durham, N.C.: Duke University Press, 2005.

Bayly, Anselm. *An Introduction to Languages Literary and Philosophical; Especially to the English, Latin, Greek and Hebrew.* London: James Rivington et al., 1758.

———. *A Plain and Complete Grammar of the English Language.* London: G. Bigg, 1772.

Behrendt, Stephen, and Eric Graham. "African Merchants, Notables and the Slave Trade at Old Calabar, 1720: Evidence from the National Archives of Scotland." *History in Africa,* 30 (2003): 37–61.

Behrendt, Stephen, A. J. H. Latham, and David Northrup, eds. *The Diary of Antera Duke, an Eighteenth-Century African Slave Trader.* Oxford: Oxford University Press, 2010.

Bewley, Christina, and David Bewley. *Gentleman Radical: A Life of John Horne Tooke.* London: Tauris Academic Studies, 1998.

Birch, Barbara. *The English Language Teacher in Global Civil Society.* London: Routledge, 2009.

Blackwell, Mark, ed. *The Secret Life of Things: Animals, Objects, and It-Narratives in Eighteenth-Century England.* Lewisburg, Pa.: Bucknell University Press, 2007.

Blair, Hugh. *Lectures on Rhetoric and Belles Lettres.* Vol. 1. Dublin: Whitestone et al., 1783.

Bonfiglio, Thomas Paul. *Mother Tongues and Nations: The Invention of the Native Speaker.* Berlin: De Gruyter Mouton, 2010.

Borlase, William. *The Natural History of Cornwall.* Oxford: W. Jackson, 1758.

Boscawen, William. *The Satires, Epistles, and Art of Poetry of Horace, Translated into English Verse.* London: John Stockdale, 1797.

Bottrell, William. *Traditions and Hearthside Stories of West Cornwall.* Penzance: W. Cornish, 1870.

Brice, Andrew. *An Exmoor Scolding; In the Propriety and Decency of Exmoor Language, Between Two Sisters, Wilmot Moreman and Thomasin Moreman, As they were spinning.* 3rd ed. Exeter: Andrew and Sarah Brice, 1746.

———. *An Exmoor Scolding, Between Two Sisters, Wilmot and Thomasin Moreman, As they were Spinning; Also An Exmoor Courtship; Both in the Propriety and Decency of the Exmoor Dialect, To which is Adjoined a Collateral Paraphrase in Plain English, For explaining barbarous Words *and Phrases*. South Molton: J. Huxtable, 1794. (See Appendix A for a comprehensive accounting of eighteenth-century editions of these texts.)

Brightland, John. *A Grammar of the English Tongue*. 8th ed. London: James Rivington and James Fletcher, 1759.

Brown, Charles Brockden. *Wieland; or, The Transformation: An American Tale*. New York: Penguin Classics, 1991.

Buck-Morss, Susan. *Hegel, Haiti, and Universal History*. Pittsburgh: University of Pittsburgh Press, 2009.

Burke, Peter. *Languages and Communities in Early Modern Europe*. Cambridge: Cambridge University Press, 2004.

Burns, Robert. *Poems, Chiefly in the Scottish Dialect*. Kilmarnock: John Wilson, 1786.

———. *Poems, Chiefly in the Scottish Dialect*. Edinburgh: William Creech, 1787.

———. *Poems, Chiefly in the Scottish Dialect*. London: A Strahan; T. Cadell, 1787.

Burwick, Frederick. "Romantic Theories of Translation." *Wordsworth Circle*, 39, no. 3 (Summer 2008): 68–74.

Camden, William. *Remaines, concerning Britaine: but especially England, and the Inhabitants thereof*. 1605. London: John Legatt, 1614.

Campbell, George. *The Four Gospels, Translated from the Greek. With Preliminary Dissertations and Notes Critical and Explanatory*. 2 vols. London: A. Strahan and T. Cadell, 1789.

———. *Philosophy of Rhetoric*. London: W. Strahan and T. Cadell, 1776.

Carretta, Vincent. *Phillis Wheatley: Biography of a Genius in Bondage*. Athens: University of Georgia Press, 2011.

Carew, Richard. *Survey of Cornwall*. London: T. Bensley, 1811; 1602.

Carey, Brycchan. *British Abolitionism and the Rhetoric of Sensibility, 1760–1807*. New York: Palgrave Macmillan, 2005.

Chakrabarty, Dipesh. *Provincializing Europe*. 2000. Princeton, N.J.: Princeton University Press, 2008.

Ch'ien, Evelyn Nien-Ming. *Weird English*. Cambridge, Mass.: Harvard University Press, 2004.

Clubbe, William. *The epistle of Horace to the Pisos, on the art of poetry. Translated into English verse. By William Clubbe, L. L. B. Vicar of Brandeston, Suffolk*. Ipswich: George Jermyn, 1797.

Cohen, Ashley. "Imperial Crisis and Geographics of Corruption in Samuel Foote's *The Cozeners*." Lecture at American Society for Eighteenth-Century Studies Annual Conference, Pittsburgh, March 31, 2016.

Cohen, Murray. *Sensible Words: Linguistic Practice in England, 1640–1785*. Baltimore: Johns Hopkins University Press, 1977.

Cole, Andrew. *The Birth of Theory*. Chicago: University of Chicago Press, 2014.

Coleman, Julie. *A History of Cant and Slang Dictionaries*. Vol. 1, *1567–1784*. Oxford: Oxford University Press, 2004.

Collier, John. *Tim Bobbin's Lancashire Dialect; and Poems*. London: Hurst, Chance, 1828.

———. *A View of the Lancashire Dialect by Way of Dialogue*. Manchester: R. Whitworth, 1746. (See Appendix A for a comprehensive accounting of eighteenth-century editions of this text.)

Craton, Michael. *Searching for the Invisible Man: Slaves and Plantation Life in Jamaica*. Cambridge, Mass.: Harvard University Press, 1978.

Crawford, Robert. *Devolving English Literature*. Oxford: Oxford University Press, 1992.

Crowley, Tony. *Standard English and the Politics of Language*. 2nd ed. New York: Palgrave Macmillan, 2003.

Crystal, David. *Begat: The King James Bible and the English Language*. Oxford: Oxford University Press, 2010.

———. *English as a Global Language*. Cambridge: Cambridge University Press, 1997.

———. *English as a Global Language*. 2nd ed. Cambridge: Cambridge University Press, 2003.

———. *The Language Revolution*. Cambridge: Polity, 2004.

Daiches, David. *The King James Version of the English Bible: An Account of the Development and Sources of the English Bible of 1611 with Special Reference to the Hebrew Tradition*. Chicago: University of Chicago Press, 1941.

Defoe, Daniel. *A Tour Through the Whole Island of Great Britain*. Vol. 3 of 4. 4th ed. London: S. Birt, et al., 1748.

———. *The True-Born Englishman: A Satyr*. London, 1700.

———. *The Works of Daniel Defoe*. Vol. 3, William Hazlitt, ed. London: John Clements, 1843.

Deleuze, Gilles, and Félix Guattari. *Milles Plateaux*. Paris: Éditions de Minuit, 1980.

Denham, John. "To Mr. Richard Fanshaw, Esq; upon his Ingeneous Translation of *Pastor-Fido* into English." In *Coopers Hill A Poeme. The Second Edition with Additions*, 21–22. London: Humphrey Moseley, 1650.

De Quincey, Thomas. "The English Language." *Blackwood's Edinburgh Magazine*, 45 (April 1839).

Derrida, Jacques. *The Monolingualism of the Other; or, The Prosthesis of Origin*. 1996. Patrick Mensah, trans. Stanford, Calif.: Stanford University Press, 1998.

DeWispelare, Daniel. "An Amateur's Professional Devotion: Elizabeth Smith's Translation of the Book of Job." *Literature and Theology*, 25, no. 2 (May 2011): 141–56.

———. "Dissidence in Dialect: Ann Wheeler's Westmorland Dialogues." *Studies in Romanticism*, 54, no. 1 (Spring 2015): 101–26.

Dillon, Wentworth, Earl of Roscommon. *Horace's Art of poetry made English by the Right Honourable the Earl of Roscommon*. London: Henry Herringman, 1680.

Drant, Thomas. *Horace his arte of Poetrie, pistles, and Satyrs, Englished and to the Earle of Ormounte by Tho. Drant, addressed, 1567*. London: Thomas Marshe, 1567.

Dunster, Samuel. *Horace's Satires, Epistles, and Art of Poetry, Done into English, with Notes*. London: T.W. for W. Mears, F. Clay, and D. Browne, 1729.

Du Toit, Alexander. "Tytler, Alexander Fraser, Lord Woodhouselee (1747–1813)." *Oxford Dictionary of National Biography*. Oxford: Oxford University Press, 2004. http://www.oxforddnb.com/view/article/27965.

Eco, Umberto. *The Search for the Perfect Language*. James Fentress, trans. Oxford: Blackwell, 1995.

Edgeworth, Maria. *Castle Rackrent, An Hibernian Tale*. London: J. Crowder, 1800.

Edgeworth, Maria, and Richard Lovell Edgeworth. *Essay on Irish Bulls*. 1802. 2nd ed. London: J. Johnson, 1803.

———. *Practical Education*. 2 vols. London: J. Johnson, 1798.

Elfenbein, Andrew. *Romanticism and the Rise of English*. Stanford, Calif.: Stanford University Press, 2009.

Elphinston, James. *The Plan of Education at Mr. Elphinston's Academy, Kensington*. London: W. Owen, 1760.

———. *Propriety Ascertained in her Picture, Or, Inglish Speech and Spelling Rendered Mutual Guides*. London: W. Richardson, 1786.

Emerson, Ralph Waldo. *The Complete Works of Ralph Waldo Emerson*. Vol. 11, *Miscellanies*. Boston: Houghton Mifflin: 1904.

Emin, Joseph. *The Life and Adventures of Joseph Émïn, An Armenian. Written in English by Himself*. London, 1792.

English, James F. *The Economy of Prestige: Prizes, Awards, and the Circulation of Cultural Value*. Cambridge, Mass.: Harvard University Press, 2008.

———. *The Global Future of English Studies*. Malden, Mass.: Wiley-Blackwell, 2012.

Englund, Axel, and Anders Olsson, eds. *Languages of Exile: Migration and Multilingualism in Twentieth-Century Literature*. Bern: Peter Lang, 2013.

Erasmus, Desiderius. *Copia: Foundations of the Abundant Style*. Betty Knott, trans. Vol. 24 of *Collected Works of Erasmus*. Toronto: University of Toronto Press, 1978.

Fairclough, H. Rushton. *Horace: Satires. Epistles. The Art of Poetry*. Cambridge, Mass.: Harvard University Library, 1926.

Fanon, Frantz. *Peau noire masques blancs*. Paris: Seuil, 1952.

Fayer, Joan. "Pidgins as Written Languages: Evidence from 18th Century Old Calabar." *Anthropological Linguistics*, 28, no. 3 (Fall 1986): 313–19.

Felsenstein, Frank, and Sharon Liberman Mintz, curators. *The Jew as Other: A Century of English Caricature 1730–1830: An Exhibition, April 6–July 31, 1995*. New York: Library of the Jewish Theological Seminary of America, 1995.

Felski, Rita. "Context Stinks." *New Literary History*, 42 (2011): 573–91.

Ferry, David. *The Epistles of Horace: Bilingual Edition*. New York: Farrar, Straus, and Giroux, 2002.

Fisher, Michael. *Counterflows to Colonialism: Indian Travellers and Settlers in Britain, 1600–1857*. Delhi: Permanent Black, 2006.

Fitzpatrick, John C., ed. *The Writings of George Washington from the Original Manuscript Sources, 1745–1799*. Vol. 27. Washington, D.C.: U.S. Government Printing Office, 1931–43.

Forde, Daryll. *Efik Traders of Old Calabar, Containing the Diary of Antera Duke*. London: Dawsons of Pall Mall for the International African Institute, 1968.

Foucault, Michel. *The Order of Things*. New York: Random House, 1994; 1966.

Francis, Samuel Ward. *An Autobiography of a Latin Reader by Samuel Syntax, Esq*. New York: Anson D. F. Randolph, 1859.

Gallant, Mary. "Slave Runaways in Colonial Virginia: Accounts and Status Passage as Collective Process." *Symbolic Interaction*, 15, no. (Winter 1992): 389–412.

Gates, Henry Louis. *The Signifying Monkey: A Theory of African-American Literary Criticism*. 25th anniversary ed. Oxford: Oxford University Press, 2014; 1988.

Giganto, James. "Trading in Jersey Souls: New Jersey and the Interstate Slave Trade." *Pennsylvania History*, 77, no. 3 (Summer 2010): 281–302.

Gikandi, Simon. "The Fragility of Languages." *PMLA*, 130, no. 1 (January 2015): 9–14.

———. "From Penn Station to Trenton: The Language Train." *PMLA*, 128, no. 4 (October 2013): 865–71.

———. "Provincializing English." *PMLA*, 129, no. 1 (January 2014): 7–17.

———. *Slavery and the Culture of Taste*. Princeton, N.J.: Princeton University Press, 2011.

Gillespie, Stuart. *English Translation and Classical Reception*. Oxford: Wiley-Blackwell, 2011.

Gillespie, Stuart, and David Hopkins, eds. *The Oxford History of Literary Translation in English*. Vol. 3, *1660–1790*. Oxford: Oxford University Press, 2005.

Gilmartin, Elizabeth. "The Anglo-Irish Dialect: Mediating Linguistic Conflict." *Victorian Literature and Culture*, 32, no. 1 (2004): 1–16.

Glissant, Édouard. *Poetics of Relation*. 1990. Betsy Wing, trans. Ann Arbor: University of Michigan Press, 1997.

Goffman, Erving. *The Presentation of Self in Everyday Life*. New York: Anchor Books, 1959.

Goldsmith, Oliver. *The Works of Oliver Goldsmith*. J. W. M. Gibbs, ed. Vol. 3. London: George Bell, 1885.

Görlach, Manfred. *Eighteenth-Century English*. Heidelberg: Universitätsverlag Winter Heidelberg, 2001.

Gottlieb, Evan. *Romantic Globalism: British Literature and the Modern World Order, 1750–1830*. Columbus: Ohio State University Press, 2014.

Graddol, David. *The Future of English*. London: British Council, 1997.

Greene, Lorenzo. "The New England Negro as Seen in Advertisements for Runaway Slaves." *Journal of Negro History*, 29, no. 2 (April 1944), 126–46.

Greenwood, James. *An Essay towards a Practical Grammar*. 5th ed. London: J. Nourse, 1753.

———. *The London Vocabulary*. 3rd ed. London: A. Bettesworth, 1713.

Grose, Francis. *A Classical Dictionary of the Vulgar Tongue*. London: S. Hooper, 1788; 1785.

Grose, Francis. *A Provincial Glossary, with a Collection of Local Proverbs, and Popular Superstitions*. London: S. Hooper, 1787.

———. *A Glossary of Provincial and Local Words Used in England*. London: John Russell Smith, 1839.

Goulden, R. J. "Smith, John Russell (1810–1894)." *Oxford Dictionary of National Biography*. Oxford: Oxford University Press, 2004. http://www.oxforddnb.com/view/article/25864.

Hamilton, Elizabeth. *Translation of the Letter of a Hindoo Rajah*. Pamela Perkins and Shannon Russell, eds. Peterborough, Ontario: Broadview, 1999; 1796.

Hammon, Paul. *John Dryden and the Traces of Classical Rome*. Oxford: Oxford University Press, 2000.

Harris, James. *Hermes: A Philosophical Inquiry Concerning Language and Universal Grammar*. London: H. Woodfall, 1751.

Harvey, Sean. *Native Tongues: Colonialism and the Race from Encounter to the Reservation*. Cambridge, Mass.: Harvard University Press, 2015.

Haynes, Kenneth. *English Literature and Ancient Languages*. Oxford: Oxford University Press, 2003.

Heller-Roazen, Daniel. *Dark Tongues: The Art of Rogues and Riddlers*. New York: Zone Books, 2013.

Heylyn, Peter. *Cosmographie*. London: Henry Seile, 1652.

Hilton, J. A. " 'Tim Bobbin' and the Origins of Provincial Consciousness in Lancashire." *Journal of the Lancashire Dialect Society*, no. 19 (January 1970): 2–7.

Holloway, William. *A General Dictionary of Provincialisms, Written with a View to Rescue from Oblivion the Fast Fading Relics of By-gone Days*. Sussex: Baxter and Son, 1839.

Hopkins, David. *John Dryden*. Cambridge: Cambridge University Press, 1986.

Horace Of the Art of Poetry, In English Numbers. London: J. Roberts, 1735.

Horgan, D. M. "Popular Protest in the Eighteenth Century: John Collier (Tim Bobbin), 1708–1786." *Review of English Studies*, 48, no. 191 (1997): 310–31.

Howsam, Leslie. *Cheap Bibles: Nineteenth-Century Publishing and the British and Foreign Bible Society*. New York: Cambridge University Press, 1991.

Hsy, Jonathan. *Trading Tongues: Merchants, Multilingualism, and Medieval Literature*. Columbus: Ohio State University Press, 2013.

Hume. David. *Essays on Suicide, And The Immortality of the Soul*. London: M. Smith, 1783.

James, Marlon. *A Brief History of Seven Killings*. New York: Riverhead Books, 2014.

Jefferson, Thomas. *Notes on the State of Virginia*. 1785. London: John Stockdale, 1787.

Jennings, James. *Observations on Some of the Dialect in the West of England*. London: Baldwin, Cradock, and Joy, 1825.

Johnson, Charles, ed. *Specimens of the Yorkshire Dialect*. Knaresborough: Hargrove and Sons, 1808.

Johnson, Samuel. *A Dictionary of the English Language*. London: W. Strahan et al., 1755.

———. *Journey to the Western Islands of Scotland*. London: W. Strahan and T. Cadell, 1775.

Jones, Sir William. *A Grammar of the Persian Language*. London: J. Richardson, 1771.

———. *Poems, Consisting Chiefly of Translations from the Asiatick Languages*. Oxford: Clarendon, 1772.

———. *Poeseos Asiaticae Commentariorum Libri Sex*. London: T. Cadell, 1774.

———. *Works of Sir William Jones*. 13 vols. Lord Teignmouth, ed. London: John Stockdale, 1807.

Jonson, Ben. *Q. Horatius Flaccus: his Art of poetry. Englished by Ben: Jonson. With other workes of the author, never printed before*. London: I. Okes, 1640.

Keach, William. *Arbitrary Power: Romanticism, Language, and Politics*. Princeton, N.J.: Princeton University Press, 2004.

Kerrigan, John. *Archipelagic English: Literature, History, and Politics, 1603–1707*. Oxford: Oxford University Press, 2008.

Kidd, Colin. *British Identities Before Nationalism: Ethnicity and Nationhood in the Atlantic World, 1600–1800*. Cambridge: Cambridge University Press, 1999.

Koelle, S. W. *Polyglotta Africana; or, A Comparative Vocabulary of Nearly 300 Words and Phrases in More Than 100 Distinct African Tongues*. London: Church Missionary House, 1854.

Knapp, Samuel. *Lectures on American Literature, with Remarks on Some Passages of American History*. New York: Elam Bliss, 1829.

Kurth, Jan. "Wayward Wenches and Wives: Runaway Women in the Hudson Valley, NY, 1785–1830." *NWSA Journal*, 1, no. 2 (Winter 1988–89:).

Labov, William. *The Social Stratification of English in New York City*. 1966. 2nd ed. Cambridge: Cambridge University Press, 2006.

Lass, Robert, ed. *The Cambridge History of the English Language*. Vol. 3, *1476–1776*. Cambridge: Cambridge University Press, 1999.

Lennon, Brian. *In Babel's Shadow: Multilingual Literatures, Monolingual States*. Minneapolis: University of Minnesota Press, 2010.

Lévi-Strauss, Claude. *Tristes Tropiques*. New York: Atheneum, 1984.

Lhyud, Edward. *Archaeologia Britannica*. Vol. 1, *Glossography*. Oxford: Printed for the Author, 1707.

Liu, Lydia. *Translingual Practice: Literature, National Culture, and Translated Modernity, China 1900–1937*. Stanford, Calif.: Stanford University Press, 1995.

Löbel, Renatus Gotthelf, trans. *Grundsätze der Kunst zu Übersetzen, ein Versuch aus Dem Englischen*. Leipzig: Mengandsche Buchhandlung, 1793.

Locke, John. *An Essay Concerning Human Understanding*. Pauline Phemister, ed. Oxford: Oxford University Press, 2008.

Lowth, Robert. *De Sacra Poesi Hebraeorum Praelectiones Academicae Oxonii Habitae.* Oxford: Clarendon, 1775; 1753.

———. *Isaiah. A New Translation; With a Preliminary Dissertation, and Notes Critical, Philological, and Explanatory.* London: J. Nichols, 1778.

———. *Lectures on the Sacred Poetry of the Hebrews.* George Gregory, trans. London: J. Nichols, 1787.

———. *A Short Introduction to English Grammar.* London: J. Hughs, 1762.

Lynch, Deidre. *The Economy of Character: Novels, Market Culture, and the Business of Inner Meaning.* Chicago: University of Chicago Press, 1998.

Lynch, Jack, ed. "Preface to the *Dictionary.* From Samuel Johnson, *A Dictionary of the English Language* (London, 1755)." https://andromeda.rutgers.edu/~jlynch/Texts/preface.html.

———. *Samuel Johnson in Context.* Cambridge: Cambridge University Press, 2012.

Lyons, Rev. "Education in Ireland. Irish Society." London: Andrews, 1827.

MacKenzie, Henry. "The Surprising Effects of Original Genius, exemplified in the Poetical Productions of Robert Burns, an Ayrshire Ploughman." *European Magazine and London Review,* December 1786. Reprinted in the annual edition of *European Magazine and London Review*: London: J. Cornhill, 1786.

Makdisi, Saree. *Making England Western: Occidentalism, Race, and Imperial Culture.* Chicago: University of Chicago Press, 2014.

Marx, Karl, and Friedrich Engels. *The Communist Manifesto.* London: Verso, 1998.

Maxted, Ian. "Brice, Andrew (1692–1773)." *Oxford Dictionary of National Biography.* Oxford: Oxford University Press, 2004. http://www.oxforddnb.com/view/article/3379.

Maxted, Ian. "Exeter Working Papers in Book History." 2015. http://bookhistory.blogspot.co.uk.

Mason, Nicholas. *Literary Advertising and the Shaping of British Romanticism.* Baltimore: Johns Hopkins University Press, 2013.

McCalman, Iain, ed. *An Oxford Companion to the Romantic Age: British Culture 1776–1832.* Oxford: Oxford University Press, 1999.

McCrum, Robert. *Globish: How the English Language Became the World's Language.* New York: W. W. Norton, 2010.

McGrath, Alister. *In the Beginning.* New York: Doubleday, 2001.

McMurran, Mary Helen. *The Spread of Novels: Translation and Prose Fiction in the Eighteenth Century.* Princeton, N.J.: Princeton University Press, 2010.

Meaders, Daniel E. *Advertisements for Escaped Slaves in Virginia, 1801–1820.* New York: Garland, 1997.

———. *Dead or Alive: Fugitive Slaves and White Indentured Servants Before 1830.* New York: Garland, 1993.

———. "South Carolina Fugitives as Viewed Through Local Colonial Newspapers with Emphasis on Runaway Notices 1732–1801." *Journal of Negro History,* 60, no. 2 (April 1975): 288–319.

Mickle, William Julius. *The Lusiad; Or, The Discovery of India. An Epic Poem. Translated from the Original Portuguese of Luis de Camoëns.* Oxford: Jackson and Lister, 1776.

Miller, David Philip. "Barrington, Daines (1727/8–1800)." *Oxford Dictionary of National Biography.* Oxford: Oxford University Press, 2004. http://www.oxforddnb.com/view/article/1529

Monaghan, Jennifer. *Learning to Read and Write in Colonial America.* Amherst: University of Massachusetts Press, 2005.

Montgomery, Scott. *Does Science Need a Global Language: English and the Future of Research.* Chicago: University of Chicago Press, 2013.

More, Hannah. *Village Politics: Addressed to All the Mechanics, Journeymen, and Day Labourers in Great Britain*. London: C. Rivington, 1792.

Morgan, Gwenda, and Peter Rushton. "Visible Bodies: Subordination and Identity in the Eighteenth-Century Atlantic World." *Journal of Social History*, 39, no. 1 (Autumn 2005): 39–64.

Mugglestone, Lynda. *"Talking Proper": The Rise of Accent as Social Symbol*. Oxford: Oxford University Press, 2003.

Mulholland, James. *Sounding Imperial: Poetic Voice and the Politics of Empire, 1730–1820*. Baltimore: Johns Hopkins University Press, 2013.

Nardin, Jane. "Hannah More and the Problem of Poverty." *Texas Studies in Literature and Language*, 43, no. 3 (Fall 2001): 267–84.

Ngũgĩ wa Thiong'o. *Decolonising the Mind: The Politics of Language in African Literature*. London: J. Currey, 1986.

Northrup, David. *How English Became the Global Language*. New York: Palgrave Macmillan, 2013.

Nussbaum, Felicity, ed. *The Limits of the Human*. Cambridge: Cambridge University Press, 2003.

Owen, John. *The History of the Origin and the First Ten Years of the British and Foreign Bible Society*. New York: James Eastburn, 1817.

Pederson, Susan. "Hannah More Meets Simple Simon: Tracts, Chapbooks, and Popular Culture in Late Eighteenth-Century England." *Journal of British Studies*, 25, no. 1 (January 1986): 84–113.

Pegge, Samuel. *Anecdotes of the English Language: Chiefly Regarding the Local Dialect of London and Its Environs*. 1803. London: J. Nichols, 1814.

Pennycook, Alastair. *The Cultural Politics of English as an International Language*. New York: Longman, 1994.

———. *Global Englishes and Transcultural Flows*. London: Routledge, 2007.

Phillipson, Robert. *Linguistic Imperialism*. Oxford: Oxford University Press, 1992.

Pincus Steven. "Reconfiguring the British Empire." *William and Mary Quarterly*, 69, no. 1 (January 2012): 63–70.

———. "Rethinking Mercantilism: Political Economy, the British Empire, and the Atlantic World in the Seventeenth and Eighteenth Centuries." *William and Mary Quarterly*, 69, no. 1 (January 2012): 3–34.

Pool, P. A. S. *The Death of Cornish*. Penzance: Pool, 1975.

Pratt, Mary Louise. "Arts of the Contact Zone." *Profession* (1991): 33–40.

———. *Imperial Eyes: Travel Writing and Transculturation*. Abingdon: Routledge, 2008; 1992.

Priestley, Joseph. *The Rudiments of English Grammar*. 1761. 3rd ed. London: J. F. Rivington, 1772.

Prude, Jonathan. "To Look upon the 'Lower Sort': Runaway Ads and the Appearance of Unfree Laborers in America, 1750–1800." *Journal of American History*, 78, no. 1 (June 1991): 124–59.

Ragussis, Michael. *Theatrical Nation: Jews and Other Outlandish Englishmen in Georgian Britain*. Philadelphia: University of Pennsylvania Press, 2010.

Rajan, Balachandra. *Under Western Eyes: India from Milton to Macauley*. Durham, N.C.: Duke University Press, 1999.

Rancière, Jacques. *Aisthesis: Scenes from the Aesthetic Regime of Art*. Zakir Paul, trans. London: Verso, 2013.

———. *Dissensus: On Politics and Aesthetics*. Steven Corocoran, ed. and trans. London: Continuum Books, 2010.

Rangarajan, Padma. *Imperial Babel: Translation, Exoticism, and the Long Nineteenth Century*. New York: Fordham University Press, 2014.

Reyhner, Allan, and Jeanne Oyawin Eder. *American Indian Education: A History*. Norman: University of Oklahoma Press, 2006.

Romaine, Suzanne. *Bilingualism*. Oxford: Basil Blackwell, 1989.

Rosenberg, Daniel, and Susan Harding, eds. *Histories of the Future*. Durham, N.C.: Duke University Press, 2005.

Ruderman, David. *Connecting the Covenants: Judaism and the Search for Christian Identity in Eighteenth-Century England*. Philadelphia: University of Pennsylvania Press, 2007.

———. *Jewish Enlightenment in an English Key: Anglo-Jewry's Construction of Modern Jewish Thought*. Princeton, N.J.: Princeton University Press, 2000.

Scheuermann, Mona. *In Praise of Poverty: Hannah More Counters Thomas Paine and the Radical Threat*. Lexington: University of Kentucky Press, 2002.

Schmidgen, Wolfram. *Exquisite Mixture: The Virtues of Impurity in Early Modern England*. Philadelphia: University of Pennsylvania Press, 2013.

Scott, Sir Walter. *Waverley; or, 'Tis Sixty Years Since*. Edinburgh: James Ballantyne, 1814.

Seargeant, Philip. *Exploring World Englishes: Language in a Global Context*. London: Routledge, 2012.

Sheehan, Jonathan. *Enlightenment Bible: Translation, Scholarship, and Culture*. Princeton, N.J.: Princeton University Press, 2005.

Sheridan, Thomas. *A Course of Lectures on Elocution*. London: W. Strahan, 1762.

Shields, John C., and Eric D. Lamore, eds. *New Essays on Phillis Wheatley*. Knoxville: University of Tennessee Press, 2011.

Shields, John C. "Wheatley, Phillis (*c.* 1753–1784)." *Oxford Dictionary of National Biography*. Oxford: Oxford University Press, 2004. http://www.oxforddnb.com/view/article/53405.

Simmons, Donald. "Notes on the Diary of Antera Duke." In *Efik Traders of Old Calabar*. Cyril Daryll Forde, ed. 1–26. Oxford: Oxford University Press, 1956.

Simpson, David. *Romanticism and the Question of the Stranger*. Chicago: University of Chicago Press, 2013.

Skeat, Walter, and J. H. Nodal, eds. *A Bibliographic List of the Works That Have Been Published, or are Known to Exist in MS., Illustrative of the Various Dialects of English*. London: Trübner, 1877.

Sloman, Judith. *Dryden: The Poetics of Translation*. Toronto: University of Toronto Press, 1985.

Sloterdijk, Peter. "Rules for the Human Zoo." 1999. Mary Varney Rorty, trans. *Environment and Planning D: Society and Space*, 29 (2009; 2001).

Smith, Adam. *The Theory of Moral Sentiments*. London: A. Millar, 1767.

Smith, John Russell. *A Bibliographical List of the Works That Have Been Published Towards Illustrating the Provincial Dialects of England*. London: John Russell Smith, 1839.

———. *Bibliotheca Cantiana, a Bibliographic Account of What Has Been Published on the History, Topography, Antiquities, Customs, and Family Genealogy of the County of Kent*. London: John Russell Smith, 1837.

———. *A Catalogue of an Unique Collection of Ancient English Broadside Ballads, Printed Entirely in Black Letter*. London: John Russell Smith, 1856.

Smith, Olivia. *The Politics of Language 1791–1819*. Oxford: Oxford University Press 1984.

Smollett, Tobias, ed. *The Critical Review; or, Annals of Literature*. Vol. 32. London: S. Hamilton, 1801.

———. "Monthly Catalogue of Poetry. *Poems, Chiefly in the Scottish Dialect. By Robert Burns. Printed at Kilmarnock.*" *The Critical Review*. Vol. 63. London: A. Hamilton, 1787. Sorensen, Janet. *The Grammar of Empire in Eighteenth-Century British Writing*. Cambridge: Cambridge University Press, 2000.

Spence, Thomas. *The Grand Repository of the English Language*. Newcastle: T. Saint, 1775.

———. *A Supplement to the History of Robinson Crusoe*. Newcastle: T. Saint, 1782.

Spivak, Gayatri Chakravorty. *An Aesthetic Education in the Era of Globalization*. Cambridge, Mass.: Harvard University Press, 2012.

———. *Outside in the Teaching Machine*. 1993. New York: Routledge, 2009.

Spriggs, Matthew. "Pentreath, Dorothy (*bap.* 1692, *d.* 1777)." *Oxford Dictionary of National Biography*. Oxford: Oxford University Press, 2004. http://www.oxforddnb.com/view/article/14692

St. Clair, William. *The Reading Nation in the Romantic Period*. Cambridge: Cambridge University Press, 2004.

Sweig, Donald. "The Importation of African Slaves to the Potomac River, 1732–1772." *William and Mary Quarterly*, 42, no. 4 (October 1985): 507–24.

Swift, Jonathan. *A Proposal for Correcting, Improving, and Ascertaining the English Tongue*. 2nd ed. London: Benjamin Tooke, 1712.

Tayler, Christopher. "Goings-On in the Tivoli Gardens." Review of *A Brief History of Seven Killings*, by Marlon James. *London Review of Books*, November 5, 2015. http://www.lrb.co.uk/v37/n21/christopher-tayler/goings-on-in-the-tivoli-gardens.

Taylor, Christopher. "'Most Holy Virgin Assist Me': Subaltern Transnationalism and Positively Possible Worlds." *History of the Present*, 4. no. 1 (Spring 2014): 75–96.

Thompson, E. P. *The Making of English Working Class*. London: V. Gollancz, 1963.

Tieken-Boon van Ostade, Ingrid. *The Bishop's Grammar: Robert Lowth and the Rise of Prescriptivism in English*. Oxford: Oxford University Press, 2011.

———. *Grammars, Grammarians, and Grammar-Writing in Eighteenth-Century England*. Berlin: Mouton de Gruyter, 2008.

Tomalin, Marcus. *Romanticism and Linguistic Theory*. New York: Palgrave Macmillan, 2009.

Tooke, John Horne. *Επεα Πτεϱοεντα*, or *The Diversions of Purley*. London: Richard Taylor, 1786; 1829.

Trumpener, Katie. *Bardic Nationalism: The Romantic Novel and the British Empire*. Princeton, N.J.: Princeton University Press, 1997.

Turley, Richard Maggaraf. *The Politics of Language in Romantic Literature*. New York: Palgrave Macmillan, 2002.

Tymoczko, Maria. *Enlarging Translation, Empowering Translators*. New York: Routledge, 2007.

Tytler, Alexander Fraser. *Essay on the Principles of Translation*. Jeffrey Huntsman, ed. Amsterdam: John Benjamins B.V., 1978; 1791.

Venuti, Lawrence. *Translation Changes Everything: Theory and Practice*. New York: Routledge, 2013.

———. *The Translator's Invisibility: A History of Translation*. 1995. 2nd ed. Abingdon: Routledge, 2008.

Viswanathan, Gauri. *Masks of Conquest: Literary Study and British Rule in India*. New York: Columbia University Press, 1989.

Waldstreicher, David. "Reading the Runaways: Self-Fashioning, Print Culture, and Confidence in Slavery in the Eighteenth-Century Mid-Atlantic." *William and Mary Quarterly*, 56, no. 2 (April 1999): 243–72.

Wales, Katie. *Northern English: A Cultural and Social History*. Cambridge: Cambridge University Press, 2006.

Walker, John. *The Elements of Elocution*. London: T. Cadell, 1781.

Wallis, John. *Grammatica Linguae Anglicanae*. Oxford: Leon Litchfield, 1652.

Watts, Richard, and Peter Trudgill, eds. *Alternative Histories of English*. London: Routledge, 2002.

Wharam, Alan. *The Treason Trials, 1794*. Leicester: Leicester University Press, 1992.

Wheatley, Phillis. *Poems on Various Subjects, Religious and Moral*. London: Archibald Bell, 1773.

Wheeler, Ann. *The Westmoreland Dialect in Four Familiar Dialogues*. London: W. J. and J. Richardson, 1802.

Whitman, Walt. "Robert Burns as Poet and Person." *North American Review*, 143, no. 360 (November 1886): 427–35.

Wilson, Kathleen, ed. *A New Imperial History: Culture, Identity, and Modernity in Britain and the Empire, 1660–1840*. Cambridge: Cambridge University Press, 2004.

Windley, Lathan. *Runaway Slave Advertisements: A Documentary History from the 1730s Until 1790*. Westport, Conn.: Greenwood, 1983.

Wojtowicz, Richard, and Billy Smith. "Advertisements for Runaway Slaves, Indentured Servants, and Apprentices in the *Pennsylvania Gazette*." *Pennsylvania History*, 54, no. 1 (January 1987): 34–71.

———. *Blacks Who Stole Themselves: Advertisements for Runaways in the* Pennsylvania Gazette, *1728–1790*. Philadelphia: University of Pennsylvania Press, 1989.

Wood, Marcus. *Blind Memory: Visual Representations of Slavery in England and America, 1780–1865*. New York: Routledge, 2000.

Wyss, Hilary. *English Letters and Indian Literacies: Reading, Writing, and New England Missionary Schools, 1750–1830*. Philadelphia: University of Pennsylvania Press, 2012.

Yadav, Alok. *Before the Empire of English: Literature, Provinciality, and Nationalism in Eighteenth-Century Britain*. New York: Palgrave Macmillan, 2004.

Yildiz, Yasemin. *Beyond the Mother Tongue: The Postmonolingual Condition*. New York: Fordham University Press, 2013.

INDEX

Page numbers in italics indicate illustrations

ACKNOWLEDGMENTS

During the time I spent working on this book, I accrued many debts. I began my research guided by Michael Gamer, Toni Bowers, and Suvir Kaul. Julia Verkholantsev and Chi-ming Yang provided crucial aid during this work's early stages. The project developed and changed through conversations with my colleagues Kasia Bartoszynska, William Coker, and Daniel Leonard at Bilkent University in Ankara. At various stages, I have been the beneficiary of generous financial support in the form of fellowships and travel stipends from the University of Pennsylvania, the University of Geneva, Bilkent University, and the George Washington University. The librarians at the Library of Congress, the British Library, the National Library of Ireland, and the National Library of Scotland have offered so much help.

Over the course of the last four years especially, this work has improved thanks to the tireless support and mentorship of my colleagues at George Washington University. Foremost among them is Robert McRuer, whose guidance and friendship have been heartening. Tara Ghoshal Wallace, Antonio López, Ayanna Thompson, Jonathan Hsy, Gayle Wald, Christopher Sten, Jeffrey Cohen, Holly Dugan, Jennifer Chang, and Jennifer James have all taken the time to read, comment, and offer suggestions or mentorship at various stages. I have appreciated Katherine Wasdin's help with questions relating to the Greek and Latin languages. Likewise, I am indebted to Washington-area scholars Patrick O'Malley, Orrin Wang, Richard Sha, and Judith Plotz for support and optimistic mentorship. Janet Sorensen, Nathan Hensley, Roxann Wheeler, and Ashley Cohen have offered essential feedback at crucial moments in this book's development. A special thanks is due to Constance Kibler for her tireless contributions to the GWU English Department's life and health. Seen from 2017, one of the developments that has become unignorable is the increasing devaluation and precarity of the humanities in the contemporary U.S. academy. Even so, I have been lucky in that the intellectual communities that I have belonged to (or skirted the peripheries of) remain generous and inspiring. I hope what I have written here relates in some way to communities of all kinds.

An earlier version of a section of Chapter 1 was previously published in "Fugitive Pieces: Language, Embodiment, and the Case of *Caleb Williams*," *Eighteenth-Century Fiction*, 28, no. 2 (Winter 2015–16). Similarly, an earlier version of a section of Chapter 2 was previously published in "'What We Want in Elegance, We Gain in Copiousness': Eighteenth-Century English and Its Empire of Tongues," in *Eighteenth Century: Theory and Interpretation*, 57, no. 1 (Spring 2016). In all cases, I have benefitted from the detailed feedback of anonymous external readers. In the same way, my work has improved immensely thanks to scholarly dialogue at formal conferences.

I thank Melchizedek Anthony, Edward Lybeer, Amy Yaft, and Kathryn DeWispelare for fail-safe encouragement over the years.

Lightning Source UK Ltd.
Milton Keynes UK
UKOW01n0608230218
318366UK00007B/290/P

9 780812 249095